CHELSEA'S

CULT HEROES

LEO MOYNIHAN

Know The Score Books Limited

www.knowthescorebooks.com

KNOW THE SCORE BOOKS PUBLICATIONS

CULT HEROES	Author	ISBN
CHELSEA	Leo Moynihan	1-905449-00-3

MATCH OF MY LIFE	Editor	ISBN
FULHAM	Michael Heatley	1-905449-51-8
LIVERPOOL	Leo Moynihan	1-905449-50-X

FORTHCOMING PUBLICATIONS IN 2006

CULT HEROES	Author	ISBN
NEWCASTLE	Dylan Younger	1-905449-03-8
PORTSMOUTH	Pat Symes	1-905449-04-6
SOUTHAMPTON	Jeremy Wilson	1-905449-01-1
WEST BROM	Simon Wright	1-905449-02-X

MATCH OF MY LIFE	Editor	ISBN
ENGLAND WORLD CUP	Louis Massarella & Leo Moynihan	1-905449-51-8
FA CUP FINALS (1953-1969)	David Saffer	1-905449-53-4
LEEDS	David Saffer	1-905449-54-2
STOKE CITY	Simon Lowe	1-905449-55-0
WOLVES	Simon Lowe	1-905449-56-9

FOOTBALL FICTION	Author	ISBN
BURKSEY The Autobiography of a Football God	Peter Morfoot	1-905449-49-6

CHELSEA'S

CULT HEROES

LEO MOYNIHAN

Series Editor: Simon Lowe

www.knowthescorebooks.com

First published in the United Kingdom
by Know The Score Books Limited, 2005

First published in the United Kingdom
by Know The Score Books Limited, 2005

Know The Score Books Limited
The College Business Centre
Uttoxeter New Road
Derby
DE22 3WZ

www.knowthescorebooks.com

A CIP catalogue record is available for this book from the British Library
ISBN 1-905449-00-3

Jacket and book design by Lisa David

Printed and bound in Great Britain
By Cromwell Press, Trowbridge, Wiltshire

Author's Acknowledgements

I would like to thank my publisher Simon Lowe for his support in the writing of this book. Simon showed a great deal of patience, humour and support and for that I am very grateful. Those days sitting over coffee and pondering on a suitable twenty players seem a long way away.

So many people have been so incredibly enthusiastic in their help with this project and I would like to thank them all. Albert Sewell for his incredible archive of photos and memories, David McCleave for his more than enthusiastic research, Steve Cook for the same reasons and to Tony Banks for his fantastic foreword.

Matt Allen, Justyn Barnes, Neil Barnett, Clive Batty for not ignoring my sea of e-mails, Rob Blake, Dougie Bruce, Scott Cheshire, Pete and Katie Collins, Louise Cook, Charlie Cooke, Kerry Dixon, Gary Double (great work mate), Micky Droy, Mike and Jill Field, Ron Harris, Allon Hoskin, Alan Hudson, Joey Jones, Tim Lovejoy, Ben Lyttleton, Louis Massarella, Hugh McIlvanney, Marc Milmo, Pat Nevin, Peter Osgood, Sam Pilger, Mark Riches, Hugh Sleight, Steve Taylor, Bobby Tambling, Rob Wightman and Geoff Young for the cover shot of yours truly. Thanks everyone.

I'd like to mention my Mum. She isn't the biggest football fan – in fact she couldn't care less, but she has always encouraged me to write. It's not quite Arthur Miller, Mum, but thanks anyway.

Once more, I'd like to finish by thanking the gorgeous Catherine. From making me porridge in the morning to kissing me goodnight, she has been an inspiration and I thank her from the bottom of my heart.

Photographs in this book are reproduced by kind permission of:
Colorsport, EMPICS, John Moynihan, Peter Osgood & Albert Sewell

Jacket Photographs
Front cover
Left Fatty Foulke, Chelsea's first cult hero, weighed in at a gigantic 22 stone, but still managed to save ten out of twelve penalties in 1905/06
Centre Gianfranco Zola, arguably the most popular hero ever to grace the Bridge
Right The mercurial, yet enigmatic wizardry of Charlie Cooke epitomises the Chelsea cult hero
Inset Inspirational skipper Ron 'Chopper' Harris clutches the silverware after that famous FA Cup replay win in 1970

Rear cover
Left Dennis Wise kisses the FA Cup, the club's first trophy for 26 long years
Right Peter Osgood, King of the Kings Road

Contents

Introduction

The crowd are as much a part of the atmosphere as the air, the rain, the sun and the mist...

Bernard Joy

This is going to sound strange, but I hope that those who read this book will close it a little disappointed. Angry, even.

Before my publisher has a stroke, let me explain. This book offers Chelsea fans the opportunity to debate, discuss and, alright, argue about the twenty greatest Cult Heroes in the club's history. Each chapter of our chosen twenty looks at that player's career in Chelsea blue and what turned them into crowd favourites. It delves behind the simple playing career sum-ups and stats with which football fans have been deluged for the last two decades or so to reveal why each of these men became living legends and examines how from legends they progressed to become part of folklore. How, with demi-gods like these, tales of their feats of derring-do become exacerbated in pub and bar conversations and as they are passed down from fathers to sons; how they tore opponents apart, cocked a snook at authority and thrilled the Bridge's crowd.

But here's the thing, when it comes to heroes and favourites the crowd is everything and within that throng, opinions differ and one man's hero is another man's donkey.

When flicking through these pages there will be some who sneer at the absence of a star who was or is everything to them. They will scoff as a player who so warmed those cold days in the stands or on the terraces is conspicuous by their absence. We could only pick twenty, but still the essence of the book lies in opinion and debate, and that is, after all, what us fans thrive on.

Tommy Lawton, England centre-forward and every post-war boy's hero, is not included. Peter "The Cat" Bonetti, that most agile of entertainers, is not here either. The feisty Scot David Speedie is missing, whilst Gianluca Vialli, the shiny-headed Italian, doesn't make it and the current day midfield maestro, Frank Lampard (who finished second equal in the list of all-time Cult Heroes as voted for by subscribers to this book – see Page 228), is overlooked in favour of the home-grown John Terry. There are plenty of others missing from these pages, of course, but I hope once the reader has got over any glaring omissions they will agree that the twenty that have made the cut represent everything that is both great and odd about this intoxicating football club.

So what does it take to be a Cult Hero? These are the players that appeal to the core of your everyday football fan. They must have that something special about them. Zola, yes. Greaves, obviously. But that doesn't have to be special in terms of their ability as a footballer, the chapters on Micky Droy and Joey Jones are testament to that. What players like Jones and Droy did have though was a link with the fans; they touched something deep inside and represent, in bodily form, the way the fans of the time felt about their club. The raw essence that drives the fan on to come and watch the game is deeply affected by men like these twenty, who, each in their own way, appeal to our sense of adventure, loyalty, fun, bold genius and in some cases absolute madness.

Chelsea Football Club is – like its current manager – special. Ever since William "Fatty" Foulke, the biggest sporting personality in Britain, signed on the dotted line and paraded himself down the Fulham Road in his dandy attire, the club has had an affinity with garish and wonderful individuals. Not to mention spending money. There are other similarities which cross the ages, not least the fact that Foulke was the first player ever to be bought precisely because he was a Cult Hero. He therefore guaranteed bumper crowds wherever he went and ensured that fledgling Chelsea commanded column inches. Sound familiar? Since 1905 the team may have faltered during certain periods, offering glimpses of success only for them then to be snatched away at the last minute, but players have always pulled on that Blue shirt with one thing on their mind, to go out and entertain a crowd hell-bent on enjoying, well, entertainment.

Wonderful goalscorers like Hughie Gallacher, Jimmy Greaves and Peter Osgood. These men represented what the club, pre-Abramovich, was all about. Troubled, but brilliant. They would fan the flames of the young fan's pulsating heart until the fires of their desire raged out of control.

Then there was Pat Nevin, a man who stood out from the crowd and who managed, with wonderful trickery, to charm the hearts and minds of an apparently hardened crowd; equally Kerry Dixon's Roy of the Rovers persona or Dennis Wise's cheeky wink coaxed fans to adulate them to the level of hero. And then there's Gianfranco Zola. At least here there is no debate. Or is there? Zola is a God as far as every Chelsea fan is concerned, so how can he be a *Cult* Hero?

These are all players who fans have taken great pleasure in paying good money to watch and then left the ground chomping at the bit to come back the next time and then the next until they were hooked. These are the men who generations of boys have pretended to be whilst playing football in the park, who adorned the bedroom walls of adolescents (and a few grown men) and who sent that shiver up the collective spine which pulled crowds in week after week waiting with baited breath to hear whether their hero's name was on the team sheet. These are the men who always crop up when seasoned supporters cite the reasons that their initial courting period developed into a full blown love affair.

Meeting some of these players was a privilege. They seemed to talk like they played. Peter Osgood was proud and handsome, Pat Nevin intelligent and philosophical and Ron Harris purposeful and a little foul mouthed. They had endured ups and down with this topsy-turvy club, but what they all had was an affinity with the place and whatever happens and however much the club changes over the next few years, that cannot be taken away.

When I met with Kerry Dixon we strolled through the ground just hours before a match. Some fans didn't notice of course, but many did. Their starry eyes opened and jaws dropped as he passed them and suddenly they were kids again as there before them, was Kerry. Their hero.

Leo Moynihan
October 2005

Foreword

Everyone has heroes and for football fans those heroes are usually from the earliest days they started supporting their clubs.

I still find it a bit difficult explaining to those who don't really understand football why I get an enormous buzz from being with players I idolised when standing on the terraces at Stamford Bridge in the early 1950s. The players who won the Division One League Championship in 1954/55 are now all in their seventies, but for me they remain my real heroes through whom I can relive my early football days and I am delighted that two of the team make this book. For the true fan football doesn't stand in isolation, it is an integral part of our lives. When we rekindle memories of great football players and moments, we also recall all those other interrelated aspects of our past both happy and sad. Leo Moynihan's book will help bring back so many of these memories.

There are few things more enjoyable than a good old argument about who was the greatest in whatever sport you care to name. Indeed there is a media industry dedicated to just such fascinating and ultimately unprovable claims. To most Chelsea fans any player who wore the club's shirt is special, but some are more special than others. Part of our centenary celebrations was the fans' vote to select the greatest ever Chelsea team and it was fun, but no-one could properly claim it was definitive. Leo Moynihan doesn't attempt to rank the players or assemble them in a team. Instead he selects players who each achieved cult status at the club and it works a treat. You don't have to be the greatest player to be granted such status, although a fair number in Leo's list do combine the both. I suppose in the end it comes down to character and that special quality that enabled each of these players to win the hearts of the fans.

No-one can take issue with Leo Moynihan that all the players he includes were indeed cult heroes, but undoubtedly he will be challenged about those he missed out. But that is part of the fascination of football and maybe he should start preparing the next volume now.

Tony Banks
Lord Stratford
(Chelsea fan 1951– to the day he drops)

Dedication

To my Dad, John. A True-Blue

WILLIAM 'FATTY' FOULKE

'OUR LITTLE WILLY'

1905-1906

CHELSEA CAREER

Games	35
Clean Sheets	10
Caps	1

MAGIC MOMENT

Legendary goalkeeper 'Fatty' Foulke's signing convinced the Football League to allow Chelsea to enter the Second Division without the club ever having played a game before

> **Some people say goalkeepers are crazy, but to me they're not crazy, they're different.**
>
> **"Goalkeepers are Different", Brian Glanville**

THE usually callous and unyielding laced-leather ball quivers in his giant hands like a soon-to-be devoured Christmas tangerine. So used to bruising the foreheads of brave centre-forwards, and stinging the unsung fingers of less equipped goalkeepers, it seems that the football finally met its match the day it fell into William Foulke's all encompassing arms.

Exactly 100 years on and the image of Chelsea's first ever custodian is still an enduring one. Nostalgia may not be what it once was, but even the most corporate-sodden football fan can still marvel at the grainy sight of a keeper, who became affectionately known to fledgling Chelsea fans as "Our Little Willy", towering over attackers and defenders alike, his long shorts straining under the pressure of his solid oak legs, pulled up high over his mammoth torso.

The notion of a Lowry-like day out at the football complete with flat caps, rattles and hearty working class banter may be over-romanticised, but here is a goalkeeper and a man whose very appearance – even a century on – manages to catapult our mind's eye into a bygone era when men were men and goalkeepers were, well, gargantuan.

WILLIAM FOULKE arrived at Chelsea Football Club in the spring of 1905. Already established amongst the Glitterati in the booming world of professional football, the goalkeeper rolled into the capital (some would say literally) with a reputation as domineering as his impressive 6 foot 3 inch and 22 stone frame.

That reputation, though, had been built in the North of England where, towards the end of the nineteenth century, Association Football had taken root and where the game had blossomed from a popular pastime into a national obsession. Football had shimmied its way out from its public school genesis to be embraced by the masses, whilst those who played the game and entertained the people were afforded a status shared by such Victorian luminaries as Henry Hook, the hero of Rorke's Drift, Sherlock Holmes, cricketer WG Grace and Captain Matthew Webb, the first man to swim the English Channel. These men seeped into the public consciousness becoming famous both to read about and look at. In 1891, some footballers – in several cases with the help of an agent – topped up their wages by endorsing products such as Oxo, cigarettes, a range of liniments and by putting their names to various ghosted columns in the thriving sporting press.

Foulke himself was – for obvious reasons – one of the most recognised and celebrated players in the game and if the trappings of that success sound frighteningly familiar, so will the reasons for his migration to the almost uncharted world of league football; the South of England. Chelsea Football Club, a new establishment bankrolled by mega-rich businessmen, were looking for the best players around to turn their dreams of becoming the best team in the land into reality. Déjà vu anyone?

At the turn of the last century, football in the capital was sparse. Woolwich Arsenal were the only team from London competing in the Football League (in fact the only sides competing that hailed from south of Birmingham were the Gunners and Bristol City), whilst their future rivals and neighbours Tottenham Hotspur plied their fortunes in the Southern League. Cosmopolitan London and in particular central London, for all its power, affluence and Imperial might, lagged well behind the industrial north. Queen Victoria had presided over an Empire of tremendous prosperity, but the city that had become the world's hub could not compete when it came to her nation's new obsession.

HAVING ascended to the throne in 1901, King Edward VII inherited a city that in so many ways was at the forefront of the world. Peter Ackroyd in his book London: The Biography highlights how energetic the capital had become just months before the birth of Chelsea Football Club:

> London once more embodied a young and energetic spirit, with a curious acquisitive atmosphere which floods the pages of urban chroniclers such as H.G. Wells. The laborious and intricate city of the fin-de-siècle seems to have vanished, together with that heavy and lassitudinous atmosphere so peculiar to the memories of the period; it is as if the city had come alive with the new century. It was the first age of the mass cinema, too, with the advent of the Moving Picture Theatre and the Kinema. The Underground lines had abandoned their steam trains, and the whole network was electrified by 1902. Motor buses, tram-cars, lorries and tricycles added to the general momentum. London was, in a phrase of the period, 'going ahead'. Where in the late nineteenth century wrote the author of *The Streets of London*, 'it had been rich and fruity, it was becoming slick and snappy'. One of the permanent, and most striking, characteristics of London lies in its capacity to rejuvenate itself... The shops and restaurants grew in size, while the tea shops became 'corner houses' and 'mansions'. There were picture domes, prizefights and soda fountains, cafes and revues, all compounding the atmosphere of a 'fast' city.

This "fast" city quickly required a football team to compliment the worldly and exotic place that it had become. If the capital was truly going to start "going ahead", and if the sprawling metropolis was truly going to re-invent itself then there had to be football; there had to be a club capable of offering the people of central London a diet of the sport that for too long had been gorged on almost exclusively by the industrial north. Fortunately there were two men; brothers and partners, who shared that hunger and whose determination and nous created Chelsea Football Club.

BUT J.T. Mears and his younger brother Augustus (or Gus) were far from mere footballing romantics with a vision of sporting prowess and success. Their motives behind establishing Chelsea FC were born from business; that was their background, that was their driving force. The sons of the hugely wealthy builder Joseph Mears (the family had been behind the development of the Fulham Embankment), J.T. and Gus had grown up around big business and big deals involving huge projects and vast sums of money. And so the idea that came to Gus Mears of a new "super-stadium" supplying regular football to affluent Londoners was as natural to his genes as it was attractive to his bank balance.

But this was no easy, overnight birth. The Mears' local stadium at Stamford Bridge near Walham Green (now Fulham Broadway) had been courted by the brothers for over a quarter of a century. Since 1877, the site had been the home of the London Athletic Club who, stubbornly, through the guise of a Mr Stunt, saw off the family's overtures. No wonder Gus and J.T. were keen. Their business nostrils had been twitched by this vast cascade of land, flanked by a main-line rail track and the Fulham Road, down which the busy hoofs of Hansom Cabs rattled by, carrying well-off locals who would surely be willing to pay to view the game that had captured so much of the country's imagination.

The Mears boys hovered over the site, but even when Mr Stunt died in 1902 they were thwarted by a clause in the contract. It took until early 1904 before they finally secured the deal that put their name to Stamford Bridge. The ball was finally beginning to roll. The brothers had their site; they had their stadium, but what now? Other options hove into view as attractive financially to the wily brothers as the creation of a football club; and potentially considerably less hassle. Along with their advisors, on 14th March 1904 they met above a pub opposite the stadium called the Rising Sun (now the Greene Room) to discuss the options. In that public house – which today, like the club, is a far more salubrious and comfortable version of its previous self – those decisions were thrashed out.

Gus – by now calling the shots – was torn. He loved football and was a fair amateur player in his younger days, but this was business. The site was prime and Great Western Railway (wanting the land for a coal yard) were willing to offer a quick profit for the Mears' new location. Tempting. Fred Parker was a close associate and the brothers' financial advisor and – with fortunate foresightedness – pointed out the longer term financial potential of a professional football club in the area.

Gus needed convincing. Football was marvellous, football was inspiring, football was making men of boys, but wasn't it also just a fad? He had serious doubts regarding the longevity of the sport. Would people in 100 years still be coming to Stamford Bridge? Parker tried hard to make the figures profitable reading, but that offer from the Great Western Railway seemed to have won the day as the meeting came to an end. As the men left the pub, the birth of Chelsea Football Club had been shelved.

Suddenly, out of nowhere, Parker let out a shriek as Mears' prize hound sunk his teeth into his fleshy right leg. "Your damn dog has bitten me," he yelped. "Damned Scotch Terrier," retorted Mears. "He always bites before he barks." Parker's painful screech was replaced by a calming laugh; and it was a chuckle that was to strike a chord with his friend. "You're the coolest fellow I have ever met," said Mears. "You took that bite so well, Fred. Most men would have kicked up hell about it." Mears stopped and wondered. Maybe he had been hasty. Maybe his was an advisor worth taking advice from. "Look here, I'll stand on your judgement about Stamford Bridge. Go to the chemist and get the leg seen to, and meet me here at nine tomorrow. Then we'll get busy." And busy they got.

Mears toyed with the idea of renting out the ground to the local Fulham Football Club, which had played its first competitive game in 1885 and built up a good reputation in the Southern League. He even went as far as proposing a rent of £1,000 per annum, but that was rejected by Fulham as too expensive. Mohammad Al Fayed's millions, like the tomb of Tutankhamun, were yet to be discovered and shown off in the capital.

SO, it was time to go it alone. It was time for Chelsea Football Club. Days later, Mears and Parker travelled to Glasgow, a hotbed for football and the home of the architect Archibald Leitch, the iconic designer of giant stadiums such as Hampden Park, Celtic Park and Ibrox.

The choice of Leitch underlined just how serious Mears and his associates were about their new project. Abramovich would have approved. He was the best and nothing else would do. He would make the stadium at Stamford Bridge the talk of London town. The Mears' brothers' plans were starting to bear fruit. But they still had no name for their fledgling club. "Kensington" was touted as was "Stamford Bridge" and even "London" – underlining just how far the owners hoped to throw their net over the capital's football supporters. However, none of these danced off Gus Mears' tongue and, after much deliberating, "Chelsea" became the chosen name.

A new club would need staff. William Claude Kirby was named Chairman (a position he would hold until his death in 1935). Alongside him worked Fred Parker, as Financial Secretary, whilst Lord Cadogan was appointed President and his family colours of light blue were chosen for the club's first kit. Things were now in place, the ground was under construction and heads were beginning to turn. "Chelsea will stagger humanity," suggested one journalist.

But before they did they would have to find a league in which to compete and the right players to do the competing.

The Football League, in 1905, was only two divisions deep and so the club decided to try its luck in the Southern League for starters. This competition housed the likes of Tottenham and Fulham, the latter's location, of course, would mean some stark competition when it came to vying for fans. The Craven Cottage club and their chairman Henry Norris, though, bore a grudge regarding the high rent they had been offered for the use of Stamford Bridge; a grudge that would have a huge bearing on the early fortunes of Chelsea Football Club. For now these affluent, nouveau riche upstarts were treading on his club's toes. It wouldn't do. Action would have to be taken. There were soon reports of Norris bad-mouthing the new club and its proprietors. Could they be trusted, did the League need their sort and were their riches earned in the correct way? These questions marred the new club to the extent that the Southern League conducted an enquiry into the dealings of Mears' new team.

Chelsea were cleared, but mud sticks and Fulham's continued mutterings ensured that Mears' application to the Southern League was blocked. What now? Mears wasn't the sort to be downbeat and if one League wouldn't have him, why not try another? Why not the Football League after all? If he was going to knock on their door, things would have to be right. He wanted to be greeted with a smile, he wanted his club to be allowed to enter and join the party, but there was a dress code and, before trying to get in, he would have to make sure that Chelsea had the right accessories to convince the League to allow admission and that meant great players. Enter William Foulke.

THE GROUND construction was coming along nicely. Leitch had designed a stadium boasting three enormous terraces, supported by thousands of tons of rubble excavated from the nearby underground line and a 120 yard long centre-piece grandstand holding 5,000 seated spectators. It would be a vast open bowl of a stadium which, when full, the club bragged, would hold 100,000 people. But it would require the right personnel to attract those sort of numbers. First of all John Tait Robertson was signed from Southern league Southampton as player/manager.

Robertson was a fine professional from Scotland who had won 16 caps for his country and who was a learned student of the game. He advised on which players should be approached and soon the likes of Jimmie Robertson and Jimmy Windridge, both promising forwards from Small Heath (later Birmingham City), were convinced to sign. But it was the goalkeeper from Sheffield United who would cause the biggest stir and prove that this new club had real ambition and credibility.

In terms of cash, William Foulke was by no means the biggest signing; Windridge alone cost a lavish £190. The £50 spent on Foulke wasn't going to break the bank, but his presence, they hoped, was going to break the hearts of those centre-forwards plying their trade in a league Chelsea wished to join. Foulke was huge both in terms of his presence and his renown. The other signings, Windridge, Robertson and another Scot, Bob McRoberts were extremely efficient professional footballers who could and would compete in league football, but they, quiet and hard-working athletes, weren't going to fill an inquisitive new stadium. That responsibility would instead fall to one man and one man only.

Foulke's bulk meant he had simply become the most heralded and recognised player around. In the 1904 publication *The Men Who Made Football* he was described as "perhaps the most talked of player in the world – a leviathan at 22 stone with the agility of a bantam." The French had got wind of

Foulke and, desperate to prove that they had the biggest footballer in the world in their ranks, wheeled out one G Soulié, centre-half for the works team of Parisian journal *Les Sports*. Monsieur Soulié weighed in at a gargantuan 24 stone 7 lbs, although he, of course, never played professional, let alone international, football. Surely then the celebrity status that Foulke enjoyed was due to more than his whopping appearance than to his ability? Not so. Foulke was more than a competent goalkeeper; in fact his distinguished performances for Sheffield United had earned him an England Cap (many thought he should have had more) and two FA Cup winners medals.

BORN IN April 1874, William Foulke was a native of Wellington in Shropshire. The Wrekin overlooks the quaint market town now almost engulfed by Telford; a hill adored by ramblers and which by only a matter of feet is now classified officially as a mountain. When it came to Man Mountains there was no such discrepancy surrounding the native goalkeeper. During the 1890s, as a teenager, he had grafted down the mines in Derbyshire to where his family had moved. Word soon spread to professional clubs of his performances for Blackwell, the local colliery team, about this giant of a stopper.

He fast became a talked about character. Stories of Foulke, even from these amateur days were commonplace. To some who had not seen him in the flesh, he took on a fairytale-like existence. Like the giant at the top of Jack's beanstalk, Foulke was seen as an ogre with the smell of Englishman's blood flowing through his gaping nostrils. The disparity between legend and myth may have been somewhat capacious, but no matter, Foulke attracted an interest that would get him out of the mines and into the relatively new world of professional Association Football.

Nottingham Forest and Derby County were local suitors, but it was Sheffield United who won his signature having offered Blackwell £1 a day for the remainder of the season. During ten successful years at Bramall Lane, Foulke both impressed and amazed in equal measure. Stories surrounding his methods and often his madness were legion and for the rest of his days and long beyond, Foulke's name would be synonymous with tall tales. His legendary status continues 100 years on and whether reality or myth, stories regarding the giant between the sticks are quite rightly referred to as "Foulkelore".

One centre-forward was lacking his teeth having contested a loose ball with the giant custodian, whilst another striker was lifted by his ankles and dunked like a digestive, head-first into the mud. The unfortunate forward in question was George Allan of Liverpool, who'd had the temerity to dribble around Foulke before finding himself making acquaintance with an Anfield puddle. Liverpool, of course, were awarded a penalty that won them the game. Back in Shefield's dressing room, Foulke was appropriately apologetic to his team-mates; he hated losing. But soon, with those apologies accepted, a large smile cascaded across the keeper's globular face. As much as he detested losing, he couldn't hide the satisfaction gained from his menacing deeds. "I made a right toffee apple out of him, didn't I?" he crowed.

For all the tomfoolery and histrionics, Foulke was also capable of turning heads for his goalkeeping ability. Whilst his appearance would at first derive cackles of laughter from fans yet to see him play, those giggles would soon be silenced by a surprisingly agile and lissom keeper. He could punch the ball safely into the opposition's half, whilst a kick from Foulke could see the weighty leather ball landing deep into the enemy's penalty box. Given his colossal size he was impossible to charge into the net, something which was still legal at the time.

FOULKE was part of a fine Sheffield United team that housed many internationals including captain and regular England half-back Ernest 'Nudger' Needham. Foulke won his only international cap in 1897 in a

4-0 win over Wales at Bramall Lane. The following season, 1897/98, the Cutlers, as United were then nicknamed, won the League title for the first time in their history with Foulke conceding just 31 goals in 30 games, the second best record in the country. He graced three FA Cup Finals saddling the nineteenth and twentieth century and proudly hung winners medals around his colossal neck in 1899 and 1902, whilst he was on the losing side in 1901 when Tottenham Hotspur became the only non-Football League team to win the FA Cup since the League's foundation in 1888.

Foulke more than played his part in the winning of those two FA Cups and his displays in the finals – particularly in the 1899 occasion against Derby County played in front of 75,000 spectators at Crystal Palace, where he frustrated the legendary Derby and England forward Steve Bloomer – underlined his very real talents.

Chelsea then, despite Foulke having recently passed 30, were signing a goalkeeper they could trust with their fortunes as well as a man whose standing in the game would heighten both their own ambitions and the credibility of their application to join the Football League. On the 29th May 1905, the League housed its annual meeting at the Tavistock Hotel in Covent Garden; an exotic choice of venue considering the League's almost exclusive Northern and Midland membership. Pipe smoke and brass music filled the air as Chelsea's anxious officials sat and waited on the sidelines, hoping that their case would be given a fair hearing.

Fred Parker was given the job of arguing Chelsea's cause. His three-minute litigation was a good one, but may have fell on deaf and hungover ears. Due to the presence of the League officials the night before, the music halls and beer parlours of London had done a roaring trade and it was hard to gauge just how much those glazed expressions were taking in. Parker implored those still listening to do the right thing. "I will not trespass on you further beyond suggesting that when you consider the points I have put before you, you will come to the conclusion that you cannot refuse us."

For those good gentlemen of the Football League there was a lot over over which to ruminate. Many of their members were put out by Chelsea's lack of previous playing record, the club had, remember, never fielded a team at this point, but some were just as keen to expand their game in the south. Whilst they puffed on their pipes and sipped on their Scotch, they pondered the prospects of this embryonic football club. The stadium was coming along nicely and their bank balance, like Stamford Bridge, was growing and impressive (they boasted £3,000 in the coffers), but it was the team, and the presence of Foulke that grabbed the eye. Mears and his associates had compiled a compelling case.

Now all they could do was wait. Chairman Kirby raced back and forth from his office by hansom cab, whilst sharing a pessimism with his manager Robertson that their efforts would again be thwarted. Parker, though, was a far more optimistic chap. He bet the perturbed pair five shillings each that they would be successful and history is yet to unveil if he ever picked up his winnings after the Football League committee announced their decision to elect Chelsea Football Club to their Second Division. Also joining them as new entrants were Hull City and Leeds City, while Stockport County returned to the League after one season in the Midland League. Interestingly, the other southern club to win election at that meeting was Clapton Orient, who had previously spent just one season in the Southern League's Second Division, where they had finished a humble eighth out of twelve. This is perhaps an indication that the Football League was impatiently swallowing up southern clubs the minute they came across them and that Parker's money had been as safe as a ball in Foulke's capacious hands.

NOW the club's officials, management and players could concentrate on making a real go at success. "Well that's that," concluded Gus Mears at a post-electoral party held near the developing Stamford

Bridge. "Now for the struggle. I suppose the first five years will be the worst." Mears' concerns were understandable, but as the squad came together in preparation for the 1905/06 season, concerns could give way to hope and in the case of their new goalkeeper, wonderment. When Fred Parker met William Foulke for the first time, his breath was taken by the enormity of the man. "My word," whispered Parker. "Darkness covers the earth."

This author's own father, John Moynihan, in his chronicle of Chelsea Football Club summed up the presence at Stamford Bridge of the newly arrived keeper. "With his ill-fitting suit, small cap popped on top of a shaven, bullet head, Foulke stalked rather than walked, carrying his bulbous belly proudly like an ostrich with a prize egg."

Foulke would have to try his hand at the strict Edwardian training laid down by his manager Robertson, but road running and sprints were not his priority. He was to be Chelsea's first captain sure, but that was due to experience and presence rather than attitude or example. No matter, the squad looked a decent one, and as the season approached, Mears and Parker hoped that the locals would flock to see how it would progress.

CHELSEA and Fulham's residents had reason to be excited about the new circus in town. Fulham had, of course, housed a Southern League football club, but this new breed seemed bigger and better and was to compete on a national stage. This particular area of south-west London had become used to theatrics, but many residents were more accustomed to the arts than sporting prowess.

Back in the 17th Century Samuel Pepys had resided in Chelsea as had Jonathon Swift and Sir Richard Steele. That tradition continued into Victorian England with prominent authors such as A.C. Swinburne and Oscar Wilde penning their works near the Fulham Road (Wilde wrote *The Importance of Being Earnest* whilst living in the area). Even Mark Twain had been inspired as a resident. In 1897, Chelsea had a fine theatre. The Grand was a luscious and elegant setting on Putney Bridge, whilst the visual arts were also indebted to artists such as Whistler and Turner who resided on Chelsea's streets.

Those streets, however, were not always the most hygienic, but by the time the new football club had been born, fans making their way to the ground could at last feel at home in their more sanitised world. In 1900, Chelsea's Chief Medical Officer underlined how far the borough had progressed in its modernisation programme: "We have much improved our sewers and house drains," he explained. "Roads have also been widened, open spaces secured for the public and some of the worst slums of old Chelsea have been demolished."

With the gentrification of the area progressing in leaps and bounds, would these locals truly take to this northern roughhouse of a sport known as football? Sport had been part of local life for years. The Queen's Club had brought both tennis and cricket to the locals whilst pigeon shooting and polo, toward the end of the Nineteenth Century, could be enjoyed at the nearby Hurlingham Club. Boxing, wrestling, running and rope-pulling were other pastimes enjoyed, but now there was something big for the locals to take a solid and communal interest in. Or so Mears and his team hoped.

AH, HOPE. For ten decades hope would prove a cruel mistress to Chelsea fans. In September 1905, it seemed that there was nothing but hope as Chelsea lost their first ever league match by a single goal at Stockport County. Foulke had, as was his prowess, saved a penalty (one of ten that season), but was helpless to stop the rebound. The laws of the game had just been changed to ensure that keepers had to remain on their line when facing a penalty kick, which handed most attackers the advantage over goalkeepers unable to rush out to close down the angle. Not so against Foulke, whose frame almost filled the goal. Against Burslem Port Vale in March 1906 he saved two penalties within two minutes, each time nonchalantly plucking the ball from the air with the ease and grace of a gymnast.

Only 6,000 fans turned up for the team's first encounter at Stamford Bridge, a game that ended in a 5-1 rout of Hull City. Perhaps the public had been put off by the awful puns in the club's match day programme (itself a luxury new item for Chelsea fans) that had asked for patience from the supporters. "[Chelsea] is only a baby as yet. Wait until it's fully grown, and then – we shall see what we Chel-sea."

Parker, though, would quite rightly argue that the game had been played on a Monday, hence the low crowd and by the following match, this time on a Saturday, the figures had swelled to 20,000 for the visit of West Bromwich Albion. It was a massive attendance for a Second Division match and Mears could sit back and slowly begin to conclude that his movement into football had been the right one.

There was no doubt that many in that first Saturday crowd had come to see Foulke. If they had enjoyed the humour of Wilde and the theatrics at the Grand, then they had both in abundance when coming to see the goalkeeper at the Bridge. The West Bromwich forwards bombarded his goal with shots and crosses that had the Chelsea defence baffled, but not its last line. Foulke belittled his own cumbersome-looking frame by throwing himself elegantly at anything that was put to him. Shots were blocked, and crosses expertly claimed as Chelsea held on for a 1-0 victory.

Newspapers described him as: "One of the curiosities of football, a wonder to everyone who visits the classic grounds of the country." And visit they did, in their thousands. It was a fact not lost on the manager J.T. Robertson. "As a draw alone, [Foulke] is worth his weight in gold," he declared. "He is a veritable wonder, and his astonishing ability has aroused a fever of interest in the doings beneath the bar for Chelsea." His opponents were no less admiring. Legendary all-round sportsman and England footballer, C.B. Fry, described Foulke as having: "a touch of genius".

Foulke's abilities quickly became the talk of Stamford Bridge as he kept nine consecutive clean sheets in the Football League, some feat for a defence only recently acquainted. And there was no doubt to whom both fans and opponents ascribed the lion's share of the praise for that achievement. Forwards lamented the lack of space available to place the ball. "You shot straight at the keeper," bemoaned the Burton United skipper at his wretched penalty taker who had missed from the spot for the second time in April 1906. "I had to!" shouted the miscreant. "There was no room either side."

Ground season tickets priced at half a guinea for men and five shillings for women and children were sold in their hundreds as the capital's new sporting baby began to truly crawl, walk and run out from its nappies. It was hardly surprising. Here was true entertainment. Music Hall, the popular refuge of the working classes was fun, but a day out at the football seemed to be able to pull a community together like no comedian or show. Music Hall was often repetitive, but the notion of football was always different. What would happen today? Who knew? And that was the buzz.

Fans were raucous and enthusiastic. A real mix of working class and Chelsea wealth would arrive at the bustling ground making themselves and their views known to all – generally unashamedly loudly. An early feature in the *Chelsea Chronicle*, as the programme was entitled, had to ask for supporters to leave any foul language at the turnstile. "Of course we do not for a moment expect to find some thousands of men with the 'football fever' on them talking like a congress of school teachers. That would be absurd. Still, there is a medium in all things. The man who cannot enjoy a little sport without howling a torrent of invective couched in terms calculated to blister the paint on the steel girders is not wanted at Stamford Bridge. Large as our ground is, we have no space for him. We vastly prefer his room to his company."

THANKS to Foulke, expletives were often replaced by wonder and awe as he pounded out of the dressing room and onto the field of play looking larger than ever thanks to his cunning ploy of having at his side the smallest player in the team, the right-winger signed from Hearts, Martin Moran. Waif-like ball boys were employed by the club. They could gallantly retrieve a loose ball sure, but more importantly they aided the intimidating illusion of Foulke's gigantic presence. He would choose the very smallest ones to stand behind his goals in an attempt to further disrupt an already nervous forward.

Jokes in the Music Halls would often centre on Foulke's size and it was here that he was given the beautifully ironic nickname of "Little Willy". Foulke himself constantly showed himself to be a man of great humour and character. Prior to defeat in that first game at Stockport, he and his team-mates were making their way through the town's cobbled streets from the railway station to the stadium (air conditioned luxury coaches were yet to be devised). There was soon a tug at the giant's trouser leg. He looked down to see a local urchin with something to say. "Eee, you'll get whacked today." Foulke looked incredulous before muttering back, "Then it will be for the first time for Chelsea, m'lad."

Referees and linesman along with opposition and even team-mates would find themselves on the end of his waspish tongue. For years officials had been forced to hide away in their dressing rooms and it wasn't a rarity to see a naked Foulke berating his way around the underbelly of stadiums seeking retribution and looking to take issue with certain decisions he felt he had good reason to disagree with. His move to the nation's capital failed to curb that temper and one referee, a J.T. Howcroft, officiating a Chelsea game against Burslem Port Vale penned his terror of coming face to face with the ire of the incredible Foulke:

> The giant goalkeeper must have got up out of bed on the wrong side, as he seemed to have a grouse against more than one opponent. Ultimately, when a Burslem player made for goal, Foulke did not bother about the ball, but grabbed the player round the middle and hurled him into the back of the net. I pointed at once for a penalty kick. Then the fun started. It took quite a time to persuade Foulke to get into his proper position and it seemed to me he was after my scalp.
>
> Eventually J.T. Robertson, Chelsea's Manager, took the bull by the horns and told Foulke to go into goal or clear out. He did not try and save the shot, but stood glaring at me. I kept a respectable distance until the end of the game, and then made my way faster than usual to the dressing room. If Foulke had put one of those large hands on me I might have been short of some of my anatomy.

Foulke's wrath wasn't exclusively for hapless officials and pertinent opponents. Even railway guards could upset the big man. On one away trip to Gainsbrough Trinity, Foulke was running behind his team, but couldn't produce a ticket and struggled to convince the guard that he was indeed a professional athlete. In one swift movement the guard was swept under Foulke's arm and carried to J.T. Robertson who could backup his argument. Foulkelore? Maybe. Wonderful? Definitely.

Referees aside, Foulke's popularity and that of his team had increased and if anything were feeding off one another. *Football Chat* magazine highlighted just how both entities were pulling in eager and willing punters. "It would be interesting to know if Chelsea's popularity is brought about by newspaper boasting, Foulke's name, or curiosity to see the team who are being provided with the most palatial home of any club playing football." The truth is likely to have been a combination of all three, but without doubt, Foulke's very presence between Chelsea's posts ensured the kind of profile and coverage which the Mears brothers must have dreamed of and which cemented Chelsea Football Club into the established order phenomenally quickly.

Success followed on the pitch as Chelsea strung together a run of results which saw them amongst the promotion challengers by Christmas. Those lucky players charged with bringing success to their "palatial" surroundings were making a real fist of the task. With their giant goalkeeper both attracting intrigued supporters and repelling opposing forwards, life for the new club both on and off the pitch was extremely promising. As well as Foulke's contribution, Chelsea's other signings were showing true class. Jimmy Windridge, the most expensive of those stars, was scoring consistently (he had bagged a hat-trick in that first ever game at the Bridge) and J.T. Robertson, as well as managing the team, was leading by example on the field of play.

Inside-right Davie Copeland and outside-left Jack Kirwan had come from Tottenham's FA Cup winning team of 1901 and were popular additions to the team, whilst Bob Mackie was a strong right-back, who so often would have the roaring voice of his goalkeeper and captain burning his eardrums. Each a good player; but it was Foulke who had fans, both at Chelsea and further afield gasping. Hype was what Mears and the club wanted and in Foulke, hype they got. On arriving at the train station of one Northern city before a game, the players were greeted by two men wearing sandwich boards that urged prospective fans to "COME AND SEE THE TWENTY-FOUR STONE GOALKEEPER!" Foulke could see the funny side and played up to his freak-show image by feigning anger. The two men failed to see the joke and dropped their boards before turning and sprinting to safety.

A RUN of five successive victories from February made promotion a real and tantalising possibility, but the team ran out of steam and could only finish third behind champions Bristol City and Manchester United, there being just two promotion spots available until the 1970s. At the first time of asking Chelsea hadn't made the top division, but they had won the hearts of the nation and wherever they went crowds flocked to see the London team and their huge custodian. A whopping 67,000 turned up at the Bridge to watch the 1-1 draw with Manchester United on Good Friday and Mears could justifiably sit watching his creation, smugly toying with his Edwardian moustache as fans crammed into his stadium to watch his team.

His ground was also proving very popular and it was not only football that had crowds making their way to Stamford Bridge. In October 1905, the All-Blacks' domineering Rugby side arrived to take on Middlesex. The tourists won, but they did manage to concede a try to their meagre opponents, a shock itself. Foulke was there to see the game and couldn't help himself by offering his corpulent services. The offer was taken as a joke, but there is no doubt that the Kiwis would have nursed many more bruises that night had Foulke tried his luck with the oval ball.

With the side competing admirably, and his popularity a linchpin to the club's fortunes, Foulke had every reason to be thriving on his London adventure. The club upped his wages and he loved nothing more than to spend his riches on another passion of his – clothes – in the boutiques that, decades before Mary Quant or the invention of the mini-skirt, scattered the streets of Chelsea.

Foulke's favourite shopping area was nearby Walham Green. Here was this unlikely fashion icon, a modern day and bloated David Beckham shopping for specially tailored fur-collared coats, extra 24-inch collars for his vast shirts – that, due to let's say exuberant perspiring, needed constant replacing – and a penchant for paisley silk scarves. The girls who served him gave Foulke special affection. Allured by his giant frame and colossal presence, they nicknamed him "Baby" and wherever he went, especially in the local taverns (The Star and Garter in Sloane Square was his favourite) heads turned.

His presence was felt wherever he went. His wife, Beatrice, who minded the shop he had established in Sheffield's Asline Road during his years at Bramall Lane, often travelled down from Yorkshire to visit and the couple would spend Saturday night at Foulke's beloved Music Hall. Before the show, it would be announced to great howls of joy from the enthusiastic crowd that the local soccer player was amongst them. Foulke had become a face, a figure amidst the Chelsea scene. In an obituary in the *Sheffield Telegraph* after Foulke's death in 1916, the sports editor recalled those days in London:

> The writer well remembers being present at one of the League games at a time when Foulke was at the height of his popularity. He had been having a particularly good time that afternoon, and at the close the juvenile portion of the crowd, as was their custom, rushed onto the ground, and surrounding the giant a thousand strong, cheered him to the echo. Then Billy amused everyone by good naturedly tucking a couple of the smaller boys under each arm and allowing another to climb his broad shoulders and be carried pick-a-back off the pitch.

When not keeping goal, when not shopping and when not socialising Foulke was, of course, eating. His more enduring nickname of "Fatty" was one well earned. His insatiable appetite has become as legendary as the man himself and stories abound of his capacity for food. "I don't care what they call me," he once declared. "As long as they call me for dinner." Legend even has it that the now well-worn terrace chant *Who ate all the Pies?* originates from this turpsichorean goalkeeper's eating habits. Certainly, Foulke once came down from his hotel room to find he was the first up for breakfast. Having enjoyed his morning meal, he roundly turned on his team-mates' portions and emptied ten further plates before anyone had shown their face. Who was going to take issue with him?

Not the fans. Droves of supporters had a new obsession and in William Foulke they had a player who drew them in and in effect made them love Chelsea Football Club. Goalkeepers have that link with the men, women and children on the terraces or in the stands. Intrinsically, the goalkeeper is a cult hero. They stand alone – like Ken Loach's young protagonist in his film *Kes*, who damply watches whilst his PE teacher desperately seeks out glory – and like the fan, can only hope that others do their job; but unlike the fan (and this is why we love them) the goalkeeper can stick out an arm or a leg and stop the opposition from scoring.

Chelsea's fans have had their fair share of heroes between the sticks. After Foulke, there was Vic Woodley, the handsome and flat-capped keeper of the 1930s. Perhaps the best of all was Peter "The Cat" Bonetti, who protected the goal with world class agility during those halcyon days of the 1960s and 1970s, whilst the Yugoslav Peter Borota entertained and traumatized in equal measure through the late 1970s and early 1980s. Eddie Niedzwiecki was a popular figure in green, while today's No.1, Peter Cech is, through his seeming aversion to high profile gaffes, a Premiership cult in himself.

But did any evoke the sort of interest and intrigue that has pursued Foulke? Will any continue to fascinate 100 years after they hang up their gloves?

BUT FOULKE'S over-indulgence in food and the long distance between himself and his family in Yorkshire would prove too much for even this colossus of a footballer to overcome. His waistline soon would hamper his ability to keep goal and Foulke lost his place in the Chelsea team to Michael Byrne. Having played a mere 35 games for the Blues (ten of those finished with a clean sheet), Foulke took the decision to seek a club nearer to his Sheffield home, wife and children. In April 1905 he signed for Bradford City, where he finished his playing career in 1907.

Many have tried to romanticise Foulke's fortunes after his playing days had finished, claiming that his last days were spent making money by saving penalties from the public on the beaches of Blackpool. It is an interesting notion. Sporting history is littered with images of its most famous protagonists having fallen on harder times. Jesse Owens running races against horses after his heroics in the 1936 Olympics; his pal, the ex-boxing champion of the world, Joe Louis, greeting and entertaining the hungry punters of Las Vegas' casinos; or George Best, swollen and bruised after another fall from his slippery wagon. Heartbreaking yes, but these tales of woe offer the everyday sports fan a warming melancholy, as if these demigods' failings in later life somehow extenuate what they achieved when in their prime.

But Foulke throwing himself onto the sand to earn small change? It just wasn't true. Instead he became a competent businessman and pub owner. Unfortunately he enjoyed one too many drinks and in 1916 died from cirrhosis of the liver (and not the Spanish flu so often alluded to).

Chelsea's first ever programme had introduced their goalkeeper as "the cheeriest of companions, who brims over with good humour", and that popularity has earned him the affection of generation after generation of Chelsea fan. Those forefathers at Stamford Bridge, who in 1905 read that their keeper "possesses all the activity of a cat, combined with the playfulness of a kitten," took him, and therefore the club, to their hearts. He had done his bit. Like a fat, succulent worm he had been the bait and the good people of Chelsea had nibbled and now were hooked on their football club. A century on, Chelsea fans still look back at images of that giant in goal, narrowing the angles like no other before or since; and like those smitten fans of a century ago, they too can refer to William Foulke as "Our little Willy".

GEORGE HILSDON

'GATLING GUN'

1906-1912

CHELSEA CAREER

Games	164
Goals	107
Caps	8

MAGIC MOMENT

On his first appearance Hilsdon blasted five goals against Glossop Town in a 9-2 win. Oh how Robert Fleck could have done with a debut like that

> **The Bishop tells us: 'When the boys come back**
> **They will not be the same; for they'll have fought**
> **In a just cause: they lead the last attack**
> **On Anti-Christ; their comrades' blood has bought**
> **New right to breed an honourable race,**
> **They have challenged Death and dared him face to face.'**
>
> **"They", Siegfried Sassoon**

IN a Leicestershire cemetery in 1941, a measly four people stand solemnly around an unmarked grave. Despite the Football Association paying for the funeral, the lack of interest is a world away from the adulation shown to the deceased man whilst in his prime. George Hilsdon is dead, but the thousands of football fans who cheered his many goals are conspicuous by their absence. It's a quiet, bleak day; a world away from the vibrant Stamford Bridge that Hilsdon illuminated during his six seasons at the young club. If those fans who idolised him from the terraces were told of his sad demise that day, they would no doubt look to the floor and conjure up images of the heroic centre-forward that they so fondly named "Gatling Gun".

Fondly is too weak a word. George Hilsdon was idolised in south-west London. His goals, his bustling style, his handsome face; all appealed to men and women alike, who warmed to his cockney charm. With William Foulke gone, Hilsdon became the darling of a crowd now completely settled into their new passion, Chelsea Football Club.

Pele once said: "without goals, football is nothing" and because of that perhaps obvious fact, those players who put the ball into the net have been afforded a god-like status. Those who have stood, sat, cheered, howled and cried at Stamford Bridge for one hundred years have had their fair share of goalscorers to dote upon. Jimmy Windridge had got the ball rolling alongside that first season's top scorer, Frank Pearson, but Hilsdon quickly eclipsed that popularity. Bob Whittingham before the Great War, Jack Cock a symbol of the roaring twenties, Bob Turnbull, George Mills right through to Jimmy Greaves, Bobby Tambling, Peter Osgood, Kerry Dixon and Jimmy Floyd Hasselbaink; so many in blue have inspired supporters through their enviable knack of finding the net again and again.

WHEN HILSDON signed in the summer of 1906, that passion for goals from the thousands making Stamford Bridge their new home from home was brand shiny new. His 107 of the beauties in 164 games in a Chelsea shirt makes for impressive reading, so it's no surprise that, having adored a man mountain sent to stop goals, the supporters now transferred their adoration to a young athletic man whose desire was for scoring them.

Hilsdon seemed to come from nowhere, earning him the temporary nickname of the "Mushroom centre-forward". Whilst Gus Mears and Fred Parker were putting together their vision of Chelsea FC, Hilsdon too was trying to get his footballing dreams off the ground. A native East-ender born at Bromley-by-Bow, Hilsdon impressed for his Marner Street school team, although, because of his mature size, he had been used as a centre-half. Soon, however, his eye for goal saw him terrorising defences rather than organising them.

West Ham had been alerted to the local prodigy when he was playing for a nearby Sunday team, Boleyn Castle FC, a club the Hammers took on lock, stock and barrel as their reserve team. 18-year-old Hilsdon quickly signed professional forms on the eve of the 1904/05 season. Despite a growing reputation and a typically East-end self-belief, Hilsdon remained in the then Southern League club's reserves where he learnt all about the harsh realities of top level football during a 10-0 defeat to Tottenham in the aptly named London Charity Cup. But Hilsdon was equal to the task and four goals in a 6-0 win over Bristol Rovers in the Western League, in which the Hammers' reserves played, flaunted his talent in front of goal.

West Ham (as they were now known having been born The Thames Ironworks) was a good place for a young footballer to learn his trade. The club's patron, Arnold Hills, who owned the local Ironworks, from which the club took that original name, was all for a puritanical approach and was fervently anti-alcohol. Even into the new century, the *East Ham Echo* referred to their local side as "The Teetotallers", and it seemed that the young Hilsdon – who would later show a fondness for a sip of whatever took his fancy – was in good hands.

Hilsdon scored on his first team debut against New Brompton (later Gillingham) towards the end of the 1904/05 season, but suffered an injury to his foot that hindered his progress and knocked him out of first team contention for some time. Having recovered, Hilsdon again found himself in the reserves and it was in a match for the stiffs in 1906 that he first, and quite accidentally, came to the attention of the new club residing at the other end of the Thames.

CHELSEA'S management and officials had been pleased with their first season's efforts, but were not about to sit around and congratulate themselves. Keeper Bob Whiting now had been charged with the unenviable task of succeeding Foulke, whilst the manager, J.T. Robertson, scurried around the country seeking new and improved footballers for a club hoping to advance their place in the English game. It was across town that Robertson struck gold the day he watched a reserve game at West Ham. The Scot arrived hoping to run the rule over another aspirant, but it was the broad shoulders of George Hilsdon that soon caught his wily eye. Robertson was taken by the young forward's direct and confident approach to the game and set about enquiring whether he could take him across town.

Chelsea were willing to spend money, that was not a problem and it rarely has been in the club's history, bar a decade spell when spending almost caused the club's collapse in the 1970s. But this was a transfer that incredibly lacked any sort of fee. Hilsdon had scored seven goals in sixteen Southern League games for the Hammers, but his injury and his young age somehow convinced the east end club to let him go for free. For Robertson it was a brilliant bit of business. Chelsea fans would hardly have paused on hearing the news of the arrival of a strong, sinewy 20-year-old as they enjoyed their summer drinks in the many local pubs in Chelsea and along the river. Come the new 1906/07 season though, those fans would be raising those very glasses to a new hero. Their first goalscoring champion and the man who set the mould for many to follow in his footsteps.

Chelsea's faithful returned for the new season in good spirits with the sun on their backs. Mears looked fondly on as they arrived in their thousands to watch their team take on the Derbyshire club Glossop as a heat-wave blasted London. Hilsdon was immediately given his chance. The team news soon got tongues wagging as the new boy was preferred up front by Robertson to Frank Pearson, the previous season's leading scorer. What on earth was going on?

For Hilsdon, such reputations meant nothing as he set about tearing into Glossop's defence and incredibly scored five goals in a 9-2 victory. That win remains a record for the club and his haul (Hilsdon also laid on four goals for his appreciative colleagues) was not equalled in a Chelsea shirt until the emergence of the equally prolific Jimmy Greaves fifty years later. More than that, a century later, Hilsdon still remains the only player to bag five goals on his Football League debut. Chelsea fans were in raptures as the heat on their brows was matched only by the warmth in their hearts for the new boy from London's cockney heartland. He had scored a hat-trick by half-time and, as the *Daily News* noted, Hilsdon was "A big factor in the brilliant display by the homesters." George Hilsdon had arrived in spectacular fashion.

His ebullience and purpose was not lost on the same paper's correspondent, who gushed at how well the new boy had performed. "He not only brought an element of dash, he showed sufficient science to warrant the assumption that he would soon 'knit' with his inside men...Some of his touches in the first half were masterly in the extreme."

East London's docks and industry were far removed from the more artistic and cerebral streets of the west. It is oft said that "the West End has the money, and the East End has the dirt", whilst common belief held that there was "Leisure to the West, and labour to the East". That, though, when it came to their footballers, meant little to the growing number of football-mad fans swarming to Stamford Bridge. Hilsdon's goals rained past keeper after keeper and with them came more and more fans, who with every passing week and every passing goal, buried him closer to their hearts.

FOOTBALL'S heroes have always been given special credence and adulation if they happen to hail from the surrounding area. Newcastle's Jackie Milburn, Arsenal's Charlie George, Chelsea's Alan Hudson and, in the modern era, Liverpool's Jamie Carragher; all have been afforded that special bond due to the proximity of their birthplace to the club. In Chelsea's early seasons, and despite his East London heritage, this affection was quickly dealt to Hilsdon. To a new set of fans at their new place of worship, Hilsdon's London roots were more than good enough for them. Indeed, given the plethora of Scots at the club, in the next issue of the Chelsea Chronicle Hilsdon was described as "living proof that to become a first-class footballer it is not necessary to be born north of the Tweed".

Stamford Bridge, after all was a far from a blinkered or bigoted place. It boasted a worldly and sophisticated charm. The vast majority of those packing into the ground were the flat-capped working classes of Chelsea, Fulham and from over the river in Battersea. However, the club could also count on the bohemian and middle-classes that inhabited the surrounding area. They too had taken to the club on their affluent doorsteps. It was a cosmopolitan support not to be found in the northern heartlands of football and if the working classes drew heart from Hilsdon's native charisma, the artistically-minded fan was drawn to his raw and stirring athleticism.

Hilsdon's style continued to reap rewards in terms of goals for his club and adoration from those who paid to watch them. His haul of 27 in that first season at Chelsea saw him selected to play and score a hat-trick for the Football League in a 6-0 win over their Irish counterparts. By February, still only twenty-one, he was playing for his country against Ireland at Goodison Park, thus becoming Chelsea's first England international. Although he didn't find the net in England's 1-0 win and thus found himself displaced for the following game by Manchester City's Irvine Thornley, to lead the attack for England was no mean feat. Chelsea's supporters' chests swelled with pride as their George outshone the likes of Alf "Blaze of Glory" Common who had become the first £1,000 player after a move from Sunderland to Middlesbrough in 1905.

Goals from all angles and from all ranges continued to flow, and soon the fans were referring to Hilsdon as 'Gatling Gun' due to the similarity of his shooting to a machine gun, like Hilsdon a new and devastating weapon. Shots peppered the opposition goal and whatever the angle the hungry Hilsdon would have a go.

A RAT-TAT-TAT of goals whistled Chelsea to promotion as they finished runners-up to Nottingham Forest, who were the only club to blemish an otherwise perfect league record at the Bridge in what had been a marvellous season. Only two years after concocting the very notion of a Chelsea Football Club, Gus Mears' team had made it to the country's top division.

The *Chelsea Chronicle*, published on the last day of the season, summed up the pride felt by all at the club's achievements:

> There is no necessity for us to perform a solo on the Chelsea trumpet. That tune has been played with orchestral effects by the full band of the public press and our legion of followers. That the Chelsea team has accomplished a wonderful feat in gaining promotion, in the second year of the club's existence, to the premier League is beyond cavil.

Whilst that trumpet sounded out over Stamford Bridge and its surrounding streets, Gus Mears, knowing how hard it would be to compete in the First Division was heard to mutter beneath his moustache his catchphrase, "Now for the struggle". Despite their owner's pessimism, the club and its employees had every right to be proud of themselves, especially as they had been left manager-less as early as October in that second season.

J.T. Robertson, whose nous had brought Hilsdon to the club, had not enjoyed the same level of success when it came to relations with those who paid his wages. The Scot had alienated himself from the board by turning up to training stinking of drink and soon the charge of picking the team was removed from his hands and taken up by those men in suits. His position was made untenable when he failed to turn up for a board meeting and with the autumn leaves still falling on the country's pitches, Robertson departed for Glossop.

For Chelsea's assault on the First Division, a new manager had to be found and their choice, David Calderhead, was to instill an amazing stability, remaining in Chelsea's dug-out until 1933. Calderhead had been the manager at Lincoln City for seven years and had come to Chelsea's attention the previous season after a Cup-tie at Stamford Bridge that the Imps had won 1-0 to end Chelsea's 100% home record. Calderhead, on arriving at Stamford Bridge was described as a "kindly, sphinx-faced Scot", and he was immediately charged with making what his boss saw as a "struggle" into a success.

Early in the season it seemed that Mears' pessimism was spot on. One win in their first eight games left the Blues bottom of the pile and so a run of four consecutive victories at the Bridge before Christmas was timely to say the least. Chelsea had tried their best to spend the sort of cash that befits a First Division club, but it was a striker who had cost them nothing who continued to be the side's much-adulated star.

Hilsdon, now an established England international who would bag 14 goals in eight internationals over the next two seasons, had no problem with the step up and strutted about the division with all the confidence of a young man aware of his position as one of the top players in the country. He thrived on the great service afforded him by other forwards such as David Copeland, who had a hand in many of his decisive moments.

HILSDON took that strut and confidence off the pitch and along the Fulham and Kings Roads where he was besieged by an adoring public. Those roads adjoining Chelsea's football club have long held attraction for the footballers who have worked there. Its bars and social life had proved the downfall of J.T. Robertson, while later the enigmatic Scot Hughie Gallacher, local hero Alan Hudson and even current skipper John Terry would be inexorably lured to the many watering holes. George Hilsdon was an early advocate of their lubricating charms.

Decades after his father's death, George Hilsdon Jr recalled just how popular his father had become: "People followed father around the streets", he said. "He scored some fantastic goals for Chelsea, beating five men and putting the ball away. One of father's assets was his strength of thigh; he was very hard to knock off the ball."

Those strong thighs were the talk of the Bridge. Hilsdon scored 24 goals in that 1907/08 season and helped Chelsea stave off the threat of relegation (they eventually finished just three points off the drop). Six of that tally came in an FA Cup tie against Worksop who were surgically removed 9-0 and to this day that result remains a record domestic cup win for Chelsea. Hilsdon also continued to shine in England white, the highlight being a four goal haul in a 7-0 win over Hungary in Budapest in the summer of 1907.

Hilsdon's goals were the remedy to a season spent battling for survival, but were enough to see crowds at Chelsea remain high. Visits from Woolwich Arsenal and Manchester City topped 50,000 and attendance figures rarely dipped below the 30,000 mark. The fan base was there, the country's most feared striker was there, but the club continued to simply tread water in a division that was proving tough. The 1908/09 season saw the club finish eleventh out of twenty with Hilsdon's 25 goals again the difference between mid-table stability and possible relegation. No sign yet of the challenge for the game's honours which both Mears and the club's fans so desperately desired.

A hat-trick in a 3-3 draw against the then leaders Everton accentuated both Hilsdon's appeal to the fans and his importance to an erratic Chelsea. His opening effort was scored within seconds of kick-off, put away with clever precision before the Merseysiders had even managed a touch. The second was more direct and underlined his muscular approach. Hilsdon picked up the ball and resisted foul after foul before lashing the ball in. His third was a cool penalty. He had given a masterclass in forward play and the press were in wonder at a player they called: "The most dangerous man on the pitch." The *Daily News* didn't stop there. "On current form I should say that Hilsdon stands alone as a centre-forward."

He stood out to the crowd and many felt that Hilsdon was somewhat carrying the side. As ever the club stated their naked ambition by reaching for the cheque book and signing Hilsdon'd fellow England international Vivian Woodward from Tottenham. Woodward was a famous and much-admired amateur. He too was one of the great attackers of his era and the prospect of a three-pronged attack with Hilsdon and Jimmy Windridge was anticipated with glee. However, as generations of Chelsea fans would so painfully discover, expectation can be eclipsed by reality and 1909/10 finished in relegation thanks to a last day defeat at Tottenham. It wasn't that the dream strike force hadn't worked; in fact they had become victims of their own success as all three players were too often on international duty and missing from league action.

So desperate had Chelsea's board been to stave off the drop that they spent thousands on players such as Derby's vastly experienced England international right-half Benjamin Warren, to keep them up. But it was to no avail. The Football League frowned upon what they saw as gluttony and unsporting behaviour and it was as a direct result of Chelsea's spending that they introduced a transfer deadline to curb such future sprees.

Chelsea's fans had every right to feel aggrieved by relegation. Despite their team's travails, they continued to turn up in their droves and a Christmas match against Newcastle United saw 70,000 at the Bridge, a British record at the time. Like their interest in the team's fortunes, the fans' love of Hilsdon refused to diminish. Woodward would become a kind of "Boy's Own" hero to many; his good looks and Corinthian manner was hard to resist, but Hilsdon appealed to the masses. He walked with them, laughed with them and sweated for them. Whilst Woodward, an architect by trade, wore an immaculate blazer, Hilsdon could be found in a smoky bar sharing a beer and a joke with his adoring public. Chelsea paid Hilsdon £4 a week, but the striker made good bonuses from the £1 per goal that Mears generously offered and he wasn't averse to spending it in the many bars of Chelsea, Fulham and Battersea. The fans loved him for it, but his penchant for a tipple would lead to his downfall.

IT IS a truth universally acknowledged that with sporting success comes unwanted attention from hangers-on and those determined to bask in the glory of others. Hilsdon was surrounded by those who genuinely admired and idolised him, but so too did he come across those eager to get what they could from his fame. For every fan who bought their hero a deserved jar, there was another hoping to get something off the relaxed star. "What wasn't widely known at the time, was that my mother had chronic asthma", recalled Hilsdon junior. "It affected her terribly – and affected father as well. He used to come home and see her suffering – it was no surprise that after a while he started taking a drink or two."

Still only 25, Hilsdon managed to cope with his growing alcoholic intake and score 19 goals in Division Two, but Chelsea missed out on promotion at the death. It was to be his last great season and soon a combination of injury and ill-living saw Hilsdon's goals (unlike his post-match glass) dry up. One commentator accused him of being "too sociable, too careless with his strength and vitality." Hilsdon's weight ballooned, his swashbuckling yet intelligent style of football was replaced by a more slumbering and flaccid approach and his one goal from ten appearances in the 1911/12 season was hardly the catalyst to his side's promotion that year.

The fans still held George in great regard. Hilsdon's socialising was the epitome of what the club had become in the eyes of a still-doting public. Music Hall gags abounded about members of the Chelsea staff and their drinking habits, which saw one unnamed player suspended for drunkenly knocking out a cab horse (and we thought Dennis Wise had issues). For Hilsdon, though, his star had been eclipsed by the goalscoring feats of Woodward and now Bob Whittingham, who had joined from Bradford City for a whopping £1,300 as part of the infamous spending spree of 1910.

Hilsdon agreed to leave in the summer of 1912 after the club quite rightly recognised his part in their formative adventures by granting him a testimonial against Fulham (the visitors won 2-0), and the £180 raised went some way to assist his faltering finances. The fans turned out to cheer the man who had switched them on to true sporting worship and begun the cult of the goalscorer at Stamford Bridge. Hilsdon had become the first Chelsea scoring centurion and to his fans it was a sad day when at only 26, Hilsdon packed up his old kit bag and made his way back to his roots and Southern League West Ham United.

The Hammers were glad to have him and, although never reaching the high standards he had so prolifically set at Chelsea, his goals did revive the club's fortunes. They finished third in 1912/13 and just like at Stamford Bridge, Hilsdon soon became a firm favourite with the fans. One of his most impressive performances in claret and blue ironically came at Stamford Bridge in January 1913 in an FA Cup first round second replay against West Bromwich Albion. The Midlanders were sent packing 3-0 and Hilsdon – no doubt in front of many who came to reminisce on his talents – scored twice. The east-ender now, despite being just 27, became known as the "Old International" and went on to play 92 games for West Ham, scoring 35 times and assisting in the development of soon-to-be Hammers legend Syd Puddefoot. But in 1914 careers and lives were halted by horrendous conflict.

In an act all too understandable, but perhaps not in keeping with his heroic image, George tried to avoid active service – being caught by the police hiding in a chicken run on one occasion. Eventually he was successfully called up, as his son recalls: "Father was still an idol when he played for West Ham, but the First World War put an end to all that. He joined the East Surrey Regiment, but it was not until the last year of the war that he had to fight. A kindly brigadier kept him out of the trenches, because he was the king of the regimental soccer and cricket teams, but then came the last big German push, and father copped the mustard gas at Arras."

Now 33, Hilsdon returned home, but never played top class football again. That gas attack meant he suffered excruciating pain in both legs and so the man they once called "Gatling Gun" was forced to lay down his weapons and quietly retire. He tried his luck in management at non-league Chatham Town in Kent, but it was not to last. George scraped a living as a teaboy on building sites, ran a pub and, on occasion, organised a dodgy raffle round east end boozers – "Mrs Hilsdon" always won. His good humour and that cockney charm, which had endeared him to so many supporters, stood him in good stead as a publican, but with the onset of a Second World War, he was evacuated from his east end home and in 1941 in Leicester, aged only 56, he died of tuberculosis.

CHELSEA supporters would have other heroes, that's the wonderfully fickle prerogative of football fans, but Hilsdon left his mark on the club. When he left, Chelsea had a weather vane placed on top of the East Stand depicting a footballer in action and that footballer was George Hilsdon. It was viewed by all as a good luck charm and there may have been something in that as, once the club took it down for planned renovations (that never quite happened), the team suffered its worst run of form and in 1983 were very nearly were relegated to the old Third Division for the first time in their history. The vane soon made a comeback, standing proudly first on the West Stand and now on the East.

Stamford Bridge, of course, is not the place it once was. To many it's a shame, to others it's just progress, but as Roman Abramovich's wind of change rages through the stadium, there is something reassuring about that twisting, turning weather vane. Hilsdon remains at the ground he helped make famous. The ball is at his feet and the goal, as ever, at the mercy of the "Gatling Gun".

HUGHIE GALLACHER

1930-1934

CHELSEA CAREER

Games	144
Goals	81
Caps	20

MAGIC MOMENT

55,000 crammed into the Bridge to see Gallacher's debut in a game that saw him score two and set-up three against Manchester United, who were thrashed 6-2

'THE MAGIC FEET'

> **Though I soon became typecast in Hollywood as a gangster and a hoodlum, I was originally a dancer, an Irish hoofer, trained in vaudeville tap dance. I always leapt at the opportunity to dance...**
>
> **James Cagney**

TODAY they are everywhere, but Hughie was the first. For decades they have flocked to Chelsea, but Hughie was the first. Be they on the field of play or watching from the stands, superstars have made their way to Stamford Bridge, bringing an extra touch of glamour and razzmatazz to an already spruce Fulham Road.

Today the champagne set are drawn to Roman Abramovich's football club like moths to his oil-fuelled flame, but that's nothing new. Lord Attenborough, Raquel Welch, Michael Caine, Robbie Williams, over the years they've all come to see the boys in blue be they Tommy Lawton, Peter Osgood, Ruud Gullit or Frank Lampard. Whilst Abramovich continues to open his well-like wallet, many more superstars will come, but Hughie was the first.

In the May of 1930, Chelsea Football Club needed Hughie Gallacher more than Hughie Gallacher needed Chelsea Football Club. He had become a football icon and was revered and admired all over Britain for his compulsive style of forward play, which had catapulted him into a new, supreme echelon of football popularity.

On Tyneside, where he captained Newcastle United, Gallacher was everything. He wore the number nine shirt and made it a sacred cloth to those fans who crammed St James' Park to see him feint, dribble and score. Yes, before "Wor" Jackie Milburn. Gallacher was a force of nature, he was the best of the best, the pinnacle looking down on a footballing world he dominated.

CHELSEA were desperate for such dizzy heights. They and their army of fans could only dream of sitting proudly on top of the pile. They strove for success, but each time they looked likely to reach those lofty and grandiose planes, they stumbled from altitude sickness and were left enviously looking up at the party above. Aside from a third place finish in the season immediately following the Great War, which can be readily discarded as a one-off due to the unstable nature of football in the aftermath of that horrendous conflict, Chelsea were confirmed First Division also-rans. Relegation to Division Two duly ensued in 1924.

What made matters worse was that their London neighbours and soon to be bona fide rivals, Arsenal, had emerged at the end of the 1920s as a new mighty force in the game; able to accept the challenge of competing with the presiding dominant forces from the North of England.

For too long that challenge had been lying dormant. Huddersfield had monopolised the Football League in the 1920s, but now Arsenal, who had managed to nab Herbert Chapman from the Yorkshire club's managerial offices, were entering the ascendancy. They won their first trophy, beating Huddersfield 2-0 at Wembley in the FA Cup Final of 1930, and in the likes of Alex James and Cliff Bastin, possessed the personnel to finally stamp some Southern authority on their Northern cousins.

But what of Chelsea? What of the club who had been conceived amidst the very notion of winning silverware for themselves and for London; but who instead had hitherto given their supporters only hope rather than truth, dreams rather than reality.

It wasn't until 1930 that they at last made a return to the top flight, helped by the form of Scottish goal-grabber Andy Wilson, who also hadn't come cheap. The British record transfer fee of £6,000 handed to Middlesbrough for the skilful little inside-forward in 1923 showed that the club's mandate for splashing cash still continued, as did its correlation with lack of success. As Chelsea now made their way toward what they prayed would be a prolonged spell in the First Division, the club's board again took the policy of flexing some financial might.

Chelsea's Doctor Frankenstein, Gus Mears had died in 1912 without ever seeing the successful monster that he had so hoped to create fully come to life. However, his long-time friend and now Chairman of the club, Claude Kirby, shared Mears' belief that Chelsea should aspire to be the best and therefore should employ the best, whatever the cost. They were to spend and they were to spend big.

IN 1930, in terms of stardom, they didn't come any bigger than Hughie Gallacher. In terms of physical stature, there wasn't much to him. At 5 feet 5 inches he was hardly the type to instill fear into a centre-half at first glance. However, what he lacked in inches he more than made up for in strength, guts, speed, temerity and sheer skill and if it was a star that Chelsea needed to illuminate their path in the First Division, then they had to have Hughie Gallacher.

Superstar? Never had this embryonic term been used in relation to association football. Superstars were the beautiful and glamorous movie actors and actresses from Hollywood who were by now not only appearing on the nation's silver cinema screens, but speaking on them too. "Talkies" were a phenomenon and those who starred in them were, by the late 1920s, beginning to wrap the tinsel around Tinseltown.

The Jazz Singer had begun the trend and those appearing on the big screens of London soon took on iconic status. Charlie Chaplin and Lon Chaney were massive hits whilst the likes of Fred Astaire, Mae West and James Cagney were about to embark on the "Golden Age of Hollywood". These were the untouchables, accessible only in your local cinema where their projected images were literally larger than life. These were the superstars.

Football? No. Football had always been about real life. Real guys, your neighbours, friends, men like you who happened to be good at this wonderful new game. Footballers weren't superstars. They could be heroic sure, but they weren't luminaries, until now. The lofty heights in which footballers could view themselves were propelled by the rising amount of money that clubs were prepared to spend on gaining the services of these young men.

"Dixie" Dean may have been the priceless goalscoring darling of the blue half of Merseyside, but big money – superstar amounts – was starting to be paid for similar talents. Both Alex James and David Jack were enticed to Chapman's Highbury for new record transfer fees and it took the first five figure sum, £10,890, for Bolton to consider selling the latter in 1928. The Chairman of the FA, Sir Charles Clegg, was incredulous at that amount and he wasn't alone. One notable and incensed bishop decried "the white slave traffic in footballers".

That, though, wasn't about to put Chelsea off. Arsenal had set the standard and if Chelsea were going to compete then they too must go for broke. So, it was Gallacher that they identified as their man, but it wasn't going to be easy. Class isn't cheap and here was a player idolised in the North East.

Why would he want to come to London, hundreds of miles from his native Lanarkshire? However, where there's a will (and an open cheque book) there's a way and perhaps that bishop had a point. It soon became apparent that it really mattered little what Gallacher wanted, his voice was redundant whilst money, as ever, talked volumes.

IN 1930, that language dictated by currency was of no interest to the average Newcastle fan. That fan simply made their pilgrimage to St James' Park in order to worship a hero who, with every weaving run and every thunderous shot played himself into their hearts. Gallacher, despite his sour-faced demeanour, despite his foul temper, or perhaps because of both them and his talent, had become, in the eyes of his fans, the embodiment of Newcastle United. There was no way he could leave.

They were wrong. Chelsea had long been admirers of the forward and indeed had tried to sign him from Airdrieonians in 1925, but he had made the shorter journey to Newcastle. This time Chelsea would get their man. For all of Gallacher's bewitching talents the enthusiasm and adoration that came his way from the terraces was often far from matched in the club's boardroom, where too often the lively Gallacher's antics on and off the field had caused them both embarrassment and bother.

Run-ins with referees, stories of drunken frolics and intermittent sendings off tested the resolve of directors and managers, who sensed that their centre-forward was in danger of becoming bigger than the club that they presided over; by implication, bigger than them. Gallacher may have brought the League title to the North East in 1927 (the club's last Championship triumph), but soon his erratic side had, to those paying the bills, become more than a little worrying.

In December 1927 Newcastle had hosted Huddersfield Town, a dominant force who had just completed the first ever hat-trick of League title wins. The Terriers were also a foe with whom Gallacher enjoyed a robust relationship. As ever, Newcastle's number nine was having his every movement checked by a Huddersfield defence hell-bent on stopping a player that they knew only too well could damage their ambitions as quickly as it took to drop those stocky shoulders and unleash a thunderbolt from those stout legs. Huddersfield went on to win the game 3-2 (Gallacher got both of his team's goals), but Newcastle were denied two rather obvious-looking penalties when twice their captain was brought down in the box.

Twice his pleas went unnoticed and on the second occasion the referee ignored his flag-waving linesman and waved play on. To the high-spirited Gallacher enough was enough. Without hesitation, he sprinted over to the referee unleashing the kind of language that made a Glaswegian shipyard sound like an episode of the Tellytubbies. The referee hadn't taken kindly to such abuse and immediately asked for his tormentor's name. Gallacher, his boyish eyes having taken on a wild expression of their own, obliged, but wanted to know the name of the official. "Mr Fogg," came the reply.

"Fogg is your name," chortled Gallacher, "and you've been in one all game."

The row continued, with Gallacher unable and unwilling to let up. The red mist had descended and the compass was lost. Even the shrill of the final whistle failed to perturb the incensed Scot. He pursued the official into his changing room to find Mr Fogg leaning over his almost full bath. Suddenly, the little boy in Gallacher emerged with deviant ease. In the same way that Gallacher's inner child made him such a joy to watch as he glided past lost defenders, he quietly stole up behind the unaware referee and kicked him head-first into his bath.

The Football Association was not amused. Gallacher was suspended for two months and Newcastle lost any chance they had of further league success, leaving the board to ponder on the future of the man so adored by their public.

GALLACHER'S drinking had increased since his move to England and tales of drunken brawls were rife. A court appearance after an incident on the Tyne and rumours of him having to be collected from a local pub prior to a match were beginning to exhaust the men in suits. Were they brave enough to cash in on their star though? For all their concerns here was a man producing the goods on the pitch and adored by those paying at the turnstiles.

In 1929, Newcastle toured Hungary and were on the receiving end of a 4-1 defeat at the hands of a Hungarian select XI. It was an angry game and tempers were running high when Gallacher, about to take a penalty, pointed predictively to the spot he was going to place the ball. The crowd didn't take to such brazen confidence and, having already been involved in another brawl, Gallacher was summarily dismissed. His walk to the dressing room was met with a cacophony of jeers, a swarm of missiles and a torrent of Hungarian phlegm.

If that wasn't enough, their hosts complained to the authorities that many of the Newcastle team had been drunk on the pitch. As ever it was Gallacher who took the brunt of any alcohol fuelled accusations and he was forced to explain to an FA hearing that he and his team-mates may have smelt of booze as they had, on that sunny day in Eastern Europe, washed out their mouths with Whisky and water prior to taking the field. Soon excuses weren't enough and that's when Chelsea stepped in.

Newcastle had appointed their first manager, Andy Cunningham, an ex-Glasgow Rangers legend, who had the task of working out what to do with Gallacher. There was fierce speculation regarding the player's future, but still many simply couldn't believe that the club would sell a man of Gallacher's ability to one of their rivals. Cunningham, though, was serious and he had the backing of a tired board.

That summer, for all his problems, the 27-year-old Gallacher was actually content at Newcastle. He revelled in the talismanic role that had been afforded him by the passionate Geordie support, the way in which the fans gorged on his every move and yes, he had considered leaving, but that had passed. He had scored 133 goals in 160 games on Tyneside, he was playing well for Scotland and despite the odd inner-battle with his own genius, life was sweet.

Gallacher returned from international duty in France with a discipline issue once again his loyal companion. He had played well in Paris, scoring both goals in the Scots' 2-0 victory, but had broken the team's curfew with a celebratory binge in the bars of the country's racy capital. He was reprimanded by the Scottish FA, but returned to Britain to be greeted with far more life-altering news. He'd been sold.

Years later, Gallacher wrote of his alarm at a move that was done firmly and unapologetically behind his back:

> A transfer from Newcastle never entered my mind with the close season holidays invitingly before me. I had been at home in Scotland only a few hours when there was a knock at the door. Two strangers stood there. They introduced themselves as Mr Claude Kirby, Chelsea Chairman, and his chief scout, Jack Fraser. 'We've come to take you to Chelsea, Hughie,' the Chairman said.
>
> 'That's very nice of you, gentleman, but I don't particularly want to go, and surely you are overstepping the limit approaching me like this,' I replied. Then came the shattering blow. 'That's all fixed, Hughie, we've come to terms with United.'
>
> "So it had all come out. While I had been playing abroad for my country, the odds had been talked over. I was brought into the deal only at the last moment. You may think I could have refused. I could. But when I felt there was obviously no future for me at Newcastle, there was only one thing I could do.

"I had a chat with the Chelsea people, but still felt far from easy at the prospect of the change. My visitors suggested I accompany them to see the Newcastle representatives. They were waiting at a Glasgow hotel. Now some of my doubts began to clear. 'Hughie, my boy, you're in a happy position at Newcastle,' I mused. It was obvious that both clubs had set their hearts on the deal, though. Newcastle were keen to release me, Chelsea keen to sign me.

"Why Newcastle wanted to let me go I never found out, but with such an attitude, I was bound to leave the club. Better sooner than later. By the time I arrived in Glasgow I knew I was going to move. We started negotiations at 11 o'clock in the morning, and before the day was out I had bounced up half a dozen times, put on my bowler and marched homewards. First, Chelsea officials pulled me back, then it was Newcastle folk in one corner, with me seated among Chelsea officials at the nearby table. Afternoon came and went. So did tea-time. Then, at last, the negotiations were settled to everyone's satisfaction. Newcastle were to receive a £10,000 fee. Chelsea had succeeded in their mission."

That made Gallacher Britain's second most expensive player, but Hughie, so often an object of desire, was stunned at the notion that a team would no longer need or want him. It hurt, but that pain could stay bottled up, for now. In public he got on with being the confident and cheeky wee Hughie that he had always been. "I did well at Airdrie," he said after the signing had gone public. "I have done well at Newcastle. I'll do well anywhere." Arrogance? In fact, he was in many ways trying to convince himself, rather then the press or the fans. The latter, after all, had every faith in him and after years of entertainment and wonderment with a football, that fealty was not without reason.

HUGHIE Kilpatrick Gallacher was born on 2nd February 1903 in Bellshill, a mining town just a short bus ride from Glasgow. His father had come to Scotland from Ireland to find work and, despite the family's Protestant roots, soon the young Gallacher had two passions, football and Celtic. Having left the Bellshill Academy, Gallacher found himself working in a munitions factory, but after the First World War, like so many others, was soon down the local pits. But it was with a football of whatever description that he became well known for in the tough, unforgiving territory in which he grew up.

It was the much-told tale of a working class boy, a ball made from rags at his feet; nurturing his talent for a sport that would eventually take him out from the filthy ravages of the coalface and into the heady world of football, where national acclaim and goodwill would wipe the grime from his eager face. Gallacher's own tale would include far more drama and tragedy than most, but, whilst a young man and with his name tantamount to footballing excellence, his was a future in which only glory beckoned.

Having starred for his country's junior teams, Gallacher signed professional forms for Queen of the South where 19 goals in his first nine games got tongues wagging. His prolific boots and swaggering style made another move inevitable. That next step was to Airdrieonians where – having got over a very serious bout of pneumonia – the impish Gallacher was, quite simply, a revelation, bagging 91 goals in 111 games.

This phenomenon helped Airdrie to three successive runners-up spots, and an SFA Cup victory in 1924, the club's only major trophy. Having scored 39 goals in that season, Gallacher was by now a full international. His game had taken his country by storm, but now his name was being coveted by those prying eyes from south of the border. In 1925 Scotland beat Wales 3-1 at Tynecastle with Gallacher netting twice. His second had the crowd purring with delight and became the stuff of legend as those lucky enough to witness his effort took great delight in relaying it to their young sons.

Children would hear how "wee Hughie" ran at the Welsh, the ball loyal only to his boot as he glided past defender after defender. Five Welsh dragons lay slain on the Edinburgh turf as Gallacher raced towards the goal with only the keeper in his way. Albert Gray, Oldham's much-approved custodian, came flying out, eager to stop the flying Scot in his tracks, but Gallacher contrived to chip the ball nonchalantly over his flailing body, hopped over him, trapped the ball and knocked it into the begging net. It was a moment everyone present savoured, with even those on the receiving end of such brilliance unable to hide their appreciation. "As I turned to walk back," said Gallacher, "I saw the Welsh players applauding me".

Such form brought an inevitable move to England in December 1925 with Newcastle securing Gallacher's signature for a fee of £6,500, which eclipsed that paid by Chelsea for Andy Wilson as the British record. His club record seasonal tally of 36 goals helped Newcastle to win the League title in 1927, but now he found himself in London, whilst Chelsea found themselves with a player not averse to a spot of bother.

Tragedy had arrived at Gallacher's door early in his adult life. He had married a local Catholic girl at the age of 17, but their first born son had not lived past the age of one. That marriage did not survive such tumultuous tests and would soon end, although not officially until 1932. By then Gallacher had become a byword for foul-mouthed temper tantrums. His fondness for oaths, like his startling ability, had been honed from a young age and his team-mate at Airdrie, Bob McPhail, noted just how irksome and lively with language Gallacher could be. "He was a selfish wee fellow, he thought of no-one but himself. He had a vicious tongue and he used it on opponents. I learned swear words from Hughie that I had never heard before."

CHELSEA had taken a huge gamble. The fans were ecstatic at the thought of seeing a player they had previously enviously witnessed at Stamford Bridge or whom they had heard about on that new invention for mass communication, the wireless, and they longed for the new 1930/31 season to begin. Their new acquisition on the other hand had doubts. He had agreed to leave Newcastle; he knew when he was not wanted, but London? Here was a city where a man could find himself in strife. There was always a buck to be made and as George Hilsdon had found even in the far less avaricious 1900s, there were always those willing to take advantage of those whose talent with a ball went hand in hand with a thirst for a stiff drink.

"I was almost a stranger when I moved to London," Gallacher noted some years later. "I had never been to happy about the South, and wondered whether I could settle down in new digs and among fresh faces." It was a tough place to be and a tough time to be there. Peter Ackroyd notes as much in *London: The Biography*: "The 1930s have in particular been anatomised as the age of anxiety, when economic depression, unemployment and the prospect of another world war materially affected the general disposition of the city....London is large enough, and heterogeneous enough, to reflect any mood or topic. It can hold, or encompass, anything..." But could it hold Hughie Gallacher?

Blissfully aware of Gallacher's misgivings, the fans relished the prospect of someone who might just galvanise their side into action. The 1920s had been a time of recklessness, frivolity and laughter. Unfortunately much of the latter was aimed at Chelsea. They were a team that promised so much yet delivered so little, a team that famously could not score goals and that was a fact not lost upon grateful Music Hall comedians desperate for jolly material. In the 1930s a popular Music Hall song entitled *The Day That Chelsea Won The Cup* alluded to events that were yet to, and more importantly, were unlikely to ever happen.

Now, though, they had Hughie Gallacher, the scourge of goalkeepers all over the land, a player who at Newcastle had scored a remarkable 143 goals in 174 appearances. Now he was theirs. But the spending did not stop there as manager David Calderhead persuaded his board to turn their wallets upside down and empty them out. In a summer of financial frolicking, Chelsea also splashed out on Gallacher's fellow Scots; £6,000 for Alec Cheyne, an inside-forward from Aberdeen and £8,500 on Alec Jackson, a wonderfully graceful forward from Huddersfield Town, who became the fourth most expensive player in British footballing history. The latter had played alongside Gallacher in Scotland's famous 5-1 mauling of England at Wembley in 1928. The "Wembley Wizards" were together again, but whilst the twang of Scottish accents eased Gallacher's transition into his new and alien home, the arrival of so many new faces upset the existing equilibirum.

CHELSEA'S squad had manfully won promotion, but they now had to come to terms with glamorous and hugely successful new team-mates. Jackson had won titles with Huddersfield, Cheyne was an acclaimed international and Hughie Gallacher was, well, Hughie Gallacher. The steady ship that won promotion had been rocked. It may have been warranted as it clearly wasn't a vessel that would guide the club into Championship-winning waters, but nevertheless the petty jealousies and clash of egos soon brought with them rocky seas.

Tommy Law, a fellow "Wembley Wizard" had been at the club since 1927 and, as skipper, noted just how problematic the change to the club's personnel became. "I was captain all right, at least until we got onto the pitch, then we had eleven captains all telling each other what to do".

The problems soon became evident on the pitch, but Gallacher's popularity and pulling power were just as apparent on the bulging terraces. Inevitably, the fixture list threw Chelsea together with Newcastle United for only Gallacher's second game in his new blue strip. The game was to be played in the North East on a Wednesday afternoon, but that didn't hinder the Geordie fans, desperate to catch a glimpse of the player they still adored. Over 68,000 fans (still Newcastle's record attendance) crammed into St James' Park whilst anything between 20 and 40,000 more were locked outside or clambered onto any free high ground that would afford them a look.

Newcastle won 1-0, but Chelsea fans could marvel in a first glimpse of their new hero when Chelsea beat Manchester United 5-3 just days later at Stamford Bridge. 55,000 Blues rejoiced as Gallacher scored twice and helped Alec Cheyne to a hat-trick, but that September day was to prove a highlight in a mediocre season as the club finished 12th, with only two other sides scoring fewer goals.

Gallacher netted 14 times, but he hadn't settled into his surroundings. He was restless and much of the training – which often somewhat monotonously consisted of running around the Stamford Bridge dog track – bored the easily fed up Gallacher. The Scot would instead ask to be able to run the nearby streets where the ever changing scenery brought light relief from the work at hand. The problem with that was that he often never returned. Days sometimes passed without any explanation and an aggrieved management could only hope that they were being spent "exercising" in the aerobic sense of the word.

The troubles continued. On a cold 1930 December day in Grimsby, Gallacher was receiving some rough treatment from over-zealous defenders. He retaliated with a wayward elbow, but soon found himself – despite the three-quarter inch strip of cotton wool he wore under socks as shin pads, such modern inventions having yet to see the light of day – needing more medical attention. He'd had enough and couldn't hold back. The referee was told clearly just how Gallacher felt about his abilities and after a cascade of bad language, Chelsea's fireball was dismissed. "Had I been forced to make a decision on my future," Gallacher later mused, "at that moment I would never have kicked a ball again." Once the FA had dealt with the incident he wouldn't kick a ball for two months.

Chelsea supporters had pinned their hopes on Gallacher's mercurial ability, flocking in their tens of thousands in the belief that he was the man who would at last bring them that holy grail, a trophy. Gallacher found that expectation a dead weight. Sure, he would do well on the pitch, but he was never going to take to the Chelsea fans like he had taken to their Geordie counterparts. He even found some of the Londoners quite fickle and was amazed at how many of the locals around Chelsea and Fulham actually had no time for their football club. Why did so many of them choose to inform the club on the supposed misdemeanours carried out by a number of the players? "Letters flooded into the club," he complained, "accusing us of all sorts of things with which we were not connected. Had the manager believed them he must have wondered whether we were ever sober."

But while Gallacher's sullen temperament plumbed new depths, on the pitch his scything runs and rapier shots continued to pull in bumper crowds. Be they fascinated by the little tank-like footballer Gallacher, or the red-eyed angry Gallacher, they still came. Footballers by the late 1920s and into the 1930s had become icons rather than just heroes. Cigarette cards were eagerly swapped amongst enthusiastic schoolboys, whilst pull-out photos were common place in new and popular publications such as *Boy's Football Favourite*, who as well as offering the fan a closer look at the country's "stars", would also take them into fictional realms where glory and adventure went hand in hand. Realms such as these:

> No-one is likely to forget the long and unflagging sequence of stories about football matches in which the lemons were poisoned at half-time, in which rascally backs hacked at the home forwards with boots containing poisoned nails, and bogus referees blew poison darts at players…[of players] who spent the week shaking off kidnappers and trying to clear his own or his father's name. It was all he could do every Saturday afternoon to break through the crooks' blockade and reach the ground in time to score the winning goal.

Gallacher was that home forward. Somehow he encapsulated that spirit of adventure. For generations Chelsea fans would take to those players who lived and played on the edge and in Gallacher they had their first swashbuckling hero, fighting his own demons, staving off the evil and meddling Football Association, whilst somehow getting to the Bridge just in time to score the winning goal.

BUT GALLACHER offered real-life intrepid incident. Many had heard of a game he had played in Belfast as a young member of a Scottish League XI, over the water to take on their Irish counterparts. Gallacher had been at his tantalising best. The crowd and opposition had been subjected to his full repertoire as, for the first 45 minutes, they were forced to endure neat flicks, sly step-overs and tantalising, teasing control.

The half-time whistle brought the home fans a certain amount of respite, but as the Scots relaxed in their dressing room a note was passed under the door stating that if Gallacher didn't stop his show-boating, he would be shot. This only incensed Gallacher and during the second half he ran his markers ragged once more, scoring five goals in a 7-3 win and leaving the field with a cheeky grin firmly in place. He had been warned to watch his back as he ventured into Belfast after the match to visit friends. Cocksure Hughie was sure he would be fine, but was instead startled when gunfire sprayed bullets over a nearby wall as he casually walked near Queen's Bridge. It was a shock, but still Gallacher had the last word. "I will have to extend my stay in Belfast," he joked. "It seems I still haven't managed to teach the Irish how to shoot straight."

Typical Gallacher. Mischievous, unnerving, sometimes liable to offend, but always engrossing. Love him or loathe him, he had style and not just on the pitch did he strut. Like the cinema heroes he had come to adore, or the jazz musicians who hypnotised him on his many jaunts along the Kings Road, his hair was immaculately styled, his suits always crisp, his tie always sharp. The Fedora hat and the gleaming spats finished off the look. Here was a man about town.

He loved the adulation that went with being a top footballer and, whilst the Shed wasn't the Gallowgate End, he still had a willing audience for whom he could perform. Fans adored him for his goals and more importantly his image. He depicted what it was to be a Chelsea man, both brilliant and confident. They'd had their heroes, but Gallacher offered something new. He had a swagger that other footballers couldn't match. Foulke and Hilsdon had touched on it, but in the depressed 1930s this Scotsman's joie-de-vivre was all-encompassing. He was a maverick; like his hero James Cagney, he was the anti-hero the public craved.

With that role came mood swings and a persecution complex. Referees continued to take the brunt of his frustrations and by the end of that first, ordinary season Gallacher was already thinking about a move elsewhere. In private he had often fantasised about teaming up with Alex James at Arsenal, but whilst a move up the Piccadilly Line excited the Scot, the Chelsea board were adamant that he was going nowhere and even turned down a transfer request submitted by the player during the close season.

To placate their enigmatic forward, Chelsea made Gallacher captain (he had also been skipper at St. James' Park during their 1926/27 Championship season) and it was to prove key as he played his most productive season for the Blues taking them to the brink of an FA Cup final and scoring 30 goals. The FA Cup run was memorable for those fans who allowed themselves to dream of a day out at Wembley. Tranmere were beaten after a replay (Gallacher scored in a 5-3 win at the Bridge) before West Ham hosted their London rivals at Upton Park. The game was played in an unnerving atmosphere as pockets of crowd trouble were accompanied by the home support giving their visitors plenty of verbal abuse and Gallacher, like all threatening opposition players, came in for the majority of that stick. With his sexuality constantly in question, he thrived on the attention. He had laughed off gunfire in Belfast, so being called a "poof" by a bunch of irate cockneys was to prove an easy day's work and Gallacher silenced their jeers as he scored with a fizzing shot. The Hammers were beaten 3-1.

Gallacher, through injury, missed the tie with Sheffield Wednesday, which was won after a replay, but he returned for the quarter-final at Liverpool, which proved a wonderful football occasion. Steam rose off a packed Kop as Gallacher stalked around the Anfield pitch with intent. He had, for a long time, relished his games against the Merseysiders and especially their Irish goalkeeper Elisha Scott and that day he ran out on top, scoring the clinching second in a 2-0 win.

CHELSEA were in the semi-final for only the third time in their history (1911 and 1915 being the other occasions) and stood a step away from the sort of day that their free-spending board had so hoped to give the fans. They avoided the favourites Arsenal, but were beaten 2-1 by Gallacher's ex-employers Newcastle in a game that by the end was a one man onslaught by Gallacher on the Geordie goal. Throughout the Twentieth Century, semi-finals and Chelsea Football Club were not the most amorous of companions and, when Newcastle took an early 2-0 lead, Wembley's towers again seemed unattainable wonders. Gallagher, though, fought like a trojan to turn the tables and his goal gave the team new impetus, whilst his drive almost got the better of his old club. Alas, even Gallacher couldn't find the breakthrough as Newcastle's keeper Albert McInroy was inspired form and kept out everything that the Scot through at him. Despite The Times commenting that Gallacher played "Like a trout slipping round a rock," it wasn't to be. Gallacher himself later bemoaned McInroy's performance, a goalkeeping display that hindered his own quest for an elusive FA Cup winners medal.

"Albert McInroy was in wonder form," wrote Gallacher almost a quarter of a century later. "When we forced corner after corner in the closing minutes only he prevented an equaliser." Gallacher called that defeat "a bitter blow" and that cup run was to represent the best of times for the Scot in Chelsea's blue. He soon lost his chum Alec Jackson, who departed amid financial disputes, and again Gallacher wondered if he would be spending the following season at the club. The French club Nimes proffered great riches, but eventually the proposed move fizzled out (although Alec Cheyne and Andy Wilson had short spells there).

As Gallacher himself was at pains to point out, Chelsea were lucky that he did. They had lost Jackson and without Gallacher's goals they would have struggled to stay up. As it was they only secured safety with a 4-1 win at Manchester City in their penultimate game of the 1932/33 season. Gallacher remained the team's life blood; his goals the difference between mediocrity and disaster.

FOR ALL that though, there were the red eyes and the late nights. Gallacher continued to prefer to stay out late than to retire early to his local back-street apartment. The drinking, whilst not affecting his goal count (he managed 19 in that struggle of a season), was a concern and soon his very presence in the area was leading to incident.

One balmy evening, Gallacher visited the cinema to see James Cagney in the appropriately named film *Public Enemy*. On exiting, Gallacher was taunted by a group of drunken Fulham fans, notorious at the time for their penchant for trouble. Gallacher took refuge in a local café but was followed in and soon the fans were pulling at his smart clothes, looking for a response and, with an image of the angry Cagney as vengeful mobster Tom Powers still fresh in Gallacher's mind, they got one.

The fight that ensued was met with a deluge of headlines with Gallacher cited as the trouble-maker, as the Public Enemy. Newspapers jumped on his behaviour and took pleasue seeing the great man reduced to a brawling lout. They cared little for the provocation afforded to the Scotsman and instead concentrate on more evidence of his wafer thin temperament. Gallacher's celebrity was complete. He had come to the capital as a sporting genius whose flair lit up the backpages. Now the newsmen who scribed the front pgaes could have their pound of flesh as his antics were scrutinised again and again. The incident was the preface to years of interest in what the players of Chelsea Football Club did in their spare time. Peter Osgood, Alan Hudson and later Dennis Wise would all have their social frolicking emblazed accross the nation's newspapers. But Hughie Gallacher was the first.

Years later, he marvellously played down the incident when he wrote, "In an argument with some Fulham fans I was getting annoyed, when a policeman came along." The truth was a little more action-packed as tables, punches and the café's produce were thrown. Gallacher, sporting a shiner, was taken to the local constabulary where he was eventually granted bail and, having stood beofre the magistrate wearing a perfectly pressed Chelsea FC blazer, he was released and forced to put ten shillings in the poor box. The club took their own action and left Gallacher out of the trip up to his beloved Newcastle. "Protests meant nothing," he said, "and I think that started our break up."

BY THE summer of 1933, Chelsea had a new manager to fret about Gallacher's behaviour. David Calderhead had retired after twenty-five years at the club and was replaced by Leslie Knighton, who had his work cut out as the team continued to struggle to find any cohesion, whilst the club began to suffer for its ambitious spending. "Trouble, then more trouble," he later bemoaned. "That is a football manager's lot, and I had my whack of it at Chelsea – at least in the early days of my work there. When I went to Stamford Bridge, the club were in a very low water financially with a heavy overdraft...[and] the work cost me many a weary day and sleepless nights."

Knighton's woes were understandable as the team still offered their fans glimpses of brilliance, but ultimately delivered only hardship. "One day they would play like men inspired," he said, "and the strongest of opposition would go crashing before them. The next day they would perform like a village side, with missed passes, wild kicks or perhaps scoring through their own goal. They were the most puzzling, yet one of the most attractive sides that patrons ever had the agony of watching lose a game."

That was the point and at the heart of that infuriation was the wee man. Gallacher, by now erratic for drink, still managed moments of genius with a football and, for all his unfulfilled promise, Chelsea's fans would still queue to see him maybe, just maybe, turn a defender inside out before unleashing the ball unerringly into the roof of a bruised net.

Knighton, rather than detesting a player cited by others as "football's stormy petrel" enjoyed trying to curb his antics and hoped that the new lady in his player's life, Hannah, may assist in some small way in curbing his wild side. To the new boss, Gallacher was a misunderstood individual. "[He] was the perfect gentleman, always sprucely dressed, always punctilious in looking after himself as a great player should and must."

The last comment might have been wishful thinking, or an early example of spin, but it was clear that Knighton had nothing for admiration for his star forward. "The boy who begun by kicking a paper ball round a lamp-post in a Glasgow slum was idolised like no other player has ever been." Knighton had every reason to enthuse about Gallacher and ensure that Hughie hit peak form as often as possible, as it was the Scot's 13 league goals that saved his team from certain relegation in the 1933/34 season, when Newcastle's last day defeat at Stoke kept Chelsea afloat.

IT WAS to be Gallacher's Chelsea swansong. He was bored in London, he was unhappy with life and incredibly, the game that had given him so much pleasure. Moves to Sunderland, Everton and Manchester United were discussed, but nothing came of them. The boyish looks, the crisp suits and the sharp hair had all begun to lose their shine. His game seemed immune to the effects of his outside life, but it was time for Chelsea to cash in.

In December 1934, Derby County relieved the 31-year-old Gallacher of his London woes, paying £3,000 for his services. He went on to have further spells at Notts County and Grimsby Town before playing out his illustrious days at Gateshead. There had been interest from the terraces right up to his last match in 1939, but after football his life continued to move along its turbulent course where insecurity and mayhem prevailed. Any player who had scored 463 goals in 624 matches would find it hard to live without the buzz, without the adrenalin rush. Without a ball at his feet to alleviate life's pain, Gallacher was, contrary to popular belief, human and he struggled.

Financial irregularities, the loss of his beloved Hannah to illness and a charge of assault and ill-treatment of his youngest son were incidents drenched in his continued problem with drink. In his fifties the suits were ill-fitting and stained, the hair receding and the hat now a cloth cap.

Contrast that with his days as a footballer, the first "celebrity" to play the game and you can imagine just how hard Gallacher's life had now become. Chelsea fans had never seen anything like him. He enticed them in their droves to watch his wizardry and to dream about how good their team could be. He hadn't brought the riches that they had desired in terms of silverware, but for the four seasons he had played, scored and drunk in front of them, he offered nothing but raw entertainment.

But just as he'd trod new ground for the footballing superstar, his life would end in a way which set the ultimate mould for subsequent self-destructive icons.

IN JUNE 1957, just days before his arranged appearance at a Gateshead Court on that charge of assault against his son, Hughie Gallacher left his house with nowhere to go, wearing a once smart, but now tattered old jacket. He looked down at the pavement as he walked toward his final destination. He approached the railway line at Low Fell station, stepped over the fence and made his way down onto the track. The whistle of an approaching train filled the air, but mattered little to this hunched and resigned man. He was unperturbed as he sat, waited and eventually stepped in front of the 12.08 Newcastle to Edinburgh express.

"Hughie of the Magic Feet is Dead," declared the next day's papers. The first superstar to grace football or Chelsea had gone, but with every bottle of champagne that is popped open at a heady Stamford Bridge today, his sparkle lives on.

ROY BENTLEY

'CAPTAIN'

1948-1956

CHELSEA CAREER

Games	367
Goals	150
Caps	12

MAGIC MOMENT

Standing in the Directors box having led his team to their first Championship in 1955, taking the applause of the ecstatic crowd

A leader is a dealer in hope

Napoleon Bonaparte

AT last they had their moment. For fifty years fans of Chelsea Football Club had been the butt of jokes. For half a century, those same fans had themselves belittled their club's chances with self-deprecating humour, but now that ridicule had gloriously transformed into silverware. Now there was nothing but pride. At last they had their moment.

The club that had been created by Gus Mears and his associates for these very instances of joy and glory had finally delivered. 50 years of jokes could end, sarcasm was replaced by festivity and snide comments silenced by cheers as the Blues were finally crowned League Champions.

Fans swelled around the Directors' box. Gus Mears would have wallowed in pride at the sight of these local people cheering on long-awaited success. He had envisaged that trophies would follow as soon as he opened those Stamford Bridge gates, but it had taken far longer than he had expected. Now, though, the dreams that had been born in a local pub in 1904 were joyously realised.

The Mears clan, of course, were represented. Joe Mears, Gus' grandson was by now Chelsea's chairman and he stood in his Directors' box, his spectacles perched on his nose and a beaming smile spanning from ear to ear. "I would like to thank everybody for the wonderful ovation you have given us today and for your support all through the season," glowed Mears. "It is not for me to say more than a few words. You want to hear from Roy and the boys, and from the one and only Ted."

The manager, Ted Drake, no stranger to Championships from his heady days as a player at Arsenal, stood proudly accepting the applause that emanated toward him and his players. "At the start of the season I was asked if we would win the Cup. I thought we might, but I thought we had a greater chance of winning the Championship," he said, a proud smirk giving way to a joyous grin.

"I congratulate all the boys and every one of my staff, office, training and playing. Right throughout they are one and all CHELSEA."

OF THOSE "boys", the crowd had formed a special bond with the goalscorer, the face of the team, the captain, Roy Bentley. He stood calmly, a tracksuit warming his toned body and a crisp blue and white check towel cooling his sturdy neck. Like a Hollywood star between takes, he paused, lapping up the adulation from those gazing adoringly up towards the men who had brought them their dreams.

There was no over-hyped, over-orchestrated pomp. It was a quiet and dignified celebration, a world away from the pyrotechnic jamboree of the club's 21st Century success. This was a different age, a more reserved time and as the shy Bentley took to the microphone an expectant hush filled the air. "On behalf of the boys, thank you all," he said unassumingly. "There is no need for me to say how pleased we are to win the Championship, but we are pleased, too, for your sakes, because you have been behind us in other years and we need your support. From the bottom of our hearts thank you very much..."

Cheers filled the April early evening sky as the fans hailed a hero. They had cheered plenty of icons at Stamford Bridge in their fifty-year history that was for sure, but not one that had delivered success. Bentley, through his leadership and goals had given the fans what they had so deeply desired and not only that; he had just acknowledged their own part in it.

For another half a century those present that day could tell children and grandchildren about the quiet Bristolian who had brought them their only championship. The class of 2005 may have altered that latter fact, but no amount of modern day hyperbole can cloud the memories of those who cheered on Bentley and the Blues in 1955.

SEVEN years earlier a 23-year-old Bentley had arrived in South-West London with very little ceremony and certainly none of the expectation that had so blighted the Chelsea careers of players before him. Stars such as Hughie Gallacher had failed to deliver the holy grail of success and there was little clue that such eminence would follow Bentley through the gates as they were opened for the new signing to stroll in and take a look around at his new place of work.

Bentley's journey in the game had taken him from his local Bristol City to Newcastle and now he followed in Gallacher's footsteps, albeit with far less fervour anticipating his arrival. As a boy he had shone with a ball at his feet and having failed his 11+ he was to leave school at 14 and make his way to Ashton Gate, via a short spell at Bristol Rovers. Bentley played some war-time football before being called up in 1942. He joined the Royal Navy and was posted on a destroyer, carrying out convoy duties in the harsh and dangerous waters of the North Atlantic.

Bentley hankered after sport though, he was offered Baseball trials whilst serving in Toronto, but it was the game of football that called and, having rejoined City after the hostilities ceased, his form was impressive enough for Second Division Newcastle to pay the not insignificant sum of £8,000 for his services. With Bentley combining in a forward line that included Jackie Milburn and Len Shackleton, the Magpies won instant promotion in 1947/48.

St James' Park offered a successful climate on the pitch, but the Newcastle air was not agreeing with Bentley. The bracing North-East wind had been known to play havoc with the more frail dispositions of southern footballers and soon Bentley became aware that he was, too easily, losing his breath in games and, far from being the lively 22-year-old on the pitch that he should have been, despite his athletic, lithe frame, Bentley was finishing games as if a veteran. Much to the glee of the country's centre-halves, his weight had dropped from a bustling 14 stone to a far less convincing 10 and a half. "I even struggled to finish a round of golf," he recalled.

Newcastle took medical advice and, whilst feeding their forward copious amounts of Guinness (often prescribed to help fortify the intake of iron) helped in the short term, it soon became obvious that they would have to release him. A move South to less harsh climes was strongly advised if the very real threat of tuberculosis was to be averted. Chelsea were the takers and in January 1948, having become the the first player to have to undergo a medical, Bentley arrived at the Bridge with a price tag of £11,000 tied to his boots.

It was the right move, but whilst the London air may have felt cleaner on his lungs, it was slightly harsher on his ears. Chelsea fans were not averse to letting their frustrated feelings be heard and players would often be subject to language that easily turned the air an even more royal blue than their famous shirts (changed from the lighter versions at the end of the First World War).

BENTLEY'S start at Chelsea was tough. "You're no fucking good, get back to Newcastle," cried one particular fan after a 2-0 defeat at home to Manchester City in the Cup. That had been only his second game at Stamford Bridge, but Bentley later admitted that very shout from the terraces had made him a more determined footballer and soon, after every goal he scored at the Bridge, he would stop and stare in the direction from which it had come.

For now, though, due to those fitness problems, Bentley couldn't settle. It was an affliction that many new signings endured. Chelsea's terraces had become a den of frustration. Home players were often lampooned from the very circles that should have been cheering them on, but for too long, those players had flattered to deceive and now they faced more than just hungry visiting teams when they ran out at Stamford Bridge.

"You're no bloody Lawton," cried an irate fan after another slow display from the young inside-forward that had failed to live up to the much-loved Tommy Lawton, recently controversially sold to Notts County for a British record £17,000. "Run back north, Bentley." Injuries, reserve football, expectant yet angry supporter; he must have pined for the restrictive air of Newcastle and now Bentley admits that it got to him. "I almost felt like packing it up," he said, "but I knew I had to fight the odds and justify myself."

Manager Billy Birrell had been in charge at Chelsea since 1939, but despite such luminaries as Lawton pulling on a blue jersey, mediocrity ruled in the immediate years after the war. The gallant centre-forward had offered some class and was idolised by young fans scouting for autographs. As ever, the expectations surrounding Lawton's arrival from Everton had not married with a successful reality, but nonetheless Bentley, however his style compared to his illustrious predecessor, was seen as a replacement for the goalscoring maestro and was under pressure to please the fans.

It was going to be hard. Too many supporters were disillusioned by what they saw every other Saturday. Too many arrived expecting to be frustrated and too many left with their dreary hypothesis firmly intact. One fan, named Shorty, wrote to the *News Chronicle* in 1950 highlighting the point. "I have been a regular paying visitor to Stamford Bridge for many, many moons, but owing to my stature (only 5ft 3ins) I never see much of the match. Why do I go? It is because that, no matter how much of the game is blocked from my view, there is the satisfaction in feeling that I have not missed much." Such humour had been commonplace for many years as the Music Hall jokes and songs proved.

Crowds, however, remained high. Chelsea had long attracted good support in terms of numbers and after the war, like so many clubs around the country, they enjoyed a boom as attendances rocketed after six long years of war. Crowds peaked in 1948/49 when over 41 million fans click-click-clicked through the turnstiles. The novelty factor brought fans flooding back and, in post-war London, with many commodities still rationed, national service introduced and its streets still littered with Blitzed rubble, football and those who played it became a welcome respite.

John Moynihan, in his history of the club, re-iterates the point. "Footballers like Lawton were necessary in that barren age; they were the monarchs of the bomb-sites, dauphins of conscripts, sporting saints in a nation pastry-eyed from dried milk."

FROM these gloomy post-war days arrived a new youth culture. Teddy Boys emerged from the Elephant and Castle; the Chelsea set and the Beatniks of Soho would soon cause outrage among London elders and, as Peter Ackroyd points out in *London: The Biography*, their arrival was a natural step. "They were all intent upon breaking free from what they considered to be the dreary uniformity of urban life still modelled on outdated systems of class and belief."

It would be some time before the ugly face of hooliganism would show itself so prominently at Chelsea, but concerns began to surface regarding the behaviour of fans. It was on the other side of London at Millwall, where the dockers watched their team, that these concerns were most rife, but Chelsea, whose fans were at this stage only verbally threatening, heeded the warning from south-east London's docks.

In 1949, Millwall were forced to publish a list of requests for their often over-zealous fans that included reminding them not to abuse the ref either verbally or physically, not to throw oranges, apples, or bricks and to remember that there are women and children present. It finished with the following strange, almost Cantona-like observation. "Think of this: As a bird is known by its chirp, so is a man by his conversation."

The chirp and the chat at Chelsea after the war was not about aggro, not yet, but instead it was the lack of success, or seemingly any hope of it that dominated the conversations on match day. Bentley found himself at a club that suffered from a long term inferiority complex. They had spent a fortune on the best, but hadn't come anywhere near being the best. Whilst optimism was at a low and heroes hard to come by, the fans were becoming organised, and thrived on the day out. They realised that their team would need a cheer or two away from the Bridge and toward the end of the forties; the Chelsea Supporters Club was formed. The new organisation was popular, but the club was unwilling to recognise them and they soon became the Chelsea (Away) Supporters Club.

The experience of watching football at Stamford Bridge was further helped by the introduction on Christmas Day 1948 of a new and improved match-day magazine. It had its critics; many believed that it was too expensive, but it became very popular and Albert Sewell, who edited the programme from 1949 to 1978, recalls how satisfying it was when it finally took off.

"No club had ever had a programme like it," recalls Sewell, "it was very exciting, but there was criticism. It was double the cosst of the old leaflet and the *Evening News* carried out a huge campaign against it. It soon cleared up, though, and the public loved it. When you come in for criticism, it's always nice when you come through. Soon Arsenal copied the idea and eventually most clubs around the country had caught on. There was no advertising at this time, just sixteen pages of football. Features, profiles, pictures. It kept me busy alright."

Through it, Chelsea's fans were brought closer to the players and couldn't get enough of news and pictures of the stars. Publications such as *Charlie Buchan's Football Monthly*, launched in 1951, brought the game and its protagonists into the homes of the fans, who lapped up the gossip as if they had suddenly been invited into the dressing room world where the smell of boot polish and liniment oil filled the nostrils.

IN THOSE early stuttering days as a Chelsea player, when his weight had dropped to a worrying 10 stone, there had been no sign that one day young Chelsea fans would eagerly flick through the pages of such magazines trying to find a glimpse of or word from Roy Bentley. But, whilst the fans initially drew little inspiration from the new signing, the coaching staff at Chelsea saw something in their acquisition that would dramatically change his game and the entire club's fortunes.

At Newcastle, Bentley's talents had been utilised as an inside-forward, but the staff at Chelsea noticed that he may be best suited at centre-forward where his physicality and footballing brain could be put to better use. Len Goulden, a useful player himself for West Ham, Chelsea and England and now Billy Birrell's player-coach, noticed that Bentley was not quite the performer he could be and suggested the new role. "You're two-footed, have pace and don't mind getting stuck in," he told the player and Birrell was happy to listen. In September 1948, they made the change and Bentley terrorised an Everton defence and scored twice in a 6-0 win. "You'll never play anywhere else," beamed Goulden, "and you'll be in the England side within a year." It took just eight months.

A few weeks later, a massive crowd of almost 78,000 crammed into Stamford Bridge to see Blackpool, a team of stars from the seaside of the north-west. Stanley Matthews, Stan Mortensen et al arrived at Chelsea and the massive attendance forced many to spill onto the greyhound track. Bentley was imperious and now, those disgruntled fans were being won round by his robust style which helped their team come back from 3-1 down to draw 3-3. The fans began to murmur hopes that this young beanpole might make a player after all.

Bentley, for all his lithe, physical attributes, was more than simply a swashbuckling centre-forward like "Dixie" Dean or even Tommy Lawton. He would drop deep to receive the ball rather than simply using his bulk to hold the ball up. It was a fresh approach to his position and one that would not become more widely recognized until the magnificent Hungarians demolished England 6-3 at Wembley in 1953, with the imperious Nándor Hidegkuti playing Bentley's role to a tee.

If it was to befuddle Billy Wright four years later then it is no surprise that static and cumbersome centre-backs, used to the rough and tumble of their day's work on the football pitch, were left confused. Why wasn't Bentley there challenging them for the ball? Why was he making them move, making them think? As Bentley's game blossomed, these questions were left unanswered. Instead he continued to wander around the pitch, his "roving" style detested by defenders, but slowly cherished by those Chelsea fans who once more allowed optimism to enter their hearts.

Equally at home picking the ball up on the wing as he was meeting a cross with a fine header, Bentley slowly became the darling of the Bridge. His was not the overnight success of a Hilsdon, nor the triumphal revelation of a Gallacher. Bentley's was a more permanent fame, born simply of admiration of his improvement. What the fan that far from politely asked him to "Run back to Newcastle" made of it, who knows? John Arlott, that most eloquent of sports observers was immediately sure of the talent that Chelsea fans were paying to see each week.

> To have been a Chelsea supporter for the past thirty years is to contemplate a meagre record of League and Cup success, but, on the other hand, it is to have seen in action a sequence of footballers who are not only great, but also unique, each with his own memorable and immediate contribution to make to a match. To have watched, season in, season out, the classic Scot Andy Wilson, the personality goalkeeper Howard Baker, the opportunist Alex Jackson, the ball master Hughie Gallacher, the goal-bursting Tommy Lawton, and now Roy Bentley, is to have known the caviar of football.
>
> Roy Bentley under way in one of his characteristic, probing dribbles sets every true football fan in the crowd – Chelsea supporter or not – on the side of the one against the many, of the gesture against utility…It is a heady thing to watch, this loose dribble of his – almost toppling with speed, in that sudden half-pitch-length burst; the swerve or turn is no more than a flicker in his headlong rush.

BENTLEY scored 21 goals in his first full season and going into the 1949/50 campaign, Chelsea fans actually allowed themselves to think that silverware was tantalisingly within their reach. Indeed it was, but as the season unfurled they would have to be content with seeing and even smelling sweet success, but cruelly remaining unable to embrace it.

Manager Billy Birrell's long-term youth policy had begun to pay rich dividends. Money, so long reserved for the big name, big fee transfers that Chelsea had become renowned for, had instead been invested in the long term outlook and a youth set-up had been nurtured. Manchester United were beaten in a fine FA Cup sixth round display with Bentley rifling a piledriver of a shot past United's keeper, Jack Crompton to make the final score 2-0.

Chelsea found themselves in the FA Cup semi-finals for the fifth time. Tom Whittaker's Arsenal, those annoyingly silky men from along the Piccadilly Line were the opposition, Tottenham's White Hart Lane the venue. For too long the men in red and white had lorded over their blue cousins, winning trophies galore before the war, but with optimism growing, maybe now was the time for Chelsea to take on the mantle of being London's finest.

John Moynihan, in his book *The Soccer Syndrome* describes the scene as eager fans queued up to buy a ticket for the game, hoping and praying that this, at last would be their moment:

> Phosphorous-coloured, dawn faces in the queue became more familiar as daylight gathered strength. The ones up front, the real fanatics, had been camping out all night, but while they were picking and scratching at spots on their faces and aches in their crutches, we at least had come from our beds…
>
> About eight o'clock a man in front of me started to talk. He was a tall, dull-faced man with a jaw so narrow that it fell away like a precipice round the edges of his blue lips…
>
> 'If Chelsea lose next week, I'll put my head in a gas oven,' he suddenly said. It was an ideal way to start the morning, something to remind us of the agonies and tensions of the game ahead.
>
> I imagined this man on his knees pressing that chinless jaw on the grill, turning on the taps, saying 'You bastards, Arsenal. You bastards.' I could sniff the gas there in the early morning as the man went on talking to a change of youthful supporters around him.
>
> 'Chelsea can't lose. Look what they did to Manchester United. They'll slaughter 'em,' said one of the youths.
>
> 'They'll win all right,' said the gas man. I've been watching them since 1920 and this is their best. Gallacher, Wilson, Mills, you can have 'em, Bentley's the bloke. Now look at it this way, his speed and shot, he's got it. Leslie Compton won't see him. But I'm still telling you that if Chelsea lose I'll put my head in a gas oven.' His companions laughed.

The gas man's optimism seemed well founded. On Tottenham's sand-pit of a pitch, Chelsea made light work of their rivals. In the twentieth minute Bentley deftly lobbed Arsenal's George Swindin in goal and five minutes later he made it two with a nifty header that made its way in at the near post. It was as if Bentley had, on this most dramatic of days, chosen to show the fans just how versatile a forward he had become.

Two up and the fans could surely close their eyes, take a drag on their cigarettes and envisage the inviting twin towers of Wembley. But lady luck was never one to wear a blue and white scarf, especially in semi-finals, and just before half time the wind of change, literally, blew in the Gunners' favour. Alan Hobey of the *Daily Express* picks up the story:

> A goal so freakish that it should be permanently installed in the Chelsea Chamber of Horrors smashed the Pensioners' dream of marching straight through to Wembley. Thirty seconds before half-time Arsenal, two goals down and with defeat sneering them in the face, forced a corner. Then the North London "miracle" happened. Without apparently a pinhead hope, right-winger Freddie Cox, taking a kick with the inside of his right foot, sliced over the ball which literally screamed towards goal. Even then it did not seem possible for Arsenal to score. But at the last split second the ball curved in and rocketed into the net. The wind

helped it...I give this goal in such detail because in my view it was the turning point of this highly dramatic semi-final.

Dramatic indeed. Arsenal, through Leslie Compton, who in the dying seconds of the game headed home a corner from his brother Denis, forced a replay, which they scraped 1-0, before going on to win the final against Liverpool. "Lucky" Arsenal were born into the nation's consciousness, while Chelsea fans were left reeling, pondering and wondering. A certain supporter may have had his head firmly in his oven, and many others would have wanted to follow suit.

Morale yet again slumped and hope was squeezed out from the club like toothpaste. The following season, 1950/51, was desperate. Where there had been dreams of a visit to Wembley, now there was only dread of a return (after 20 years) to the Second Division. With four games left, Chelsea languished four points behind Sheffield Wednesday and six behind Everton. The season had been so dire that there seemed no hope of redemption. But Chelsea beat Liverpool thanks to a product of that youth system, Bobby Smith, who would become a star at Tottenham seasons later. Then Wolves succumbed before neighbours Fulham got the same treatment at Craven Cottage. The hosts missed a pillowcase of chances and Chelsea fans mockingly sang a late 19th century ballad, *Dear Old Pals*.

This left Chelsea level on points with Sheffield Wednesday and two behind Everton, with the clubs desperately close in terms of goal average. The final game saw 40,000 fans cram into Stamford Bridge hoping the team could pull through. Bentley scored twice, as did Smith, as Chelsea hammered Bolton 4-0. Sheffield Wednesday kyboshed Everton 6-0, a result which condemned both clubs to the drop as, having reached for their pocket abacuses, the fans were gleefully informed that Chelsea had stayed up, although only thanks to a fractionally (0.44 to be exact) better goal average.

THE FOLLOWING season was less dramatic, but heralded the end of Billy Birrell. He was a keen student of the game and a deep thinker and he knew that now the time was right to bid farewell. Things had become mundane at the club and they had to change. His successor was former England and Arsenal centre-forward Ted Drake.

Under the Hampshire-born Drake, a new dawn would finally arrive at Stamford Bridge, but for Bentley the sun had already risen and was beating down on his glorious career. Having won over the Chelsea fans, his form had convinced the England selectors that he was worth a place in the national team. In May 1949, Bentley took his place alongside Stan Mortensen and Tommy Finney in an England forward line. Chelsea fans looked on with pride.

But Bentley's fledgling England career followed a similar path to that at Chelsea. On his debut the team were beaten 3-1 by Sweden in Stockholm. He would have to wait for another chance, but when it arose, Bentley proved his worth scoring the winning goal against Scotland at Wembley in April 1950, a performance Bentley himself described as his best for England. That was enough to earn a place in England's first ever World Cup squad for the 1950 tournament in Brazil. There he was fated to feature in one of the most notorious results in football history as England were diabolically star-spangled by a novelty United States football team. Ridicule followed and Bentley had to wait two years before winning his next cap.

Chelsea fans, though, took most heart from a hat-trick their striker scored against the Welsh in 1954 at Wembley. A few days later, Tottenham were the visitors at Stamford Bridge and Bentley was perturbed by the huge cheer that rose from the crowd as he walked onto the pitch. "What the hell's going on here?" he thought. Everyone was standing and applauding and he could only wonder who was receiving an award. "It didn't dawn on me. Every time I touched the ball, another cheer went up, then at the final whistle, the penny dropped that everyone inside Stamford Bridge was cheering me."

Bentley was modest, but in terms of real quality and belief so was the squad. 50 professionals were employed at the club when Drake arrived in December 1952 and changes would have to be made. The first casualty under Drake though was no lacklustre footballer, but the Pensioner emblem that, for so long, had been the face of Chelsea Football Club. The white-bearded gentleman decked in medals and donning the famous red uniform was, and in many ways still is, the face of the club, but Drake wanted to make changes and quickly.

Fans and papers were up in arms about the old man's imminent departure, but to Drake the Pensioner had invited ridicule. So often a torturer himself of the Chelsea defence (he once scored four at Stamford Bridge for Arsenal), Drake had heard all the old jokes that his new club "played like Pensioners." Drake, for so long a winner, didn't want to be associated with such mockery. "I'm pensioning him off," he declared and was equally quick to answer the argument that "Chelsea will never be the same without the Pensioner." That was exactly Drake's motivation. "I don't want Chelsea to ever be the same."

DRAKE'S first match as manager at Stamford Bridge was a frustrating 1-1 draw with Derby and the impatient home support dished out boos and jeers toward the players, who were clearly suffering from a lack of self-belief. Drake sat and took his new home in, listening to supporters so scarred they found it hard to give support to their own team. Drake wondered about these supporters, who could be so polite to visiting teams, but so detrimental to their own. Something would have to be said.

"You folk may be rightly proud of your title as 'Football's Fairest Crowd,'" Drake remarked in his programme notes for the next home game. "But for my part I would like to see not a little, but a lot more partisanship in favour of Chelsea. All too many people come to Stamford Bridge to see a football match – instead of to cheer Chelsea.

"Please prove me wrong, but it's my opinion that over the years too many bystanders have gone out of their way to grouse, jibe and grumble, to pull the club down rather than say a good word for Chelsea. And for years now, the players must have been thoroughly sick of all the music hall publicity that has gone before.

"Let's have more people eating, sleeping and drinking Chelsea. Let's spread the spirit of Chelsea across London...don't tell me the crowd can't make a difference."

Drake's plea was to the common man on the terraces. He was right. Many of the fans were locals who ambled down to the Bridge and as a neutral watched an entertaining game of football. Actors such as Richard Attenborough, writers such as Laurie Lee, painters such as Johnny Minton, they all flocked to the ground, but Drake was concerned about the reputation of his new club as a luvvies' hang out. The passion that he had been used to at Arsenal simply wasn't there, but then Arsenal's fans had become accustomed to something that their counterparts at Chelsea felt was never going to come their way; success.

Those "grumblers" weren't going to go away over night, especially as results remained stagnant and relegation was once more narrowly avoided in that first season of Drake's tenure thanks to a last game victory over Manchester City. The loudly opinionated amongst Chelsea fans, who shifted about in their expensive seats, did not heed Drake's request. Still they came. Still they moaned.

The mood on an average day at Stamford Bridge in the early fifties reflected that of London itself. A thick smog had descended on the capital, and, like the dreary Chelsea fans, locals found it hard to see a bright future in a town where many bemoaned an atmosphere that was akin to "the end of the world."

So often crowds at winter football could only make out hazy shadows, battling the elements as well as trying to convince those who had paid to watch, that theirs was a future worth believing in. Alan Ross, a poet and football correspondent for the *Observer* summarised the atmosphere at one match:

> Chelsea and Stoke, once again clutched in an Octopus-like struggle in the murky depths of the First Division, played a goalless draw at Stamford Bridge yesterday...At the present rate, one, if not both of these teams will go down to the Second Division next season, and neither, it must be admitted, look at the moment look good enough to remain where they are.
>
> If the quality of play at Stamford Bridge was negligible, this match was nevertheless a memorable visual experience. It began in a light veering fog, which laid a transparent silky screen across the ground. Although the players remained coated with curious, clinging dew, most of the play was clearly visible throughout the first half. Sometimes a thick wave of fog made the stadium seem like a film re-construction of a gas attack for a World War I epic; then, in a clearer spell, the teams moved in a kind of ballet among the clouds, the ball lost from sight, but whole sequences of intricate passing preserved from the fog and given a special beauty.

SO OFTEN, that special beauty was in the form of a certain Roy Bentley. Chelsea's own lighthouse shone through the smog, offering hope and quality. The beacon in blue had once more scored the goals that kept the club away from the jagged rocks of relegation and remained the one hope for disgruntled fans. Bentley himself had now truly taken to the supporters. Their unpartisan tendencies, derided by the new manager, had struck a chord with a player who had been so used to the fanatical qualities of his previous employers. "At Chelsea, I found the supporters were more appreciative of good football, whoever it was being played by."

Bentley, through his class, endeavour and form now had a mutual-admiration with those hard-to-please fans. They thrived off his spirit and his courage. Bentley was a footballer who could tantalise with a fine touch, but also enthral with a boisterous surge. Bolton defender Malcolm Barrass discovered that Bentley could not be intimidated. Barrass was a heavyweight stopper not perturbed when it came to kicking forwards. Bentley, though, thrived on his attentions, giving as good as he got and often having the last laugh with a goal or two against the Burnden Park club. Bentley was told by Bolton's Nat Lofthouse whilst on England duty that Barrass was worried by a day's work marking the Chelsea player.

That comradeship between star striker and fans was noticed by Drake who often, along with the veteran full-back Johnny Harris, invited his player on golfing days where they could discuss intricate plans to improve Chelsea's form. Drake soon made Bentley his captain, a popular move on the terraces and in the dressing room, although one which drew some criticism from outside Chelsea ranks. "Some people in the game think that it is far more difficult for a centre-forward to captain the side than it is for a central defender or midfielder," Bentley noted. "Because I liked to drop back and help defend, I could still bark out my orders and keep the players on their toes. Ted would often say that if I led by example, then it made captaining the side that much easier because the other players see how you're playing and match your effort."

Bentley would run out onto the pitch with an authoritarian swagger. The players followed him with gusto and as he settled into the job, the team began to mimic their captain's vigour. Results improved.

The club sailed in calmer waters and finished a healthy eighth in 1953/54. Bentley, as ever, finished the club's top scorer (a feat he would achieve in all eight of his seasons in blue), but now he was being well served by new recruits. His supply came from winger Eric "Rabbit" Parsons, who had at last begun to show his true class, while Johnny McNichol, a sneaky Scottish inside-forward, had been Drake's first signing from Brighton and was beginning to justify his place in the team.

Drake, a keen student of all things football, had also gone into the amateur game and recruited some untapped talents. Inside-forward Seamus O'Connell had played for Bishop Auckland whilst closer to home, winger Jim Lewis and half-back Derek Saunders arrived from Walthamstow Avenue.

It seemed that maybe, just maybe, Drake's vision of a "New Chelsea" might just take shape. Bentley was seen by outsiders as a man who deserved success and, like Chelsea itself, it seemed wrong that this gallant centre-forward was not ladened with medals. John Arlott bemoaned that very fact: "Fewer of the great honours of football have come his way than have gone to some workmanlike players of much less character."

AS THE club embarked upon the 1954/55 season there was a feeling that fact was about to change. It was a feeling, it must be said, exclusive to Stamford Bridge and its home dressing room. The might of Wolves and Manchester United, managed by football moguls Stan Cullis and Matt Busby respectively, were dominating the English game. Drake, though, saw something in his men that indicated a possible new name on the old Championship trophy. "The spirit is here that I have always wanted," he told the fans at the beginning of the campaign. "Not only inside the club but among you, the supporters ...and that's great...I am confident that we can match the best...the lads are the happiest and the nicest bunch I could wish to have with me."

Early season defeats at home to Preston and Everton offered little in the way of confidence in Drake's words and it seemed yet again that Chelsea fans would have to leave their hope at the turnstiles. But another loss to Manchester United at Stamford Bridge in October offered chinks of light. Chelsea languished in twelfth place, but gave a fine account of themselves against Busby's "Babes". They pegged United back to 2-2, but then their rivals drove on for a 5-2 lead.

Bentley rallied the troops and the lead was cut to 5-3. 6-3 United, 6-4, 6-5. It was incredible, but time ran out and Busby's men were victors. "Wow," yelled an impressed American tourist. "Some ball game!" Chelsea had, even in defeat, gained support and merit from their fans. This team were worth shouting for rather than at, and, despite some further defeats that late autumn, soon the good form would garner welcome points.

In early December, Wolves, the champions, led Chelsea 3-2 at Molineux with a minute to go. To complete a fairytale turnaround, Bentley netted the winner in the last seconds with a sublime run and cool finish past Bert Williams. Chelsea had won against the strongest team in the land. Confidence, for so long a stranger at Chelsea was now draped in Blue and White. By the New Year they were fifth, but poised for a run that would bring the title into their arms.

"After Christmas everyone was on song," recalls Bentley. "Defeats became draws and draws became wins. There were fewer points dropped and Chelsea ran up an unbeaten run of ten games in the closing weeks. Manchester United and Wolves couldn't compete with us after Christmas and New Year."

The side's resolute belief in themselves was summed up in a rescheduled midweek game at West Bromwich Albion on a February frozen pitch. The Baggies took a two goal half-time lead in front of 7,500 hardy fans, their fingers stinging from the cold air. Chelsea though, had plans to warm things up.

Derek Saunders pulled one back. Only ten minutes remained when Peter Sillett netted twice, before Bentley scored another of his 21 goals that season to seal the win.

Chelsea stormed to a 4-2 win at White Hart Lane, and a week later Wolves, still favourites for the title, arrived at Stamford Bridge for what was now a crunch match in the championship race. Teams like Wolves had come to Chelsea in the past, expecting a tough game, but finding the ride comfortable among the less than passionate crowd. Things had changed. Chelsea fans had woken to a fine sunny morning knowing that a victory would put them firmly in line for silverware. Soon after breakfast they poured into the ground, truly believing that it was their team that was worth shouting about. And shout they did. Stan Cullis' men were greeted by a roar that must have rocked the passing buses on the Fulham Road, let alone the black country men in their football boots.

Blue balloons filled the sky as Bentley led out his team. The game, though, unlike the atmosphere, was tense and tight. Players were hampered by that age-old English problem where fear of making a mistake rules over natural match-winning instinct.

It seemed to be rolling toward a goalless draw, a result the visitors from the Midlanders would have gladly accepted, when, with fifteen minutes left; high drama. Wolves captain Billy Wright used his arm to clear a humdinger of a shot by Seamus O'Connell. The referee drew howls of anger from fans when he awarded a corner, but after much argument and disorder he changed his mind and gave the obvious penalty.

It was Peter Sillett who netted from twelve yards (a moment he described as the most terrifying of his life) to be besieged by team-mates as tears flowed freely and joyously among the giant crowd. Chelsea were almost there. A newspaper strike meant that the moment wasn't recorded, but those present headed home, beaming at the consequences of a famous result.

A DRAW with fellow title-chasing Portsmouth was another important point and after a 3-0 win over Sheffield Wednesday at the Bridge, fans and playes alike patiently waited for news of the south-coast team's fortunes. 1-1 came the cry. Chelsea had done it! In their Golden Jubilee they had won themselves the most desired of birthday presents. The championship was theirs!

Fans were not to be restricted to the terraces. The usual post-match greyhound race would have to wait as the athletic mutts were seen off the track by whippet-like supporters desperate to give thanks to their heroes. "Only the Blues, to carry me by..." was sung by the fans as Bentley, their quiet yet forceful hero, gave his thanks and sent them on their way into the early London evening where, depending on their background they mused over the joyous events whilst supping beer or champagne. The players sipped their own bubbly before quietly boarding the tube and heading home.

It felt good. But club chairman Joe Mears, then President of the Football League, followed advice from the League secretary, Alan Hardaker, and declined the opportunity as Champions to take part in a new pan-European club competition, the European Cup, believing that it would interrupt the defending champions' League programme the following season. As it turned out, that campaign was never going to reach the heady levels of the previous May.

Bentley continued to score goals, but his days as a Chelsea player were strangely coming to an end and fans were dismayed to hear in August 1956, that their championship-winning hero, despite being just 32, was off to nearby Fulham. Bentley wasn't one for whining and instead he packed his bags and made his way with dignity toward Putney Bridge. Young fans could only wave fondly at a departing hero who they would, one day tell fond tales of glory about to their own disbelieving grandkids.

CULT HEROES can so often be the troubled genius or the flawed whizz-kid with a penchant for booze and provocation. Chelsea, by its culture, financial clout and geography has attracted such aggrieved souls who entertain and infuriate in equal measure. Bentley was different. His cult lay not at the bottom of a glass or in the arms of a Kings Road beauty. His cult lay instead with that famous old Football League Championship trophy. He had got his hands on it and in doing so had given the fans what they so craved. His goals were one thing, but the success they brought was another.

"No longer could they call us the Clown of Clubs" said Bentley. "Now we were the Champions Club." It wouldn't last of course (this was Chelsea), but Bentley's name would remain the benchmark of league success long after the trophy had made its way to other cabinets.

In 2005, Chelsea were once more crowned champions. As the class of 1955 were ushered proudly onto their old stomping ground the loudest cheer was reserved for Roy Bentley, their captain and a man whose 150 goals in 347 games were matched only by Peter Osgood and bettered only by Kerry Dixon and Bobby Tambling. It was a moment that the great man said, "Left me with a warm glow for the rest of the week."

The dog track had gone, as had the old terracing, but the memories hung in the air like Pathé newsreels. Bentley, their big handsome hero, their captain was back and it was as if he had never been away. John Arlott sums him up. "Others, perhaps, will make more goals, score more goals, but they will not leave behind, when they finish, such memories as Bentley, that eager forward, profiled like a head on an antique coin, poised for assault, against odds, perhaps, but so dazzlingly quick that no defence opposing him could ever relax."

ERIC PARSONS

1950-1956

CHELSEA CAREER

Games	177
Goals	42
Caps	0

MAGIC MOMENT

After Eric's two goal display against Sheffield Wednesday, the day Chelsea clinched the 1954/55 League title, the crowd chanted for 'Rabbit'

'RABBIT'

Any activity becomes creative when the doer cares about doing it right, or doing it better.

John Updike

A hush descends on Stamford Bridge as the ball makes its way excitedly toward Eric "Rabbit" Parsons. He controls it with ease and then, whoosh, he's away and that expectant silence on the Shed is replaced by a vivacious roar. His bright yellow hair against his royal blue jersey gives the illusion of an American Cavalryman speeding with purpose toward an Apache battlefield in the merry month of May. The crowd thrive on these moments as Parsons' muscular legs carry him past defender after sorry defender before he unleashes a devastating cross or shot that more often than not will test a keeper's resolve or tempt a lucky centre-forward.

That lucky player was of course, Roy Bentley. His many goals were numerously assisted by Parsons, who, by the time the glories of 1955 came around, was a fixture and favourite at Stamford Bridge. Bentley may have been the crowd's darling; the captain with the square jaw, the goalscorer with the broad shoulders, but Parsons was different. He lacked the cigarette-card good looks of Bentley or the aura of a superstar, but his effort, his speed and his blistering will to win made him a firm favourite with supporters who were, and would always be, smitten by raw effort.

Bentley, by his very presence and talent, demanded admiration and hero worship. Parsons, on the other hand, barely courted it. His name would not be the first to be mentioned on the pages of history books chronicling Chelsea's story or their first Championship, but to those who stood on the terraces whilst he plied his trade and who would eagerly chat over a pint on the Fulham Road, his name was always at the fore; as if Parsons himself was there alongside them, cheering on the team or shouting the next round of beers.

THE PEDESTAL reserved for footballing icons can be an unsteady place to stand. Many have fallen from its great height with a bang and a dent to their inflated egos. Parsons would never have that problem. He preferred to see defenders at his feet than the Chelsea public and it was that determination to get at and beat players that almost unwittingly won him the affections of his club's fans.

As he picked up the ball whilst hugging the right touchline, expectation exuded from fans and team-mates alike. The latter would manoeuvre into place, ready for the next phase of attack, whilst the former drew breath in hope. Chelsea fans have long been spoilt by players who could do just that. Parsons' pace and skill offered hope on a drab day, his broad smile shed light on a smoggy afternoon. Charlie Cooke, Pat Nevin, they would later excite and please in the same way. Today Arjen Robben in full flight, attacking a wide-eyed full-back invites a similar intake of breath. *Something* is about to happen and when Parsons prepared to take flight it was advisable not to blink.

The speed that so enthralled and excited the supporters was apparent in Eric Parsons from his early days growing up in Worthing, Sussex. He was clearly a gifted athlete, but rather than simply running, he used his fleetness of foot to great effect whilst playing the game that he truly loved. "I did a lot of sprinting and was the 220-yard champion of Sussex and a member of the Worthing Harriers," recalled Parsons. "I loved running, but I always wanted to play football."

Whether or not that desire would turn into reality was still questionable as Parsons, approaching the end of his school days, pondered his career and future. He had shown an aptitude for art, and a life designing posters beckoned before a game in 1937 for Worthing Boys opened the eyes of football scouts to the talented athlete's ability.

It was played at Second Division West Ham's Upton Park and the 15-year-old Parsons impressed the Hammers' manager Charlie Paynter. He saw enough in the strong youngster, then playing at centre-back, to make enquiries. "We'd like to sign you Eric," said Paynter. "You'd better see my teacher," came the reply from the excited youngster. "I already have." Parsons' parents were approached and design's loss was soon football and West Ham's gain.

WEST HAM nurtured their exciting protégé, giving him run-outs in a local team that played on Hackney's famous Marshes. It was on that renowned sea of football pitches that Parsons' attacking qualities began to flourish. He scored goals, he created goals and by the time he was playing wartime football for West Ham and the Armed Forces he had been converted to an exciting inside-right.

"I converted to a winger in the forces," he said. "I was in the British Army of the Rhine team which played all round Europe entertaining the troops immediately after the war." During the hostilities, Eric made his debut for West Ham in a 1943 wartime fixture against Southampton. Parsons was only 20 and so, come the end of the war two years later, he was still a relativley young man who could look forward to a career in the game rather than bemoaning the loss of one due to War.

Parsons returned to the east end of London and was entertaining the appreciative West Ham crowd, who took great delight in a burst of speed that had even the most hardened of London Dockers gasping like a schoolboy. It was on those chirpy terraces that the name "Rabbit" was first assigned to Eric Parsons. It was more than apt as he darted about the pitch in short, damaging bursts. Now aged 26, his form and his name had started to invite interest from clubs in loftier positions than West Ham. Chelsea, as ever, were at the front of the queue, sniffing out a possible new acquisition.

It seemed a brave move by a club that too often had got it slightly wrong in the transfer market. Parsons had injured his right knee at Blackburn whilst playing in West Ham's claret and blue and had undergone surgery to remove his cartilage. It was an ill-timed incident for a player who seriously harboured international ambitions. Parsons had travelled with an England party to Scandinavia in 1949, the tour on which Roy Bentley had made his international debut, and played for the B team against Helsinki. The game was won 4-0 and Parsons won the man-of-the-match award. He followed that up with a goal in another 4-0 win, this time over The Netherlands in Amsterdam. Full England honours beckoned, but it was never going to be easy.

English selectors were hardly sweating when it came to talented wingers and with Preston's Tom Finney, Blackpool's Stanley Matthews and Wolves' Jimmy Mullen in their prime, they would eventually overlook Parsons and his supposed dodgy knees.

Fortunately, Chelsea's management didn't share the selectors' concerns and after four years, 152 appearances and 35 goals for his cockney employers, Parsons trod that well-travelled path from east to south-west London. George Hilsdon of course had pioneered the move, but today, a novice to the game would be forgiven for thinking that West Ham is Roman Abramovich's feeder club. A place where youngsters like Glen Johnson, Joe Cole and Frank Lampard spend the pubescent years of their career before maturing into Champions at Stamford Bridge.

Chelsea manager Billy Birrell was confident in his new signing. Here, he thought, was an attacking option that would provide his new centre-forward, Roy Bentley, with some much-needed service. Birrell was so confident that he convinced his chairman to part with £20,000, a club record fee that in November 1950 was not that far short of the British transfer record set by the £26,000 paid by Preston to Sheffield Wednesday for inside-forward Eddie Quigley just a year earlier.

THE AUTUMN of 1950 gave way to another winter of discontent at Stamford Bridge. There had been signs of improvement, but that FA Cup semi-final defeat to Arsenal the previous spring had seemingly knocked the stuffing from Birrell's revival and again the grey clouds of mediocrity hung over the club and its supporters.

Relegation was narrowly avoided, but with Parsons a regular onlooker; not what was expected from such an expensive acquisition. That knee injury played on his mind and affected the confidence that so aided his dynamic game. Instead of working his way into the team and the affections of the crowd, Parsons spent those early months in the reserves, just another player in a huge and bulbous squad. In fact the rare outings he had in the first team were more memorable in the early 1950s for the cowboy-like bandana he wore over his face to keep the thick London smog from his lungs. Fans would not have been surprised – such was the inept performances of the team – if the whole squad had adopted a similar disguise.

Parsons' displays were hardly the sort that would have the fans urging their manager for more. The reserves seemed like the right place for a player who was perhaps going to be yet another in a long line of anonymous and expensive flops.

In later years, the likes of Peter Houseman would face that same dilemma in having to convince cynical fans that first impressions can be deceiving. What they see from the comfort of the stands must not be taken as gospel. Houseman, also a winger, struggled to impress both manager Tommy Docherty and supporters initially, but persevered to become not only a favourite in a spoilt crowd, but also a linchpin in the squad that won domestic and European honours in the early 1970s.

Like Houseman under Docherty, Parsons couldn't find the form to impress Birrell. The club were stuttering and it would take the arrival of Ted Drake to reaffirm both the team and Parsons' fortunes. Chelsea fans had been promised a rabbit, but in Parsons they became more accustomed to a hare, beaten and embarrassed by the tortoise. That, though, was about to change.

1953/54 was a seminal season. A post-Christmas surge by the club saw them finish a healthy eighth and persuaded Drake that this team might just be able to challenge for some real honours the following season. A major part of that progression was Eric Parsons. By now a vital cog in a wheel that Drake hoped would roll his team towards silverware.

So where did it all go right? As Drake stamped his own will to win on the club, individuals who, whilst clearly talented with a football at their feet, but who had struggled to show any sort of cohesion or regular form, started to buy into his theory that success wasn't a million miles away. Parsons was the very embodiment of that turn-around. A microcosm of the club itself; a struggling, but extremely gifted individual, who, with the right guidance could be at home amongst the best.

"I thought Ted was a good manager," said Parsons some years later. "He had faith in me and I knew exactly what he wanted. He said 'Eric, I want you to get down the wing – if you don't, I'll get someone who will,' so I always played that way." Suddenly the ambiguity surrounding the winger had gone. Parsons knew what was required of him, the manager knew he had a player eager to please him and the fans at last could delight in the winger's skills that only a couple of years earlier had caused England selectors to crane their necks for a closer look.

The knee that had played such a devious part in Parsons' derisive form had been well looked after by Chelsea's medical staff. Halfway through the 1953/54 season he at last felt like the player who had coaxed Billy Birrell into spending such a large dollop of Chelsea's cash. The club had started the season in a sluggish mood. Two draws and five defeats – including an 8-1 drubbing at Wolves that today remains the club's heaviest defeat – was hardly the sort of form that Drake envisaged for his "new Chelsea", but he still told anyone who would listen that better times were on the way.

"Sometimes you come away from a game knowing you have lost and that is all there is to it," he said after a 5-2 defeat at league leaders West Bromwich Albion in October. "I am not given to flattering my boys in my comments, but I feel that if they continue to show the same spirit and play this type of football there is no doubt our turn will soon come." A week later, Liverpool were beaten 5-2 at the Bridge and from there the remaining 27 fixtures brought 13 victories and the team finished in their highest position since 1920.

The new, improved Eric Parsons darted down the touchline with purpose. Matthews, Finney, Liddell; these men had whetted the appetite. They had shown fans how deadly a good winger could be. Chelsea supporters, in their fair-minded way, had flocked to the Bridge so often to see these men playing for the opposition, but now they had their own. Parsons' injury was behind him and instead of dreading public opinion, he opened his morning paper to find his manager gushing about how good his right-winger was. Parsons was desperate to repay Drake's faith in him, and Drake took extra time to assist his player and offer advice on just how he thought he should be playing.

AS THE 1954/55 season kicked off, Parsons was that most lethal of animals; a supremely confident footballer. The supporters now impatiently waited his turn on the ball, as did Bentley, who marauded into the box anticipating Parsons' delivery. It was the era of the winger and centre-forward. Matthews and Finney tricked their way past gormless full-backs before whipping the ball inch-perfectly onto the centre-partings of a thankful Stan Mortensen or Charlie Wayman.

Parsons was slightly different. He would beat his man with similar grace, but often knocked low drives into the opposition's penalty area for his captain to sweep home. Fans couldn't get enough and with every good result bought further into the idea of Drake's "new Chelsea". Gone was the Pensioner, gone were self-torturing worries of failure, gone were the big, expensive star names and in their place were professionals giving their all. With that came a mutual respect between player and fan that had long been absent.

"I don't recall many of the goals anymore," Parsons has said. "I do remember the fans though. What tremendous support the Chelsea fans gave us. There were so many people inside Stamford Bridge every match that they had to lock people out frequently and to play in front of seventy thousand fans became almost normal.

There was a huge bank on one side of the ground, which looked fantastic as I was running down the wing. Unfortunately, when you're playing centre stage and making sure you're switched on to your team-mates, you don't get the chance to absorb the atmosphere that a crowd of that size generates."

The championship season generated an average of over 48,000 fans and they crammed themselves into Archie Leitch's old stands that had survived not only years of fans frustratingly stamping their boots, but also two World Wars. Even training was a joy for the reborn Parsons. His game was based on that fleet turn of foot, and in training he spent his time running and running and running. "I absolutely loved it," he enthused. "We would start by going out for a long run, every player at the club, and get back after about an hour and do a lot of sprint exercises, which was really my cup of tea."

As Chelsea rampaged closer and closer to the title, "Rabbit" Parsons was the dynamo of the team; his pace, the fifth gear that his team could call on when all else had failed. Drake recognised the tool he had in the box and used it to bring the best out of others such as the new youngster in the team, 20-year-old Frank Blunstone. The recent signing from Crewe played on the left-wing and was quick, but not in Parsons' league. Drake had them running together in training. Often Blunstone was treated like an opposition full-back and left trailing in his team-mate's wake.

Blunstone himself was to become a popular and vital player in Chelsea's forward line for 12 years. Jimmy Greaves once opined that he had "a heart the size of a cabbage", but in those early sprints with Parsons he felt nothing but a twinge of humiliation. "I couldn't get near him, and I wasn't slow," said Blunstone. "After twenty yards he'd be another ten yards ahead of me. The manager thought that running with him would help me out, but it used to frustrate and embarrass me, he was too quick and I know he used to toy with me, pretending to let me keep up for a while before showing me his heels."

At the end of that season Blunstone was one of three Chelsea players capped in the same England team against Portugal, alongside Peter Sillett and Bentley; a real honour for a club who now in Spring headed the table after a 1-0 win at Cardiff and harboured serious championship ambitions.

"ADMIRAL" DRAKE'S was now a cohesive combat unit. In goal was Bill Robertson, reliable and solid and, after an ankle injury half-way through the season, replaced admirably by Charlie "Chic" Thomson. At full-back were Stan Willemse and Peter Sillett, who were also dependably deputised by the old man of the team, Johnny Harris who managed enough games to warrant a medal.

The half-back line constituted half-back Ken Armstrong, a strong player who would win an England cap, and Ron Greenwood, a future England manager and sturdy centre-half. His deputy, Stan Wicks, was a constant prickly thorn in the side of centre-forwards. At left-half was Derek Saunders, the flame-haired amateur from Walthamstow who, along with Parsons was the only ever present in that Championship side.

Blunstone was joined on the left by the inside-forward Les Stubbs, the owner of a mule-like kick. Bentley of course was at centre-forward, whilst Parsons' partner on the right-side of the attack was Johnny McNichol, a silky Scottish ball player who weaved intricate magic with Parsons and provided so many goals. With the likes of Seamus O'Connell and Jim Lewis more than able members of the squad, it was no wonder that even the might mustered by Manchester United and Wolves could not stop the championship making its way along the Fulham Road.

The skills of Parsons, McNichol, Bentley and Blunstone were backed up by the steel of Armstrong, Wicks and Willemse. There have been better championship winning teams (Chelsea's total of 52 points remains the equal lowest winning total for a 42 game First Division season alongside that of Arsenal's 1937-38 side), but the hard graft that they all put in and the way in which they organised themselves and each other had fans swarming to the ground every other week and made this Chelsea side worthy champions. Not least because they had delivered when so many of their predecessors had failed.

So what of Parsons' role? Playing in all forty-two-league games that season is testimony to his supreme fitness and will. His ability to provide goals was best portrayed in the famous 4-3 win at Wolves. Trailing 3-2 to the reigning champions with only moments left, Parsons was not going to wilt. He had forged his way all game through the Molineux mud, and was already the man-of-the-match before he picked up the ball in his own half, stormed past several challenges and crossed perfectly for Les Stubbs to equalise. It was magical wing play and summed up the new, improved Parsons. As for the new, improved Chelsea, Bentley got a last minute winner and the tide of the title race had turned.

Parsons chipped in with eleven vital goals. Crucially, often Parsons was a game's first goalscorer. His were the strikes that brought the big cheers, as deadlocks were broken and hope ignited. Parsons' efforts were often spectacular shots from range; goals that would heighten his popularity. But it was his last two goals of his best ever season that had the crowds screaming his name. They came in the penultimate match, the last at Stamford Bridge, and in the victory that finally won the First Division Championship for his Chelsea.

Sheffield Wednesday were the visitors. They had long been relegated, but, with the usual abandon that afflicts doomed sides, they had won their previous two games and couldn't be taken as the pushovers that so many of the supporters hoped they would be. The expectation weighed heavy on the players' shoulders and the team began tentatively. It was Parsons, a player who for so long had been unable to release the shackles of an expectant audience, who broke the deadlock before half-time with a fine, but rare, headed effort. That was that. A Peter Sillett penalty and then – the icing on the blue cake – a late Parsons strike after good work from Blunstone, sealed both the win and "Rabbit's" place, under their blue rosettes, in the hearts of Chelsea fans everywhere.

With the result from Portsmouth and the championship confirmed, the fans tumbled onto the dog track. The greyhounds, whose night's work had been unexpectedly cancelled, could only stare and whimper as hoards of supporters set about doing what the canines had hoped to do; chase the "Rabbit".

As the players, management and directors took the applause and gave their thanks from the stands, a quiet request became a boom from those crammed below. "We want Rabbit! We want Rabbit!" came the cry. It was a wonderful tone and one that quite rightly summed up the impish winger's contribution to the season and to Chelsea's history.

THAT DAY saw Drake thanking the fans for a level of support that had turned his new Chelsea into a much harder outfit to beat. The fans had changed, the team had changed and in turn, Parsons had changed. Each one complemented the other and now each was at the peak of their powers. Parsons' name was chanted because he underlined that progression from also-ran to champion.

He now stood still; a blue and white towel round his neck like a prize fighter having won the heavyweight crown (it was believed that these towels would help players, like boxers retain heat and mositure at the end of games) and a shy grin across his friendly face. The fans wanted him to speak, but words weren't Parsons forte. He instead waved and followed his team-mates into the Directors' Box for a well deserved drink. "We had champagne," recalled the new hero. "I was interviewed by Eamonn Andrews on the radio and then I just sat there in the ledge and let the fans shout my name." And shout they did before making their own way home for numerous and hearty parties.

Like his Chelsea, this was to be as good as it got for Parsons. 1957 saw a terrible epidemic of Myxomatosis. Dead rabbits littered England's countryside, but a year earlier Drake had unleashed his own form of the disease when he unceremoniously sold his right-winger to Brentford where Parsons remained until he retired from league football in 1960. Parsons played nearly 500 senior games, not bad for a player blighted by a World War and two nasty injuries (he broke his leg at Griffin Park).

For all of his other endeavours however, the winger will be rightly remembered for his role in the Chelsea team that, in their jubilee year, won their first piece of silverware, their first ever Championship. Every lightening run, every powerful dribble, every inviting cross and every scorching shot had the crowd wanting more. Every moment had the crowd wanting "Rabbit".

JIMMY GREAVES

'GREAVESIE'

1957-1961

CHELSEA CAREER

Games	169
Goals	132
Caps	57

MAGIC MOMENT

Greavesie's four goals against Nottingham Forest in his farewell game saw fans invade the pitch to hoist him aloft and confirm his legendary status

I set my star so high that I would constantly be in motion toward it.

Sidney Poitier

THE presents had been opened, the Christmas bird had been stuffed and goodwill had been passed to all men. Now it was time for the match. Christmas day fixtures were the norm in the 1940s and 1950s and Chelsea fans in great numbers lapped up their yuletide helpings of association football.

Healthy attendances flocked to Stamford Bridge looking for some Christmas cheer. With this being Chelsea, although that merriment wasn't always in the Blues' favour, but many a fan could sit and recall memorable occasions on December 25th. In 1946, Chelsea were beaten by Preston North End, who boasted an enthusiastic Scot named Bill Shankly and a useful, but fairly unknown, young winger called Tom Finney, who scored both goals in a 2-1 win. Two years later, Tommy Walker bade his farewell to Stamford Bridge before heading home to his native Scotland. Walker had been a favourite with the crowd, a classy international, but now he was off. Chelsea lost 2-1 to Portsmouth.

Typical Chelsea, but no matter. Football at the Bridge on Christmas Day was like Brussel Sprouts; it could leave a bad taste in the mouth, but somehow was tradition. In 1957, supporters made their way to the ground (for what turned out to be the last of those Christmas matches at Stamford Bridge) in typically large numbers and in good spirits. The new sound of Rock 'n' Roll had brought a spring into the step of many fans who had taken to rocking around the clock and were happy to wear appropriately coloured suede shoes.

With the sounds of the new fad ringing in their ears, Chelsea fans were snaking their way along the Fulham Road hoping that their manager, Ted Drake would give them the gift they all craved and play the young, goal-scoring sensation who had burst onto the scene and who, even at the tender age of seventeen, had become the darling of the terraces. Glory to the newborn king!

Despite his incredible start in the first team, Drake had chosen to rest the young forward, fearing football overload. It wouldn't do. Chelsea's fans, the fizz having evaporated from their Championship bubbly, wanted this boy to play; they wanted to see a player who pointed to a remarkable future and allowed them to escape a mundane present. News filtered through quickly. Jimmy Greaves would play. It was going to be a wonderful morning after all, and they'd be back in time for a roast lunch.

The usual cigarette was replaced by festive cigars, cheeks were rosy after a celebratory morning dram, whilst the thought that the young boy could once more produce the kind of mesmerising form that had forced all football eyes to focus again on Stamford Bridge, warmed the heart like no new Christmas sweater ever could.

Greaves himself had become a restless figure for the six weeks that Drake had forced him to "take off". The youngster craved his football and yearned to score goals. It was apparent every time he got on the pitch and was an attitude that would endear him to those in the stands who themselves wished they possessed his extraordinary gift for scoring goals. That morning, Portsmouth would find out the hard way. That morning, Greaves would underline that he wasn't a boy who could be rested. His place was on the pitch, wearing blue and winning games and he set about the Pompey as if picking a succulent Turkey right to the bone.

Greaves scored four times, his first on the quarter hour, a long-range drive that sliced through the grass and into the corner of the net. It was always the corner of the net. There was no need for great power, there was no need to split the ball's laces, instead it was caressed into the angles with all the precision of a mathematician.

Goals flowed at both ends, but Greaves' quadruple ensured Portsmouth were beaten 7-4 and fans skipped home longing to recite to their families, over Christmas lunch, tales of marvel about the messiah sent from heaven; one that scored goals. The football didn't end there. Boxing Day would see the reverse fixture played at Fratton Park, and the next day Chelsea lost 3-0. Bloody typical.

THE "OLD UNPREDICTABLES" (as they were known to their weathered fans) were up to their old tricks. Ted Drake had long since lost the consistency from the team that had been crowned champions. Those players had begun their exodus from the club within a year of lifting the crown as the manager put his faith in young, raw talent and a decent scouting and youth set-up. Greaves was the very heartbeat of that decision, he was the very reason to again feel hope, the excuse for fans to shuffle eagerly to the stadium, rather than to trudge both leaden in foot and in heart.

It was the same old story. The club misfires, trophies, like hope, are lost, but then along comes an individual so sparkling, so effervescent that you as the fan *must* be there every week, you *must* witness his genius so that one day you'll be able to say, "I was there…" Jimmy Greaves was that individual. He became the only reason for many fans' presence. A gravitational pull exuded from his young frame. Each time his left foot was cocked a hush fell and goals flowed.

He looked like butter wouldn't melt in his mouth. The foppish hair, the cheeky east end grin, the knowing glint in his eye that back then had been untouched by success and its dangerous trappings; the chicken-like legs engulfed in the baggy shorts of the period. Put a ball at his feet however, and he became the devil incarnate. Defenders were made a mockery of as he swerved and slalomed past the most useful of rear-ends before dispatching the ball with that evil precision. Goals were his business; no, his lifeblood. He once admitted that he physically yearned to score and Chelsea's fans were immediately hooked. The team's fortunes were almost secondary.

JIMMY GREAVES was born in Dagenham, East London in February 1940 amidst the rumblings of the Luftwaffe's almost nightly devastating deposits. He was a small child, but he excelled at football, kicking a tennis ball heartily around his streets until said ball had split. He was always a striker. There was never any other position for Jimmy Greaves to play. His shape and form, his movement and eye demanded that he partake in the role of goalscorer. Primary school, secondary modern, Dagenham schoolboys, Essex schoolboys and then their London equivalent; all benefited from his record-breaking form and soon Greaves had scouts clambering over each other to grab his attention.

West Ham, Tottenham and Chelsea (the three English clubs he would eventually play for) were all keen, but cockney eyes were once again drawn to Stamford Bridge. Their chief scout, Jim Thompson, was renowned for his work with young footballers and having concentrated more and more on their youth teams, Chelsea had become renowned as the club for any aspiring young footballer to join.

Greaves knew of Les Allen, a fine and much talked about schoolboy footballer. Allen had chosen Chelsea and had no regrets and neither would Greaves (both would play together in later years at Spurs). Chelsea were delighted. Thompson – a former Chelsea player of the 1930s – had seen many good youngsters in his time, but the day he spotted the wispy young Greaves, even he was inclined to immediately get on the phone and call his boss, Ted Drake.

It was 16th October 1954 and that day Drake had bigger issues on his mind. His Chelsea team had just been beaten 6-5 by Manchester United. A loss maybe, but it was the game that had underlined, to him at least, the potential of his would-be champions. He picked up the phone without letting his scout get a word in edgeways. "Seamus O'Connell got three on his debut, Jimmy," said Drake. "We still went down 6-5 though…I tell you Jimmy, you just missed the game of a lifetime."

Thompson took it all in. But images of the five goals that he had seen a fourteen-year-old score that afternoon remained tattooed on his mind. "Maybe so," he said. "But I've just seen the player of a lifetime." Greaves was on his way, a schoolboy maybe, but one teetering on the very cusp of greatness.

For now such lofty ambition was obliged to hide behind pubescent pimples, as the mundane apprenticeship of the young, pro footballer had to be adhered to. Greaves had shown much aptitude not only for football, but to his studies and therefore rather than simply painting the stands and washing boots, he was asked to carry out his apprentice's duties in the club's office.

There he aided the chairman and the secretary and in many cases, the players. John Sillett, the brother of Peter, who had played such a huge part in the 1955 Championship winning team, took the young office-boy to one side with a request. Greaves was in charge of the luncheon vouchers for the nearby greasy spoon *Charlie's* and Sillett hoped to persuade the young apprentice that he should slip some their way. "I'm not suggesting that you steal them," said Sillett innocently. "Them vouchers are imprisoned in that office. I want you to liberate them." The Sillett brothers (hardly the Krays) would sell on these vouchers and Greaves would make a bit of extra cash, whilst also getting to know the men, whom soon, on the field of play, would come to rely on that very slippery nature of his.

When not scamming in the office, that bare-faced cheek was mischievously causing havoc on the youthful pitches of south-east England. Greaves was a revelation. In 1956/57, the youngster scored an incredible 122 goals for Chelsea youth and reserve teams. Yes, 122 himself, in one season.

IT BECAME clear that soon this boy would have to make the step up to the first team. He had played a smattering of reserve team games that season, but how long could the "Wonder Boy" (as he was affectionately known) be left out of Drake's stuttering team?

Drake's champions had split up and potentially great players such as Bobby Smith had been sold. The only light in the darkness seemed to be the new floodlights that illuminated the old ground for the first time in March 1956, when Sparta Prague were the visitors. Otherwise things at Chelsea were perhaps not quite banal, but certainly routine. The club needed an injection. Drake had been inspired by Matt Busby's dedication to young talent and had hoped to bring similar fledgling success to London. Greaves then would be perfect. Wouldn't he?

Drake, a man who would become increasingly erratic in terms of decision making, was somehow not fully convinced by the 122 goals accredited to his young striker. If the player's time in the youth team and reserves was a job interview then surely only the most hardened or insane of employers would have doubts about showing him to his new office. Now it was time to offer – or not – professional contracts and Drake called Greaves into his office, amazingly still undecided.

They chatted and Drake said he was unsure and if he did get a contract then no signing-on fee would follow. Greaves left the meeting confused. Hadn't he done enough? How many goals could he score? Jimmy Thompson pulled up. "What's wrong, son?"

"It's Ted Drake," said Greaves. "He doesn't want to sign me."

"Leave this to me." With that Thompson made his way with all the purpose of his playing days into Drake's office and returned ten minutes later with an assuring smile. "You'll get that contract, son."

He did. He even got a £50 signing-on fee, although Greaves himself believes that may have come from Thompson's own pocket.

Was Drake mad or a genius? Mad, if he didn't see the potential he now had under his command, a genius if he was trying to keep the youngster's feet on the ground. Either way, Greaves was in the first team squad that began training for the 1957/58 season.

THE YOUNG man did well on a pre-season tour to Holland with the youth team and when he returned to train at Stamford Bridge he was delighted when advised to get changed in the home team dressing room, a pleasure reserved only for those harbouring real first-team ambitions. There he disrobed amongst players he had only read about in his *Charlie Buchan* annuals. He would sit quietly, whilst Frank Blunstone, John McNichol and Les Stubbs, all members of the Championship squad, changed in front of him. He would get a wink from the knowing Sillett brothers, but other than that, he was on his own.

Out on the pitch though, with a ball as his companion, he was like a veteran. One afternoon the club hosted a series of trial games where first team members would take on fringe players in a match open to the public who paid a small fee to come along and cast their eye over the season's prospects. 15,000 fans had made their way through the sunny streets of south-west London to see the match and Greaves took his place in a side designed to test last season's first team delegates.

Greaves was hungry. The match was but minutes old when he took the ball in his stride and set off toward those very men who had hitherto ignored him, the ball fixed to his feet. "Get rid of it!" shouted Ted Drake from the sidelines. Greaves continued. "Get rid of it. Get rid!" came the cry. He swivelled past one reputation after another; his mixture of deft movement and blistering pace bemusing opponent after opponent.

"Get rid! For Gawd's sake, pass the bloody ball!"

Ian McFarlane, a giant of a defender, felt confident he could check the boy's impudence. He too was left lonely and confused before Reg Matthews in goal came rushing out to narrow any angles. "GET RID!" came the cry from Drake now tinged with desperation. Greaves instead dribbled around the England custodian and rolled the ball into an empty net, leaving mouths agape around the entire stadium. Greaves strolled off amid the silence, looking over at his exasperated manager.

"You never told me who to."

Jimmy Greaves had arrived.

The flair, the cheek, the sheer skill had been unleashed on an adoring Stamford Bridge public. "I thought there were about 15,000 supporters in the ground," said Greaves recently. "But judging from the number of people who, over the years, have told me they were present when I played in that first practice match and were first to spot my emerging talent, the crowd must have been nigh on a quarter of a million."

Who could blame them? Greaves would become a hero, albeit a fleeting one. His brief spell in Blue was a whirlwind of skill and goals. Chelsea fans can be forgiven for wanting to say they were present on that day to witness the explosive beginnings of a career that would reach for the stars.

FOLLOWING that Greaves was always going to start the season in the first team. The opposition were Tottenham, the venue White Hart Lane. Debuts have long been the mark by which Chelsea players have been judged. He may not have scored the incredible five that George Hilsdon notched in 1906, but the young Greaves did manage a performance so vivid and fresh that it had fans, pundits, players and the gentleman of the press alike gushing disbelieving expletives.

Greaves scored Chelsea's goal in a 1-1 draw and tested Tottenham's Danny Blanchflower to the point that the Northern Ireland skipper enthused that he had just played against "the best youngster I have ever seen". The understandable hyperbole continued on the nation's back pages. Charles Buchan, in the *News Chronicle* was in no doubt about the new talent. "Young Jimmy Greaves gave such a brilliant display on his debut that I think he may rival the performance of Duncan Edwards, Manchester United's left-half who became the youngest player to play for England. Only seventeen years old, Greaves showed the ball control, confidence and positional strength of a seasoned campaigner. It was the finest first-ever League game I have ever seen from any youngster."

News quickly spread. Chelsea had a new impish hero with a cheeky grin and a deadly finish. Artful Dodger? That's too easy. Goal-poacher? That's like calling Van Gogh a doodler. No, what Chelsea and its fans had was a master in the art of finding space and the craft of putting the ball where it was supposed to be; in the back of the net. Fans flocked, cramming in to see the slight, waif-like boy-man with a cheeky teenage grin, but a huge talent. Men wanted to be like him, women wanted to mother him. Mostly.

If Greaves was exciting the crowd, then the team itself was infuriating them. Goals were being scored, but they were also being given away with alarming and often comic ease. Greaves himself recalls a goal that they conceded to Everton. "I still rate it as one of the all-time unforgettable goals. If there had been action replay machines around those days I am sure they would be showing it as a comic classic. A long shot from an Everton player slipped under the body of keeper Reg Matthews. Reg scrambled up and chased the ball, hotly pursued by Peter Sillett, who thought he had a better chance of clearing it. They pounded neck and neck towards our goal. Reg won the race and then, instead of diving on the ball, elected to kick it away. He pivoted beautifully and cracked the ball dead centre-straight into the pit of Sillett's stomach. The ball rebounded into the back of the net and Peter collapsed holding his stomach. The rest of us collapsed in laughter."

Such joviality was never far away from Stamford Bridge in the late fifties and early sixties. A new London was emerging from the rubble left by Hitler's raids. Prosperity was up and a young resurgence blossomed amidst a desire to escape the post-war gloom. In Greaves' first season, attendances rose by seven thousand to 38,000 despite Chelsea finishing eleventh.

To the young fraternity, here was a kid, only a little older than themselves, who they could identify with and worship. To the older punter, this meek-looking little striker with the baggy shorts made them dream that they had a new Alex James in their side. The shorts, the dribbling and mazy runs, all pointed to the great Arsenal man of the 1930s.

Greaves scored 22 times in his debut campaign and his second season, so often the tough rock upon which less talented players founder, was even more dynamic. He only missed one game and scored 37 goals. Crowds rose again to over 40,000. How they loved their goalscoring hero, but Chelsea finished fourteenth. The problem was Greaves simply couldn't always outscore the opposition. However many he managed to net, Chelsea's defence too often managed to let in even more.

FOR THOSE wanting entertainment during the 1958/59 campaign, this was the place to be. Newcastle were beaten 6-5, but Bolton hammered Chelsea 6-0. 3-3 draws were commonplace. Chelsea were never in danger of relegation, so fans could stand and joke at their team's frailties whilst marvelling at the skills of their young inside-forward. To the old-time purist, Saturday at the Bridge was once again a frustrating place to be, but for the young and carefree, a little more unaccustomed to the hair-tearing idiosyncrasies that go with supporting Chelsea, these were wild, fun days as fans of the club that the

Daily Sketch dubbed "The Dr Jekyll and Mr Hyde of the First Division". Other publications agreed. "If it's goals you want to see, see Chelsea," joked *Soccer Star*. "Goals are what Chelsea deliver unfailingly, at either end of the pitch."

Greaves by now was being touted as a future England star. He had represented the England Under-23s (predictably, he scored on his debut) and now full international honours beckoned. At the close of that goal-laden 1958/59 season, Greaves took flight with Walter Winterbottom's youthful England squad on an ill-fated summer tour to South America. The side lost their first game 2-0 to World Champions Brazil in Rio and so the youngster from Chelsea was called for. He couldn't stop another defeat, but he did score a clever goal in a 4-1 mauling at the hands of Peru.

The England skipper, Billy Wright, was under no doubt that England had a new Lion in their midst. "It was good to be there to witness the start of another great England career, this time of the chirpy cockney Jimmy Greaves...His goal was the only face-saving thing of an otherwise disastrous match."

Wright knew all about Greaves' game from a pasting that his Wolverhampton Wanderers side had received early that same season. Wolves were the champions and so 61,000 fans packed Stamford Bridge to glimpse Stan Cullis' great side, but it was to be their own new star who stole the show, scoring five times in a wonderful 6-2 win, the first of three occasions on which he would equal George Hilsdon's club record of five goals in a game. It was a day that symbolised Greaves' ascendancy and style. He ghosted about the flat Wolves defence, scoring with that trademark ability to place the ball into the net rather than to slam it. He sneaked about looking for and invariably finding space and before a defender could react he had, first time, put the chance away.

Billy Wright retired that summer and the press were quick to suggest it was Greaves who had shown him that the twilight of his career had turned into dark midnight. "That was nonsense," said Wright. "There wasn't a defender on earth who could have held him that afternoon."

Playing in front of over 60,000 fans against the Champions, an England debut alongside his nation's luminaries such as Johnny Haynes, Bobby Charlton and Billy Wright, it didn't matter. Greaves was unfazed, his nerves untouched and he actually thrived on the pressure and the occasion. The bigger it was, the more dangerous he became.

He was genuinely unmoved by tension. He would sit calmly in the England dressing room as Walter Winterbottom elaborately discussed the day's tactics. Different passing moves and concise modes of play were gone over before the manager finished saying, "At the end of all that, Jimmy will score a goal." The forward didn't blink. He continued to tie up his boots before looking up and dryly asking, "Do you want me to score that with my right or my left foot."

GREAVES had style. By the start of the 1960s he was the nation's goalscorer. Chelsea fans could look upon him with pride. He had been brought up at their club and he was their gift to the country. Their team wasn't going to get them noticed, but Greaves and his goals would. Five goal hauls against Preston and West Bromwich Albion headlined another season of goals; 29 in all in 1959-60. To Greaves it was simply his job. "My trade is scoring goals," he would say. "I love scoring. I would rather play badly for 89 minutes and score the winner than play well for 90 and not hit the net."

It was once said that "Goals pay the rent". If that is true then Greaves was living in a penthouse flat in Mayfair. He couldn't stop scoring and the fans couldn't stop loving him, and it wasn't only mere fans. Prominent sports-writers Terence Delaney and Maurice Edelstone, who was also once a manager at Reading, wrote a book looking at the major forces in the English game at the turn of the decade. Johnny Charles, Stanley Matthews, Tommy Lawton, Len Shackleton and Billy Liddell were, of course, included in a book named *Masters of Soccer*, but there included in the pages was a chapter on the 19-year-old Jimmy Greaves.

Delaney and Edelstone made their way to the Bridge before a European match (Chelsea had qualified for the new Inter-Cities Fairs Cup tournament in 1959) against Ville de Belgrade to meet the new sensation. They chatted to Jack Oxberry, the club's stout trainer. "Oh yes," he said, "he's a good-un Jimmy Greaves."

"What do you have to teach him?" asked the inquisitive writers.

"Nothing. You can't teach him anything. He's a natural…He learns from playing."

Soon this deadly executioner joined them in the club office that not so long ago he was helping organise. "There was a tap at the door and the face of a cool customer appeared around it – a shrewd, alert face, sharp, and a little paler than you would expect, very much a Londoner's face; his close-cropped hair stood up spikily above his forehead. He could be quite a comic, we thought, but at the moment his expression was simply pleasant and polite."

What the writers found was not a sporting thoroughbred, hell-bent on world domination, but a young kid in love with the game and ecstatic to be doing what he was doing for a modest wage. "Who was the one player you admired as a boy?" they asked.

"Len Shackleton."

"Why?"

"Why? Because he was…he was just good." It was simple. It didn't need explanation and nor did the reasons behind the Chelsea fans' love of him. He was just good.

As the pair left the office with Greaves they were swarmed by a deluge of supporters wanting a word or a signature:

> Many of them carried so much evidence of being Chelsea supporters that they were almost entirely concealed; blue and white scarves muffled their necks and chins and fell below their waists; there were players' names knitted into the white bands; one wore a blue and white tam-o'-shanter that fell over his eyes and ears as he ran; their lapels were smothered with pin-badges bearing the faces of the team; most were eating, some carried rattles, nearly all had autograph books, of various sizes. They pulled at Greaves, waved the books and their pencils under his nose; he was late, he had to force his way through them. They followed him with cries of anguish. 'Jimmy! I've been waiting!' 'Jimmy – you said you would last week.' 'Just this one, Jimmy – oh Jimmy!' They were only a few years younger than Greaves. It's a great thing to be a hero at nineteen.

Greaves was more than just a hero. His ability and his goals meant the fortunes of the club rested on those young shoulders. He was carrying his team-mates and it began to play on his mind. "We were labelled 'Drake's Ducklings' and had more potential than any other team I ever played for," admits Greaves. "But you need experienced players to help draw out the potential, and we were just a bunch of kids playing it off the cuff and often coming off second best. It was like being at Butlins, a real holiday camp atmosphere. Our lack of success did nothing to harm the dressing-room spirit and even in defeat you would find us falling about laughing at things that went on at the club. We were still kids wanting to grow up."

Those kids had talent all right. The youth team went on a wonderful spell of winning the South-East Counties League again and again, but the same success couldn't be continued in the big league. David Cliss was a sharp inside-forward, Barry Bridges a dynamic centre-forward. Peter Brabrook was a skilful, pacy winger, whilst toward the end of Greaves' time at the club a young Bobby Tambling got his chance and showed plenty of potential when it came to scoring goals. His time would most certainly come, but for now, under Ted Drake, the "Ducklings" seemed lost amongst the hard pond-life of the English First Division.

In 1959/60 Greaves' 29 goals helped Chelsea finish eighteenth, a remarkably low position for a team that boasted such a striker. Again there were ups, Peter Bonetti made his debut, as did Terry Venables, and Tottenham were beaten 1-0 at White Hart Lane, a result that cost the North Londoners the title, but again there were downs, culminating with Wolves walloping them 5-1 on the final day of the season.

FOR THE fans it was a case of "what if?" What if they had a defence to match their forwards and what if they had a manager who could bring out the best of the players he had urged the club to nurture? They were not alone. It was getting to Greaves too, who later suggested that, as nice as Ted Drake was, another man would have brought better times to the Bridge. "I think if Bill Nicholson had had the team, it would really have got somewhere...If you'd taken some of the managers of the day, like Bill Shanks, who was just up and coming, or people like Harry Catterick at Everton, or Harry Potts at Burnley, they probably would have done very well with that Chelsea squad."

That same squad, though, was very much stuck in the mud, clinging desperately to the sturdy pole of Greaves' goals, while he himself was beginning to wonder about his future at a club who couldn't muster a challenge for the game's honours. Things might have to change. He was now 21, a man. His life (eerily like Hughie Gallacher's before him) had been struck by grief in 1960 when his four-month-old son Jimmy Junior had died of pneumonia and he now knew he must take care of his wife, Irene and their other young children.

Greaves was now a fully fledged national celebrity having scored two hat-tricks in the 1960/61 season, the second coming in England's 9-3 ritual slaughter of Scotland at Wembley in April. In all he notched 11 goals in the season's five internationals. With superstardom just around the corner, Greaves started to realise that his footballing world may have to branch out from its SW6 roots. Things came to a head, in Greaves' mind certainly, when the team were beaten 2-1 in the FA Cup by lowly Crewe Alexandra. It was an embarrassing defeat, one which could not even raise a chuckle from the most sadistic of fan. It had come off the back of 6-0 and 6-1 defeats by Manchester United and Wolves respectively. Greaves was going to have to have words.

He finished with 41 League goals that season, a club record that remains a seemingly unattainable figure at Chelsea. The team scored ninety-eight times in the First Division, but conceded one hundred. That was Chelsea, that was the norm. Fans put up with it, however much it had them gnawing on their scarves, but could Greaves? Should Greaves?

He asked himself that question and the answer was "no". He loved the club, he had named his house after them, but he went to Drake suggesting a move. It wasn't formal, it wasn't so he could get more money, it was simply a genuine plea and after a while Drake listened. Tottenham were keen, who wouldn't be, but the Chelsea Chairman, Joe Mears (grandson of Gus), and his manager were loathe to sell him to any rival, let alone a club that even then were despised by the Chelsea faithful.

IN 1961, Italian football decided to lift a ban on foreign players. The stylish clubs from Turin, Rome and, of course, Milan wanted the best and eyes immediately turned to Greaves, the Gucci loafer of English footballers. A transfer to a foreign club would suit Chelsea and they pushed for the move, but Greaves was less convinced about a life abroad. Whatever his trepidations, he may well have gone during that season as it seemed to be his only option, but the embargo remained up until the summer; the inevitable would have to wait.

Chelsea's hierarchy busily pushed the deal through, pleading poverty and drooling at the proposed £80,000 on offer. Financially it was a wonderful opportunity for Greaves, a player only just getting used to the abolished maximum wage in this country, but he harboured many doubts. He told the Chairman he couldn't bear to move his family out to Italy. He was a simple Essex boy. He didn't look for the high-life, he didn't look for glitz, fans loved him (for now) for that wholesomeness to his play and this didn't feel right.

Chelsea, though, had already received part of the fee and the response was a simple one. "There's no ifs or, buts about it, you gotta go, Jimmy, you gotta go." The days of player power were decades off yet. That was that, the public knew, the press knew, the clubs knew and now Greaves knew. He was bound for Italy whether he liked it or not. There was one last game left of what was to be his final season and fortunately it was to be at Stamford Bridge, where crestfallen fans could come and say their goodbyes to the man who had made their trips worthwhile.

No man is bigger than the club? That day one man was.

The opposition were Nottingham Forest and 23,000 fans made their way to the ground desperate to get a last glimpse of their departing hero. Each one of them clung to his every move, his every touch. It had been a drawn out affair. Would he stay, would he go? Think Steven Gerrard, but this time the local hero *was* leaving.

GREAVES' status as a hero in his susequent career changed like the phases of the moon, for whilst he continued to score goals (he set a new England record of 44, which has only twice since been surpassed), his football and life was tinged, rightly or wrongly with the scent of booze and misdemeanour. What Chelsea's supporters can look to with pride is that they had the original version of the man. They had the untainted Greaves (a player whose shot was likened by the writer Geoffery Green to "someone shutting the door of a Rolls-Royce". They had the boy with a spark and a brashness, the boy with – and this word isn't often used to describe the club's sometimes anarchic employees – purity.

His game was like a hypnotist's clock, sliding from one side of the pitch to another as spellbound punters waited for a darting move that invariably ended in a goal. On this occasion, they ended in four of them. Chelsea beat Forest 4-3, and Greaves bagged all the goals in a flurry of deadly finishing. For the fans it was a sad goodbye; like a final parting with a recent ex whom, while waving farewell, strikes you, through tear-filled eyes, as the most beautiful person you have ever and will ever know.

Greaves himself would miss those fans, he would miss the club. It was and remains the fondest of places for a player who always carried that star quality with him wherever he went. Things got hard, but he kept that cheek, that charm and never forgot where those qualities were first nurtured and so deeply cherished. "Chelsea: it's a name. It's probably the greatest name in the world: Chelsea, you think about it." He later gushed. "What does it conjure up? It conjures up the best part of the biggest city in the world. Chelsea! It's magical."

That afternoon was bewitching and the fans cascaded onto the pitch to say "Farewell" to their hero and the two feet that for four years had been their magic wands. They hoisted him onto their shoulders and hauled him around their arena. "They carried me off like I were the FA Cup," he later joked. Greaves, as ever was right on target. To those fans, that is exactly what he was. He was their trophy, their shiny possession, their glittering jewel.

BOBBY TAMBLING

'THE GOALSCORER'

1958-1970

CHELSEA CAREER

Games	370
Goals	202
Caps	3

MAGIC MOMENT

His five goal display at Villa Park in 1966 equalled the club record for goals in a game alongside Hilsdon and Greaves, but Bobby still thinks he should have had more!

> **Hey! Mr Tambourine Man, play a song for me,**
> **I'm not sleepy and there is no place I'm going to.**
> **Hey! Mr Tambourine Man, play a song for me,**
> **In the jingle jangle morning I'll come followin' you.**
>
> **"Mr Tambourine Man", Bob Dylan**

CHELSEA'S all-time record goalscorer is a content man. Sitting in his living room in southern Ireland's County Cork, he overlooks a beautiful river strewn with cruising yachts as the July sun sets on another lazy day. Green rolling hills and friendly taverns are a world away from the hullabaloo of life on the swinging and hip Kings Road of the 1960s. "People ask me why I live over here now," says a relaxed and friendly Bobby Tambling. "I tell them that if they looked out of this window and saw the view, they would immediately know the answer to that."

Tambling's need for the quiet life cannot be ridiculed. For thirteen years he thrived on the honour of being a Chelsea footballer and with that came goals, lots of them. The 202 he scored in 370 games remain a club record and whilst today Roman Abramovich can pour zillions of pounds into acquiring the world's most eminent goal getters, it is unlikely that the nomadic modern footballer would stay long enough to challenge Tambling's heroic work.

Throughout the 1960s, Bobby Tambling found himself firmly in football's rat-race. Like an overworked commuter, he would come into work everyday knowing that his goals were needed if Jimmy Greaves' spirit was to be exorcised from the club's terraces and to ensure that Chelsea's renaissance in the swinging decade was to continue under manager Tommy Docherty.

Not only that. Through his prodigious talent for putting a football into the back of his opponent's net, Tambling made himself the darling of a club who epitomised the coolest confounds of cool-Britannia. London was the place to be, and Chelsea was at the gyrating, pulsating heart of it. That general lifting of post-war gloom had continued throughout the 1950s, but now had risen to new levels of affluence and well-being. Young men no longer had to endure National Service and the rigid rigmarole that went with its polished boots and harsh haircuts. Music continued to whip a zealous youth into a frenzy whilst fashion became a way of life. Mary Quant opened her trendy boutiques (which would have delighted Fatty Foulke) and the Kings Road became the place to be seen. Quant designed clothes that summed up the vibrancy of the time and hoped her clothes "were much more for life – much more for real people, much more for being young and alive in."

Being geographically and spiritually at the centre of this cosmopolitan cool, Chelsea Football Club took on that same mantle and thousands flocked to the ground; a place they felt both young and alive in. The football on show and the vigour of the men playing it added a fizz to this most effervescent of London boroughs. Football Club luminaries such as Terry Venables, George Graham and later Peter Osgood quickly became movers and shakers amid Chelsea's growing set, but Tambling was more the silent, modest type. The place rocked, the fans had a gas, but the team, inevitably for this almost-but-not-quite football club, couldn't pull off a major victory. Like many a young lady in Quant's mini-skirt, Chelsea fell short of promised expectations.

That was undoubtedly part of the Blues' charm, it always had been. They tantalised and they teased without quite giving all that they promised, but Tambling, the Hampshire-born striker, eschewed that image. He was a man far more content to score goals than to strut and score on the Kings Road.

Whilst Terry, George and Peter's devilment was akin to Frank, Dean and Sammy; Tambling was more of a Tony Bennett; the quieter one who got on with making records that today remain intact, popular and unlikely to be broken. "We were a trendy club in a trendy area," says Tambling. "It wasn't my image, though. I was far less outgoing than some of the others. Terry and George loved all that side of things and let's just say they played up to the image of the club. They were the men about town, but at the same time both were fantastic pros. They did like all the music, the suits and a little drink, but I wouldn't say they went overboard. They knew what they were being paid to do."

IN 1957, when a 16-year-old Tambling arrived at Stamford Bridge, Chelsea remained more cloth-cap than rat-pack. Under the pragmatic Ted Drake, Chelsea had won their title and Stamford Bridge was now – amid a glut of goals from the impish Jimmy Greaves – clearly a place where youth could have it's say. Whilst it was Drake who was entreated with the decision of who should play in the first team, it was Jimmy Thompson, the club's chief scout, who was charged with casting Chelsea's net to catch those suitable to fit in.

Tambling came to Thompson's attention whilst starring for East Hampshire Schools and it wasn't long before the country lad's door was being knocked upon by the big-city club. "I was only 13 when Jimmy Thompson approached me," recalls Tambling. "I was living on the south-coast and suddenly there was a knock on the door and there's Jimmy of Chelsea Football Club standing there, without even a phone call to say he'd be coming, just 'Do you want to sign for Chelsea?' It was crazy."

Tambling, though, had scored enough goals at schoolboy level to catch many eyes and already had represented England juniors against Ireland in 1956. Portsmouth, Reading, Wolves and Arsenal were keen, but as ever it was Chelsea, armed confidently with a real promise of first team football that got their boy. "Under Drake the club put a great emphasis on youth," says Tambling. "Other clubs had youth policies, but often didn't really use them. Chelsea had attracted a lot of youngsters and so it would have been pointless if they had not had a look at them and, of course, in time they did." For those impatient for a chance in the first team, Jimmy Thompson had a way of making young footballers feel like they were not only the future, but also the present. "Jimmy was a bit of a rogue. A lovable rogue, mind. He had all the chat and would make you feel good. You felt you were the only schoolboy player that Chelsea had ever watched or wanted."

That, of course, was not the case and through their shrewd recruitment, the club found themselves with no shortage of talent for the youth team coach Dick Foss to work with and mould into players the club and its long suffering fans could count upon for the decade or so to come. Foss himself had enjoyed a modest playing career, having signed for Chelsea before the war from Southall where he turned out at inside-forward, but his time was interrupted by the hostilities. Now he passed on his coaching skills to the new generation, many of whom would go on to represent not only the club, but their countries too.

"Dickie was great," says Tambling. "We were all coming from different parts of the country and were all top-dog in our particular area. There could have been some egos, but Dickie would sort you out and you had to fall into line. Our Youth team was amazing. If we hadn't won five or six nil it meant we had had a bad day. It was the club's 100th year party recently and I don't think there were many there with an FA Youth Cup medal. I'm very proud of that one."

Tambling and Chelsea won that honour in 1960. The club should have taken the crown in 1958 when they faced Wolves. Despite Greaves' goals they let a 5-1 first leg lead slip to lose infuriatingly 6-1 at Molineux in front of 50,000 fans. That had affected everyone – "I thought they were pulling my leg when I heard," says Tambling, who was at the club, but not playing. By 1960 the youth set-up boasted several players who would become legends. Peter Bonetti, Terry Venables, Allan Harris; they all played alongside Tambling as Everton (who included future internationals and League title winners Howard Kendall, Colin Harvey and Joe Royle in their line up) were beaten 5-3 over two legs in that final.

By then, though, Tambling was used to the big time. He had plundered 33 goals in the 25 games that constituted his first season in the youth team. His seven hat-tricks that year would entice the most conservative of managers, but Drake had already dithered over giving the prolific Jimmy Greaves a pro contract. Just as with Greaves, though, Tambling was eventually handed a deal and, in February 1959, along with fellow youth team starlet Barry Bridges, he made his debut at the Bridge against West Ham, the team that for so long had competed with Chelsea for the title of Football's most eminent production line.

"What an exciting time," purrs Tambling. "What you must remember is that the forward line that day had all grown up together. Jimmy, David Cliss, Barry, Me and Peter Brabrook; we were all pals and so it didn't seem a nerve-wracking prospect at all. That was until we got into the dressing room and Ted started to talk about what he wanted us all to do. I thought 'Christ, I shouldn't be here. I'm in the wrong place; I'm not up for this.' We played well though and we got a good result."

TAMBLING over the years would delight Chelsea's faithful with his honest and modest ability. Now, 40 years on, those same qualities remain and us authors looking for some self-hyperbole are left with an almost coy account from a footballer without conceit or arrogance. Yes, the club did play well that day in 1959, yes they won 3-2, but Tambling – who had yet to play a single moment in the reserves – scored the opener after only fourteen minutes, making senior defenders such as John Bond look incredibly ordinary in his callow wake.

The youngster just got on with it and was aided by Drake's devotion to keeping those young feet firmly on the ground. "He was very good like that," recalls Tambling. "He never pushed too hard or too fast. One week I'm in the first team in front of 45,000 and the next I'm back in the juniors in front of ten."

Tambling's football would flit for a year or so between 50,000 and the Shed, and one man and his dog. The crowd were more than pleased by another youngster showing apt talent. Their eyes were firmly fixed on Greaves, the boy who, on his young frame carried all their hopes and dreams with his endless stream of goals.

They weren't alone. Tambling himself would sit and marvel at Greaves' skills like a rookie policeman in awe of his Detective Inspector. "Jimmy was so silky," says Tambling. "To watch him against very organised defences was great. I'd watch from the stand and he'd pick them off one by one. He'd run around four or five defenders like they were nothing but training cones."

Tambling had a good run in the first team during the 1960/61 season. It was Greaves' last at the club, but alongside Tambling, plenty of goals ensued. The main man however was bound for foreign shores and the fans, through their salt-watered eyes, would be looking for a replacement to fill their hearts. Bobby Tambling would be that reluctant hero.

He blushes at comparisons with Greaves. He was always aware that contrasts were inevitable, but for the meek player who remained behind, the idea that he could replicate the skills of a man he, like most who witnessed him, had drooled over was insane. "It's like comparing a thoroughbred and a beach donkey," laughs Tambling. "We were so different. I knew that and so I didn't put too much pressure on myself. I knew my game too well to do that and I hoped others would too.

"I was going to take over the scoring mantle. That's normal. It was obvious, though, that we were different players. Jimmy was an individual. He could be playing absolutely crap, get the ball in the last minute on the half-way line and "Boom" he's scored. However, *I* needed the team to be playing well if I was going to do well. My skill was to get on the end of good football and finish rather than making things happen on my own."

IN TIME though that's exactly what he was – on his own. And, like it or not, Tambling became the man who the fans hoped would stretch out an arm and take the baton from the departed Jimmy Greaves. Life without Greaves was hard on Chelsea supporters, emotionally as much as anything, as they struggled to cope without boasting the genius goalscorer amongst their ranks. But life without Greaves proved harder on the team. Drake was struggling to knit his young players together. They showed incredible talent and promise, but at times lacked guidance and their youthful vigour too often mutated into fledgling immaturity.

By 1961, from the 1955 Championship winning team, only Peter Sillett and Frank Blunstone remained. Drake himself seemed drained and lacklustre after so many years of trying to make the club a constant force. Reflecting his fatigue, Chelsea won only one of their first six games – a 2-0 victory over Manchester United, which included a Tambling strike from distance – and so the visit of Sheffield United required a steadying influence. Chairman Joe Mears, along with his board decided that Drake might need some help. Tommy Docherty, a granite-like 33-year-old Scottish pro from Glasgow's Gorbals, was plucked from Arsenal and given the role of player/coach.

It was to prove a major move for the club, but went unnoticed on the terraces as the fans were too concerned with Chelsea's problems on the pitch and how they were going to recover from Greaves' departure. To Tommy Docherty though, it was a wonderful opportunity. Mears had asked around his many contacts about the countries unused young coaches. Walter Winterbottom, England's manager offered two names, Jimmy Adamson of Burnley and Docherty.

At his first interview, Chelsea immediately got a taste of the man who would turn the club around. Forthright and to the point, Docherty made his mark. "When I was asked my opinion of one of the other two men in for the job, I said jokingly, 'If you appoint him, you'll get a hearse, not a coach!'"

Docherty got the gig – Drake greeted him with a handshake and the declaration that "you weren't my choice, I wanted Vic Buckingham" – but before he could set about his work on the training field, he was asked to help out on the pitch against the visiting Blades.

Docherty was at left-half, but the day belonged to the 19-year-old Tambling who bagged a hat-trick in a 6-1 win. It was a high, but still there were too many lows. Defeats at West Ham and Cardiff and a home draw with Blackburn Rovers at the end of September meant that Drake, the man who had brought the Championship to the Bridge had to go.

He had slowly but surely replaced his famous tracksuit with suit and tie and found it harder and harder to relate to players who now, after much wrangling, had managed to abolish the maximum wage and in some cases were earning £100 a week. On his arrival in 1952, Drake had rid the club if it's old "Pensioner" image and dragged them to modernity and glory. Now time was again moving on and the club needed fresh impetus and ideas. The Board resolved, in the usual Chelsea fashion, to appoint a big name who would bring guaranteed success. Although why they should think such a thing existed in the manic world of football boggles the mind.

In the meantime though, Joe Mears turned to Docherty; merely as a stopgap, mind. "Mr Drake is leaving us by mutual consent," the Chairman said to the eager Docherty. "If you are willing, we would like you to take charge of all matters concerning the players." Docherty jumped at the chance. "Would I just?" he declared. "The Chairman didn't have to ask me again. This was a dream come true, even if I was to be a manager in all, but name."

TAMBLING, gradually becoming the shining light in a sky clouded by the dual departures of Greaves and Drake, recalls this period as one which exemplifies Chelsea's split personality as far as fans are concerned. "We always gave them their money's worth," he laughs. "There would be four or five goals when they came to see us. But who knew at which end! Of course after 1955 they thought 'This is it, we're going to dominate now', but that simply didn't happen back then. Nowadays it's only a couple of teams who win things, but back then it was passed around. United and Wolves were good, but other clubs always had a look in. Burnley, Ipswich, Spurs, it was widely contested."

Maybe so, but as far as Chelsea were concerned that open contest was lacking an important ingredient, namely them. In fact Docherty could do nothing to curb the slide and "his" team – despite Tambling's 20 league goals – finished bottom of the table. Mears and co, though, had seen something in the determined Scot and, in January of 1962, offered him the job permanently. "From now on," he jokingly told his players hastily gathered in the dressing room after training, "you will call me 'Mr Docherty', they've made me manager."

After 32 years of First Division football, it was time to regroup and attempt to spark a quick return to the top-flight, and for those youngsters at the club who had excelled at youth level it was time to step and be counted. Tambling for one was excited. "We were all young. Blunstone, Upton, Sillett, they were there, but the rest of us were only around 21. If you talk to the old supporters they would tell you that that was the time Chelsea started to turn in the sense that the club had a side for the future and could be long-term challengers"

On paper it looked good. Bonetti was arguably the finest young keeper in the country, the two full-backs, Peter Shellito and new boy Eddie McCreadie, were regarded as tough nuts to crack, whilst the young Terry Venables, Barry Bridges and Albert Murray were more than exciting prospects. But who would lead them? Frank Blunstone or Frank Upton might have been the obvious, experienced choices, but Docherty had other ideas.

Whilst casting a canny eye over his relegated side, Docherty was drawn to his young inside-forward. On the eve of that year's FA Cup Final, Tambling had been picked to play for the young England side against the seniors, a game played as preparation for that summer's World Cup in Chile. Tambling performed manfully and his maturity shone that day. "[Tambling] was the most consistent, and therefore, the most dependable man in my squad...at twenty," Docherty recalls.

Tambling got the armband and, remarkably for one so young and in such a specialist and high pressure position, continued to score goals at the same rate. It was now that the fans truly sat up and noticed a player who could lead them out of the Second Division. "A lot of the older players left," says Tambling. "I think the Doc wanted to completely turn things around. The training intensified and the senior men at the club were given a choice; play his way or play for another club.

"Some left, but a couple stayed and said, 'Ok, Boss. Let's get on with it then. Let's do it your way.' That pleased the Doc. He wanted to create a completely new image and us youngsters were a big part of that. He came up with me as his choice of captain and I was as shocked as anyone. Shocked, but very, very proud."

To the fans, just as the Beatles' sound heralded the start of the Swinging part of the Sixties in fashionable Chelsea, this was an exciting new dawn. Tambling and Bridges were banging in goals whilst McCreadie, Shilleto and Bonetti, for the first time in a long time, were keeping them out. By Christmas 1962, the club had a seven point pillow at the top of the Second Division table.

Soon though the winter came, a winter that put the freeze, not only on the nation, but seemingly on Chelsea's promotion bid too. The club had spent some time in Malta training away from the icicle-clad streets of London, but when the campaign re-started their momentum had been left behind on the Med and things got tough. Four games were lost in a row and the lead at the top disappeared.

TAMBLING was still scoring goals and his talents had been noticed by the new manager of the national team, Sir Alf Ramsey, and in November 1962 he made his England debut, although playing at outside-left against Wales at Wembley hardly gave him the best opportunity to shine. It was the first of only three caps, but they were always going to be hard to win with Greaves now his competitor for his preferred position of inside-left. With the climax of the season approaching, Tambling's goals still flowed from his predatory feet, but, just as Greaves had done, Tambling watched as goals began to leak at the other end. Chelsea's return to the top flight, which had seemed assured for most of the campaign, was now in severe doubt.

Stoke and Sunderland, the other two teams challenging for promotion, were two of the three remaining games of the season and the first, a home match against the Potters, still being served by the tantalising talent of 48-year-old Stanley Matthews, ended in a 1-0 defeat. The Sunderland match took on vital importance and Docherty was going to pull out all the stops to get the right result, however ugly it got.

Up front, spring lambs, Bridges and Murray were dropped, as was Graham Moore. In came the more rough and ready Derek Kevan and Frank Upton whilst Frank Blunstone and the pint-sized veteran Tommy Harmer joined Tambling in the front line. All five were sent out with explicit orders to harass Sunderland's centre-half Charlie Hurley.

Flying tackles, not seen from most forwards in those days, followed. And in packs the forward line made the afternoon thoroughly uncomfortable for defenders and Mackem followers alike. From Tambling's corner, Harmer scrambled the ball in with his crotch, but they all count (later he nicknamed himself Tummy Harmer). The famous Roker Roar became a squeak and the Blues headed south with both points.

Chelsea, of course, were famed throughout the land for never doing things in an easy fashion. That result in the North East, though, marked a change. The young team had gone to a very hard place to play and they had won, and won ugly. It proved to all that here was a team capable, in an intimidating atmosphere, of putting in the hard graft and battling for a result. No more fancy dan Chelsea. The era of hatchet Chelsea was born.

The following Tuesday brought Portsmouth to the Bridge for the last game of the season with a win necessary to clinch promotion. After two minutes, Kevan scored and from there on in it was the Bobby Tambling show. He scored four times in a 7-0 mauling. The goals may have not been scored with the nonchalant genius of Jimmy Greaves, but with each competent and deserved effort, Tambling played his way into the hearts of the fans. Only two seasons earlier, those very supporters had watched Greaves score a quadruple as a farewell present and carried him off the field, tinged in sadness. Now, they hoisted Tambling upon their shoulders. He was more than just the team's goalscorer, more than just the captain, he was the talisman who had sent the club straight back to the First Division and the fans straight back to heaven. His 39 goals that season had whitewashed the memories of Greaves and the despair of relegation. "[The fans] adored Jimmy, everybody did, he was a genius," says Tambling. "They realised, though, that I was honest. The fans had understood maybe that it was Jimmy who had basically kept us in the First Division and when we went down Tommy got us youngsters in and we came straight back. That pleased the fans who appreciated that this was a team game and us new boys were exactly that, a team. Not individuals. We were blue, blue, blue and they got behind us. They loved us. The fans were with us from that point."

CHELSEA started the next season competently, but Tambling was suffering a promotion hangover. He went the first 13 games without a goal and Docherty began to wonder about his captain's levels of concentration. "It was the longest barren spell of my career," recalls Tambling. "The Doc felt that the burden of the captaincy was affecting me. The team was doing well, but I couldn't score. He took the armband from me and hoped I could get on with doing the job I was paid to do. The next game at Ipswich I got two, so who was I to argue?"

The team continued to improve and fifth in their first season was a fine base for Docherty and the team that were dubbed as "Docherty's Diamonds". Some, like the new captain Terry Venables, shone whilst others, such as McCreadie and his new full-back partner named Ron Harris, continued to be the rough kind. Within Docherty's gems, there was a great combination of styles, but a collective will to win and to entertain that brought much joy to the thousands who once again crammed the Bridge.

In the summer of 1964, an elegant striker named George Graham arrived from Aston Villa for £5,000 and with that Tambling was moved to a wider position, but his selfless and industrious style of play helped the club to push for honours. In 1965, the League Cup was in its infancy; the brainchild of a Football League hoping to raise further revenue for the cash-strapped clubs of the lower leagues. It shared the same level of supposed intolerance that its modern day version is afforded, but, as Tambling points out, as far as the team were concerned any silverware would do. In the fifth League Cup Final Leicester City were beaten 3-2 over two legs with Tambling scoring Chelsea's opening goal in the first leg, but only 20,000 fans had attended that game at the Bridge.

"It was nice to get something in and we thought it was the start of something big." So did the fans. With the team playing a flowing game that for so long had been absent and with such young men playing it, the fans hoped that this was the team that would offer more than just a flash in the pan.

Tambling remained the club's iconic figure. On the newly named Shed (more of which later), where singing was becoming that much more prevalent, the words to Bob Dylan's *Mr Tambourine Man* were changed to fit Tambling's name. With "Hey Mr Tam-ber-ling Man" echoing around its stands, Stamford Bridge once again became a cool place to be. Titles were competed for (Chelsea finished in third place, five points off Champions Manchester United in 1964/65) as were the latter stages of the FA Cup, but frustratingly the club couldn't break into the top two or get past that blasted semi-final stage.

In the Cup, Liverpool, a club on the rise under Docherty's fellow countryman Bill Shankly, enjoyed some tussles with the Blues. In 1962 the Merseyside club, then on the way to the Second Division title, had knocked out Docherty's soon-to-be relegated Chelsea 4-3 at Anfield. In 1965, though, Chelsea were confident of gaining revenge as the two met at Villa Park in the semi-final. So confident, in fact, that captain Terry Venables printed a Cup Final magazine before the game. Shankly, of course, got hold of the magazine and, by pinning it on the wall, his team-talk was done. Liverpool won 2-0.

The following year though, Chelsea were again asked by the draw to travel to Anfield in the Cup. Liverpool took an early lead, but this Chelsea team were now mature enough to compete, even in front of a fervent Kop and equalised before half-time through a new young forward named Peter Osgood. The second half was one of Docherty's finest moments as the Cup holders were beaten in their own, fortress-like back yard thanks to a goal from who else, but our man Tambling. He received the ball, played an incisive pass to Graham before making a fine run to latch onto the Scotsman's cross and head past the onrushing Tommy Lawrence.

In the boardroom, Chelsea's chairman was asked to spare the Merseyside club the price of a stamp. "We were due to send the cup back to the Football Association next week," said Liverpool's Chairman. "Do us a favour and take it back with you, you've earned it anyway."

Soon afterwards Manchester United arrived to play a league game at the Bridge. Their players matched those in blue when it came to being en vogue as Law, Charlton and especially George "El Beatle" Best had just seen off Benfica in Lisbon in the European Cup. This, though, was a Chelsea team up for a challenge and within four minutes Tambling had scored and Chelsea were two up. Game over.

But Chelsea once more lost their FA Cup semi final, this time 2-0 to Sheffield Wednesday. And once again Docherty's Diamonds failed to get their hands on major silverware.

IN SEPTEMBER 1965 Tambling became only the fourth man in the club's history to surpass the 100 goals mark (Hilsdon, Bentley and Greaves being the others), but it was the following season that he had his finest hour; well, hour and 10 minutes actually.

On the 17th September 1966, the country was suffering from a World Cup winning hangover. Wingers were no longer the required ingredient in the First Division hot-pot and fans were missing the flair of yesteryear. Tambling had found that to his cost as he'd played in one of England's warm up games against Yugoslavia prior to the finals themselves. To make matters worse, Chelsea fans had been forced to listen for weeks to how West Ham had won the World Cup whilst none of their own boys had been part of the country's most raucous footballing shebang as Tambling, Hinton, Venables, Bridges and Osgood had all fallen by the wayside, culled from Ramsey's initial squad of 40. That day in Birmingham, though, reminded his loyal fans that here was a player still worth cheering on. *Hey Mr Tamberling Man* echoed around Villa Park as Bobby set about the Villans' defence with the keenness that always endeared him to the Chelsea faithful.

"I got a video of that game recently and what I had forgotten was that Villa were top of the league that day and we were second," recalls Tambling. "We went up there and slaughtered them. I've always thought that they must have been crap, but they weren't, they were good." Tambling scored five goals, "I could have stood on my head that day and scored". It was a display of which both George Hilsdon and Jimmy Greaves would have been proud. Tambling shot from distance and sniffed about the six-yard box in equal measure and was unfortunate not to go on and at least equal Ted Drake's age-old record of seven goals in one game.

"I went off with twenty minutes left," recalls Tambling. "I'd already scored four and I had been indicating to the bench that I should come off because I had a niggle in my knee. Johnny Boyle broke down the right and so I went with him and watched whilst he beat two or three defenders before crossing it to me and I just had an open goal to slot my fifth"

"People thought I should have stayed on and gone for Ted's record, but it never crossed my mind. Maybe I should have. It's lovely to remember days like that and it is well documented in Chelsea's history." Villa fans were equally impressed. As their conquering visitor hobbled off having helped himself a famous quintet, one fan stood up and cried, "I think he's declared!"

THE CHELSEA of the mid-60s were established as a fine, competetive team and Tambling a fine goalscorer. He was a subtle player. His goalscoring record was wonderful, but he was far from a Bentley or later, a Dixon. They were broad-shouldered, barrel-chested hunks of men who would power ball their way onto the end of inviting balls. Tambling was different. He would ghost into the box. Like Greaves he would come from deep, choosing wide positions as the catalyst for deadly runs. Unlike Greaves he had a thunderbolt of a shot, it fizzed off his boot and belied his gentle nature.

It was that five-goal haul at Villa that set Tambling up to better Roy Bentley's all-time goalscoring record, as he now stood just two goals shy of equalling it. That must have put him under pressure? "No, I wasn't funnily enough. In fact I recall very little of that time," recalls Tambling. "There was some press attention, but by then I was in my mid-20s and confident, unless something drastic happened that I was going to beat it."

The fans' hero was so close and Tambling could delight in the fact that they were right behind him, willing him on to history. "The fans were always on my side. I never ever got any stick, even when things weren't going well for the team or for myself. Some players don't have to do much wrong for fans to get on their back, but fortunately I was popular. As I approached the record there was a feeling from the terraces that they wanted me to get it, but you must recall these were very different times.

"Nowadays there is so much more awareness of statistics and situations like that due to all the publicity and all the television. TV crews will talk about it and therefore fans will, but back then there wasn't many games on telly. At best you would be on the *Match of the Day* highlights programme about four or five times in a season. I recall the game we won when I broke the record, but strangely I can't recall the goal." Well, Bobby, it was against Manchester City, who hosted Chelsea and were torn apart 4-1, with Tambling's single effort enough to put him top of the Stamford Bridge pile, where today he still proudly remains. His record bears comparison with any Chelsea goalscorer. He bagged 50 more goals than Bentley despite playing only four more games. He may not have matched the goals per game ratio of a Greaves or a Hilsdon, but Tambling played over 200 Chelsea games more than Greaves; and anyway he far outstrips Osgood and Dixon on goals per game too. There is no doubt about it, Chelsea's quiet, less-then-flamboyant goalscorer was one of the deadliest in the history of the game.

FANS poured down the Fulham Road to see Tambling's goals and live in the reflected glory of fashionable Chelsea and by now had a new West Stand from which to enjoy the talents of Messrs Bonetti, Harris and Osgood. The mushroomed hunk of terrace that had so appealed to Gus Mears back in 1905 was replaced by an all-seater stand. It wouldn't cripple the club like its east side equivalent in the late 1970s and that was down to the crowds, whose continued support paid for its construction and then some. Attendances had steadied at an average around the 35,000 mark, but receipts were up. The club was doing nicely, thank you.

Fans turned up bringing more than expectant smiles and a rattle. Blue flags were becoming en vogue in SW6. Vendors outside the new West Stand soon began selling different paraphernalia that could highlight a fan's allegiances. Very popular were the cheap looking badges with grainy black and white photos of the club's heroes. Hordes of jackets were pinned with Tambling's unassuming smile. In the not too distant future these oh so trendy fans would adorn Crombie overcoats and Dr Marten boots with tokens of their esteem, but for now, in a still relatively innocent age, the badges would do.

The players would cross the dog track onto the pitch amid a hum of excitement as the waft of roasted peanuts competed with the stench of expectancy for the fans' nostrils affections. John Moynihan describes match day:

A large new group of fans started going along to watch Saturday's match at Stamford Bridge, and down the Fulham Road to Craven Cottage; various showbiz and other glossy customers emerged wearing fur and leather and with tiny cheroots pressed between refined thumb and forefinger – articulate property dealers, inaudible starlets, chauvinist actors, fledgling models, unshaven members of the rag-trade, solemn artists, rural antique dealers. On match days, they dropped everything else and made for the football ground.

A diverse bunch maybe, but they were bound together by a collective will to see this fine group of young men fulfil their obvious potential and bring a major trophy to the club. In 1966/67 it looked like that may be a distinct possibility. Chelsea finally reached the FA Cup final where they would meet their old rivals, Tottenham Hotspur. Cigars were primed, champagne was chilled and pints poured. It was the first time two London clubs had faced each other in the showpiece event and was dubbed "The Cockney Cup Final."

Chelsea had started the season well. Tambling had scored those goals at Villa Park and with Peter Osgood emerging as an equally fine goalscorer, the team found themselves sitting on top of the league in October. The latter, though, broke his leg in a challenge with Blackpool's Emlyn Hughes and didn't play again that season. The club, despite 28 Tambling goals, slumped to finish a disappointing ninth.

In the Cup, though, Chelsea proved that on their day they were a match for anyone. The mighty Leeds United – who would continue to play a role as Judas in Chelsea's history for years to come – were their semi-final opponents and surely after two successive defeats at this, the cruellest of stages to lose at, it would not happen again. It didn't. Osgood's replacement Tony Hateley powered a header into the net to ensure that at last the club were on their way to Wembley.

AN FA CUP Final. An occasion for all to savour; more than a match, a day out. A sunlit May Day where memories are forged and heroes made. Not this time. Chelsea players and fans alike will have wanted to forget the occasion, as the Cockney Cup Final became only a knees up for those in the lily white of North London.

Chelsea froze. Spurs, galvanised by ex-Blues Jimmy Greaves and Terry Venables were never ruffled and won 2-1, more comfortably than the scoreline suggests. Tambling managed Chelsea's late consolation, but a goal at Wembley in the Cup Final has hardly left lasting memories for its scorer. "The team that day wasn't as good as the team that had been knocked out cruelly of two semi-finals in the two previous years. That's how I see it," recalls Tambling.

"I don't know why, but we looked inexperienced and nerves got to a few of us. We were too relaxed maybe. Tommy was great like that. He was a joker and he kept the nerves away by making all the gags. It was fun time and it seemed to work, but when we actually hit the ground and came out onto the pitch the nerves kicked in and we played like a side that hadn't ever been in a big game before.

"My own game was awful. It was chronic. I had always done well against Spurs; always scored, always played well, but that day it didn't go for me. I'm not taking anything away from Spurs, they had a good side. Joe Kinnear played well at right-back. I ended up marking him and that is wrong."

Docherty had been surprised by his main goalscorer's off day, but he soon had more on his mind. A row about tickets for the Final, a new, distant Chairman (Joe Mears' death had seen Charles Pratt take the helm) and some dodgy results at the beginning of the following season saw the end of the cantankerous Scot's six-year reign. His Diamonds may not have twinkled as brightly as everyone had hoped, but to the fans who cheered and laughed every other Saturday, they will be forever remembered as entertainers – and Docherty as the bringer of hope.

FOR TAMBLING, the disappointments of Wembley were confounded by an abdominal injury that kept him out of the majority of the following season. By now Osgood was vying for the fans' attentions, but the 1968/69 season – Tambling's last full campaign – proved just how good a player he was as again he finished the club's top scorer with 18 goals. None spectacular, but all finished with the skill of a clinical goalscorer. Under the new boss Dave Sexton, Tambling was being utilised far more as an out-and-out winger, but even that mattered little to a man who had an unquenchable thirst for goals. He would dart down the wing and then, in a flash, cut in and take aim. More goals followed, but so did continued injury problems.

"I did my cartilage, but didn't have it diagnosed quick enough and was out for 10 weeks," he recalls with a grimace. "By the time I was fit the team had changed. Youngsters such as Alan Hudson and Peter Houseman had got in and taken their chance. The team was winning and so how could Dave change things?"

Tambling was typically stoical about his fate and with fond memories he left for Crystal Palace on loan in the January of 1970 before signing permanently the following summer. By then of course, Chelsea had won the Cup at last, but without Bobby Tambling, their greatest ever goalscorer.

"Chelsea was my life, my whole life. When I go back I always get such a good reception. I don't know why, I'm just an old fella now, but those fans don't see that. They are marvellous." What Tambling forgets is that there will always be a cheer reserved for the man who has given them more goals than any other player in their illustrious history.

In the 1980s Kerry Dixon threatened Tambling's record, but to no avail. Tambling remained Chelsea's top man "They're the facts aren't they?" he says without conceit. "They look like they will be a top team for some years, but will players stay long enough to beat it? There have been players good enough to beat it, but will they stay long enough? Did you know that I never scored for Chelsea after the age of 28? That's amazing." Yes Bobby, it certainly is.

RON HARRIS

1961-1980

CHELSEA CAREER

Games	795
Goals	14
Caps	0

MAGIC MOMENT

The famous night Ron lifted the FA Cup at Old Trafford has gone down as arguably the most iconic in Chelsea's history

'CHOPPER'

Speak softly and carry a big stick; you will go far.

Theodore Roosevelt

AT an age when most teenagers are marking the estate wall or each other's necks, a 17-year-old Ron Harris found himself marking Stanley Matthews. It seems fantastical to think that the player that an awe-struck Stamford Bridge would eventually name "Chopper" was ever a boy, and Stanley Matthews was the earliest of advocates to testify that there was nothing juvenile about his marker that day in 1963.

Matthews' Stoke City came to London in May that year having closed the gap at the top of the Second Division on a previously rampant Chelsea. London's blanket of ice had put an end to the Blues' domination and now places in the top flight were fiercely up for grabs.

Stoke, still inspired by the shuffling feet of a 48-year-old Wizard of Dribble were challenging hard for promotion and their headline act guaranteed a big crowd at the Bridge. Fans would swarm to most grounds to see the old magician, who, like a footballing-Gandalf, would conjure trick after mesmerising trick that belittled the ageing process.

Tommy Docherty, though, had a plan. Allan Harris was already part of his back line, but tonight, his younger brother, Ron would be asked to keep the old man in check, whatever it took. Matthews had grown used to the close attention of wannabe full-backs, looking to make their mark, quite literally, in the game; and later in his authorised biography by David Miller he talked of those bruising times.

"I wasn't expecting an easy time from any of the Second Division full-backs; not for a moment. And I soon found them coming in as hard as ever, some tougher than the First Division, like the Harris brothers of Chelsea. But I was still pretty quick, I still had confidence."

With that self-belief, Matthews tricked his way down the wing and helped his team to a crucial 1-0 win. It is no wonder that in his book, Matthews cited the Harris brothers because that day the younger of the two dished out some treatment that even his own supporters – who one day would cheer his every kick of both ball and man – took issue with. These were far less partisan days and Stamford Bridge, despite Ted Drake's best efforts, continued to house a polite set of football enthusiasts.

"That was a strange match," recalls Harris. "The Doc told me to go out and stop Stanley playing, but he was still a good player. He set up the goal and they won, so 1-0 to Matthews. As good as Stanley was, he was a bit of a moaner. He didn't like the attention I was giving him. Eddie McCreadie and myself dished out some stick and I started getting comments from the Chelsea fans.

"I suppose it was the last time they were going to see Stanley and to them he was still a hero because of all his exploits over the years with England and that Matthews Cup Final thing. I, though, had a job to do and I got on with it. It was odd getting booed from my own fans, though. Still, they won the game, no harm done." Matthews' ankles and shins might have disagreed with Ron and the old winger later recalled the youngster's exuberance. "He was trying to kick me here, there and everywhere." Ron Harris had laid down his marker.

Despite the defeat to Stoke, Chelsea won promotion by finishing runners-up to the Potters (Harris' resolute performance during the decisive win at rivals Sunderland was pivotal) and top flight reputations meant little to Chelsea's new defender. The harder they came the harder they fell and, whilst labelling Harris purely a spoiler is a disservice, he got on learning the First Division ropes as an opponent's shadow. "Big names meant nothing to me," says a gleeful Harris. "I was young and I just went out there and tried to do my best. Tommy often used me as a man-marker and I just tried to concentrate on the job at hand. I was trying to stop them from playing. It frustrated people and frustrated away fans. I began to hear things getting shouted at me and I knew I must be doing my job."

The "job" was conducted with un-relinquished vigour for nearly twenty years and his total of 655 league games in the blue shirt is unlikely to be matched, despite Frank Lampard's 21st Century efforts. Throughout Harris's tenure as Chelsea's top hard man, opposition attackers came, saw and limped. Former hero Jimmy Greaves, George Best, Rodney Marsh, Ian St John; fine players, but that mattered little to Harris and the fans who, having initially booed his rough treatment of a footballing god like Matthews, would come to idolise the man and his methods, adulating him in a song that glorified Harris' hardman image and propogated the rumour that he "Put Iodine on his studs.".

Peter Osgood is no doubt that Harris was the man among men. "There was only one governor and I'm just glad he was on our side," he laughs. "Chopper inflicted pain and he enjoyed it. He was very good at it. I have never seen anybody so hard and so ruthless on a football field.

"We were playing a Brazilian side and they had this little left-winger who was good. Chopper was playing at right-back and this kid starts playing all the olé stuff. He was flipping it around Chopper, nut-megging him, the works and after about 15 minutes of this nonsense Chopper goes, 'Ossie, roll me one.' So I played him this tame little 50-50 pass. They're both going for it, Ron puts on the brakes and makes it about 60-40 in the Brazilians favour who reckons it's easily his ball, and then, crack, Chopper speeds up and the kid's on a stretcher. Out of the game. 'Took the grass, Os,' he said with a smile.

IT WAS a time when men were men and shin pads were for girls. Flare players and hard men were in abundance and something had to give. Norman "Bites Yer Legs" Hunter was one of many yeomen in Don Revie's Leeds United side and he recalls Harris with a wry fondness. "Luckily Ron and I didn't come into contact too much because of our similar positions. That suited me I can tell you. I'll never forget his challenge on Eddie Gray in the first ten minutes of the FA Cup Final replay at Old Trafford. Eddie had given Chelsea the run around in the first game and Ron let him know he was about. In fact Eddie was admiring his own pass when Ron took him out with a crunch. Today it would have been a straight red, but back then we didn't even ask the refs to send people off. We just sorted it out between ourselves."

Retribution was always around the corner and centre-forwards played knowing full well that their post-match ankles would resemble rotting apples. Peter Osgood (though a striker, a man still able to look after himself) is in no doubt that Harris made his own life that much easier.

"It was a tough time. Defenders would dish out some rough stuff and there were plenty of hard men. Smithy [Tommy Smith], Norman [Hunter], in fact take your pick from that Leeds team, but I'll tell you what, none of them could live with our man. Ron was the hardest of the lot."

Hard, uncompromising, unflinching and hell-bent on both winning and, arguably more importantly, nt conceding, a Harris tackle could shake a stadium like no rock-band ever has. And Chelsea's fans loved and respected Harris for it. No questions asked. No quarters given. In this new-found era of glitz and glamour liberally mixed with grit and brute force, Harris epitomised Chelsea's sterner side. A grit which had needed to be instilled for years and that manager Tommy Docherty achieved by blooding the likes of Ron Harris, Eddie McCreadie and John Dempsey. But there was a time in his teenage years when Harris was, perhaps not wet behind the ears, but slightly damp. As ever it had been Jimmy Thompson, the Blues' own pied piper, who had sweet-talked him to make sure that Chelsea were his club of choice.

"My brother (Allan) had signed a few years before me and I would go down there and be the ball boy for every home game," says Harris (it is questionable whether William Foulke would have agreed to having the young Harris behind his goal. Even as a boy he would have failed to make the gargantuan goalkeeper look at all imposing). "The feeling was that if they felt you were good enough you would be given the chance at the age of 17 to have a go in the first team.

"That's why lots of youngsters chose Chelsea, because they were the club who were going to give you a go. West Ham were the other. Both gave youngsters a chance and then it was up to you."

Under Dick Foss's guidance in the youth team Harris' game was cut and polished until it became evident to all that here was yet another diamond, if somewhat of the rough variety. The youth team's success made life easy for Chelsea's newly appointed first team manager Tommy Docherty, but his enthusiasm for watching these kids blossom never waned.

IN APRIL 1963, just weeks before introducing himself to Stanley Matthews, Harris captained his country's youngsters in an International Youth World Cup which England won with aplomb. Docherty took all his Chelsea players to Wembley to watch the final and it was the left-half who shone as a certain player for the future.

England's right-half in that competition was a young Tommy Smith and he recalls how good his team-mate was. "Put it this way, we played the Netherlands and beat them 5-0. Next up came the champions, Romania and we won 3-0. The third game we beat Russia 2-0, then we beat Scotland 1-0 and in the final we beat Northern Ireland 4-0. We never let a goal in. It was a half-decent team that one, and Ron was a massive factor when it came to stopping goals."

Docherty had no doubts and that very night waxed lyrical to a reporter about the player he had under his wily command. "Ronnie, at 17, is a far better player than I was at 20 with Celtic. He knows more about the game than I did." By then, Harris had already tasted first team action and had already devised a style of play that he felt was most required.

"I made my debut against Sheffield Wed and we won 1-0. I had captained the 1961 youth side to the FA Youth Cup [in fact Chelsea won back to back Youth cups in 1960 and 1961] and I signed as a pro at 17 and was immediately in the first team. It was something I had waited for and sure there were nerves, but it seemed natural. Mind you the first team was a different ball game. The pace is so much quicker and you're playing against great players. Wednesday had England internationals Tony Kay and Peter Swan. I had orders from the Doc though; let them know I'm around early. I did and I got a pat on the back to say 'Well done'. So, I thought I'd better do the same thing the following week."

A legend was born and Ron Harris' name and game became the talk of terraces and dressing-rooms alike. In fact Docherty's entire young team made their collective presence felt. They finished a highly promising fifth in the table in their first season up, 1963/64, as Harris' own progress mirrored his side's fortunes in the First Division.

A HIGHLIGHT of that season was knocking Tottenham out of the FA Cup; a pleasure that would never lose its shine on Chelsea's terraces. The side had earned a 1-1 draw at White Hart Lane to bring Spurs back to the Bridge. Britain's pre-eminent goalscorer of the day, and arguably of all time, Jimmy Greaves, returned to his roots as part of the glamorous north Londoners, who'd won the Cup in consecutive seasons in 1960 and 1961 and were a class act amongst top flight sides. But any sentiment was reserved for those fans amongst the 70,000 throng who could still recall the forward's hip-swivelling exploits whilst wearing blue. Harris had no such concerns. The past was now resigned to fading *Charlie*

Buchan annuals; he had that job to do and he did it. Greaves was subdued and Spurs were beaten 2-0 in front of a rapturous crowd.

Greaves would always struggle against the team where he made his name. "He never crossed the halfway line when he played us," laughs Osgood. "He was too scared of Chopper!" Banter aside, Harris did seem to have something over Greaves and unlike so many – arguably better players than himself – he managed to shackle the demon goalscorer who only notched one goal against his old employees in thse games.

On one occasion, Tommy Docherty requested that Harris give Greaves a good kick early on to slow him down. "But boss, I might be sent off."

"Don't worry about that son. They'll miss him, more than we'll miss you!"

The fans at Stamford Bridge were warming to a player, who whilst lacking the skills and frills of past heroes, gave his all for their cause. Thus Harris set the mould for his successors in the hard as nails and wearing blue stakes; Micky Droy, Doug Rougvie and the two Welsh Jones boys, Joey and Vinnie.

Despite his vicious streak, the fun-loving set amongst Chelsea's supporters still found that sense of excitement and entertainment in Harris. It wasn't all about pretty boys like Venables and George Graham making pretty patterns, a big part of enjoying the day was watching Harris wind up for a tackle and ducking from the subsequent shrapnel. The crowd they were a-changing at the Bridge.

IN THE dressing-room the popular young Harris was known as "Buller". Peter Osgood explains. "He was always talking bullshit. He couldn't help it and it wasn't long until we all knew him as 'Buller'. I remember once we had a match between ourselves and I was getting some harsh treatment from John Dempsey who had a bit of a Bobby Charlton thing happening with his hair. 'What you playing at, John?' I asked, but 'Bang', he's kicked me again. 'John, I'm warning you, if you do that again I'm gonna have to hit you.' John looked well angry before explaining himself. 'I know what you've been saying, Ossie. Ron told me that you've been spreading rumours that I have to use lacquer in my hair.' I'm thinking 'When did I say that?' and Ron, about 50 yards away is in hysterics. That was Buller for you."

If it was Buller behind closed doors, on the pitch Harris had earned another nickname and one that has stuck ever since. Those fans so adoring of his robust challenges were in no doubt. "I had become one of their favourites," says Harris with pride. "They came up with 'Chopper' because of the way I tackled. They used to say I would scythe the people down and so 'Chopper' stuck. More people today know me as 'Chopper' than they do Ron."

Harris wasn't the first footballer to be awarded such a momentous and descriptive nickname. He'd been preceded by at least two decades by Stoke City's infamous left-back John "Jock" McCue, whose wild eyes betrayed the insanity his challenges often bordered on. But Harris was unique in that fans essentially substituted his first name for his new monicker. He became simply "Chopper" Harris.

Plus his legend became perpetuated as, not only were his tackles winced upon and enjoyed by those attending the games, but also by those safely resting in the armchairs, as from August 1964, the BBC broadcast a new show called *Match of the Day*.

DOCHERTY'S diamonds had made fine progress and, along with the equally glamorous Liverpool and Manchester United, under his guidance Chelsea were the talk of a swinging nation. "We had a good young team and they were exciting times, recalls Harris. "I think the team, Shilleto, Tambling, Venners, it was exceptional. I think Tommy split the team up through impatience. If he had waited and persevered then I'm sure we would have won the title with that bunch. There were some clashes of characters, but if you ask me that team in the 1960s was the best I ever played in, and that includes the team in the early 1970s."

Docherty's impatience that Harris describes often stemmed from an impulse to act, whatever the consequences. The most revered incident between Docherty and his fun-loving criminals happened in 1965, when Chelsea, having to play a couple of games in the north-west of England based themselves amid the bright lights of Blackpool.

A cynic might suggest that Docherty was courting trouble simply by his choice of barracks. Those players who had brought such optimism and excitement to the Bridge liked to relax with a drink or two. It had always been the way. George Hilsdon and Hughie Gallacher had in previous decades and Alan Hudson and Dennis Wise would follow. To play for Chelsea is to socialise for Chelsea and this lot were no less fond of a tipple. So, putting them among the festivities of Blackpool and hoping they'd behave was like asking Hugh Hefner to go to bed with nothing but a mug of Ovaltine.

Temptation loomed and whilst tales vary, the crux of the "Blackpool incident" was that eight players – Terry Venables, Barry Bridges, George Graham, Eddie McCreadie, John Hollins, Bert Murray, Marvin Hinton and Joe Fascione – stayed out partying well after their curfew and were spotted by the hotel porter, slipping in via a fire-exit. Docherty had thought that his Diamonds had settled in for the night after an evening at the cinema. The porter informed Docherty of the players' misdemeanours and the boss made his way to each room to round up the perpetrators. John Hollins lay there under his covers as Docherty snorted angrily over his twitching midfielder. "Get up, John!" There was no movement, but Docherty wasn't born yesterday. The wily Scot pulled back the covers and there was Hollins, like a naughty boarding school boy, fully dressed in jacket and tie.

Docherty had had it. He told his revellers that he'd ignored the problem for too long and that this time – despite that this was a Wednesday night and the game wasn't until Saturday – he was sending them all home. To many it was harsh, to Docherty it was essential, but to Chelsea it meant the beginning of the end for the team that had promised so much.

For Harris, it meant that the captain's armband was on its way to his ample bicep. Docherty, as tough a player as he was a manager, saw a lot of himself in Harris and when it came to replacing Venables (their relationship deteriorated after Blackpool and in May 1966, Venables was sold to Spurs) he had no concerns about the youngster's aptitude for the job.

"Terry knew he had been on borrowed time and it was a case of waiting for his move. There were no problems between Terry and myself. Tommy gave me the opportunity because he had taken such a liking to how I played and that I went out there every week with the same enthusiasm that he had for the game and for the club." Harris though, whilst not one of the Blackpool eight, scoffs at the idea that he was the manager's puppet. "I wasn't a goody-goody. I would go out as much as anyone, but later I'd select my moments and do it when we were away from London, on tour or on away trips. I wasn't going to shit on my own doorstep. I was captain and had a bit more responsibility to set good examples. In the 21 years I was there I didn't get in trouble once, I didn't ask for a transfer. I was more than happy to give 110% week in and week out."

This then was truly a new kind of Chelsea hero.

A LEADER of men on the field and in the dressing-room, Harris was soon the focal point of a set of fans becoming as partisan and as vocal as any in the country. The match programme for a non-descript 2-2 draw with Leicester City in September 1966 included a letter from a C. Webb of Essex. "From now on we wish the Fulham Road End to be called 'The Shed'. That is the section where the fanatics stand and, while we are all fanatics, why don't more people come in the Shed and join in the singing and chanting, instead of just at big matches like last season's Fairs Cup? If we could have that support all through the league and Cup, we could have won them both. This year we must have this attitude at every game, so please help us make 'The Shed' as fanatical as the Kop."

The example set by the packed mass of terracing at Liverpool was being taken up by fans all over the country and Harris himself got excited by the many trips to Anfield. "I loved playing in front of the Kop. I think they are the best crowd you can go and play in front of. They love their club, but they appreciate the opposition. It could be soul destroying when you're losing 4-0, though, with minutes to go and that bloody song, *You'll Never Walk Alone*, comes blaring out."

At last, Chelsea's fans were taking up the war cry first sounded by Ted Drake in the early 1950s. Their new enthusiasm for making a day out at the football more of an interactive event meant that Harris and his team had a new level of support, a level that would lift the roof off Gus Mears' old stadium; a place that had been too friendly for too long.

The long tradition of fans changing ends at half-time to be behind the goal that Chelsea were attacking was becoming antiquated and obsolete. "You didn't want to see defenders, you wanted to see goalscorers," remarked one fan. But that too, with Harris now established as one of the most popular men in blue, was a thing of the past.

Fans in the Shed would cheer, they would swear, they would be loud and they could be cruel. Ted Drake would have approved and his successor was more than pleased to have a home ground where guests were far less cordially treated. With Stamford Bridge's capacity falling from 70,000 in 1962 to 62,000 with the inclusion of the new West terrace, the place was in need of a more robust atmosphere and the fans didn't disappoint.

They had learnt from their Scouse cousins that the medium of song was the best way of expressing their love for the team and perhaps in homage to their teachers adopted a Beatles track and soon the Yellow Submarine had been shaded an appropriate colour. "We all live in a Blue Submarine!" screamed the Shed.

Individual players were afforded a special mention and a more and more vocal crowd took joy in harmonising the name of the players in particular favour. Opposing players, foolhardy enough to foul a member of the Chelsea team were left quaking in their boots as the Shed gleefully informed them that "Chopper's gonna get ya, Chopper's gonna get ya."

THE MENACE that Harris offered appealed to many on the terraces, a place that by the late-1960s had become a more and more aggressive place to watch your game of football. Chelsea fans again cite those pioneers from Liverpool as starting a trend, this time organised football "aggro".

"The players were aware that there was that bit more trouble, but like any walk of life, you were always going to get a few idiots," says Harris. "It wasn't only Chelsea though, every club had a rowdy element, and every club had guys who would go to matches and smash things up. That was just part of the era."

The football "special" train had allowed fans to travel en masse and whilst places such as Millwall's Den had seen sporadic outbursts of violence, this new wave of fans had extra-curricular activities specifically on their minds. One fan, in Clive Batty's book *Kings of the Kings Road* recalls the day at Easter 1965 when Liverpool fans arrived with intent. "[They] caused a lot of trouble in the Shed end. Loads of fans climbed over onto the dog track from the Shed and then it spilled all round the ground."

Soon, the polite and hearty day at the football was a thing of the past. Scars were gained and worn as badges of honour as rival factions tried to out do each other with brazen attempts to "take" a rivals particular End. Another fan, again in Batty's book sets the scene.

"I was in the Shed once, around 1967/68, when all these fans came in wearing blue and white scarves. I thought it was a bit strange because there was so many of them in a big group. Then, all of a sudden, I got a whack on the side of my head. They were Arsenal fans in disguise and, of course, once everyone realised there was a huge fight."

As vivacious as London was in those "swinging" days, it also had a more violent and sinister underbelly. Tower blocks, which had been thrown up seemingly willy-nilly since the relaxation of the maximum height limit on buildings in the capital in the 1950s, offset the boutiques. Whilst a night vandalising was the Saturday night option for those youngsters not affluent enough to be living it up in the capital's clubs. Crime in London tripled in the twelve years after Chelsea's championship season of 1955 and adds to a sense that all was not as groovy as so often reminisced upon.

These angry young men, in their different guises – Mods and Rockers would soon be most notoriously accompanied by the Skinhead – brought a new edge to a Saturday at the football. Women were scarce. *Charlie Buchan's Football Monthly* ran a special "female fans" letters page where club gymnasia were requested to convert to nurseries on match days, but those pleas fell on very deaf ears. Strange then, that in decades to come the likes of Dennis Wise would take their offspring up the steps of Wembley to lift the FA Cup.

THE SECOND half of the 1960s, though, were far less paternal times and the nation's youth, gorging on instant gratification like no generation before, were not going to be told what to do and how to do it. Ron Harris, whilst a responsible captain, decent bloke and underrated footballer, appealed to these new supporters. As the fledgling football fan had been drawn to William Foulke's sheer novelty and the artisan to Hughie Gallacher's troubled brilliance, the fan making the Shed his new home took an obvious shine to Harris' wrecking ball technique. He vented their anger for them and they loved him for it.

It continues today. Football fans, especially of the British variety love to see a player's effort, they love to see a player sweat blood. A photo of Terry Butcher awash with crimson blood is as iconic to us as the image of Johan Cruyff perfecting his turn in the 1974 World Cup is to the Dutch.

That is our nature. There is no escaping that fact. Chelsea fans, whilst always admiring a player who could offer something special for them to chat about over a beer on the Kings Road, are no different, and indeed could be said to lead the way throughout their history in the new fads and fashions on football's terraces. Even today, with squillions at the manager's disposal, they will raucously cheer at raw effort. Shaun Wright-Phillips made his home debut in August 2005 against the old enemy Arsenal. Here is a young player (who cost a cool £21 million) regarded as one of the finest young talents in the country, but the loudest cheer that comes his way is when he tracks back and sends Ashley Cole, a player who Chelsea fans believe wimped out of joining their club, crashing to the ground. Wright-Phillips like Harris before him (I grant they are not the most obvious of bed-fellows) was simply doing on the pitch what those who watch week in and week out wish they could, and that includes the rough stuff.

THE ATMOSPHERE and the attitude on the terraces was not the only new phenomenon at Stamford Bridge under Tommy Docherty as manager and Ron Harris as skipper. The club that Gus Mears had built to bring not only success to the surrounding, affluent streets, but to London as a whole was now strutting its stuff around Europe.

Not that Chelsea were arrogant new kids on the block when it came to taking on distinguished overseas opposition. The club had entertained the Dynamo Moscow side that had toured and enthralled Britain in 1945. Twenty years later they were invited to play the West Germans, as part of the latter's preparation for the 1966 World Cup finals. 32,000 Germans were shocked to see their side – containing a number of the men who would face England in the World Cup final, including Franz Beckenbauer and Uwe Seeler – lose 1-0 thanks to a Barry Bridges strike.

With that sort of form, Chelsea finished the 1964/65 season in third place with the mantle of the top London club and therefore were invited to play in the newly formed Inter City Fairs Cup the following season. The competition featured only one club per city for the first decade or so of its life before becoming the UEFA Cup which we now today. It was another adventure and another opportunity for Docherty to gauge just how good this team were. The idea of watching differing styles at the Bridge appealed to the Chelsea faithful and the first round draw against Roma must have had fans salivating at the idea of watching the silky Mediterranean skills of the Italians.

Reality proved very different. Chelsea's fans witnessed a bloodbath as "I Lupi" (the Wolves, as Roma are known) gave as good as they violently got. Chelsea played brilliantly, winning 4-1 (Terry Venables bagged a hat-trick in one of his last games as captain). Eddie McCreadie had been sent off for a blatant punch, but as he sat, close to tears in the dressing room, his shins dripped with blood; a testimony to the provocation dished out by the Romans.

Roma were themselves incensed and Chelsea were in for a torrid time as they made their way to Italy for the second leg. The Roman press ran stories that their officials, when entering the Chelsea dressing-room to congratulate them on their win, were spat on and thrown out. Such propaganda fuelled their irate crowd who booed every touch and threw so many missiles that the pitch looked like a green-grocer's; with pears, apples, oranges and tomatoes all covering the penalty areas.

Chelsea held firm and left the stadium with a 0-0 draw and famous victory. That, though, was just the start of their fun in Rome as, despite a police escort, their coach was set upon by a baying mob. "They smashed that coach to pieces," recalls Harris. "It was quite frightening actually. They weren't throwing stones, these were bricks coming through the windows. What can you do? We just got on the floor and hoped that no one got hurt. I suppose I could have started throwing things back, but I was too frightened."

THE FOLLOWING round saw the Austrian side Wiener SK easily dispatched (Chelsea were getting used to this) and next up was another massive occasion; a trip to northern Italian giants, AC Milan. The "Rossonieri" were only three years away from being crowned Champions of Europe and in their skipper, Cesare Maldini, boasted the golden boy of Italian football. But reputations meant little to either Docherty or his enthusiastic young side and they left the San Siro 2-1 down, but well in contention.

For the return, 60,000 sardine-like fans crammed into Stamford Bridge and revelled in their team's football that outshone the floodlights and lit up the SW10 sky. Chelsea won 2-1 and in those days before penalty shoot-outs, a replay followed in Italy thanks to Milan winning the toss of a coin.

The press corps were in no doubt about the quality of Chelsea's performance, many even ignoring their hip-flasks in an attempt to grab the nearest Thesaurus and come up with the most appropriate of superlatives. Bernard Joy of the *Evening Standard* was on hand to describe the evening.

> Chelsea tried all the moves against Milan...short passes, long cross-field passes, decoy running, overlaps, individual breaks, short corners, long ones, wall passes. In those early,

> breath-taking minutes they overran Milan and their grim defensive scheme, and forced them to disgorge two goals, more than they had given away in any previous match that season. Venables was the showman of the match; [Marvin] Hinton outdid Maldini as a sweeper centre-half; the dark head of Graham was always menacing; and Ron Harris relentlessly mastered Amarildo, the Brazilian World Cup star.

Post Blackpool-incident Chelsea, led by their new skipper, took the confidence they had gained from the game at Stamford Bridge and battled to a 1-1 draw. Extra-time couldn't distinguish the two and so it was down to another toss of the coin, this time to decide the actual winner. Harris and Maldini met in the centre-circle, the coin was tossed and this time landed in favour of the Blues.

The European adventure continued in Germany as Munich 1860 were dispatched 3-2 on aggregate and now it was yet another massive fixture against Barcelona in the quarter-final. 70,000 Catalans were drawn to the Nou Camp by Chelsea's growing reputation, but the Spanish team took a 2-0 win into the second leg. In a way that score-line was a victory for Docherty's men as Harris admits that it could have been ten.

If Barcelona had been charitable in their own giant backyard, then they were even more so back at the Bridge as another bumper crowd saw two own goals allow Chelsea back in the tie. Again it would have to be replayed and again Chelsea were forced to travel back to their opponent's country. This time there was no repeat of the heroics of Milan, as Barcelona had clearly paid more attention at finishing school and dispatched the Londoners 5-0.

It had been a great learning curve, but, thanks to that incident on the North West Riviera, Docherty's Diamonds were about to be broken apart and sold to the highest bidder. Chelsea fans had been given a glimpse of success, but, as seemed perennial until the modern era, it had been kept at a safe distance.

Look, but don't touch seemed to be the rule and in the following season, 1966/67, Docherty's last, that flirtation again stubbornly refused to be consummated. This time the FA Cup offered herself, but again Chelsea's sweaty palms were unable to wrap themselves around that which they most desired.

The holders, Liverpool were beaten at Anfield, and Leeds were dispatched in the semi. At the tender age of 22, Harris would be the youngest man to lead his team out at Wembley for an FA Cup final, but that would prove to be the highlight of a miserable day. At ten to three though, Harris was only concerned with the hitherto most memorable day of his life.

"That was hard to explain," he says. "You have to be there walking up the tunnel and listening to 100,000 people making that much noise to really know how that feels. The atmosphere was incredible and whilst the day turned sour, I can still take something from the occasion."

Sour is right. Tottenham's 2-1 win was the beginning of the end for Tommy Docherty and the club captain was about to answer to a new Boss. "We went out to Bermuda to play some pre-season games," recalls Harris. "He had a pop at the ref, he didn't like the new Chairman Charles Pratt, he was suspended by the FA, the results didn't go great at the beginning of the new season and so the board had their excuse to sack him."

SO WHAT of the new man? "Dave Sexton was a thinker and a tremendous coach. The Doc was more of a motivator and wore his heart on his sleeve, but Dave was far keener on learning the game and passing on information. Tommy would blast and Dave was far calmer in his approach. As captain, though, I had no concerns about the change. I got the backing of any of my managers to captain how I felt fit."

In Harris, Sexton had a leader on the pitch, a man that both the players and the fans looked up to. He may not have had the panâche of the modern day or celebrity footballer of the late 1960s, but he had the grit and the determination that Sexton demanded. It was that attitude that drove the club on into the new decade via a seminal season; one that today, amid all the success and glitz, remains an iconic campaign for Chelsea fans.

"We loved it," says Harris. "Chelsea had achieved nothing for a long, long time. Pop music was great, players played with a smile. It was very enjoyable time. Good luck to the players today, but if you ask most Chelsea fans, they will relate with that team of the early 1970s. I think, that in years to come, that got up Ken Bates' nose."

1970 was Chelsea's Waterloo. The year that all that promise and all that class came to fruition. The year that the club no longer got nervous around that beauty called success; instead they combed back their hair, confidently strolled across the dance floor, took her by the arm and whisked her off her feet.

The Championship itself should have been won (one win in the first nine games put the kybosh on a wonderful late run of form that catapulted them into third place), but it was the FA Cup that again held the team's attentions and it was Harris who would finally become the first man in Chelsea Blue to get his hands on the famous trinket.

The team's intentions had been made clear in a quarter-final match against Queens Park Rangers at Loftus Road. Their west-London neighbours had made their way into the top flight and now harboured not only Rodney Marsh, but also a number of ex-Chelsea players including Terry Venables and Barry Bridges.

Chelsea won 4-2; they were brilliant and for Harris personally, it was a case of a "job" well done. "I was told to keep Marshie quiet and loved it. I knew him very well, I used to play for Hackney schools with him. He had a moan up, but then everyone had a moan up when I was marking them."

Marsh himself sniggers as he recalls that day and the man who kept him so unusually quiet. "Ron was one of the hardest defenders. He was a terrific man-marker. I spoke to him last week and he said that we were about 50-50 in terms of who came out on top, but it was never even, I got the better of him about once.

"Ron was relentless, he was a simple footballer who knew he was cut out for certain jobs and just got on with doing them. Oh Christ, that Cup game at Loftus Road was a hard one. He marked me right out of the game. Al the hype was that I would cut them to pieces, but with Ron as my shadow I didn't see the ball."

Watford, the surprise conquerors of Liverpool that same day, were easily beaten in the semi-final and Chelsea were back at Wembley. This time Leeds United, on a quest for an incredible Treble, would be their opponents and when it came to battles, not many teams relished their meetings like these two.

Don Revie's men were prone to harbouring a grudge and still felt hard done by after Chelsea's slim victory over them in the 1967 FA Cup semi-final. That sense of resentment wasn't going to disappear amid Wembley's grandiose surroundings. The game – due to England's World Cup campaign in Mexico – was played on a grey April afternoon and the recent Horse of the Year show meant that the pitch was more like a sand-pit than the lush green turf that these occasions merit.

"It was always going to be a tough match," recalls Harris. "Both teams had their footballers, Bremner, Lorimer, Osgood, Cooke, but both teams had three or four players who could kick and dig. They knew they would be in for a tough game. The tougher the game got, the tougher those players became."

On this occasion those players would have to become very tough. Twice Leeds took the lead at Wembley, but twice Chelsea came back to equalise. For the first time a Wembley FA Cup Final would have to be replayed and it was up to Old Trafford for round two.

Eddie Gray, Leeds' Scottish winger had given Dave Webb a torrid time at Wembley (it was even suggested that when Webb went to shake Gray's hand at full-time, he missed). Action would have to be taken and it was Harris who would move out to right-back to make sure that the same time, space and courtesy was on this occasion withdrawn.

Harris' early crunching statement of intent upon Gray's right-leg was just a prelude to the most blood thirsty of Cup Finals. 28½ million television viewers tuned in for the horror show (the sixth highest British television audience and the second best football match – only the 1966 World Cup final has drawn more). Here was real-life drama with no need for the make-up girl or a special effects department. Here, the blood was genuine.

"This was no match for weaklings," wrote Geoffrey Green in *The Times*. "As the sun dipped out of sight over Old Trafford's mighty stands, it seemed to take with it flaming streamers of the day; and it left behind a bonfire."

Norman Hunter, no shrinking violet himself, recalls the game with a wince and Harris, who thrived on his role in "stamping" out the threat of Gray today admits that it was tough game in a rough time. "If players today could see some of the things that went on then they'd be shocked."

Hunter too talks of just how different those days were. "A little while ago, a current referee watched a video of that game and did an analysis of it from a modern-day refereeing point of view. He said afterwards that had he been in charge that day under the instructions given to referees now, he would have sent four or five of us off and shown ten or eleven yellow cards. I have also watched the video and I have to confess that there were some horrendous tackles flying around."

THAT is now though and this was then. Mick Jones gave Leeds the lead once more, but in a dramatic second-half Peter Osgood and Dave Webb (a centre-half for the night) gave Chelsea a famous victory.

Harris wiped the blood and mud from his hands and lifted the trophy. "The only disappointing thing was that I didn't get to do that at Wembley," says Harris. "That was a shame. Leeds, though, were a great side, they really were. They could have won the treble that year and ended up with nothing. We did so well to win. Perhaps we were a bit fortunate, but we came back three times and not many people did that against that Leeds team."

Fans flocked to the Fulham Road where an open-top bus paraded the team and the trophy to a hungry and giddy crowd. These were unprecedented scenes in this part of the footballing world and they answered any doubts that Gus Mears and his colleague Fred Parker may have had in 1905 regarding the longevity of the sport's popularity and their wisdom in creating a football club called Chelsea.

It didn't end there. Harris went on to captain the side to its first European trophy the following season as Real Madrid were beaten in the final of the Cup Winners' Cup. That victory under the gaze of Athens' Acropolis was to be – for a quarter of a century – the pinnacle.

Under Sexton, the team that again should have built on its own success instead took a wrecking ball to its own foundations. Vital players fell out with the management and left, whilst an eager board did it's best to better the club, but with almost catastrophic financial consequences.

THROUGHOUT the turbulent 1970s Harris remained at the club. His role in the defence changed to that of a holding midfield man, but his commitment never ceased. Half-heartedness was not a term that he knew that much about. Times, though, were tough.

"Some of the players fell out with Dave," recalls Harris with a tinge of melancholy. "Ossie and Huddy had transfer requests granted and then the side seemed to lose all that momentum. One or two new faces came in and they didn't work. Chris Garland, Bill Garner, Keith Weller. They never did as well as they did at their previous clubs. The new stand was bleeding the club dry and things became hard. We were playing in front of perhaps 7,000 people and it was tricky. There was no atmosphere and that was depressing."

Managers came and went, as did Chelsea's First Division status, but Harris remained. The Scot, David Hay, a club record signing, had jeopardised his position in the team in 1974, but, as ever, the challenge was met with a grunt and steely determination. From 1977, Harris' last three seasons in the side were as a regular. His final campaign saw the 35-year-old rack up his fourth ever-present campaign in the league. But when he retired in 1980, sadly the loss of his services was sadly overshadowed by the plight that the club now found itself in.

Harris left for Brentford where he would have a spell as player-manager, but the game that he had put so much raw effort into couldn't contain a man desperate for a challenge. In 1984, Harris went his own way and made a vast amount of money improving and selling an old golf course. Never seeing eye to eye with Ken Bates, Harris was not a regular at Stamford Bridge under Chairman Ken's regime, but today he is greeted with a cheer by those who recall his enthusiasm with awe.

RON HARRIS was the catalyst for the style that the club became famous for. Those silky players with a glint in their horny eyes owed everything to their captain, the man who made it all happen, the man who won them the ball, without whom they would have been nothing.

To this day supporters recall "Chopper" with passion. Even the limpet fan, who knows little of the club's history and clings on to Chelsea while the club oozes money and trophies under Abramovich, knows Chopper's name. There is no doubt that those he played against and marked will not forget his close attentions in a hurry. Liverpool's Ian St John recalls facing Chopper with a nostalgic grimace. "What I remember most about Ron," says St John, "is that he always put Vaseline on his eye-brows. He said it was to keep the sweat from dripping into his eyes, but I think it was to make himself look that bit meaner. Ron, you didn't have to try any harder. I can vouch for that.

"He wasn't one of those guys who would whisper in your ear. He wasn't a talker, there was none of that 'I'm going to get you mate,' none of that. That was for wimps. No, Ron was a silent assassin."

George Best always seemed to thrive on the attentions of his era's hard men, but Harris' attentions left those fascinated by the Ulsterman as frustrated as anyone. In the 1960s one photographer was sent to take promotional shots of Best in action for United, but unfortunately the opposition were Chelsea. The snapper happily took his pictures, but was left with not one useable shot. Sure, Best looked his usual handsome self, but in each picture there was Ron Harris, at his arm, chipping away at the great man's game and spoiling his image.

That was Harris. That was Chopper.

"I tackle hard," wrote Harris during his reign of terror. "I go into a tackle hard and I admit I have tried to soften a suspect opponent (suspect for courage that is) by letting him know early on in the game that I am a hard man." Yes, Ron. That you are.

PETER OSGOOD

'THE KING'

1964-1974
1978-1979

CHELSEA CAREER

Games	380
Goals	150
Caps	4

MAGIC MOMENT

Charlie's cross was tasty and inviting, but how Ossie thundered his flying header past David Harvey in the Leeds goal. Chelsea's name was on the Cup

The first time that I appeared on stage, it scared me to death. I really didn't know what all the yelling was about. I didn't realize that my body was moving. It's a natural thing to me. So, to the manager backstage, I said "What'd I do? What'd I do?" And he said "Whatever it is, go back and do it again."

Elvis Presley

IN a sleepy south-coast pub enjoying a chilled bottle of white wine, the King of Stamford Bridge relaxes with his thoughts and memories. The beer garden is illuminated by an English summer's day as Peter Osgood takes a sip of his drink, leans back in his chair and like a mischievous schoolboy thinking about *his* moment, gives a wry and knowing grin. "It all seemed to happen in slow motion."

Slow motion? In the 1960s and early 1970s things at Stamford Bridge weren't usually prone to happen in slow motion. Usually a flash of blue kit and dark wavy hair would usher in another Peter Osgood goal whilst a lightening dart to the bar would lead to a fresh vodka or a pretty blond, but usually both. Slow motion? What could he mean?

"My goal at Old Trafford against Leeds in 1970. It all happened in slow motion." Ah, the goal. Having twice trailed at Wembley and found the equalizer in that FA Cup Final with just twelve minutes left and then having fallen behind once more to a Mick Jones goal in the replay, Chelsea surely couldn't come back a third time. Could they? Not against this Leeds team. "Charlie [Cooke] and Hutch [Ian Hutchinson] had done well out on the right and I've drifted into the box. Charlie knocked in one of his specials and from there, everything seemed to stop.

"It was a very weird feeling. I'm diving for the ball to head it, but I'm waiting for the keeper to come because I wanted to know where to direct it. Gary Sprake didn't play at Old Trafford, it was Dave Harvey in goal. I think Sprakey would have come out and clattered me, but Harvey went to come and then stepped back, so he was on his back foot and I could pick my spot. It was so simple. I thought I was offside because there was nobody near me and I seemed to have so much time. I thought 'That'll do.' Superb."

Chelsea were back in the game once more and from there you may as well have started ironing the blue ribbons. Leeds were a team of winners, but now the thought of defeat was a companion at each of their weary sides. Jack Charlton to this day blames himself for the equaliser and in his autobiography spoke of why he hadn't been on hand to prevent Osgood's moment of devilish inspiration. "I'd been waiting on their goal-line for a corner kick when one of the Chelsea players – someone who'd better remain nameless – whacked me in the thigh with his knee. After the corner was cleared I started to chase him, way over to the right. Then the ball was knocked in long to our box and I started to run back, but I was still hobbling after the whack in the thigh and I couldn't get there in time to stop Peter Osgood heading his goal."

Chelsea had matched Leeds at their own sly game and now were firmly on the front foot. Charlton remarked that from there it seemed that it was destined to be, there was something in the stars over Manchester that night, and Chelsea's name was proverbially on the cup. They had marched to Wembley with real purpose and proved that, whilst a little too erratic to be League Champions they could beat anyone on their own wonderful day.

IF CHELSEA circa 1970 epitomised everything about the club, with its style, its flair and its sometime preference to shoot itself in the foot, then it was Peter Osgood who epitomised that team. His goals, his ability to offer something out of the blue, along with his tendency for fun, a drink and a cheeky smile wooed Blues fans into awestruck adulation.

To the tune of *The First Noel*:

The Shed looked up
And they saw a great star
Shooting goals past Pat Jennings
From near and far
And Chelsea won
And the star of that team
Was Peter Osgood
Osgood, Osgood, Osgood, Osgood,
Born to be King of Stamford Bridge

Osgood's ascension to that throne was inevitable. Those fans had long adored a man who could score goals in style; Hilsdon, Gallacher, Bentley and Greaves had become icons not only due their prowess in finding the net, but also due to the aplomb with which they sent the ball there. In Osgood they had that and more. His 150 goals in 379 appearances glittered the ten years he spent entertaining his loyal subjects. His was a glorious reign; one those who witnessed from it's coronation to abdication today still take pleasure reminiscing about. And therein lies the mark of the enduring Cult Hero. One who still mists the eyes of fans 30 years after his exploits. Those men, those heroes are few and far between and they live long in fans' memories, becoming legends in the process.

IT WAS at Queen's Park Rangers' Loftus Road in that season's much-hyped quarter-final that Osgood had scored a hat-trick as if to remind all present that West London belonged to him.

"That was on a mud bath," recalls Osgood, that smile edging onto his lips once more. "What made it more memorable wasn't beating QPR, although that was nice, it was scoring a few past their keeper Mike Kelly. I'd done a coaching course a few weeks before and he'd been in charge of it and failed me. As I knocked the last one in I ran past him and shouted, "Stick to fucking coaching!"

That was Chelsea style.

Dave Sexton's boys romped on to Wembley, thrashing Watford. "We went to White Hart Lane for the semi and won 5-1. Like at QPR, Spurs' pitch was shit, all bare and bumpy, but we'd managed to get nine goals in the two games. We're thinking how good are we going to be at Wembley on that lovely pitch. 'We're going to be the business'.

"As it turned out it was an awful pitch, but because we were two great footballing teams there were still goals. If it had been a good pitch it would have been four each. They say they murdered us, but you watch it again. We didn't half have some chances and they must have cleared about three or four off the line. It was a good game."

Now, in extra-time at Old Trafford it was Chelsea who had taken strength from the previous 220 minutes of football. That strength was manifested in big Dave Webb who climbed highest at the back post and headed the ball into the Leeds goal. Chelsea were ahead and this time it was for keeps. Leeds were strong, Leeds were tough, but now Leeds were beaten.

"They were probably one of the best club sides we played against. They were awesome. They had eleven internationals in the team. The thing with that Leeds team, though, was that they were bullies. They couldn't bully us, mind. They couldn't bully Chelsea. Even the skilful lads like Charlie weren't frightened. Holly [John Hollins] wasn't going to be intimidated was he? He was strong. Not dirty like they were, just very strong. It was the guys at the back, though, who gave it back. Webby, John Dempsey, they don't take prisoners. Chopper, enough said. And Eddie McCreadie, he was worse than all of them, I think. He was nearly as bad as Harris. Fit as a flea and strong as an ox."

Those granite men were the base, but Osgood and his more glorified team-mates further up the pitch were far from soft touches. "We'd have backed ourselves against anyone, even Norman Hunter and Jack Charlton," says Osgood. "Up front we had Tommy Baldwin, Hutch and myself and we would dish back whatever we got. You had to against Leeds. They also had Paul Reaney who was tough and Terry Cooper. He could be a bit snide, Terry. He could hit you late."

Now, though, all the rough stuff could be forgotten. Now was the time to savour and wallow in the glory. The hard work against the hard team was done. "When Webby scores that was it. Jack Charlton and Norman just sat down. They'd lost. Mentally as much as anything. We'd come back three times, but there was no way they were going to do the same. Not after leading both games for so long."

CHELSEA had done it, they had won the FA Cup; only the third major trophy in their history. If the Championship success of 1955 had been greeted by enthusiastic, but polite applause and a round of drinks, this was going to be different. Chelsea, circa 1970, had changed and now was to witness a party that so many in the area had longed to host.

John Moynihan recalls the fervour of an unforgettable night and a club who at last had the razz to go with its matazz:

> In Chelsea it was like Armistice, VE and Coronation nights rolled into one – those who remembered Chelsea with affection from the old Music Hall days linked arms with younger ones, who could just recall dad raving about Roy Bentley. Every little side street from the World's End to Fulham Broadway had a private party... 'Darlings, wasn't that fantastic?', Dickie Attenborough yodelled in more sophisticated places, actor friends ready to raise a jar of champers. Dickie, Chelsea director, distinguished actor, hero of *The Angry Silence*, was hardly reticent now – his smile lit up the towpaths of his homeland, Richmond, where the Mears family had once run cut-price coaches for local fans to Stamford Bridge. The show business world rejoiced – Michael Crawford and Terry Stamp walked tall. Had it really happened? Yes it had – Chelsea had won the Cup!

As Chelsea's luvvie-set got on with clinking glasses to a famous victory, the players that had got them there hurried to their own festivities. The team stayed in Manchester that night and made it a home from home. Soon the locals were revelling in the player's cockney charm and Osgood set about mingling. "What a night. I'll never forget it," purrs Osgood, that glint firmly in his eye. "We all went to this fantastic night club and I pulled this blonde bird, an absolute darling. What a stunner. I was walking along John Dalton Street at six in the morning with this girl and she turns and says to me, 'You've given me the best night of my life. Being with you guys, the champagne, the dancing. It's been brilliant and now I am going to give you the best morning of your life.' Happy days.

"We got to my room – make that we ran to my room – I open the door and there's ten of my mates all over the place, passed out. She took one look, gave me a kiss, and left. I never saw her again. Bastards!"

She may have been the one that got away, but for now there were others to think about. An army of fans awaited their heroes' return with baited breath and by the time the train pulled into Euston station, the shenanigans of the night before had been forgotten.

Well, almost.

The glory, the celebrities, the champagne, the girls; the fall-out from Chelsea's Cup win had all the hallmarks of the trendy football club, but there, standing waiting for the players and the staff was a reminder of the past. "All the Chelsea Pensioners were there waiting for the train in full regalia and with tears rolling down their cheeks. That was magical. There they were in their pristine red uniforms, dripping in medals and real emotion. They had come to see us back into London and that's when the hangover and the glory wore off and I realised that we had truly done something special."

For years The Pensioners had symbolised the club, to many they still do, and there they were as timely reminders of what the club had been. Like images of William Foulke filling his goal, or George Hilsdon's weather vane, the old men in red were the club's heritage and for the moment Osgood understood the marriage between the club's traditional past and its alluring present. The nickname might have been done away with by Ted Drake out of necessity to unburden the yoke of failures past, but Chelsea's new-found success had its foundations in the very fabric of the being of the club. Flair, skill and some of the best players around. Although this Chelsea team was for the most part homegrown, unlike its counterparts in most eras of the club's history.

As the open-top bus processed regally through the thronged streets of Chelsea, Osgood waved to his legion of fans, the Cup and a cold beer never far from his grasp. "To be part of that day was something I'll never forget," recalls Osgood. "What capped it was that I had done it with a great group of lads. It was a special squad and we remain great mates to this day. I keep in touch with them all.

"If you talk to fans today they'll say they may have been only six when we won the Cup, but that remains their fondest memory. At the centenary do in August 2005 our table was packed all night. People were coming up to us constantly. We were back together, Catty [Peter Bonetti], Charlie, Chopper, Huddy, Tommy Baldwin, Webby. We were back.

"Webby said that night that it makes it all worthwhile. What we did back then still means something and that is a very nice feeling. They have the old Lion back on the shirts now just like we wore. They still play *Blue is Colour* (the song recorded by the club for the 1972 League Cup Final against Stoke, which reached no. 5 in its 12 weeks in the charts and has remained a stirring battle cry for Chelsea fans ever since) and that is because we brought such a good time to the club."

BY THE time a young Peter Osgood was learning to love the game of football, Jimmy Thompson – the man who's antennae for young talent was Chelsea's secret weapon – had left, but still the net held firm and brilliance made it's way to SW10. In Osgood's case there was initially a lack of competition for the lanky but gifted teenager. "I was captain of Berkshire and captain of Windsor. You'd leave school and all the scouts would come to county games, but nobody fancied me. I had a trial for Reading as I was local, but their manager, Harry Johnston, only said, 'We'll call you, son.'

'That's funny,' I thought, 'I'm not on the phone.'"

Osgood, despondent, got on with a labouring job and playing for his local teams. Fortunately, he was surrounded by people who saw something in him and fortunately those people were Chelsea mad. "My aunts' husbands, uncle Horace and uncle Bob were involved with my team, the Windsor Corinthians. Bob was Chelsea mad, he had named his house after them and he wrote to the club and got me a trial.

"I also had one for the Arsenal, but tore up the letter thinking if I can't get in at Reading, then I've got no chance at Highbury. My Uncles, though, weren't going to let me not try out for Chelsea and they said they'd take me down. It was to be a half an hour trial and I asked if I could have mine early as I had a big cup game in Windsor that afternoon.

"There were about 200 kids and I played for 25 minutes, the great Dick Foss blew his whistle and called me off. I'd scored a goal and thought I'd done OK. "Thanks for the 25 minutes," I said.

"What do you mean?"

"Thanks for the trial, I really enjoyed it, goodbye."

"Would you like to sign for Chelsea?"

"You're joking?"

"There's ten scouts here looking to get at you and we want you at Chelsea."

"Dick had a great eye for a young player and he saw in that 25 minutes that I was worth giving a go. You have to look at balance and brain. Pace as well. The strength will come."

OSGOOD was in, but continued to work on building sites whilst travelling from Windsor to play in the youth team alongside the likes of Johnny Hollins and Peter Houseman. "I was lucky to work with such good players. I got a phone call from them saying that I had to report to Stamford Bridge on the Wednesday for the junior floodlit cup final against West Ham. They had Harry Redknapp, Johnny Sissons, Marty Britt, good players. We won 3-1, I scored two goals and did very well. I got my medal (I still have it) and then the next day I was back making the tea on the building site."

Eventually, that tea would have to make itself as Tommy Docherty asked Osgood to sign for the club full-time for £10 a week. It took nine months for him to break into the first-team, but whilst it would be nice to say after those nine months that a star was born in an instant, Hilsdon or Greaves-style, it would take a while for opinionated Chelsea fans to recognise what they had in their midst.

In December 1964, the awkward-looking youngster sat on the bench, anonymously watching his team eek out a 2-2 draw in a League Cup tie at Fourth Division Workington. Tommy Docherty (or "The Boss" as Osgood still refers to him) felt that the replay was the time to blood his young forward and like so many before him, Osgood shone on his debut, scoring both goals in a 2-0 win. It didn't have the impact of Hilsdon's five against Glossop or Jimmy Greaves' one-man show at White Hart Lane, but it was a good start. "It was a horrible night, very foggy, but I got those two goals. 'Well done, Pete,' said the Boss. 'By the way, you're back in the reserves next week.' That was that."

Things were never going to be handed out on a plate, not with the array of young talent at Docherty's disposal, but a player of Osgood's talent couldn't sit on the periphery for long. Docherty knew it. His ascension wasn't going to be easy, though. The fans had their favourites. Bobby Tambling was scoring goals with his eyes shut, whilst Barry Bridges brought a suave swagger to both the Chelsea and England attacks. The boy from the home-counties would have to prove he was worth the fans' time and effort. The Doc had such faith that he shuffled his pack and moved crowd favourite and centre-forward Barry Bridges to outside-right to accommodate Osgood and the switch provoked plenty of dissension from the stands. "The crowd were getting at me big time," chuckles Osgood. "They loved Barry and Bobby back then you see. The Boss, though, soon said to me 'I don't care what happens, I don't care how much this crowd moan, I'm going to give you ten games.' Now that is a lovely thing for a player. It took the pressure off and I knew if I went out there and was myself it would come. I was again surrounded by such great players. Peter in goal, Terry Venables, Houseman, Bridges, Tambo, Shilleto. They were great. The fans, though, saw this new kid on the block and were concerned that I would rock the boat."

Docherty was not a manager to be swung by outside opinion and immediately saw something in Osgood that merited such a leap of faith. He later described the moment he clapped eyes on the boy who would be King:

> Think back through the past to the youngsters who, from the first moment they were spotted, all concerned – except perhaps themselves – realised that here was a natural. Cliff Bastin, Tom Lawton, Stanley Matthews, Tom Finney, Johnny Haynes, Jimmy Greaves, Alick Jeffrey, Jimmy Mullen…a few more; they all had something which stamped them apart, that elusive stardust which heralds the greatness to come.
>
> That is what I saw in the beanpole Peter Osgood from the first moment I saw his casually deceptive amble across a football field, that sinuous shift which took him past an opponent, who, left with a baffled look on his face, turned to gaze almost in awe. It was all done without a trace of conceit. Indeed, to Peter it was all a game.

Such effervescence would have appealed to Docherty who genuinely got a buzz from witnessing the playfulness of his young team. The manager, though, was still smart enough and shrewd enough to know when Osgood's callow qualities should be used and when they should be laid temporarily to rest. One such occasion was during the Fairs Cup campaign of 1965/66.

Osgood had played in the battle against Roma at the Bridge and had impressed Docherty, who later described him as, "Striding leisurely through all the froth and bubble of this burning game." The atmosphere of the night was far more ugly and the manager was concerned about the return in the eternal city. Osgood for one had no complaints. "The Boss pulled me aside and said, 'I'm not taking you because it's going to get nasty and you're too young.' He was right, it did and I felt he knew what he was doing."

Despite that, Osgood was becoming a pivotal part of Docherty's plans and as the European adventure continued, he tried his hand at terrorising some of the best defenders on the continent. "I played in Milan and that was brilliant, super," recalls Osgood. "The great Karl-Heinz Schnellinger of the West German national team was playing for them then and he marked me, or he tried to anyway. I played well against him and scored a vital goal at the Bridge."

GOALS, goals, goals. But for Osgood these heady times were offset by the fact that he was just a kid and things were moving very quickly indeed. "I was still a little star-struck. Suddenly you can buy a house and you were given a car. It was crazy and people go on about the players today and the money they earn. People look at George Best and Gazza and call them wasters, but those people who say that don't know, they don't realise how much your life changes overnight and it can be hard to handle."

Osgood pleased his manager by getting married at the age of seventeen and by becoming a father at eighteen, but such happy families were not allowed to get in the way of club business. "We were about to go to Australia on a six week tour and I said to the boss, 'I can't go.'

'Why not?'

'My wife is expecting while we are away.'

'Did you sign a contract?'

'Yes, Boss.'

'Well, you read it, because you're coming, son.' That was that, so my first son was born while I was away. We were gone for ages. We walked out of Heathrow and my son was standing there, shook my hand and said 'Alright, Dad.' That's how long we were gone!"

Osgood was a family man, but that sense of trickery and even brazen cheek that Docherty was so drawn to never dispersed. "The Blackpool incident" had cast a shadow over the spirit of the club, and while Osgood was away with the England youth team and so missed the shenanigans, Docherty had no doubt that had he been in the country, Osgood would have needed a telling off. "In Blackpool eight of them went out and got caught. Simple as that. The Boss said to me when I returned, 'There would have been nine sent home if you had been there.'

'Too bloody right', I thought."

Not that circumstance got in the way of Osgood's brushes with indiscipline. On one away trip, he and his friend, the young centre-half Marvin Hinton, were out past their curfew and opted to scale the hotel's drainpipe and return unnoticed through an open window. Unfortunately for the two night-owls that window took them into the chamber of their sleeping Chairman, Joe Mears.

That was part of Osgood's make-up. Alan Hudson is on record equating his team-mate and friends' supreme confidence to sheer arrogance, but it was that which took him onto the field with a belief that he could score, no matter which team provided the opposition or the reputation of the defender. It was an attitude that brought success, goals and, ever more quickly, the love of his fans.

IN 1966, Osgood scored a goal at Anfield that helped knock Liverpool, the holders, out of the FA Cup. Suddenly his name, whilst being sung on The Shed, was being whispered about on opposing terraces as someone who could damage their team's chances on any given day. With that fear comes derision and the chants of "Osgood, No Good" that predictably made their way around the country when Chelsea were in town were clear signs that here was a player worth talking about.

In fact having taken on a strong West Ham team that included Bobby Moore, and laid on four goals in a 6-2 win, Roma – just weeks after having been knocked out of the Fairs Cup by Chelsea – came in with an audacious enquiry about bringing this embryonic hero to Italy. Docherty, though, was in no mood to negotiate. "We wouldn't dream of selling Osgood any more than Brazil would sell Pele. Peter isn't for sale to anyone – not even if they offered us £500,000."

Strong in the air and tidy with the ball, Osgood was your archetypal centre-forward, but with a twist. He would, in many ways like Roy Bentley before him, drop deep and start attacks in his own half where his ability to beat men and create space baffled the most regimented of defences. Equally, faced with the likes of Dave McKay, Norman Hunter and Tommy Smith, Osgood had to be brave and able to look these monsters in the eye to let them know they were playing an equal.

"Not many got the better of me," says Osgood proudly. "Spurs' Mike England was the hardest I played against, I reckon, and he often kept me quiet. When I left Chelsea I went to the US to play for the Philadelphia Furies and who am I up against on my debut? Mike bloody England. The first few minutes I thought I'd let him know I wasn't here to be knocked about and went over the ball on him and gashed his knee. The next thing I know I've got to have five stitches over my eye as he's come in with the elbow. He was a great player, Mike."

IRONICALLY it was that desire to compete full-bloodedly with his contemporaries that led to Osgood's first footballing set-back. Chelsea were playing Blackpool when Osgood lunged for a tackle with Emlyn Hughes. "He came and he done me. I was a bit naïve and went in with him and you could hear the crack right round the ground.

"My first thought was 'Fuck'. The trainer, Harry Medhurst was on and his son Norman had joined him on the staff. This was one of his first games and he started looking at my left leg. 'Norman, it's my fucking right leg and I can tell you myself, I've fucking broke it.' He looked at my right leg, went all white and almost fainted. We needed two stretchers! One for me and one for him!! It wasn't funny then, though."

It may not have been amusing – Osgood was cut down at a time during the 1966/67 season when Chelsea and their forward were blossoming and both looking the best on offer in the First Division – but that sense of humour never diminished even in the ambulance away from Blackpool's Bloomfield Road.

The attendant on board, clearly not a follower of football, enquired of the name of their new patient.

"Peter Osgood."

"What position do you play, Peter?" asked the medic.

"I'm the best fucking centre-forward in the world, but at the moment you'd better put me down as Wasgood."

Osgood was far from the model patient. He began playing golf with his uncles whilst still in a plaster and Docherty once found him and the also injured Peter Houseman playing football in the dressing room, each kicking the ball about with their fit legs. Journeys into the West End with his many pals when he should have been resting with Harry Medhurst at the Kensington Palace Hotel brought the statutory £80 fine (a wrap on the knuckles that was each time greeted with that charming smile and a declaration that it would never happen again).

But Osgood's antics only endeared him further to Docherty who loved his spirit, but the Scot had less time for many others in his squad and, having fallen out with one too many players and officials, Docherty departed early in the season of 1967/68.

"We started that season off and lost 7-0 at Leeds and 5-1 at Newcastle," says Osgood. "6-2 to Southampton at the Bridge, though, was the last straw. The boss was again doing things his way and he put young lads in at Spurs to mark Ron Davies and Martin Chivers. They got murdered. Martin scored four and Ron got two. The boss was stubborn, but I would never fault him for that as he was great to me and he brought so many of us on. I think that team had far more potential than the 70s team. If the Boss hadn't fallen out with some of the lads we would have gone on for years and years."

Docherty's last big occasion for Chelsea had been the 1967 FA Cup Final, a frustrating day for the club and for Osgood who sat injured watching his struggling team-mates. "That day would have been perfect for me. I was getting used to massive games and never had a problem with Milan, Highbury, Old Trafford and I'd have loved Wembley. It wasn't to be for me or the team. That was a massive shame."

Osgood regained his fitness, but had arguably lost the pizzazz that had seen him swagger onto the scene. He didn't become an ordinary player, he had too much about him to ever be ordinary, but the broken leg slowed him down and he had to re-model his game accordingly.

CHANGE for Osgood as a player reflected the change the squad underwent with the installation of a new manager. Dave Sexton, a well respected member of Docherty's coaching staff, who had arrived via Fulham and Arsenal, inherited a fine, if lively, group of players, but got on with fine-tuning it to his requirements. It was work that often left him with burnt fingers as he set about trying to bring into line the more care-free elements of his side.

"Myself and Huddy [Alan Hudson], we would have got in any side at the time, I don't care what anyone says. We were gifted. Dave had been a very average centre-forward and he soon looked at us as wasters.

"We were flair players and that meant we couldn't turn it on every week. We wished we could, but we would win you more games than we would lose. Charlie, Huddy, they could create, they could give me the perfect ball and I scored." If anything went wrong, though, Huddy and me got the bollockings. We lost 3-0, 'What were you two doing?' Sexton'd ask. 'What about the defence?' we'd reply."

Those disputes would later come to a head, but for now Sexton's changes such as recruiting Dave Webb and John Dempsey bolstered the defence, whilst Tommy Baldwin sharpened the attack. The team grew together on and off the pitch, sparking the era which is fondly remembered today as Chelsea's halcyon period. And at the very hub of it all was Osgood. The King of the kings of the Kings Road.

IN FEBRUARY 1970, Osgood won the first of only four caps for his country and he made Alf Ramsey's squad for the World Cup that summer. That squad has now gone down in popular opinion as better than that which actually won the trophy in 1966 and with strikers such as Geoff Hurst, Martin Peters, Allan Clarke, Jeff Astle and Francis Lee it is perhaps no surprise that the 23-year-old only managed 42 minutes on the pitch as a substitute. With Hurst still England's main striker, Osgood was cast alongside Jeff Astle as chief reserve and spent most of the time on the bench. The pair shared together, two Kings in one room. However Astle's musical obsession eventually preyed on Osgood's nerves. "Jeff played the 'Spirit in the Sky' single over and over again on the record player we shared. It drove me to the point where I had to destroy the deck just to get some peace!"

If Osgood felt he was being blooded for a long and fruitful international career ahead he was wrong. Being the era of the wingless wonders, Osgood was never going to receive the kind of service he did at Chelsea from Charlie Cooke and the half hour or so he played in the 1-0 group win over Czechoslovakia proved to be his last in an England shirt for over four years. Then he was tried in an experimental side selected by Joe Mercer after Ramsey had been sacked for failing to lead England to the 1974 World Cup Finals. England lost the friendly 1-0 at home against Italy and Osgood was cast into the international wilderness.

But in 1970, Osgood's involvement in Mexico went some way to appease Chelsea fans who'd had to endure four years of West Ham's supporters wallowing proudly in "Their" World Cup win. With FA Cup success to celebrate, Chelsea remained the place to be, and Osgood remained the player to see. By now his characteristic bushy sideburns had been carefully cultivated to confirm to the trendy new long-haired look of the 1970s. Osgood was the chic, hirsute man about town and was very much in demand.

Raquel Welch, like so many celebrities, was drawn to Stamford Bridge whilst filming in London with life-long Chelsea fan Richard Attenborough [making *The Magic Christian* in which Raquel played the Priestess of the Whip]. Osgood recalls the tale. "Lord Attenborough – a lovely chap, 'Call me Dickie, Ossie,' he says – he was making a film with Ms Welch and he brought her along as a guest. She'd said she'd like to meet Peter Osgood. I don't think she really knew who I was, but Terry O'Neil, the photographer, used to do all my shots back then and he would do all the fashion shoots and the film stars and he'd taken snaps of Raquel. I got her a kit with the number 9 on it. My number. I still dream about her wearing it now.

"We played Leicester at the Bridge and drew one each the day she was there. I had an absolutely fucking diabolical game. I'd met her beforehand and had given her a kiss. Maybe she made me lose my concentration. The new East stand was being built and the boards were up so you could hear the fans a bit more. I was taking a throw on as she was leaving midway through the second half and she shouted, 'Bye Ossie'. I stopped and waved, 'Bye Darling.' Dave Sexton is going nuts in the dug-out, pulling his hair out. I got such a bollocking when I got in."

CELEBRITY was part and parcel of life at the Bridge. The players lived their lives to the full, enjoying every minute of their fame, whilst the manager pulled his greying hair out. It was a clash of wills and the stand off on the Kings Road between Sexton and his players lasted for years.

"We were still young lads growing up," says Osgood. "The guys today have the papers following them around and we never had that, not like them anyway. We never went fighting, though, and we never went 'roasting' girls. When we said 'Would you like to come back to bed with me?', they'd say 'Yes', so I don't know what today's players are saying. Whatever it is they're using the wrong lines.

"The Kings Road was our patch; Alexandra's, The Drugstore, The Seven Bells, The Trafalgar. They were great pubs, swinging pubs, and we had great times. We played hard and we worked hard."

That hard work paid off again in 1971 when Chelsea reached the final of the European Cup Winners' Cup. The players knew that on their day they could beat anyone, home or abroad. They weren't a team who were consistent enough to win the title, but put them in a situation that demanded something special and they invariably would come up with the goods.

Club Bruges were the opposition in the third round and the Belgians inflicted a 2-0 defeat on the Blues across the channel. Osgood had been suspended for that first leg, but was due back for the return. "George Best went up to the FA and got away with whatever he'd done, but the guys at Lancaster Gate said, 'the next one, we're going to hammer'. Who is up two weeks later, but muggins here. I had three bookings, that was it. And they gave me a £150 fine and a 6 week suspension. I could not believe how harsh they'd been. Sexton and the Chairman Brian Mears came over and Brian said, 'My father was very respected here, Ossie. We're going back in there and we're going to appeal. We're going to fight this all the way. I got fucking eight weeks! Thank you, Mr Chairman."

But the ban did not apply in Europe and Osgood returned to score two in a 4-0 demolition of Bruges at the Bridge. It was a night that today lights up Osgood's face. "That was a massive night, massive. I'd say the fans made as much noise that night as they had at Old Trafford in the Cup Final. They went beserk and I won't forget it."

It set Chelsea on their way and, having knocked Manchester City out in the semi-finals, they found themselves in Athens to face the might of Real Madrid. Osgood travelled to the Greek capital nursing sore knee ligaments and doubted his availability for the match.

"I told Dave that I wasn't fit, but he brought in the club doctor and they said they could sort it out with an injection. They didn't force me, but at 24 years old and with the chance to play in a European Final against Madrid, you're going to try anything. I lasted about 85 minutes. I'd scored a goal, but I had to come off. The injection was starting to wear off and I couldn't go on. I'm sitting there thinking "Hold on, boys, hang on and I've scored the winner in the Cup final."

"They'd even brought the cup out and put it on the table. Then Madrid went and equalised with twenty seconds to go. My head was in my hands. 'Dreadful.' I thought 'This one ain't ours. This must be how Leeds felt.' You think that it's all against you. The lads battled on, though, and after extra-time we're told the replay will be on Friday, two days later, when we'd been expecting it to be the following week. 'You're having a laugh!'

IN OSGOOD'S mind there was no way that knee was going to be strong enough in two days and, having been given Thursday to relax, he sat, a forlorn figure with his leg dangling optimistically in the hotel pool. Then Charlie Cooke came over and uttered the famous words, "Fancy a drink, Ossie?"

The answer was affirmative. Why not? He wouldn't be playing the next day after all and why not let a couple of vodkas numb that particular pain. "We should have been going home with the cup and having that same reception as the year before, but we weren't, we had to play again and I wasn't going to be fit. It was the fans that you so wanted to play for and win for. They had travelled over in their thousands and most were sleeping on the beach."

For now, though, there was a bar-full of cocktails to sink and Osgood must have looked at his knee and the Acropolis as the sun set over Athens and wondered which was the greater ruin. The following day, whilst Charlie and Tommy Baldwin shared his hangover, the club doctor again approached Osgood and he wasn't handing out headache pills. "He said they could do the injection again, so why not? In it went again, fucking big needle it was and that cortisone didn't half burn as well."

Fuelled by substances of varying kinds, Osgood took to the field and again set about the Real Madrid defence. The Chelsea fans, sand still in their hair, cheered a great goal by John Dempsey before Osgood made his mark once more. "I got a pass from Tommy Baldwin. He wanted to play a one-two, but having received his pass I dropped my shoulder, and went to shoot. 'Fucking hell, Ossie,' he shouted, but as it nestled in the top corner he went, 'Great goal, Os!'"

Chelsea now had a two goal cushion and Osgood could limp off once more having done what he did best, but again from the bench he had to witness a harrowing finale as Madrid pulled a goal back and laid siege to Peter Bonetti's penalty area.

This time, though, Ron Harris and his defence held firm and Chelsea had conquered Europe. Osgood, as winning goalscorer, was the hero and the team returned to London that next morning to another wild reception. "As a player you don't get bored of those days. It doesn't matter that you've done it before. Once you've savoured a day like that you want it again and again. It's just as enjoyable and to see the fans lining the motorways was a wonderful sight."

BLUE was the colour and now an attentive continent were catching on. These were the best of times. Fans and players could wallow in what had been achieved, but unfortunately the manager, looking in from his more conservative world, wondered where it was all leading.

Sexton was growing increasingly frustrated with his star players, who he felt were far from pulling their increasing weight. Rather than building his team around Osgood and Hudson he began to make changes; changes that didn't necessarily demand their silky presence. They, after all, were testing his increasingly short patience and the booze culture at the club had many fans wondering what adventure they would read about next. Osgood was arrested for raucously celebrating the League Cup semi-final win over Spurs in 1972, the charges were dropped, but it was just another in a long line of incidents involving the players, the drink and the law. "Then we got beat by Stoke in the League Cup final and things really went wrong from there," says Osgood. "We lost all momentum and it was over. The new stand was needed, but it didn't help. The game was changing and Brian Mears realised that hospitality was taking off at football and whilst it strangled the club financially you could see why the Chairman did it. The thing is you have to get it right on the pitch whilst all that is going on and we couldn't get it right. I was struggling with motivation and the team was being fiddled with, which didn't help."

Osgood was intermittently moved to midfield and couldn't help but go through the motions. "It was ridiculous. If you're playing badly you should be dropped and able to freshen up in the reserves. Don't play us out of position. That affected us."

OSGOOD, though, remained a major feature of Chelsea's culture both in the dressing room and on the terraces. Sexton may have been pulling his receding locks out, but, in late 1973, he still thought enough of Osgood to surprisingly ask him to be the club captain. Osgood was as shocked as anyone.

"That was strange, yeah. Ron Harris had done a silly thing. At the training ground he stood up and took a piss in the communal bath with Dave still in it and, as you can imagine, Dave went nuts. He called me in and said, 'I don't want Ron as captain, not after that.' I told him, that Ron was our captain, he'd always been our captain and we look up to him. He leads us and I don't think I'm right for it. He said 'Think about it.' So I said I would."

Shortly afterwards Chelsea lost 1-0 at Liverpool and were preparing for a trip to Sheffield United when Sexton again called Osgood into his office. "On the Monday Dave called me in to say 'I'm making some changes and you and Huddy are dropped,' he said.

'Thanks very much'. So I've gone from captain to reserves in two days."

The battle lines had been drawn as Osgood took his place training with the reserves and their coach, Dario Gradi. It wasn't long, though, before Sexton requested Osgood returned to train with the first team. By now, though, Osgood was in no mood to be accommodating. "'What's the point of that when we're not going to be playing with them?' I asked. 'If you don't like it,' said Dave, 'Go home.' 'Fine', so that's what I did. As I'm walking away, Huddy said, 'Is that the same for me?' 'Yes.' So he walks out too, but he ended up asking for a move right there and then.

Cult heroes often leave in a manner befitting their high-profile status and for these two irascible icons it was never likely to be the fond handshake and gold-plated carriage clock. The mud-slinging began straight away. That night the *Evening Standard* ran the story saying that Osgood and Hudson were demanding a move. "They'd been tipped off. I didn't tell them and I hadn't asked for a transfer. Dave must have done it. When I did leave and it came to a tribunal, it was made clear by the club that I had asked for the move. I hadn't, of course, but they still stopped my 5% from the fee. That was the sort of stubborn bastard he could be. I wanted to make it clear to the fans that I wanted to stay though. I even went and asked for a new contract. Dave said he would go and ask the chairman, but he never did. I did everything I could."

IT WASN'T enough and the Chelsea team that had offered so much were now breaking up. Their long-suffering fans once more having to watch a hero depart as Osgood made his way to Southampton. When Chelsea visited The Dell in 1974 their fans booed his every touch. "They were singing 'What a waste of money.' That hurt. Then we knocked them out of the FA Cup in 1977 and they were gutted. They knew they were missing a good player, but that's life."

After winning the FA Cup once more with the Saints in 1976, Osgood later had a spell in the United States. "I played in Philidelphia which is the arse-hole of the world. Benjamin Franklin has on his tombstone, 'Rather here than Philadelphia' and he was right. "Fucking horrible place". But soon the chance to return to Stamford Bridge arose as the club was under new management and in 1978 the King returned in a blaze of publicity and hope. His fiefdom was not what it once was, however, and whilst hoping to play sweeper under manager Ken Shilleto, he ended up enduring traumatic and short-lived spells under Danny Blanchflower and then Geoff Hurst. Things turned sour once more.

"Geoff was the reason I packed up. He was Danny's coach and I felt he just sat there and waited for Danny to get the sack without really helping him. I couldn't believe it. When Geoff took over he said he had 16 players in the squad and I was number 16. He thought I wasn't fit. I wasn't having that. I told him he'd been there three months and if I wasn't fit surely that was the coach's fault.

"I told him that he had stabbed Danny in the back and I can't stand for that. I was picked for the reserves the next night and I told him that I'd play then, but after that I'm picking up my cards and was leaving. 'I've heard that before,' he said. On the Thursday I did exactly like I said and walked out.

"I saw Geoff recently and it was OK. He helped me to get in the England squad back in 1970 and we were always very close then. Our wives were close, we'd go on holidays, roomed together at times in Mexico, but I just felt he let himself down at Chelsea a bit. I'm sure he agrees."

AND THAT was that. Osgood had gone. Long live the King and all that, but this acrimonious departure was as symbolic that Chelsea's glorious reign was over as any other incident. The team were on the precipice of disaster and the Kings of the Kings Road, with their suits and their side-burns, were now only memories. Four years after winning in Europe the club were relegated; consigned to flitting between the top two divisions and between financial hardship and disaster for two decades.

Osgood's image, though, will never diminish. He had it all. He would drop off and receive the ball before causing havoc. He could pass, shoot, he'd tackle, he could head the ball like Tommy Lawton. He would drop his shoulder and leave defenders on their arse. He once volleyed the ball unerringly past Bob Wilson in the Arsenal goal. It was a great finish and Osgood need offer no less to the fans than that clenched fist and gritted teeth, "Pick that out!" Osgood would score goals like that, salute his adoring fans, give a wink, get suited up and go to have a few jars with the boys, all before whisking a blonde off her feet and onto a Kings Road dance floor. You had to love him. And Chelsea's fans did. He was their King; the very essence of Chelsea.

How Chelsea could have done with Osgood's goals, his charm and his forthrightness to lift the spirits during the dark days. There are innumerable "What ifs" in sporting history. But in football, the stark contrast between the Chelsea of 1970 and 1980 begs the question "What if Osgood, Hudson and Cooke had stayed?" Could Chelsea have continued to beguile their fans with the swagger which had characterised the glory days? Would Osgood have broken Roy Bentley's club goalscoring record?

But for all that, legends are built as much on the 'what might have been' as the reality and there is no doubt that for the vast majority of the generation of fans who lived through Osgood's sovereignty, Ossie is and always will be King. Like all good monarchs, Osgood himself appreciates the role his loyal subjects played in his success. "It was nothing but a pleasure to play in front of those terrific fans. They were wonderful in fact. They cheered us when we were down and they cheered us when we were winning. They won the Cup for us in 1970, because we kept going when we were losing because they kept singing."

The mutual admiration endures.

CHARLIE COOKE

1966-1972
1974-1978

CHELSEA CAREER

Games	373
Goals	30
Caps	16

MAGIC MOMENT

Under the Acropolis in Athens, Charlie wrote his own Iliad in the Cup Winners' Cup Final of 1971, running the show as the mighty Real Madrid were beaten

'THE CAVALIER'

When you run out of red, use blue!

Pablo Picasso

WEEKS and months had passed, but still that winning feeling remained. Life had moved on and there were new, fresh moments to relish, but still that winning feeling remained. The summer nights had grown long and that early spring evening in Manchester back in April seemed a world away. Time to move on? You must be joking.

In the summer of 1970, Charlie Cooke, that artistic Scot found himself in Mexico enjoying the most memorable of World Cups. His country of birth were not participating whilst his country of work were rallying to defend their crown of World Champions. It was a summer in footballing heaven, the first broadcast in colour to a world able to receive on expensive new colour TV sets and one when iconic images of the world game were being formed.

Bobby Moore perfectly timing a tackle to dispossess Brazil's Jairzinho, Gordon Banks somehow manoeuvring himself like an eel across his goal to prevent Pele's goal-bound header, Pele and Bobby Moore swapping shirts, Gerd Muller's goals, Carlos Alberto ramming the ball on the run into the Italian net and lifting Jules Rimet for the last time; all are now bedded into the very fabric of the game, but that summer Cooke still had other things on his mind.

At his hotel he sat by the pool, one leg dangling in the cool water, his toe flicking the water as if juggling a spellbound ball. Others may want to talk about Brazil's flair, Italy's dour catenaccio tactics or England's chances of retaining their crown; Cooke, though, still wants to reminisce about a chillier night thousands of miles away in Manchester when his Chelsea side won the cup. "Ossie was incredible," he tells his companions who are intrigued by that wonderful cross of his. "He made the ball as he wanted to knock a hole right through Manchester."

Peter Osgood had powered in Cooke's perfectly executed cross to level at 1-1. Chelsea were back in the game and soon they would win it through a Dave Webb header that sent man mountains Jackie Charlton and Norman Hunter crashing to the turf. It was an epic struggle, one that Chelsea had had to dig deep to triumph in, but their sheer will saw them through. The original game at Wembley was at times a dog-fight with the players on both sides who relished the uglier aspects of the game allowed to flourish, while those gifted, like Cooke, with an ability to cajole the ball into obeying orders were far more subdued. "Subdued?" he laughs.

"You mean knackered from trudging up to our knees in Wembley's turf – change 'turf' to 'ankle deep mud' – that day. The Horse of the Year Show and heavy rains the previous week had made the field deep and dead, something that wasn't easily seen from up above with the turf on top reasonably green and just a few darker spots showing its true character. Think back to Jack Charlton's goal and you can surely remember the ball bouncing towards the line and Eddie Mac swinging his right boot to clear it like he'd done a zillion times before in his career, but the ball didn't bounce on the dead turf as Eddie and we all expected and Leeds were a goal up.

"As for the robust Leeds defenders they were as dead-legged as we were, I can assure you. They should have won that Wembley game, I'll give you that, but we were giving at least as good as we were getting at the end with Ian Hutchinson's physicality wearing them down and we could even have snuck a win at the death. That's how much the game had changed by that point."

During extra-time, Cooke began to play. The pitch was never going to allow him to demonstrate just how fleet of foot he could be, but as the game wore on and defenders tired he came into it and by the replay he was back to his tantalising best. "Tantalising best may be overstating it," he tells me, speaking from his American home where he now works coaching kids.

"I felt pretty good and I think, like every other player on the field, I was ready for anything that night. My cross for Ossie's goal was a thing you dream about and his finish topped it beautifully. When I took the ball over from Hutch I saw Ossie out of the corner of my eye. I figured it'd have to be a slow floating cross if I was to get it in where he could strike on goal and at the same time give him enough time to get to it. When my chip was on its way I remember thinking, 'Go on Cookie, that's a nice ball.' And of course Big Ossie laid himself out like a platform diver in an Olympic final and smashed it home and the rest, as they say, is Chelsea history. It was a great goal, though I say it myself. Pin-point set up and glorious finish.

"After that I felt slowly but surely it was only a matter of time. We were feeling better about ourselves the longer the game went, putting the Wembley nightmare behind us and getting on with what Chelsea was all about then. Doing it whatever way we had to do it. Pretty if pretty worked, but ugly if need be. Remembering how many tackles around the throat there were in that game I'd say this was one was definitely ugly, but a great battle and a wild and happy and rumbustious night for sure."

The kind that legends are made of.

35 YEARS on and memories of the night are blurry, but back then all the best nights were exactly that. Chelsea players were used to such blow-outs, but not the glorious reasons for having one. The Championship win of 1955 was in a more sedate time, but now, showered, hair combed and flares pressed, it was time to raise a glass or two to Chelsea's Cup.

"I honestly can't remember too much about that evening. We were out of town and due to go back the next morning. What happened at the team hotel between the end of the game and the next day was wild celebrations and toasts and the usual champagne spraying and toasting malarkey that occasions like that bring on. I think the Las Vegas advert over here goes "What happens in Vegas, Stays in Vegas" and would be a good tack to take here, if I could actually remember any of it of course."

If the memories of such times are hazy, the fans who followed the club's fortunes will never forget the contribution of Charlie Cooke. He was the artisan, a player who played the game as if in a park with his mates. Cooke loved to beat his marker, he would beat him and then come back to beat him again. It could be cruel, but mostly it could be wonderful. Looking back, it was certainly inspirational.

COOKE had long been a popular and highly esteemed player in the Scottish League. Aged 18, he was present at Hampden Park for the 1960 European Cup final when Real Madrid mesmerised a more than decent Eintracht Frankfurt side. Like all of the 120,000 spectators that day Cooke went home in a trance, wondering about the show that Puskas, Di Stefano et al had just put on.

Cooke had been spotted by Aberdeen two years prior to that final and went on to play 125 games before moving on to Dundee in 1964, after Alan Gilzean was sold to Spurs. At Dens Park Cooke was hailed as one of the most gifted players in Scotland and it wouldn't be long before those prying eyes from south of Hadrian's Wall would try to entice Cooke to follow that much travelled path to England.

But Cooke so nearly did not move South. Jock Stein, manager of Glasgow Celtic and doyen of his art certainly wanted to bring Cooke to his all-conquering club. However, with Cooke being a Greenock Protestant that was never going to happen, but oh how he would have loved the chance to work with a player he saw as epitomising all that was spine-chilling about the game he loved. Hugh McIlvanney, that most prominent of sportswriters recalls talking to Stein about the subject. "Jock said to me once 'I would never tap anybody up for Celtic.' I laughed and said, 'Jock, you'd tap up your own grandma if it helped Celtic', but he wanted Cooke. 'I know how to play him though. I'd have him running up the middle.' He said that 'nobody in the game carries the ball at speed like Charlie Cooke, except George Best and he's another species.'

"He would have him running through the middle because in Jock's view there was nothing deadlier than a player who could do so. Like Di Stefano. Charlie wasn't quite a Di Stefano, but that's the best method of applying Charlie that Stein fancied because he could take two men out of the game by running through the two of them.

"I do think a man like Jock might have been able to get Charlie to find more in himself. Maybe, though, even Jock, among the greatest managers who has ever lived, would have struggled to have got him to apply himself week in week out."

IT WAS 1966. Cooke was about to be named the Dens Park club's Player of the Year when Chelsea boss Tommy Docherty, a fellow Scot remember, made his move and offered big money to a player who had long put off making a move to England. Now the time was right. Docherty was in no doubt. He'd had to deal with the "Blackpool Incident", his relationship with midfield and social linchpin Terry Venables seemed unavoidably doomed and it wouldn't be long before the England international was making his way to Tottenham. In Cooke, he saw a man who could step in and bring a similar fizz to the side.

Replacing a hero can be hard, but Cooke was blissfully unaware of all the shenanigans taking place in the corridors of power at Stamford Bridge. "I was aware that it was assumed I'd been bought to replace Terry, but neither Tommy Doc nor anyone else at the club said as much to me," recalls Cooke. "I really only knew what I read in the papers in Scotland and that hadn't been a lot as English football didn't get a lot of coverage in the Scottish sports pages in comparison to the Scottish league scene. So I was aware of the team and that it was going well, but knew next to nothing of the internal relationships within the club or its own grapevine."

Dundee received £72,000, a record Chelsea sum paid for a player, but again, the laid-back Cooke wasn't going to allow that to pressurise or spoil his big move. "It was something I was quite proud of, although that kind of self congratulation was short-lived in those days as record fees were being touted almost daily. It was something I enjoyed for a short period and fun while it lasted."

As for Docherty, he had flown personally to Scotland to guarantee the move went smoothly and in the Royal Caledonian Hotel in Edinburgh, the deal was finalised. "I had seen Charlie play on a number of occasions," Docherty said later. "I particularly liked the way he had teamed up with George Graham in the Scotland Under-23 team."

That was a good sign, but Cooke's arrival was reported to have caused problems in the ranks, fuelling some ill-feeling between established players unsure about this wonderfully talented new arrival. He was good. Very good and that meant places were under threat. The press heard that Peter Osgood for one was peeved by Cooke's presence, even stating in lurid headlines that there had been a dressing room punch-up.

Docherty was having none of it. "There were several red hot rumours that when Cooke arrived, Osgood resented him so much that there was a punch-up, ending with one or the other on the floor, depending on who told the story. Well, there was a fight that's true...but it was one of the greatest mock fights ever seen at The Bridge. It took in even those closest to the scene! Actually, the pair are good pals and understand the need for each other's play on the field. There never will be any trouble between those two, they respect each other too much."

COOKE made his debut in a Fairs Cup match against Barcelona at Stamford Bridge. It's not an occasion that he can immediately reminisce about. "I hate to say it, but I don't remember much at all about that game. I know it sounds strange, but there are other much less publicized games I remember far better, although I also have to admit my memory is like a sieve even at the best of times."

For players such as Cooke times looked tough. England had just won the World Cup and Alf Ramsey's "Wingless Wonders" were seen as a new and efficient way of winning football matches. Could a man at his best when enticing defenders wide before beating them and whirring the ball into the penalty box survive in such conditions?

"I realised Sir Alf's wingless wonders would affect the game, but didn't realise how much," recalls Cooke. "It was a victory for system soccer, and it spawned a slew of copycats. It's a way to play without having too many specialists, I suppose. Just rotate a core of hard workers in midfield behind hard running front men who will 'work the channels' and hope you can outwork and out luck the opponents. Basically what most clubs do today.

"The biggest kick in the pants to specialist players and individualists was the omission of Jimmy Greaves in the 1966 Finals. Greavsie was the most dangerous scorer in the England ranks, but didn't get a sniff in the finals in favour of the more workmanlike Hurst and Hunt. It's ironic that today the wealthiest of the Premiership clubs are fighting to pay king's ransoms for players from abroad in the Greavsie "misfit" mould."

Cooke's team-mate Dave Webb himself commented in 1970 on the hangover from England's famous win. "I'm firmly of the view that the game suffered in this country though England winning the World Cup in 1966 and creating a monument at which too many worshiped without question, but, with equal conviction, I believe that football will save itself because there are so many personalities in the game strong enough to throw the lifebelt."

Cooke was no doubt one of those players. In 1967 his dynamic play helped Chelsea to the FA Cup final and in 1968 – as his approach continued to fight off the spirit of efficiency – he won the club's Player of the Year award, voted for by his bedazzled fans. To come to the Bridge and watch a man taking the ball and running at defenders and beating them was thrilling. As he received the ball, a murmur would make its way around the vast ground, and, as he confronted his marker, that murmur would evolve into a crescendo of noise as his quick feet took him beyond his bewildered assailant. "The Chelsea Cavalier" had arrived.

But in 1967, Docherty left the club under a cloud and his departure was particularly poignant for Cooke, who had clearly thought the world of him. "I missed the Doc because he was the manager who signed me and never at any time showed any loss of faith in me," he recalls. "He was a laugh a minute with a gift for stinging repartee and the life and soul of things wherever he was. I liked him and will always be grateful for the chance he gave me and the confidence he showed to plonk down the record fee for me.

"Dave (Sexton, the man promoted from coach to the manager's chair) was quieter, more pensive and deliberate and less of a gambler than Tommy Doc I think. If Tommy Doc was the frontier cowboy, Dave was the shrewd back office accountant. When Dave first arrived he offered me a chance to move. I told him "No" and subconsciously I think I set out to show him. I think I did OK for I was voted Player of the Year that year and followed up with another a few years later in my second spell at the club. When players get arguing the final checkmate retort is "Put your caps on the table". I always figured playfully that if it ever came to an argument with Dave I'd just put my Player of the Year awards on the table."

IN 1967, this author's own father John Moynihan, a football correspondent for the *Sunday Telegraph*, where he also worked on the literary pages, was introduced to Cooke in a South Kensington watering-hole by Hugh McIlvanney. My father, a Chelsea nut, expected to talk football and about the day's game, but instead met a player more interested in literature. They spent the evening drinking and discussing the merits of their mutual favourite author F Scott Fitzgerald and what they both agreed upon wholeheartedly was his strongest novel; *The Great Gatsby*.

It could be argued that throughout his career Cooke suffered from occasional bouts of the football equivalent of writer's block. Like many a winger he could marvel and traumatise in equal measure, but when he lost a lot of form in 1969 and was dropped, it played dreadfully on Cooke's mind. He was a deep thinker, not the usual footballer, but instead a young man prone to deep and enquiring gazes into his own psyche. That season, Hugh McIlvanney conducted an interview with Cooke in the *Observer*. It was a telling account of a troubled soul.

"[Cooke] is plagued by fundamental contradictions, worst of all by the dark suspicion that he is a hero without a role, that excitement associated with his name is a capricious invention of the public, an aura to which he is simply not entitled," wrote McIlvanney. "Cooke is never short of a problem. He is introspective about being introspective, frightened of being seen as a poor man's Hamlet or, more probably, a Greenock version of James Dean, to whom he bears a noticeable physical resemblance."

The writer goes on to quote Cooke who tellingly begins by speaking of himself the player in the third person.

"People say that Charlie Cooke is a nutcase. He keeps making a great big psychological issue of everything. Why doesn't he just get out there and play with that ball? That is what he is supposed to be about. Listen, by the time I was 15 it had been decided that football would be my life. I was a junior player then, mixing with old men who had been the game for years and there was never any doubt that I would go on and be a professional.

"Since then I have not loved my life. I have been led through my life by this talent that I'm supposed to have. It's as if there was a ring in my nose and someone was dragging me along. Maybe that is why I can never make my mind up about this game, whether it is the greatest thing in the world, or a garbage game. Who knows what I might have been? I might have been a good writer or a good architect or I might have been the biggest no-user in the gutter full of meth, but the point is I have never had a chance to find out.

"I have been stuck with this football thing. It's like having a retarded childhood. I'm 26, but in a lot of ways I feel like a wee boy. In this game you can still be an adolescent at the age of 30. Everything is done for you. Plane tickets, train tickets, meals – everything is organised for you. You don't live your own life at all.

He continues. "People get the idea that you are worried about what will happen to you when you are finished with the game, when nobody wants to know. That's not what it is at all. I'm worried about now, about whether the whole thing is worth the candle.

"You can say it's the same for everybody, that everybody has these doubts, journalists and everybody else, but the difference is that you are riding a horse that you have schooled carefully and you know just what it's going to do, how it's going into the fences. I'm riding a bucking bronco and I don't know from one minute to the next what the hell it is going to do.

"You get out there on a Saturday afternoon and it can go either way. One guy might have got his head down and worked hard and another guy has pissed it up and the fellow who has behaved badly may be the one who plays well. I'm not saying it doesn't help to work and try hard, but the point is that it's all to do with mood and whether you feel like it at 3 o'clock on a Saturday afternoon. You tend to tell yourself 'Alright Chas, it's always come before – it will come again,' but obviously there's going to be a time when it doesn't come.

"And the terrible thing is I don't know whether that would be such a horrible thing. It's a diabolical strain to go out there for 42 Saturdays in a season, knowing that you have to go at that full-back and try and paralyse him. The first day you feel great, but then you think that when you beat that guy there are 41 others standing in a line behind him waiting for you. Jesus!"

Incredible stuff that highlights this enigmatic, but alluring character. Fans too couldn't quite make their mind up about him. Cooke had god-given skill, but it wasn't always utilised. You were with him or against him. He knew it and it worried him. "He had phenomenal skill," recalls McIlvanney today. "His juggling with oranges was amazing and with the ball he was phenomenon. That was one of his worries. He was concerned that he'd be regarded a circus turn rather than a footballer. There were people in the game who thought he was profligate and he wasn't a team player.

"Charlie worried and I remember talking to Paddy Crerand. Paddy himself was a very practical player, brilliant in his way, but the kind of guy that Charlie feared would look down on him because he was just a trickster. Paddy confirmed that most people didn't take that disparaging view of him. He said that they [at United] would look at a team-sheet and think, so and so, OK, he's OK, but then you would come to a name and you'd all think 'Christ, he could be a problem' and Cooke was one of those. If he's on his game we are going to be in trouble. Some players were non-descript and you knew that either way you weren't in bother, but not Charlie. He was viewed as a threat and measures were taken to try and stop him."

ON HIS DAY, despite his lack of self-belief, Cooke could be devastating. Days after Christmas in 1969, Chelsea travelled to Crystal Palace for a league game. Tottenham and Arsenal had been recent visitors, but it was Sexton's men in blue who attracted the biggest audience, a Selhurst Park record crowd of 49,489. Palace went one up, but having run off the Christmas cheer, Cooke set about taking apart his festive hosts.

A flowing move brought an Osgood equaliser, but it had been a dribbling Cooke deep in his own half who had orchestrated the flowing move and, whilst Osgood got three more in a 5-1 win, it was Cooke who tormented and weaved his way about the wintry scene.

Chelsea's fans may have fallen in love with Cooke's refreshing approach when he was on his game, but what of the players? Osgood laughs when recalling the highs and lows of his old team-mate's style. "Charlie could be great. The best thing about him was if you were winning 1-0 you could get the ball out to him and that would be it for five minutes. Charlie would keep the ball dribbling about the pitch, wasting precious time. The problem there was that if we were 1-0 down he would get the ball and do the same thing!"

At times, Cooke had been utilised in the centre of the pitch, but from there he could not attack packed defences. With the emergence of the teenage Alan Hudson and the graft of Johnny Hollins, Cooke could move back out to the right and create mayhem from the flank, turning and getting in behind defences. Again and again at Palace he drew defenders out, feinting his way into space and causing havoc, from which Osgood had his fun.

Fun, that word seems to pop a lot when analysing Chelsea Football Club of the late 1960s and early 1970s. Cooke had arrived with perfect timing with the Kings Road beckoning a fun-loving young man to come in and join the party.

"I didn't think any of us needed to be told where the partying was going on in those days. We were a partying team, some of us anyway, no question and I can assure you we'd have found our own way to a party without any sticky notes or map directions, but it was also a fun time. We were being successful on the field and working hard on the training field to stay that way, at least I was, so I don't in many ways regret it. Some of the occasional excesses maybe we could have toned down a bit, but we were young guys in the centre of London's party scene and it would've been a miracle if we hadn't been enjoying some of it.

"Life was the tops. The Bridge was usually packed and I was playing out of my skin and having a blast every week. I worked my butt off in training, enjoyed great social times with my room mate Tommy Baldwin and looked forward to every game.

"The great thing when it's going well like that is you get to the point where you feel you can handle anybody and you don't care who the opposition is. When you're going well they're all the same and it's a great feeling. There were some opponents that I thought the world of even if they gave us tougher times than we maybe wanted. George Best, Tommy Smith, Emlyn Hughes, Peter Thompson. Steve Heighway, Bobby Charlton, Johnny Giles, Billy Bremner, Pat Jennings, Dave Mackay, and many more. Great players all and I'm proud to have played against them."

The upbeat Cooke was now on top of his game and crowd-pleasing was what he did. In 1970, after the FA Cup win, he was asked about his ambitions in the game. "I'm just happy to dodge along...play nice and aggressively...play well for the fans. As time goes on I'd say each game seems more exciting than the last."

Fans would have no argument there. "Charlie Cooke for Prime Minister" was one prominent banner at the Bridge. The Shed would come alive as they sang:

We'll drink a drink a drink
To Charlie the king the king the king
The saviour of our football team
For he invented professional football
And now we're gonna win the league

The club never did. Sure, the team could be nothing short of wonderful to watch, but the consistency that would bring that title remained elusive. It frustrated but didn't surprise Cooke, who today recognises the current squad's attributes that were lacking in his own class of 1970. "While we were a terrifically stylish team that on its day could compete with the best and beat them, we were also inconsistent and didn't do what Chelsea do so well now and take close to maximum points from all the teams below them. That's why they won the Premiership with a record points total. We used to play well against the toughest opposition, but drop valuable points against sides we should have handled easily."

In European competition that theory stood firm. On the continent each game was against new and challenging opposition. Here, Chelsea's players always had something to prove and in 1970/71 those peacocks had ample opportunity to parade their brilliant feathers.

The final in Athens was a cagey affair, but as the game progressed Cooke began to probe at his marker with increasing purpose and success. He started the move for Osgood's goal and despite Real

Madrid's equaliser, he, in the replay, continued to be the likely spark. Cooke had enjoyed sharing those cocktails with Osgood by the hotel pool only the night before, but no matter; it was the Spaniards who were suffering.

"It was another replay like Old Trafford and, although I don't ever remember making that connection in my mind, I think maybe we were thinking subconsciously it was in the stars for us. We thought we had done enough to win the first game and in no way were we intimidated or in awe of Madrid by that point. In the second match I remember being so happy for John Dempsey, who had been such a key, unheralded figure in our defence, when he scored and our confidence grew as we moved towards the final whistle. Madrid were maybe not what they had been, but I think we showed in both games we were deserved winners."

Hugh McIlvanney covered the game for the *Observer* and recalls just how dangerous Cooke had been in Greece. "The other players were all praising him and I remember being in a shop in Athens the following day and some of the Madrid players were in there. One of them said to me, who was that number 4? (Cooke had played number 10 in the first match, but then switched to 4) They couldn't believe how well he had played in the middle of the park."

The writer went on to pen his report on the game, citing how well David Webb had played in defence, but leading with Cooke's fine form. "If Webb was the one who did most to save the tie, Cooke did most to win it. The Final, with its exotic setting, its offering of opponents whose name is synonymous with the arts of the game, was made for him. His pride was roused and that, when he is fully fit, is enough to make him one of the most exciting players in the world."

Cooke's team-mate and the winning goalscorer in the final, Peter Osgood agreed. "When Chas is in that mood, he is one of the best footballers that ever played," Osgood told McIlvanney. "I think I've got skills, that I can take geezers on, but when Charlie's going like that I don't think I'm quoted with him. That's why we get so sick when he goes out some Saturdays and wanders about in a dream. If he did justice to himself all the time, there would be nobody in the game to touch him."

WHILST he was more than happy to have the vote of the faithful, Cooke recalls having to dodge the more unsavoury aspects which surrounded the game at the time. "Remember there was a lot of crowd misbehaviour back then and often we'd get to away grounds or even to the Bridge way early to avoid possible problems. Same with after the game. We were usually sliding out of back doors or side doors to avoid the inevitable crowds and occasional hassles and heavy police cordons moving groups looking for fights away from trouble spots.

"We used to meet fans on the trains coming back from away games. They were usually pretty boozy and boisterous by that point with lots of singing and chanting. I think it must have been pretty uncomfortable and even threatening for other passengers, but no matter what might have gone on earlier in the day the fans were excited to be on the same train as us.

"It wasn't so bad in the bars around Stamford Bridge after the games. It seemed that each season we'd find a new quiet place tucked away on one of the side streets or mews near the ground or Putney Bridge where we could let our hair down relatively undisturbed. Then with my mate Tommy Baldwin and his partner Gabrielle and my wife Diane we'd meet up with friends and sometimes journalists such as John Moynihan, Hughie McIlvanney and maybe Lew Gardner and blather ourselves into the night."

1971/72 was the season when Sexton realised this team, for all that cup success, wasn't going to bring home the Championship. He was left exasperated by their sometime overly free-spirit and,

Fatty Foulke's bulk peaked at 22 stone, but it seemingly didn't restrict his agility and it certainly helped scare the living daylights out of opposing penalty takers, with incredible results

If there was any doubt about Foulke's imposing presence then this picture of Chelsea's first ever team dispels it. He stands literally head and shoulders above ever other player

George Hilsdon became Chelsea's first England international after a barnstorming season which saw him leather in 27 goals. He bagged 14 goals in just 8 internationals

Legend has it that 'Gatling Gun' Hilsdon was immortalised in the form of the weather vane which now adorns the East Stand at Stamford Bridge

Hughie Gallacher shows off his Magic Feet and the style which made his the most sought after signature in the country. Needless to say Chelsea shelled out megabucks to secure it

Just one of Gallacher's many Achilles heels was his propensity to argue with referees. Here he disputes a disallowed goal against West Brom, which the referee has ruled out for offside, in typically hostile fashion

The first league title in Chelsea's history was celebrated in classically 50s style, with speeches through the tannoy and three cheers. Here captain Roy Bentley (centre left) shakes hands with manager Ted Drake (behind microphones)

It wasn't just in 2005 that Manchester United players were forced to clap Champions Chelsea out onto the pitch for their final home game of the season. Here captain Roy Bentley leads his legendary team out at Old Trafford

Eric Parsons living up to his nickname of 'Rabbit' by haring down the wing to send across yet another centre for Roy Bentley to score

Jimmy Greaves shows the shooting style and eye for goal which turned him into the archetypal cult hero

Greaves is carried shoulder high "like the FA Cup" off the Stamford Bridge pitch by his adoring Chelsea public after his four goal farewell

Chelsea fans celebrate one of Bobby Tambling's club record 202 goals

Bobby Tambling preferred the more sedate out of hours activity of owning a sports outfitters to carousing with the kings of the Kings Road

Possibly the most iconic image in Chelsea's history. Ron Harris thrusts the club's first FA Cup into the Manchester sky

Another day at the office for Chopper; booked again

It doesn't get any cooler than this.
Raquel Welch slips into sharpshooter
Peter Osgood's number nine kit

Proof that winning trophies gets you girls. (From left)
Peter Houseman, Peter Bonetti, John Hollins and John
Dempsey revel in the spoils of winning the 1970 FA Cup

Ossie and Chopper proudly display the Cup Winners' Cup after surviving a drinking session
to defeat Real Madrid in a replay in 1971

For decades Chelsea fans had been forced to watch their heroes depart whilst still at the peak of their powers and the sale of Peter Osgood was no different. Protests continued well after his and Alan Hudson's departures

A drop of the shoulder, a shimmy and an insouciant chip are all that Charlie Cooke needs to beat the world's greatest goalkeeper Gordon Banks, in goal for Stoke

The Daddy of the Kings Road, Alan Hudson, shows off the style that made him a cult hero and fall out with a succession of managers

That Hudson goal at Coventry. Defenders lay sprawled in his wake – and then came the celebration

Tongue out in typically determined fashion; Ray Wilkins as Minnie Driver remembers him

Micky Droy works out before breakfasting on razor blades and iron filings

The fearsomely bearded Micky Droy – no believer in reputations – clatters into a challenge in typically forthright fashion against Nottingham Forest, who would become European Champions at the end of this 1978/79 season. Chelsea finished rock bottom of Division One

Joey Jones cracks in a shot against Portsmouth in Chelsea's promotion season of 1983/84

Jones the Fist acknowledges the Shed End, the spiritual home of Chelsea hardmen

Pat Nevin relaxes at home in his flat; part New Romantic, part art collector and part footballer

Nevin's photo from the Full Members' Cup Final programme reveals his own individual style and a cracking 80s haircut. David Speedie did not approve

Kerry Dixon celebrates in his usual fashion, with both arms stretched out to the skies. This time Derby County are the sufferers

Dixon the pin-up flashes that alluring smile of his, which disguised one of the deadliest goalscorers in the club's history

Chelsea have just won the 1997 FA Cup, their first major trophy for 26 years and the fans cannot hide their delight, mobbing their hero Dennis Wise

Wise lifts the last FA Cup at the old Wembley Stadium, accompanied by his son, Henry

Dirty Dennis gets to grips with Arsenal's equally tenacious skipper, Patrick Vieira

When it comes to being cool, Ruud Gullit was the past master. Not many dreadlocked men can get away with wearing a sweater like this

The man who somehow launched his own range of underwear without facing total ridicule poses in relaxed fashion having taken over from Glenn Hoddle as manager

Gianfranco Zola volleys home the winning goal in the 1998 Cup Winners' Cup Final to defeat Stuttgart and win Chelsea an unprecedented third trophy in a year

One of the few cult heroes who have left Chelsea after fulfilling every promise and securing silverware by the sackful; Zola bids farewell at a typically humorous press conference

Despite the arrival of the Abramovich era their captain and talisman, John Terry, remains the figurehead of the team, giving everyone hope that it's not just about the money

And whenever another trophy comes to rest in Roman Abramovich's boardroom cabinet at Stamford Bridge there are plenty of youngsters ready to let the world know who exactly it is that they idolise amongst the all-star team

despite a League Cup Final appearance that ended in defeat at the hands of Tony Waddington's Stoke, changes began to be planned. Osgood and Hudson would depart shortly, but incredibly it was Cooke, much to the annoyance of the Chelsea faithful, who was the first to leave.

In September 1972, Sexton accepted an offer for Cooke and Paddy Mulligan from Crystal Palace as new faces Billy Garner, Gary Locke and Ian Britton arrived. "The club was in trouble on and off the field," says Cooke. "Money was short because of the construction of the East Stand, the results were anything but good and they got an offer that, all things considered, they couldn't refuse for Paddy and myself. I think Paddy and I both went because the club's acceptance of the offer disappointed us. Once Chelsea had made it clear they were willing to part with us, I think we both wanted to get on with it."

Life at the Bridge had been sweet. Now it was over. It must have been hard? "It wasn't that hard because it was still in London in fact not too far from the Bridge. It was still a London club which meant less domestic upheaval than there would have been to go elsewhere. But it was hard in that Crystal Palace had been struggling for a long time and our arrival didn't change that any. So soccer-wise it was a tough go that never seemed to get any better. I believe there were some quotes about fans being unhappy, but you'll always find those if you look hard enough. Remember both clubs were in trouble at the time and fans will accept most things I think when the chips are down."

AT SELHURST Park, the chips were down and doused in vinegar. It was tough. Palace were relegated in a season Cooke describes as "one only of heartbreaks." Malcolm Allison arrived to attempt to change their fortunes and that meant the end of Cooke's sixteen-month stint with the club. By then Alan Hudson had departed Stamford Bridge and the team, as well as the fans were lacking in known quality. In January 1974, Cooke could return, but would he want to?

"That was the easiest decision of my life. I wanted desperately to go back as my days at Selhurst Park were numbered under Malcolm Allison. Palace were still struggling and Malcolm wanted new blood and it suited Malcolm and me both. Chelsea had gone through a tough transitional phase too and were still in a rough patch so it was no gimme, but I was delighted to return. The fans were fantastic. I don't know what they expected, but they acted like I'd never been gone. It was heart-warming and I think I repaid their welcome with some decent displays for the next couple of seasons. I think I may even have snuck in another Player of The Year award there too."

Sure, some fans didn't think that Cooke's style of play was what their struggling club needed. They were invariably the few who had never taken to that "Cavalier" approach. To those who had marvelled at his first spell at the club there was only joy. Cooke himself was interviewed soon after his return against Derby (a 1-1 draw at the Bridge) and couldn't disguise his delight at being "home".

"I hadn't played a full game for three weeks and I thought I might run out of puff, but by the end I wanted to go for another 45 minutes. The Chelsea crowd were special. They've always loved me. At Crystal Palace, if I played brilliantly – which wasn't often – they just about let me get away with it. There were days over there when I wanted to throw my shirt at one of them and tell them to get on with it, but at Stamford Bridge they would clap me just for standing up in a strong wind."

Despite Cooke picking up from where he left off, that strong wind he mentioned had begun to swirl around a troubled football club. Financial difficulties remained and that first season, attendances were down by around 10,000 on those at the time of Cooke's initial departure and despite his Player of the Year performances in 1974/75, the club were relegated. "The financial troubles of the club were public knowledge and results were bad and everything had the feel of a beleaguered ship. The young fellows when I came back, ably led may I say by, 'Butch' Wilkins doing a fantastic captain's job, were in a sense learning what they were all about. They could all play or they wouldn't have been there in the first place. Jock Finneston, Kenny Swain, Gary Locke, Ian Britton, Graham Wilkins and a bunch more."

Eddie McCreadie, Cooke's old stable-mate was by now manager and in 1977, he led the team back to the First Division before quitting due to a pay dispute. Cooke's days were numbered as manager after manager came to the club hoping to raise the bare bones. Cooke did enjoy a 35 minute role in the club's 4-2 win in the FA Cup over European Champions Liverpool in 1978, but that was one of his last run outs in the blue of Chelsea, the blue he had helped make famous.

"I loved the club and the fans," he says. "They were always fantastic to me and exhilarating to play in front of when they're chanting your name. I don't think I can remember them giving me any stick really. Sure there was always the individual comedian who'd get you laughing when they'd tell me to "pass the damned ball Cookie", but never any concerted catcalling I can recall ever."

THE DAYS when Cooke would glide across the pitch before gliding across the Kings Road ended in the summer of 1978, when he followed that well-trodden path to the football pensioners' playground of the NASL in the States. But Cooke's legend still lives on in the hearts and minds of those fans who fell in love with his cheeky back-heels, nutmegs and scything dribbles.

"It would be terrible not to take the chance to thank every one of the fans for their support that made all the difference to us. When we were back for the Chelsea Legends team dinner in May 2005 I got to say "Hello" to many of those fans and it was moving to hear how the old team affected them and how much we meant to them.

"It was more than just the results. We were young and maybe brash, but skilled and exciting in full flow. I even get chills thinking about some of the games and Ossie's headed goals, and Chopper and Eddie's killer tackles, or Johnny Hollins' 25 yard shots, or Catty – the greatest keeper of them all for me bar none – saving our bacon many a time."

Cooke was an odd one. Brilliant, but often able to make a fan pull their hair out, simply because they knew more than anyone just what their man was capable of. More often than not, though, there was that drop of the shoulder and a blistering movement that would take him either side of another punch-drunk defender to set up a goal, or score one himself.

His fellow Scot and grand entertainer Jim Baxter summed him up neatly; "That Charlie Cooke. If he sells you a dummy, you have to pay to get back into the ground."

ALAN HUDSON

1968-1974
1983-1984

CHELSEA CAREER

Games	189
Goals	14
Caps	2

MAGIC MOMENT

His goal against Sheffield Wednesday in March 1970 saw him leave defenders strewn all over the place and the ball in the back of the net. Thank you very much and goodnight

'THE SCOUT'

There are two kinds of talent, man-made talent and god-given talent. With man made talent you have to work very hard. With god-given talent, you just touch it up once in a while.

Pearl Bailey

AT 18, Alan Hudson had it. Whatever that something special is that a young footballer needs to get by in his strange world, Alan Hudson had it and he had it by the bucket load. Without a concern for where he was and whom he was doing it with, Hudson breezed through his early days as a footballer with all the confidence and panâche of a young man completely at ease with the magnitude of his newfound situation.

Those socks lay nonchalantly around his ankles whilst his long hair settled on the very shoulders that had taken so effortlessly the burden of the new role that he had acquired as Chelsea Football Club's gifted new conductor. As he dictated play and orchestrated those around him, the glint in his eye was formed. It was a twang of mischief that would eventually hamper Hudson's career, but take that glint away and you lost half the player.

That was his trademark; a self-belief that would, as a teenager, catapult him into the stratosphere. It was the summer of 1969. The summer of love. Woodstock was hosting its festival, "free-love" was the watchword of a generation that gazed through a haze of cannabis smoke to see man step on the moon. It was a young man's time, the youth of the day were making their own decisions and the establishment would have to get used to their liberated point of view. Alan Hudson epitomised that world and that attitude. His game was a form of footballing "free love," and his gifts with the ball had Chelsea fans wondering once more about their own possible lift off toward the heavens.

They weren't alone. For one so young and so raw, Hudson had seasoned pros looking on in awe. The club's England keeper, Peter Bonetti described him as, "The best prospect I have seen at his age with Chelsea or any club – he has matured so quickly." Dave Webb, that no-nonsense defender couldn't help, but gush, "This Hud is going to be some player. Well, he already is, isn't he? If ever I saw a boy who's got it all set up for him, he has with his talent. What a future he should have."

SHOULD is a dangerous and sometimes cruel word in the world of professional sport. Expectations are too often not met and dreams are left as only dreams, but as 1969 turned into 1970, Alan Hudson had it all layed out in front of him and even those firmly in the game's positions of power had been drawn to his every gracious, gliding move. In March 1970, when Chelsea beat Queens Park Rangers 4-2 in the quarter-finals of the FA Cup, Hudson was inspired. He swivelled, he passed, he shot, he tackled and the watching Sir Alf Ramsey – building a squad that he hoped would defend the country's status as World Champions in Mexico – was suitably impressed. "There is no knowing what this boy might achieve," said Ramsey in his clipped tone. "He could become one of the greats."

Hudson was Dave Sexton's youthful vigour. The side Sexton inherited was good, but in Hudson he now possessed a young talent exploding onto the scene, a scene that the young footballer always felt he had been destined to boss. Having beaten Watford in the semi-final of the FA Cup, Hudson could look forward to a final appearance and the very real prospect of playing in the World Cup. Then came a league match at West Bromwich Albion. Chelsea were probing the upper reaches of the First Division, but it was a fairly innocuous fixture and an even more innocuous moment that changed Hudson's season, career and in may ways, his life.

"It was Easter Monday," recalls Hudson. "There was no-one near me, but I came down on the floor hard and went down the biggest fucking hole in the Midlands. Straight away I knew. Straight away I knew I was out of the Cup final, the dream was over."

35 YEARS on and the hair is not as thick, that glint in his eye has been dulled somewhat by time and excess, but the swagger remains. He strolls into a Tapas Bar on the New Kings Road like an ageing cowboy. The waiters, enthused by a love of both Spanish football and Chelsea, know him well and he chats to them with ease as we sit down to discuss his heyday on these very streets.

He reminisces fondly, stirring his vodka and fruit juice with the arm of his reading glasses. Time has passed, but the subject of that injury and its consequences rolls back the years and now the voice is cracked and the eyes become misty.

"I was so devastated," he says as if discussing events from only yesterday. "Not only would I miss the Cup final, but I had those real hopes of playing in Mexico. I found out years later that I would have played if I hadn't been injured. A journalist, Ken Jones, had told me in the hope that it would make me feel better, but it just made me feel worse. I could have replaced Bobby Charlton instead of Colin Bell in the quarter-final against West Germany, kept the ball and helped us through that last 20 minutes. Instead I watched it at a mate's house with a few beers.

"The Cup final too, that was so hard. This was the squad's big moment, this is what we were trying to achieve and I was missing it. No-one could have helped me through that time. No-one. I don't think the lads, Ossie, Tommy Baldwin, knew or quite understood how down I was.

"I couldn't even stay up at Old Trafford for the party afterwards. I couldn't go on the team bus, nothing. I couldn't go on for a while. It's very hard to put into words just how bad I felt. The reception back here was the worst. There I was standing in a pub on the Kings Road as the bus went by with my team-mates and the Cup."

To literally miss the bus must have hurt. The Kings Road was where Hudson had grown up. These were his streets, he had learnt to play the game here, he had watched the game here, but now he was missing the moment of glory, the moment he got to show all those that he had shared his formative years with, just how far he had come.

ALAN HUDSON was born on 21st June 1951. His father was a Fulham fan, whilst his Mum's side of the family were dyed in Blue. His dad, a decent player himself, was always going to win that struggle and Hudson found himself at Craven Cottage, cheering on the team, but delighting in the unpredictable charms of Johnny Haynes and a young Rodney Marsh.

Haynes, especially, left his mark on a boy enamoured by his way of doing things. The England man stood out from the crowd. Fans drew their breath and waited in eager anticipation of his next pass or shot and as the young Hudson stood on the terrace by the famous old Cottage, he realised that that was how he wanted to play.

Hudson's dad saw a lot of Haynes in his son and took him to Fulham who had training sessions for local young talent. "They soon said that I was too small to make it there," he says. It was the usual mistake and Hudson senior was having none of it. "My dad said, 'You are all idiots.' There was a fella called Arthur Stevens taking the training and my dad said to him, 'You're not too big yourself. My son is only 12 years of age and is going to grow.'

'Bring him back when he has,' said Stevens.

'You fucking idiot,' reiterated my Dad."

And so it was off to Stamford Bridge where the diminutive but gifted young Hudson hoped to make the grade at the club that was only a corner kick away from the prefab in which Hudson had been brought up. "You needed to be able to handle yourself around here. If you couldn't stick up for yourself around the World's End Estate then you were in trouble. I was never one to start fights, though; I was too busy playing football. I still have a drink with some of the guys I grew up with and they say today how far superior I was to everyone else with a ball. I never knew that. To me it was just a game and one that I loved. There is such a fine line between making it and not."

HUDSON had the gift that with a swivel of the hips widened that fine line. He had that ability that would push him forward, but like many players his talent needed that extra shove and Hudson got it from his father. "There were times on a Tuesday night when I didn't want to go over to Chelsea. My dad would give me a clip round the ear and say 'you're going whether you like it or not' whereas I would have preferred to have played in 'the cage' by the prefab with my mates. 'You're going to Stamford Bridge.' I'd got no choice. Maybe if my son had had my father he would have made it as well because he was very talented. Dad wanted me to be what he wasn't. He had played non-league for Wimbledon and Wealdstone and I was very lucky that he pushed me the way he did."

Hudson's father believed in his boy and installed a confidence in the youngster which bred into cock-sure arrogance and it would be Fulham who would live to regret their lofty discriminations. "We were coming home from Highbury one evening and Bobby Robson, the manager at Fulham got on the train. My dad weren't shy and went over and said, 'Bobby, my lad here is an apprentice at Chelsea.' Bobby didn't turn around or anything and acknowledge me, which I thought was a bit off. He could have said, 'Why not come to Fulham' as we were fans. He didn't, but if he had by then I don't think I would have gone. Once you're winning things at Chelsea and wearing the blue strip it feels good. The Doc was the manager, Dick Foss the youth team coach, it was a great place and whilst you wonder if you will ever make the first team, it seemed the exciting place to be.

"I remember when I signed pro forms in July 1968. We met Dave Sexton and Dad said, 'Please don't try and teach my son anything, because he already knows more than you.' Dave, who was an introvert, must have walked away thinking 'another nutcase then.' Dad saw the maverick in me and loved taking me to Spurs when Fulham were away to see the likes of Johnny White, Jimmy Greaves, Dave MacKay. The only way to become a great player is to watch great players and my Dad made sure I did just that."

Chelsea once more had their boy. Jimmy Thompson, their pied piper, who had unearthed talented youngsters on behalf of the club since Drake's era, had gone, but still they were capable of picking up the best in young talent. Dick Foss was on to hand to work with and, in Hudson's case, nurture young talent, but they also had to deal with a knee condition that had unknowingly been with Hudson from a young age. Two bones in his knee were not fusing together and rest would have to be endured before he was fully able to compete. Frustration was replaced by joy though in 1968 when he was able to get on and play with the other youngsters and work his way quickly into first-team recognition.

IN LIGHT of Hudson's subsequent frolics as a footballer with a penchant for good times, the circumstances surrounding his debut were extremely ironic. It was late January 1969 and having picked up a niggling injury with the reserves, Hudson lay on the treatment table whilst Harry Medhurst went about his business as club physio.

"It was a Friday afternoon when the phone rang in Harry's room," recalls Hudson. "Harry wasn't one for many words and there he is with the phone saying, 'Yes, no, no, OK, yes, yes,' before putting the phone down.

'That sounded bloody interesting, Harry,' I said.

'That was the manager wanting to know if you're fit or not. If you are, you're playing tomorrow. '

'Bloody hell."

Dilettantes amongst the first-team had chosen to wash down their post-training lunch with a few bottles of vino... a few each that is. "The lads were sitting in Barbarella's restaurant just a few hundred yards from the ground getting hammered. Someone had grassed them up. Sexton went down there and found them sitting and drinking at the table. Charlie Cooke fell over and I was in."

The next day, Hudson, only just 17, ran out to face Southampton at the Dell. The axe had dropped and a number of new faces got a run out that day, but Sexton's ploy backfired as Chelsea were routed 5-0. "Now it's funny; but it wasn't funny for the 90 minutes I can assure you. It could have been fifteen. I don't know where I played to be honest. All over the place I think. I can only imagine that the guys were pleased that Dave had been proved wrong and that he shouldn't have played the kids, but they also would have been upset for us. I was never ready for first team football, not back then."

THE EARLY months of the 1969/70 season proved to be Hudson's launch pad. Injuries might have played a part in his selection, but the enthusiasm and the desire that he showed when given a chance convinced Sexton that this kid would be the real thing.

"First-team football took a while to get used to," says Hudson. "I don't think that I or Dave knew how far and how quickly I was going to progress. I remember how hard the first six to ten matches were. Physically I had to strengthen up, and so I did a lot of extra training. I over-trained in fact. I stayed and trained harder and for longer than anyone else.

"I enjoyed it. In time I wasn't happy unless I was the best player that day. That was crucial to having a good career. I had to aim for the top. Young Frank Lampard impresses me so much because he has the right attitude, he wants to be the best and nothing else will do. He's improved himself and become better and better and now is regarded by many as the best. And to be considered on a par with, or better than, Stevie Gerrard is quite something.

"For me, playing regularly in the first team was a dream come true. That knee condition had looked like it would keep me out of the game for a long time. Suddenly I am in and doing well and those guys whose boots I was cleaning and who I thought so much of as players were now my team-mates and I'm celebrating goals with them. I've got photos of me when there is a goal scored and I'm always looking in awe, slightly set back because I was still so shocked to be in the position I was in. I couldn't believe it."

THAT position was centre-midfield and not only that, Hudson was slowly becoming the team's playmaker, not bad going for a kid in a team awash with men capable of making the play. His partner in the middle was the piston-like John Hollins. As footballers and men they were like chalk and cheese, but it worked as they complemented each other perfectly; Hudson's thoroughbred to Hollins' workhorse.

"Holly was our ball winner. Everyone would say you need a Hollins or you need a Ron Harris, which is probably right. People keep telling me how important Makalele is to the team today, but I can't see it myself. They keep telling me he is vital so I suppose I'd better go along with it. I suppose he helps Frank get going, but I struggle to appreciate those players. I wasn't very complimentary about Holly in my book (*The Working Man's Ballet*), but I don't think we could have or would have swapped him for anyone else at that time. Leeds had Bremner and Giles who were both super players. They had great balance and had a bit of nastiness to get by.

"John Hollins would never hurt anyone in his whole life. He had the enthusiasm, though, and even in his thirties he acted like an 18-year-old. He still does. He's still as silly as ever. It was a dream for him too, remember. He was playing with greats and letting them get on with things. George Graham, Charlie, myself, he was lucky to be in with so much talent.

"The big argument I had with Holly was the night he missed the penalty against the Swedish team Atvidaberg just months after winning the Cup Winners' Cup. He used to take all the penalties and free-kicks just because he wouldn't go out drinking, so he reckoned he had steady nerves. That was all. 'Let me take it,' I said, but no. I had already scored that night and if I'd taken the penalty it would have been 2-1 and we would have won the cup again (Defending cup holders Chelsea went out on the newly instituted away goals rule). Little things like that stay with players."

THAT WAS to come. For now, in the early months of the 1969/70 season, Chelsea fans delighted in the balance of their team's perfect marriage of flair and grit. In Hudson, they not only had a young player to pin their hopes on, but also a young man who grew up on their own, fairly mean, streets. "The Cage" that Hudson learnt to play football in was like so many estate pitches. Bomb-site playgrounds were full of kids playing under the dim streetlights, whatever the weather. Here was where children grew to love the game, most would take that passion to the terraces, some took it all the way to the centre of the club's midfield.

Hudson, though, actually found that by being the local boy in the team, his position of favour among the fans was harder to gauge. "It was difficult being a local lad. It was strange. Chelsea fans used to chant all the players' names as they ran out. One after another they would sing a name, but it was rare they did mine. A mate of mine used to say, 'They don't sing yours, Alan, not because they don't think much of you, they love you, it's because you're one of them.' I used to stand on the Shed, I lived around the corner and knew most of the guys there. You cheer the untouchable heroes don't you? Why would they shout my name? They all knew me. Either that or they thought I was shit!"

If they did they were in the minority. Sir Alf gave him an under-23 cap against Scotland in 1970, just weeks before that ankle injury. And now we know that after just a season of first team action, Ramsey considered Hudson good enough to make the trip to Mexico. Yet Hudson was living a modest life, staying in a flat with his uncle and aunt just yards from the Bridge. His wages were still those of a reserve team player, but the boy with the flowing locks was beginning to make a stir both among the press and the ladies. In August 1970, the *Evening Standard* sent a female writer to meet him and her first impressions were that he looked, "Elegant, though a bit spotty."

Callow blemishes aside, Hudson was getting used to his newfound fame and the trappings of success. "I think I have expensive tastes," he told the Standard. "Everything I look at seems to cost a ton. I pay £50 for my suits – well you like the best don't you? I've got eight suits, six pairs of shoes and three or four-dozen shirts tucked away somewhere, good shirts. I love clothes." De rigueur taste for the archetypal Kings Road smoothie.

The followers of Chelsea had always been followers of fashion. Indeed, with the fur-lined-collar-wearing Fatty Foulke as their fashion leader, for Chelsea's fans style had always been the byword in what their heroes simply had to have. And in the young Hudson they once more had a man with a taste for the nightlife and all its wonderful trappings. Girls took a shine to his flamboyance and his wayward persona. He was his own man, the sort a coach couldn't coach and therefore the sort your dad wouldn't approve of.

"I never tell a girl what I do," he told the *Standard's* reporter. "Never ever, unless she's really local and she's got an idea. I've said I'm a window cleaner before now. I don't like taking girls out. I'd rather go out with my mates and have a laugh and finish up with them, you know."

His team-mates knew all right, and it was that partying side of him off the pitch, as well as the ability to create chance after chance on it that so endeared him to those amongst his team-mates who styled themselves as the kings of the Kings Road. The majority of the squad shared those wants, desires, foibles, lusts and weaknesses, but importantly were blessed with enough talent to still be amongst the best players in the land.

"We thought we owned Chelsea," laughs Hudson now. "It was a trendy place to be, but it was our playground. Whenever we finished training we would go for lunch. There was nowhere we couldn't go and there was nothing that we couldn't do. We walked around the place and we owned it."

THE ROUTINE was set and with their playground primed they would move in for the kill. "We'd arrive back to Euston after an away game and head straight for the Markham Arms on the Kings Road. We'd go in there, about ten of us players and the girls would start mingling, but we would talk football for about an hour. We talked about the game that day, where we went wrong, where we went right. Dave Sexton never believed that, but it was true. We did. The chat was football for ages, but then, all of a sudden at about 10 o'clock, that was it. No more football, 'Let's go boys' and it was time to unwind and chat to the girls.

"You'd run out at the Bridge knowing there were loads of celebrities there. Terence Stamp, David Hemmings, all the cool people, Sean Connery. We knew they were all up in the long bar up the top. We knew how much these famous, A-list celebrities wanted to be *us* and that was wired. They were in awe of us. We were in awe of them, but they would have swapped places with us. It's not till later that you realise you would swap with them because they go on forever."

To the hip crowd, Hudson had the look, the style and the image. Here was an athlete who was well aware of his image, but not in the modern sense of tying up rights in the contract or merchandising either his name or goal celebration. "I was a young man enjoying life. I had been influenced by many players as a kid, but the one that stands out is Denis Law. He had his shirt outside his shorts, he would roll his sleeves up and when he scored would just lift his arm carelessly. All those little things I took in. I'll do that if I ever make it. I always had the style didn't I?"

In short, Huddy, as he had become known, was just cool. As cool as the celebs he entertained. In March 1970, Hudson scored a goal at Stamford Bridge against Sheffield Wednesday that had fans daring to compare him to Jimmy Greaves. He picked up the ball deep in his own half and went and went and went, leaving countless defenders wriggling on the turf like worms in his wake before slipping the ball unerringly into the net.

It wasn't a fluke, only weeks before at Coventry he had scored a replica and celebrated in style behind the goal in front of thousands of jubilant travelling fans. "I picked the ball up on the edge of my own box and done the whole lot of them before slipping the ball in. What was funny was I ran behind the goal and the lads were going mad. I had come of age and was now as good as Charlie and Ossie. The crowd went nuts. All the players had celebrated with me and we were running back for kick-off. Ossie was with me, and as we were jogging he said, 'Fucking great goal, son. Let's go back and have it again.' So we've run back to our fans and celebrated again. They loved that. They went mad. 'Fucking brilliant, son,' Ossie said. 'Nearly as good as the one I got at Burnley last year!' Bastard."

IF THERE was competition for style on the field, it easily overflowed into their social lives and in Hudson, the squad found a young man willing to take up the awesome burden of social secretary and ensure that their post-match lives were never drab. After all this was his turf. "I was called The Scout because I would go out looking for the best afternoon drinking clubs, the best pubs, the best restaurants. They would ask young Alan, 'Where we going today, Scout?' Dave Sexton hated that nickname."

There was plenty that Sexton didn't approve of, but there was little he could do about it. These young men were on top of the world. They were FA Cup winners and the following season, 1970/71, saw them winning in Europe. The players just clicked. "I can't think of anything else I would have rather been doing at that time, or any other people I would have rather been doing it with," says Hudson.

"To be able to train, to be in the dressing room with the banter and then to socialise with them was extraordinary. They should have made a film of it in Hollywood, the things we got up to." One occasion stands out.

"The night we were on *Top of the Pops* in 1972 summed us up. We were at the BBC filming our bit for *Blue is the Colour* and we ran riot. We had booze in the dressing room and we were running about causing mischief. There was a band there named The Sweet, they may have been Number One. Their lead singer, Brian Connolly, had this long blond hair and we ran in and sprayed him with hair-spray and put lacquer in his hair. It was a riot. Very bad behaviour.

"By 11.30 that night we had a load of Pan's People, the glamorous dancers on the show, with us holding our hands, including the married ones who shall remain nameless. We all went down to Alexandra's and had a right good party. People must have seen us, a load of Chelsea players and Pan's People, it was a marriage made in heaven."

Alexandra's was the regular haunt for Hudson and his team-mates. Hudson's brother had cleaned the windows of the place and informed his brother, The Scout, that here was a place worth frequenting. "It was run by these gay guys who from the minute I went in there became Chelsea fans. I brought Ossie along and from then on it was our place.

"You can imagine Dave getting the phone call from one of his spies saying that his boys were all in a restaurant with Pan's People. Bloody hell, he would have gone mad. Those spies couldn't keep up with us though. There were only so many places they could follow us, but also Dave's imagination and paranoia got the better of him."

SEXTON could only do so much. The team had brought the club and its fans success, but to the manager they were wasting their talents. The way he saw it, these players had responsibilities and were wasting his and their time. Needless to say the players saw it differently. And they were good enough to both enjoy their fame and never stop giving to the cause.

"Basically, here was a manager who didn't know how to handle us all. He'd wanted to be what we were, but hadn't been and so got frustrated by us. To him, we had all this talent and were abusing it."

Perhaps the success they had gained wasn't enough for the manager. Sexton had a fine group of players, capable of brilliance, but they were never going to win the Championship. The team's inconsistency over a season saw to that. They finished third in 1970 behind an Everton team that, whilst not offering the same in terms of individuality, had a team ethic that took the title to Goodison Park.

Post-1970 the team began to drift. "Ossie was suffering with injuries, I had my ankle that was still playing up and Chopper and Eddie McCreadie were going blind. They couldn't see a thing. If you look at the one goal at Wembley in the 1970 FA Cup Final against Leeds, they are both on the line and the ball sneaked between them. They just took a swing at it and missed. Neither could see the bloody thing. Eddie was almost totally blind!

"Everton were strong in 1970, there was Liverpool who were coming on again, there was Arsenal, and of course Leeds. I still say that our ground was against us. It was far too open. It took a lot to get an atmosphere. The Shed made life easier because they made a noise, but if those boys had been on top of us and the opposition in today's ground making the noise they made back then, we would have been unbeatable.

"No excuses, but that ground was seen as a nice place to play by opponents. The crowd made noise, but they were so far away. The only time you noticed them was at night matches because of the light. The game came alive then. On a Saturday it was hard work."

Having won the Cup Winners' Cup, Sexton set about trying to change the team's attitude and that meant changing personnel. The culture that had become such an integral part of his team had got to him. But to the men involved that was as much part of their make-up as the blue kit and the white lion they felt they wore with such pride.

"We weren't drinking any more than we always had been. We were doing nothing different, but Dave started digging us out and looking for scapegoats. What annoyed me about Dave Sexton was that the kind of courage the lads showed against a team like Leeds was fucking incredible and he never commented on that.

"Dave should have seen that character, and said 'Whatever you guys do, keep doing it and keep showing that strength. I'm proud to be your manager.' If he'd done that we would have stood back and thought 'We're all in this together.' Dave wasn't in it with us though. Nothing that was said by Dave in those two finals would have won us the trophy. It was down to the boys on the field."

THE MORE the manager complained, the less likely it was that his strong-minded players would fall into line. In 1972, the team reached the League Cup final, but the defeat to Stoke was to be the last such occasion for the club for an extremely long time. The glory days were over.

Hudson was struggling to train regularly due to that niggling ankle and consequently – along with too much good living – his weight became harder to keep in check. Sexton brought in Steve Kember from Crystal Palace and whilst his arrival was not as a direct replacement for his wayward star, it was a move that the manager hoped would act as what he saw as the necessary kick up the ass.

"I was taking a few Mondays off because Saturdays were getting longer. How I was out so long without any money I don't know. People were buying me drinks I guess. You'd get bought all these drinks and then on the Saturday you'd hear someone shout, 'Oi, Alan, I know why you're crap today, I bought you a load of vodkas for you the other night!' That was odd."

The fans could, like their manager be frustrated (they named the era "The Wonder Years" as they wondered what had happened to their great team), but still they had ample to reason to take delight in Hudson's sometimes wonderful talent. It wasn't easy for Sexton or the fans, but for Hudson these were hard times. Frustrating times. Hudson had wanted so badly to get on with using his given skills, but now due to circumstance and his fondness for fun, things weren't what they might have been.

"Coaches say 'Don't do that' and 'Do that.' When they start speaking like that they lose you. You can't coach great players. You need organisation for when you lose the ball, but you can't tell great players what to do when they have it. Matt Busby couldn't tell George Best how to play. You say nothing, you leave George alone. Osgood was the same."

Hudson, remember, was still a young man and still capable of genius, but his single-mindedness and an incredible self-belief was to upset those charged with coaching and selecting him.

His next controversy saw him fall out with Alf Ramsey over being selected for an Under-23 summer tour as opposed to the full England squad.

"Ramsey banned me for three years. I was training with the England team and Bobby Moore told me I would be playing and there I am; I'm overjoyed. When Alf picked the team I wasn't in it. I was gutted. Thanks, Bobby. I looked at him and he couldn't believe it. I wasn't happy and I wasn't going to go on an under-23 tour. 'You've got no chance.' Chelsea were going to Barbados on tour and that to me was a far better option. Sexton was surprised, but I wanted to be with my club not the Under 23s.

Ramsey phoned me and said, 'Young Hudson. Is this true? Are you are not coming?'

'No. I've got better things to do.'

'Excuse me?'

'I have better things to do. My wife's pregnant and all that is more important than coming away with you.'

'You'll take the circumstances,' he said in that elocuted voice of his.

'Fine. Fuck ya.'"

IT WASN'T until 1975 that Hudson won his two caps, but he was never going to be a regular in an England team that time and time again ignored the more gifted, but unreliable footballer. "It wasn't till Alf got the sack that they dropped the ban. I was then so lucky that Don Revie got the job – not. Talk about out of the frying pan into the fire."

It wasn't all gloom. In 1973, Chelsea went on a run in the FA Cup that suggested they could again claim the country's showpiece event, but as ever it was those pesky men from Arsenal who thwarted their progress at the quarter-final stage. A 2-2 draw at Stamford Bridge meant a trip to North London and a game that reminded all present of Hudson's brilliance. He controlled the midfield alongside Kember, but poor refereeing and the wily grace of Alan Ball saw the Gunners run out 2-1 winners.

Hudson's flashes of brilliance were becoming fewer and further between and too often he found himself forced to hug the touchline rather than pulling the strings in the centre of midfield. "I wasn't brought up to play out wide, but Sexton saw me as the best option. If Charlie [Cooke] was injured we had no-one and he thought I could do a job, but I wasn't a player to just do 'a job'. He knew I was pissed off. I was out of it. I couldn't play."

To Hudson it was another example of bad man-management from Sexton and the relationship between these two very contrasting men was near breaking point. "Dave was a good coach. The thing was I didn't feel I could be taught. You might think that's arrogant for a 22-year-old, but it's a simple game made complicated by too many. Don't knock the genius in your team, that's why people come through the turnstiles. Fans don't want to see a team just winning. They want to see the skills. They want entertainment. They want class.

"He always pointed the finger at me and Ossie. It was mainly my fault because I used to pass to Ossie so much. He thought because we always went out drinking together that was why I passed to him. It wasn't. It was because he was our best goalscorer and we'd developed this great understanding.

I said to Dave one day, 'I thought football was about giving the ball to your best players?' and he couldn't answer that. He didn't like how easy we found the game and that we couldn't be coached."

THE TWO partners in crime were both struggling, both playing out of position and both seen by Sexton as microcosms for why his great team hadn't achieved all that it might. Today Hudson stares out onto the New Kings Road and wonders about that time. "I think I'm a little deeper than others in the game. I think about why this happened and how that happened. I look at things and study why things went wrong. I don't ever say I was an angel, but there are two sides of every coin and we didn't have a coin."

In truth, Hudson and Osgood were not the only ones, but they represented the best, the potential that Chelsea never fully realised back then and therefore they were the butt of everyone's frustration. Hudson himself recognises just how widespread the good times were. "I once said to the then Chairman, Brian Mears, that it was his fault. He couldn't understand that at all. I told him he should have listened to the players and certainly not agreed to sell his best two. Brian listened to Dave, sold us and then a year later sacked Dave. Is that clever business?

"Brian apologised because he was more caught up in the team's success than even us. He would say I've had more women because of this team than probably you, Alan. He was the Chairman of Chelsea and it cost him his marriage, he told me. That's a load of fucking good, ain't it? I wouldn't have minded if he had given us some cash to go with his good time!"

Hudson's time was up at Stamford Bridge. Like Osgood he was dropped from the first team after he arrived late for training one too many times and was banished from a trip to Bournemouth.

"We were leaving on the Monday and I had been out with Ossie on the Saturday. He had said he'd pick me up and drive me to training. We were due in that morning and in the afternoon we were going to the south-coast. Anyway, he's forgotten to come by and I'm at home and well late for training. I called a mini-cab and walked in knowing Sexton would go mad. I can't say what he called me, but I wasn't going to Bournemouth. I never said a word and I wasn't going to drop Ossie in it."

It was obvious that Hudson, like Osgood would have to move on.

HUDSON was only 22 when he left Stamford Bridge in 1974, a young man with a young man's zest for life. He joined Tony Waddington at Stoke, where he enjoyed a wonderful debut against Liverpool, which their manager, the legendary Bill Shankly, described as the best debut performance he had ever seen.

But the temptation to enjoy the early hours at the Stoke players' regular local haunt in Hanley, The Place, could not be avoided. "That debut was incredible. Some said it was the best they'd seen. I don't know how I managed that because I moved up to Stoke and in with Geoff Hurst and his wife. The club didn't want me in a hotel, but still I was out. I wanted to rest before the Liverpool game, but on the Monday Geoff took me to a club where I met my new team-mates. Those first few days were like a ritual welcoming ceremony. Jackie Marsh, Terry Conroy, those boys could drink and by the Thursday I was at last looking forward to an early night.

"The phone goes and Geoff picks it up and I heard him saying. 'Alright, we'll see you in half-hour'. Oh no! 2.30 every night we left the club. I was in there more than on the training pitch."

Hudson did well at the Victoria Ground and won his England caps before moving to Arsenal where he finally played in an FA Cup final in 1978, albeit a losing one as Bobby Robsons' Ipswich won a poor game 1-0. Things didn't work out with the manager Terry Neill and after the statutory spell in the United States, he rejoined Chelsea in 1983, but despite being only 32 failed to make either an impact or an appearance.

He did prove he still had the swagger and the style by rejoining Stoke in January 1984 and helping the club to a miraculous escape from relegation. The pace may have gone, but the eye for a defence-splitting pass and the calm manner in which he could run a top flight football match single-handedly remained.

ON THE occasions Hudson returned to Stamford Bridge with Stoke he copped the obligatory abuse from his one-time worshipers. It wasn't the kind of thing that bothered him, but what about his time at the club? Surely there were regrets? "I can honestly say that I put 90% of my failings down to that injury. I couldn't live up to what I had done before that and I couldn't train properly. I was always on ice and resting. I was so depressed and all because of that one silly moment at West Bromwich. I fucking hate that place."

But there is always a silver lining in any particular cloud and because of that injury and the extra training he'd put in as a "small" footballer, Doctors told Hudson after a car ran him down in 1996 that his strength had saved his life. The set-backs that he faced as a young man have made him strong and able to stand up to the slings and arrows that life can throw at you.

"When I had my accident I told myself 'This is just another struggle, a harder one, but just another struggle.' I got through and came out of the intensive care unit when others wouldn't. You have to dig down deep and find strength from somewhere and I think it's because of all the blows I took in my life and that includes that bloody ankle injury."

Despite an admirable outlook, that step into a hole at the Hawthorns rankles like never before. "That fucking hole. The Beatles song, *A Day in a Life* where they mention 'four thousand holes in Blackburn'. That always makes me laugh. Whenever I hear that song I think of my version. 'One fucking hole in the Midlands.'"

There will be fans who share his frustration. Here was a young man who should have done just about anything he wanted. It didn't work out as it could have done, but what those supporters have is the eight months in which he dazzled them with an array of talent that the whole world should have appreciated. In those months that saddled the 1960s and the 1970s, Hudson offered the perfect tonic to the ending of the "Swinging" decade.

Those are the months that we must recall and rejoice in. Those are the months that Alan Hudson had it. Big style.

RAY WILKINS

'BUTCH'

1973-1979

CHELSEA CAREER

Games	198
Goals	34
Caps	84

MAGIC MOMENT

His 30 yard chip against Hereford at the Bridge in 1977 provided an early glimpse of the class of Chelsea's young captain

Are teenage dreams so hard to beat?

"Teenage Kicks", The Undertones

FLASH photography fills the night air as the world's greatest players glide from their tinted windowed, chauffeured cars. Minders assess the scene whilst glamorous girlfriends excitedly shuffle toward the red-carpet where footballers and Hollywood regulars are side by side for an evening of congratulation.

It could be argued that an imaginary red-carpet has cascaded down the Fulham Road for decades welcoming the rich and the famous to Stamford Bridge. Tonight though, it is football in general that is attracting the stars, with gongs handed out to add to already bulging trophy-cabinets.

Autograph hunters' pens compete with television microphones for the guests' attentions. Over the years, football has been called "the beautiful game" and "the people's game." Now, through a steady process of amalgamation, it is clearly "the beautiful people's game."

This evening's inaugural FIFPro awards ceremony is no different. A world team is named, as voted for by the world's players (although Roman Abramovich may have used the evening as a recruitment drive) and celebrities gush about their love of the game and for those who play it. Chelsea Football Club, arguably the most glamorous name in world football in 2005, is of course well represented. Frank Lampard, John Terry and Claude Makelele have all made the team, and are joined for the night by team-mate and England starlet Joe Cole.

Minnie Driver, the Hollywood actress and no stranger to the tack of such occasions, stands up to dole out an award, taking time (thank God) to ignore the autocue and alters the mood completely. "I grew up supporting Chelsea," she reveals. "My hero back then was Ray Wilkins."

It's a wonderful moment. Ray Wilkins? To a generation of football fans Ray Wilkins was that balding midfield player, "The Crab", know for his incessant sideways passing, the very embodiment of the secure professional who deals only in percentages. To another, younger generation, Ray Wilkins is that nice, if slightly monotone, TV summariser, who thinks everything is "Super", or "Triffic."

They, though, would all be wrong. Ask Miss Driver. Ray Wilkins was far more than that. Ray Wilkins was a hero, a glamorous hero nonetheless; one who appealed to the burly fan on the Shed and future glamourpusses alike. From the ages of 17 to 23 Wilkins was Chelsea's great white hope. Not since Jimmy Greaves' spotty young face burst onto the scene had a player offered so much and borne the mantle of club saviour on such youthful shoulders.

INEVITABLY, like Greaves, Wilkins would have to move on to better himself and ultimately he offered only hope where there was none. But in the mid-1970s Wilkins acted as a parachute for the everyday Chelsea fan. The club was in free-fall, but his talents, his boyish good looks and his zestful leadership at least brought some good times and cushioned that descent.

Young "Butch" (a nickname he earned from his father at birth) was lorded in the local pubs as a player who might just bring back those great days of 1970 and 1971. Cool girls could take down their posters of Donny Osmond and David Cassidy and replace them with his image; blonde hair flowing onto his snug blue shirt. Yes, flowing blonde hair. Our Ray was a bit of a looker in his day; fashionable to boot. Back then Wilkins was a skilful and trendy new player, but in time Wilkins has come to mean much more to the Chelsea faithful. He represented a time, not the happiest of times, mind, but a time when a trip to the new Bridge was far from joyous, far from inspiring, but in the young captain there was a light. Whilst he was playing, their Chelsea still had that touch of class. That swagger that had made it so cool to support the Blues remained through him and seemingly him alone.

The early years of the decade had seen manageable cracks between Dave Sexton and his headstrong – or as he saw it, licentious – players turn into destructive and gaping chasms. Peter Osgood, the King of Stamford Bridge was dethroned, whilst Alan Hudson, that most stylish of mavericks, joined him through the gates. It couldn't have been easy for Sexton. These were great players, these were the men who brought a glint to the team's eye and the fans loved them; cherished them. In Hudson's case, selling him meant selling the club's playmaker and it caused a furore. Particularly as he had departed for Stoke. Stoke, for heaven's sake. Were players moving on to better themselves at Stoke? But amid the raised eyebrows, Sexton had inside knowledge of a youngster in his ranks who would soften the blow of Hudson's departure.

For so long, Chelsea had been known for giving youth its eager chance. From Greaves to Hudson, nearly two decades of Chelsea greats had been reared in-house and as Sexton looked to build a new team, he again hoped that a new crop would represent another perfect harvest. At the beginning of the 1972/73 season Steve Wicks, Ray Lewington, Gary Locke, Ian Britton, Graham Wilkins and his younger brother Raymond were all waiting in the wings; and, like the soon to be built East Stand, represented a hopefully golden new dawn for the club.

IT DIDN'T quite work out. As good as those kids were and as modern as the new stand looked, both failed to ignite the club into the class-A categories that the ambitious board had dreamt they might. Be you a moneyman or a hungry fan, these were frustrating times. Did Ray Wilkins do enough to replace the likes of Hudson? To many he alone could never replace that era when Blue truly was the colour. "I don't think he was half the player Huddy was, but that's only my opinion," says Ron Harris. "I think Ray was very lucky to do what he done. 90 games for England, that's a lot."

Harsh? Perhaps, but some fans shared Harris' pessimism not for Wilkins per se, but for the era that had gone from silver to grey very quickly indeed. Fans, though, could see in Wilkins that glimmer of glories past; in him they could dare to fantasize about a brighter future. It wouldn't work out, club and player wouldn't last together, but ask those fans who stood on the Shed or sat in the new East Stand in the mid-to-late 1970s and they will tell you, Ray Wilkins dared them to dream.

We saw it in flashes later in his career when he earned wider exposure for Manchester United and England. Who can forget his scything dash downfield and curling shot into the top corner of the net to put Manchester United 2-1 ahead in the 1983 FA Cup Final against Brighton. It wasn't a crab-like Ray Wilkins who dinked the ball over a Belgian defence rushing out to catch England offside and then volleyed in a spectacular opening goal in the 1980 European Championships either. To many he is more familiar as the holding midfielder, but in his time he could turn it on too.

The son of a decent footballer (his father represented the Army alongside Tom Finney and went on to play for Brentford, Bradford Park Avenue, Leeds United, Nottingham Forest and Hearts), Wilkins made his debut as a substitute in a 3-0 win over Norwich City at Stamford Bridge in October 1973, only a month after his 17th birthday. The team was littered by those men who had made Chelsea great and so for Wilkins, who, at the time, was still cleaning their boots this was the start of something wonderful. He made his full debut later in the season in a win over Spurs at White Hart Lane and from there the fans were hooked on following the progress of this prodigious talent.

It was daunting for Wilkins, though, in those early days. Hudson may have gone, but that only left one midfield berth for which he would have to compete with John Hollins, Charlie Cooke (although soon on his way to Palace), and Peter Houseman. The great thing about Chelsea, though, was that if you were good enough it mattered little about the novelty of your birth certificate. "You get opportunities in life and its how you take them," Wilkins said in Rick Glanvill's book *Rhapsody in Blue: The Chelsea Dream Team*. "I was very fortunate that there were certain people at Chelsea at the time, Dave [Sexton] included, who felt it fit that I should get a game."

BUT SEXTON'S reign was over. The man who had brought the FA Cup as well as European success to the club was sacked in October 1974 as the Board panicked, thinking that events on the pitch weren't going in the direction required to match what they thought they were achieving off of it. By then Wilkins had gone from lively young substitute to integral playmaker, pulling the strings of the team and the heartstrings of young, hopeful fans.

Ron Suart, a well-liked coach took over, but relegation – a filthy word that would have been laughed at down the Kings Road bars frequented by Messrs Osgood, Hudson and Bonetti – was a real and all too concerning possibility. The 1974/75 season had begun with optimism with the opening of the new and improved East Stand. There was much to look forward to as fans filled its vast space. This was a stand for the future; a future that would see the club develop into one of the country's finest. Then the game started, newly promoted Carlisle won 2-0 and the season had its precedent firmly set.

A 5-0 defeat at Newcastle was followed in December by a 3-0 reverse at home to Queens' Park Rangers before a 7-1 hammering at Wolves in March had fans wondering just where it had all gone wrong. Ron Stuart was moved upstairs and his coach, one Eddie McCreadie, the tough-tackling and much-adored Scot, went to his Chairman and asked for the job. Brian Mears felt it the right move, it was a decision that was to prove vital for Wilkins' development.

DESPITE Chelsea's on-field problems, that development looked as though it would need only the finest of fine-tuning. In May 1975, while fans pondered their club's fate as they battled to stave off relegation, Wilkins captained the England under-18 team to a Mini World Cup victory in Switzerland. England beat their Finnish counterparts in the final with a team that included future luminaries Glenn Hoddle, Peter Barnes and Alan Curbishley, as well as Chelsea starlets Steve Wicks, Tommy Langley and John Sparrow. Wilkins, though, stood out, his leadership qualities and maturity belying those tender years.

A vital 2-0 defeat at White Hart Lane at the end of the season effectively condemned the club to the ignominious depths of Division Two (Spurs finished just one point and two places higher than Chelsea), but that possibility had been on the cards for weeks. Now McCreadie could take stock of his squad and hoped the fans would stay with him. The night before that game at Spurs, McCreadie approached Wilkins and informed him that he wanted him to be the club's new captain. Peter Bonetti had reclaimed his green jersey from Welsh international John Phillips, John Hollins was still there, as was Ron Harris, and record money had been paid for Celtic's David Hay, but McCreadie wanted to build a new team and take the club away from the imposing shadow of its glorious past. Wilkins was fresh, he was new, the fans loved him and the players respected him. He was perfect.

"The senior players couldn't have been more supportive," said Wilkins recently. "I did worry a bit initially, but I knew them all as people, not just as footballers, and they gave me an enormous amount of assistance. There were times when I didn't feel quite up to the job, but Eddie McCreadie had the utmost confidence in me, so I just went for it. I went through good periods and not such good periods, when you lose your form and you couldn't get it back, but those older players were always there for me." Harris, Bonetti, Hollins; they got on with playing with and aiding their new skipper. They were there for him as they had always been there for the club and tried to do for McCreadie now what they had all done together for Tommy Docherty in 1963; get Chelsea straight back into the First Division.

IT WASN'T going to be easy. Those fans who wondered about this new young side and its new young captain were patrons of a troubled football club. Relegation was one thing, but now very real financial problems were circling the Bridge like beady-eyed vultures. The club found itself £3.4 million in debt and attendances had slumped (the chairman, Brian Mears, later wistfully concluded that if they had played hold-music on the phones at Stamford Bridge, "It would have been Dire Straits").

In 1972, the year's attendances had been 815,000 at the Bridge; in 1976 it was down to 399,000 – a drop of over 50%. The reasons were twofold. The club's capitulation from trophy winners to Second Division also-rans kept locals and glory hunters away in equal proportion, whilst the widely reported threat of trouble in SW6 had away fans thinking twice about their visit. It was a dour time. Former top dogs Chelsea finished a nowhereland 11th in the Second Division in 1975/76 and those who made the trip to shout on the team found themselves with very little to get excited about. After all who *could* get excited about a dreary goalless draw against York, when just up the road QPR were making a serious attempt to wrest the League title from Liverpool's grasp with flowing football and silky skills à la Chelsea of old?

Except Ray Wilkins gave them something to get excited about; the skipper, the gifted-one, the player who ran onto the pitch looking like he was born to wear the famous blue jersey. A throwback to Osgood, Hudson and Cooke. He lifted the spirits. Like a post-match pint he had it in him to numb the pain. In 1975/76 Wilkins was an ever present and finished top-scorer with 12 goals.

He was the club's heartbeat – make that pacemaker – for this was a heart in need of a good deal of assistance. McCreadie had Wilkins playing in "the hole" off the front-runners, Teddy Maybank and Bill Garner, dictating the attacking impulses of the side and getting into the box as often and as menacingly as possible. It was hardly the role of a player who would later in his career earn his nickname of "The Crab" for his tendency to move the ball sideways, but Chelsea's Ray Wilkins was a very different animal. Here, he tickled opposing defences, probing at their weak spots, trying to open them up and invariably succeeding. To fans, especially the younger breed, he was a fresh-faced demigod, one that would cast away the darkness and let there be light.

Admiration for his form had filtered through to nearby Lancaster Gate and an England debut was inevitable. In May 1976, the national team played in a tournament in the United States and Wilkins got his chance in a memorable 3-2 win over Italy. Still only 18 and the club's youngest ever captain, Wilkins proved he was more than just an inspiration on the pitch. After returning from that stateside sojourn, the teenage England international was brought along by chairman Mears to talk to inpatient creditors. Ron Harris, Dave Hay and Garry Stanley were also present, but no-one put Chelsea's case forward as well as the captain. He remembered names, spoke succinctly in the manner he does on TV now whilst summarising games and set Mears up for the club's most important speech since Fred Parker in 1905 put forward the fledgling team's attributes to the Football League. Like Parker, Mears was successful and managed to buy the club time, space and a future.

McCreadie used the breathing space well. He knew that his young team, if it was going to prosper, needed to add an edge to their game. "After the first year I talked about how I'd like the players to be a bit more aggressive," he said. "They weren't brought up at a Fourth Division team to kick the ball half the field. All these kids were brought up to play the game, to pass the ball – the most important thing in the game – and to do it with quality. And in the Second Division they came up against a little bit of the hard, physical side of the game. And it hurt. So we talked about it and I told them, 'You're going to have to kick a bit of ass here.'"

With his old pal from schoolboy football, Ray Lewington, adding that steel alongside him in central midfield, Wilkins and Chelsea first found their feet in the Division and then began to run. McCreadie, an incredibly popular manager as he sat in the dug-out dressed like a Vegas pimp, created a team worthy of his and the club's past. The youngsters brought a sense of style and, as rumours spread of this resurgence, fans began to fill the ground again to see for themselves if the tales were true. Were Chelsea back?

IT SEEMED they were. Wilkins, revelling in his free role, started the season in imperious fashion. He left the everyday grind of midfield play to his comrades and got on with creating and scoring, a world away from the holding role first envisaged for him by Dave Sexton. Again Wilkins was an ever-present and again got himself amongst the goals, this time netting nine times and winning himself the crown of London Footballer of the Year along the way.

The exuberance of youth lifted the gloom over Stamford Bridge. The team was wiping the floor with the opposition and playing with a smile on its face that was easily imitated in the stands. Back-heels (Wilkins beautifully did so to lay on a goal for Jock Finnieston against Oldham), flicks and goals pulled in heaving crowds who created a deafening noise. 55,000 crammed into the Bridge to watch a 2-0 Boxing Day derby victory over Fulham, Hereford were beaten 5-1 in a game that included a sublime Wilkins chip from 30 yards still regarded by many as his finest Chelsea goal, whilst over 42,000 turned up to see the league game against Southampton, the FA Cup holders, which Chelsea won 3-1.

That day, Wilkins set up two (once more Finnieston was the lucky recipient) and scored one in a game that Mike Langley of the *Daily Mirror*, not the easiest man to please, gushed that "Butch Wilkins did everything for Chelsea except sell programmes and pump up the match ball."

Promotion was secured with a 1-1 draw at Wolves and celebrated vivaciously with a last fixture of the season at home to Hull City. It was a jubilant day, unexpected in light of the previous two seasons, but now Eddie McCreadie's young guns, marshalled by Wilkins, had once more given the fans something to shout about.

And how they shouted. 44,000 turned up at the Bridge. The good times were truly back. Chelsea waltzed to a 4-0 victory on a day when the fans could wave goodbye to the Second Division and say "Hello" to what they hoped was a bright future. Wilkins himself was supremely confident, his career was ahead of him and his team were turning it on. "We're going to shock a few people next season," he crowed. "We're not going up to the First Division to survive. We're going to attack. Chelsea will help make football tick again."

IT WAS 1977; the Queen celebrated her silver jubilee whilst the youth of the day were working themselves into a punk-fuelled frenzy. The King, Elvis Presley, had died and it was time to look forward to new beginnings. A rebirth of popular culture. Like today, football was in need of a shot in the arm. Liverpool Football Club did their bit weeks later, winning the European Cup, whilst Chelsea were hoping that their comeback would be as sleek and well received as Elvis' 1968 version. Their team had that same well-oiled look about it. Like Elvis, they were aware of a glorious past, but had a twinkling eye on the reinvented present and a new future. Would it work?

As seemingly ever, a new dawn at Chelsea was greeted with cloudy skies and tempered moods. Again like Elvis' comeback, Chelsea's version was short-lived. The world had changed and just as new, fresh punk bands abounded, playing energetic, vivacious music, Chelsea discovered that, despite their return to the big time, they had been usurped from their crown of kings of glamour.

It didn't help that the club's alarming propensity to shoot itself in the foot reared its ugly head once again. Eddie McCreadie, the manager who had brought the glitz back to the old place, found himself preparing for the new season whilst locked in contractual disputes with the club that would eventually see him resign and make a new life for himself in the United States. "I will not let this club go to the wall," he had said on taking the job and true to his word, he had turned the place around, but now the club that he had played for, coached and managed had let him go. Bloody typical.

McCreadie was reported to have asked for a ten year contract, one that could not be met and so once more the managerial turnstile at Stamford Bridge click, click, clicked. This time Ken Shellito, another former player and now the youth team manager who had nurtured much of the first team into the talents which had won promotion, stepped into the breach just as the season beckoned. The fans might have been concerned, but McCreadie's departure didn't stop the huge wave of optimism which had enveloped the club since their return to the top flight.

THE CLUB'S merchandise was flying off the shelves, sales bettered only by Liverpool and Manchester United. Those clubs might have Kenny Dalglish, they might have Lou Macari; but Chelsea had Ray Wilkins. He was the face of the club, the man on the teenage walls on mugs, pens and bedspreads and in adult hearts.

Sure Osgood, Hudson and Bonetti had been shining starlets, but their brilliance was surrounded by and even overtaken by the glory of the whole team. Wilkins illuminated a dull, grey period in the club's fortunes when any chink of light was magnified tenfold and grabbed by eager fans desperate for reasons to be cheerful.

Their pride in their young captain, especially over the summer of 1977 was born from his development at their club. Wilkins himself later spoke of just how much a home-grown player can connect with the everyday football fan and how vital it is that a club has that link. "I have to say I feel happy and sad in equal measure for youngsters coming into the game now," he said recently. "Happy that they have the chance to learn from some of the best players in the world and sad that we don't see many 17-year-olds playing first team football these days.

"I was lucky, I had my chance, but now it's not nearly so easy which is sad because the fans like nothing better than a home-grown player. They like their club to spend money, but, most of all, they like a youngster who has come through the ranks. They can identify with him."

That was what the fans were so desperate for. That heady team of Kings Road regulars had been and gone in a whirlwind of brilliance and troubles, so who better to take on the mantle of hope than a more sedate youngster who had learnt his trade right under their noses? Wilkins, a quiet sex-symbol and pin-up wasn't seen out in the area's basement bars, but he threatened to be as flamboyantly Chelsea on the pitch as any of his predecessors.

THE 1977/78 season under Shellito's guidance didn't offer the revival that Chelsea's Second Division performances had promised. But Wilkins continued to offer pride in his play and his leadership. By now he was a regular in the England set-up and was a school-kid's reason to hold his or her head up in the playground whilst others ranted about their own team's exploits and at the pitiful fortunes of Chelsea.

The Blues at least averted a quick return to Division Two by finishing 16th, but Nottingham Forest, a side that had come up with the Blues (finishing third, three points behind them in the Second Division the season before), won the League Championship. Brian Clough had executed his plan to perfection, whilst Shellito – a man with the best of intentions – struggled to give the fans what they so craved. In fairness he'd had little chance to prepare and had to assert his authority, tactics and style of play on a group of players who had achieved success under another man. That Chelsea survived is bordering on an historical anomaly, but early in the next season, 1978/79, Chelsea and Shellito were struggling and both were looking doomed. Come Christmas, Shellito had gone and relegation looked a certainty. The Chelsea board, showing particular eccentricity, appointed Danny Blanchflower, a wonderful player and now football journalist, but manager of Chelsea? Eyebrows were raised toward the ceiling.

The Ulsterman couldn't stop the inevitable and Wilkins, for the first time, had to deal with immense disappointment. His form had dipped toward the end of 1978, injuries had blighted his run in the team and he even found himself taking the odd Valium to ease the strain that had begun to take its toll. It didn't stop there, Wilkins' older brother Graham had also been a regular in the team, but, having scored two own-goals against Bolton, had become the butt of much of the cruel chants from a frustrated section of the crowd.

The hiccup in form was temporary of course and there was no doubt that Wilkins was Chelsea's shining light, but he was an England international now, could he remain in the lower leagues and harbour continued aspirations to play for his country? The fans who once more faced a downward spiral hoped that he would stay. If seeing a home-grown player prosper is fantastic for any fan, then seeing him blossom at another club is as painful as anything that this sometimes cruel game can throw up.

WILKINS was keen to stay. He wanted to rectify the situation. Blanchflower, though, was shrewd enough to a) realise the value of such a player to the struggling team's coffers and b) let the fans down gently by allowing them to think that here was a player who had to move on in order to better himself.

"It's bad business to sell your assets," someone remarked to the manager.

"But nobody wants to buy our liabilities," quipped Blanchflower. In the club's magazine on the eve of the 1979/80 season he told depressed fans that "Ray Wilkins wanted to leave. He 'thought he could do better' for himself somewhere else. I did not want him to believe this was true, but in my heart I knew he could be right. With smarter and more experienced players around him, it could help his game develop, but there is no way I would have thought like that if Chelsea had not been in debt. Then we could acquire the kind of players he needs around him. So by helping Ray Wilkins on his way, he will be helping us reduce that debt."

The Chelsea bank account was credited to the tune of £825,000 (a club record) when Manchester United, now under the stewardship of a certain Dave Sexton signed Wilkins from under the noses of both Everton and Ipswich. It was a massive move for Wilkins, but years later he was adamant that it was actually Blanchflower who suggested that a move was the best for all concerned.

"Danny pulled me [aside] and said that he thought it was best for everyone concerned – God bless him – and he just put it to the board that they should let me go," said Wilkins. "Obviously at the time I didn't fancy that at all. Because I was with my mates. We'd gone down, and I wanted to help them come straight back up again, like we had before. But once Manchester United came in for me, there was not much of a decision to make.

"A lot of people put two and two together, with Dave being there, that it might be Manchester United, but it was after the Cup Final, Man U versus Arsenal, that Dave came in. I was very sad to leave.

I didn't really want to leave. I love London, and I'd only just got married and we were very, very happy. And although we'd just gone down, we felt that we could get back up. Looking back, I'm pleased I didn't ask for a move, because I go back now and there's a pleasant reception. When I meet fans they ask me if I wanted to go, which is natural, typical Chelsea support, but Danny made it clear he didn't want me around, and he got loads of money at the time: £825,000 was a few bob."

All very well, but once more, in a theme as recurring as Petr Cech clean sheets, the Chelsea fans had to wave farewell to a reason for coming to football. Like Greaves almost twenty years earlier a genuine hero was off to pastures new. Supporting this club was cruel, the team wouldn't come back up, not for a while and a spell of real strife was only just around the corner.

YEARS later Wilkins would return as Gianluca Vialli's assistant, but by then to a new crop of fans he was the nice guy off the telly, slightly balding and a little bit dull. By then he'd also been through incarnations as the voice of Tango adverts, "The Crab" and as one of England's finest playing exports to Italy's Serie A. But to those who had got their teenage kicks from watching and worshiping the young Wilkins; he was the very reason they had fallen in love with football à la SW6.

Minnie Driver is not alone in thinking back and recalling Ray Wilkins controlling the game, golden locks flowing over his shoulders, waving at the crowd and looking every bit the world star. "Triffic".

MICKY DROY

1970-1985

CHELSEA CAREER

Games	313
Goals	19
Caps	0

MAGIC MOMENT

Micky's lion-hearted performance in a vital relegation battle at Bolton in 1983 saw Chelsea win, stay up and move on

'THE GREAT BEAR'

> **The ultimate measure of a man is not where he stands in moments of comfort and convenience, but where he stands at times of challenge and controversy**
>
> **Martin Luther King**

BY the early to mid-1980s young fans on The Shed had a new look about them. "Wedge" haircuts sat proudly above a wide range of European sports brands. Lacoste or Sergio Tacchini jumpers were worn over faded jeans or jumbo cords, and Nike or Adidas trainers were a must as the terraces were now places on which it was essential that you looked cool. The English game back then was awash with foreign labels rather than foreign players, as style became the name of the game. And the right labels got you the right kudos and that was vital. The Soccer "Casual" had arrived, a new youth sub-culture that was prevalent at grounds around the country. Paulo Hewitt, biographer of those leaders in all things youth and cultural Paul Weller and Oasis and a former NME journalist to boot, called the Casuals, "One of the biggest working-class youth-cults ever".

For those in their number who stood on The Shed their clothes were offering more colour than the club they came to support. Things hadn't been going well since Dave Sexton's team had disbanded in the early 1970s; Hudson, Osgood and Cooke had long since gone and now, amid continuing financial plight and on-field disillusion, times were tough. The club's captain – who as a player was as far away from flash continental fashion houses as you can be – was Micky Droy. His beard and his brawn stood him out from the crowd; and certainly from the archetypal Chelsea hero who had preceded him. But by the 1980s Droy was an institution at Chelsea; he had been there for over ten years, week in and week out heading, defending, putting his body on the line, rippling muscle and sinew and risking life and limb for the fans. He was more Army and Navy than Burberry, but as a fan you couldn't help but adore him.

Those fans still have a soft spot for Droy. He was a big, bad defender who gave his all for their cause. In a sense, Droy became a mythical creature. One can't help but describe him in those terms. Think of the Minotaur, the creature from Greek mythology, a giant of a man with a Bull's head and you are almost there. Like the Minotaur, Droy was, as captain, handed the task of guarding the labyrinth that Stamford Bridge had inadvertently become. Fans' dreams had been lost for years in the gloom of the place, but the sight of Micky Droy guarding their penalty box filled their hearts with the knowledge that at least their side would battle and put up a fight for the cause, giving his all, no matter what the cost to himself, or his opponents. And because of that the fans bestowed possibly the greatest complement a Chelsea footballer can have by chanting the same song in praise of Droy's thunderously stout tackling as had accompanied "Chopper" Harris' reign of terror; "Micky's gonna get ya, Micky's gonna get ya" reverberated around the Bridge, scaring the pants of more than one suspect opponent.

Was Droy really that hard? Where did myth end and reality begin? "When I was playing at Wrexham," laughs Joey Jones, "I saw him stamp on somebody's face." Droy was tough, not necessarily dirty, but he'd do what it took to prevail. That was the way of the bone-rattling, rough-house 1970s when Droy grew up into this mountain of a man. Mention his name today to one of his then admirers, who now wallow in the club's riches and success, and you'll find a smile radiates across their face. As they recall Droy in his pomp, throwing himself bodily into challenge after challenge.

THAT POMP began in 1970, that most special year in the life of Chelsea Football Club. The FA Cup was won and Micky Droy brought his 6 foot 6 inch frame through the gates at Stamford Bridge. He would stay for fourteen seasons; fourteen of the most chaotic, up and down years in the club's history. New teams, new managers, new stands brought age-old problems, but there was Droy; a mainstay through it all, his bulging frame the only constant in a turbulent time.

Tim Lovejoy, Chelsea fan and presenter of Sky's *Soccer AM* was a young man on the West Stand's Members' Benches back then and recalls Droy fondly. "That was right at the beginning when I started watching Chelsea, " he says. "I just remember Micky being the most solid defender. He was like a rock. What I remember was him just heading the ball, a lot, and he wouldn't have to leave the ground. These days defenders try and bring the ball down on their chests and try and take it, but Micky just headed it back from where it came. He would stand there, his legs rooted to the ground and just whack it with his head back up the ground. He was a hero back in the day. As a fan you demand the old 110% effort from your heroes. That is the important thing and that's what Micky gave you."

MICKY DROY hails from Islington, the borough north east of the Bridge that houses the nemesis that is Arsenal FC. Droy was a fan of the Gunners, he played for the district and as a youngster he trained with the Highbury club, but it didn't work out. "I actually packed up football for a little while after that and then a mate of mine asked me to play on a Sunday team," he tells me. "That led to some amateur football and from there I started playing for Slough."

Droy talks to me from his Islington home and sounds under the weather. He has a heavy cold, but you just know he's going to beat it. "The guy who was the manager at Slough, Tommy Lawrence, was quite friendly with Dave Sexton. We played Chelsea in a friendly and they must have seen something in me they liked and they asked me to sign. At first I said "No". I was happy with what I was doing. I enjoyed my football at Slough and I was working down the Caledonian Road for a big American tiling company called Armstrong's. I was getting paid for doing both and so I felt it was a risk to give all that up and turn pro. What if it didn't work out?

"So, I turned them down and carried on. Three months later I played for a representative side against the Army. Chelsea were there and this time made me a much better offer. It was tempting. I had a word with my old man and he said I should go to see the bloke at my work and ask that if it doesn't work out with Chelsea could I have my old job back. Well, the fella was as good as gold. I was 19. If he had said "No", I wouldn't have left and come to Chelsea." A generation of football fans weaned on watching the leviathan antics of Droy can therefore thank a manager in a tiling company on the Caledonian Road.

Chelsea was a hotbed for style and for glam. Droy was a giant of a young man, coming from non-league to the big-league where top players and internationals resided with that nonchalant swagger that all had become so accustomed to. Hardly his scene, so it was bound to be tough. After a few training sessions with his new colleagues, a couple of them (Peter Bonetti and Peter Osgood) only just home from playing in that summer's World Cup in Mexico, initially had their doubts about the new boy. He was massive, but could he play? "Micky looked the worst footballer I've ever seen," laughs Ron Harris today. "He wasn't the most cultured player, but then again nor was I and what he did over the years was he worked at his game, played with good pros and turned out to be one of the best findings for the team and for the club as a whole."

Droy himself admits he isn't one to be fazed by much. You just have to look at him to see that is probably very true and he settled into the Bridge, undaunted by the murmurings about his abilities.

"There were a load of internationals there in 1970 and they had just won the Cup, but they were really nice guys. Friendly, helped me settle, they were as good as gold."

DROY spent the first half of the 1970/71 season inconspicuously – or as inconspicuously as a 6 foot 6 inch hulk can – settling into his new surroundings. Fans knew little of him before February 1971 when he made his debut in a league match at Wolves. For those supporters Dave Webb, John Dempsey and, of course, Ron Harris were their giants at the back, each a terrier-like defender protecting the goal as doggedly as if guarding a juicy bone.

Droy ran out at Molineux for an unremarkable match, but he was in and whilst those travelling fans wouldn't have rushed down the M1 to tell their pals about a new phenomenon in their rearguard, he hadn't disgraced himself. "I don't have many memories of my career, but I have been reminded enough times that my debut was against Wolves," he says. "We got beat 1-0, I remember that. Things don't faze me generally, but I had only played eight or nine reserve games. I was used to a couple of hundred people, suddenly I'm running out in front of 30-40,000. I was nervous, but you are playing with good players and if you're good enough you'll soon find out."

Dave Sexton clearly had faith in the young man. He wasn't to become a regular just yet, but when it mattered and when it was a necessity, he answered the call. Before the 1971 European Cup Winners' Cup semi-final against the holders Manchester City, Chelsea had an injury crisis. Eddie McCreadie was among the wounded and so Droy stepped in for the first leg at Stamford Bridge, playing alongside John Dempsey in the heart of the defence. It was a tense occasion, one that the home side won 1-0 to set themselves up for a place in the final in Athens against Real Madrid. "I hadn't been in the pro game long and so strangely didn't realise how important it all was. We had some injuries and we won. It was great to be involved," says Droy.

He travelled to the Greek capital, but Droy wouldn't make the substitute bench. His time had come just too late for European glory, but he recalls the trip vividly. "We drew the first game and everyone thought we would be coming home and the replay would be played the next week," he says. "That's what we had been told, so we all went out on the piss that night, and then the next day we were informed that we would have to stay and were playing the game the following night. Some would have gone out even if they had known, mind, but not all of us."

The trophy was of course, joyously won. Chelsea returned home to another heroes' reception, but that was as good as it was going to get for a long time. Sexton broke up his mischievous but brilliant team and would himself soon be asked to leave as the club's board switched on a conveyor belt that would bring manager after manager and problem after problem.

DROY by now had broken into the first team, grabbing a starting spot by the scruff of the neck and hung on to it with grim determination for over a decade, fighting off all comers to keep his place. He managed 30 starts in the 1973-74 season, Sexton's last, and his no-nonsense style of play, whilst poles apart from what some fans were accustomed to cheering on, was at least appreciated by stunned supporters, struggling to come to terms with the departure of the club's glitterati.

The success that Sexton's tenure had brought had excited Chelsea's fans and directors alike. The board, under the guidance of Chairman Brian Mears, decided to rebuild his great-grandfather's ageing stadium, built back in 1905 by Archibald Leitch to house champions, into a modern ground that would suit what they saw as one of Europe's biggest clubs with massive, capacious stands to hold the legions of new Chelsea fans. It was a risk and it would badly backfire.

The first stage of the redevelopment, the enormous East Stand, opened amid great press furore for the start of the 1974/75 season. But far from heralding a new dawn of ever-growing crowds, ever better players and ever more trophies, it was to prove a nightmare which would almost bring the club to its knees. Under Sexton's replacement, temporary manager, Ron Suart, the club suffered some disastrous results and were relegated. Unthinkable. Somebody hadn't read the script that Mears and his colleagues firmly believed should have involved Hollywood glitz and glamour.

In 1905 Mears' great-grandfather Gus had gazed around his brand, sparkling new football club and sighed. "Well, that's that," he said looking at his huge bowl of a stadium. "Now for the struggle. I suppose the first five years will be the worst." He was wrong. Having been relegated in 1975, the club would have to endure the toughest eight years of its history. They would almost go broke and they would almost sink down into the Third Division. Fans would desert, but just enough would stay. Micky Droy just stayed and it was his efforts that warmed many a chilly season.

"I had become a regular then and I liked playing there," says Droy in typically forthright fashion. "I liked Dave [Sexton], and I liked the club, it was very nice. Then Dave went, but I didn't know much about the politics behind the scenes. The money, the new stand. A lot of players left because it was obvious that we couldn't afford other players and so we lost some good men. To be fair, you can understand. It was a difficult time.

"It was all about what was happening behind the scenes. The Mears family and all that mob, no fucking idea at all them lot. They got all these big ideas about building stands, but never realised the implications of it all. It's all well and good spending all that money on things like stands, but what about the team? It's the team that people come and see, not some new high-rise structure. They were all too busy sitting up in their board room eating cheese sandwiches and having a cup of tea."

As stars left and kids replaced them, the new East Stand was hardly brimming full with either fans or confidence. "After Sexton had gone and many of the players from his great team, they decided to bring in a load of kids. The thing is, you can do that with a couple of them. That's OK, but you can't bring in six or seven kids to play. It ain't going to work, but we had no money, so what are you going to do? You have to play somebody. If you can't afford to sign someone then you'll have to play a youngster. It was difficult and the crowd got the needle and so times were rough."

THE EMERGENCE of Eddie McCreadie as manager in 1975 lightened the mood somewhat. He built a team that, whilst short in experience, at least attempted to strut like the sides that McCreadie himself had starred in, albeit it in Division Two. A new away kit had the crowd chanting "Eddie McCreadie's red and white army", but as I say it was a strange time. There was a brief bubble of hope as Ray Wilkins and Jock Finnieston had fans wondering and hoping and promotion was skilfully won in 1977. Micky Droy missed much of that campaign due to injury and illness, but by now he had become a popular figure on the terraces. Albeit almost by default. "I think some fans looked at me and thought, well, I could have left when others went, but I didn't," he says. "I had offers to move elsewhere, but it's not like today, you can't just bugger off. If I had put my foot down I could have got a move, but I didn't because I liked playing at Chelsea. The fans understood that and I think that's why they were on my side. They knew I was loyal."

Clive Batty, Chelsea fan and author of *Kings of the Kings Road* was a regular at the Bridge back then and agrees that the supporters understood that here was a man unwilling to jump ship, however sinking the feeling might be. "Micky was very loyal to Chelsea, later in his career especially, when he was in the reserves. He turned down moves to other teams, partly because he and his family were settled in London, but also because of his genuine affinity for the Blues – and that was despite being an Arsenal fan."

As well as that loyalty, Droy's game was itself a reason to hold him dear. When the new East Stand was opened his was the only clearance that would ever send the ball spiralling right up to its vertigo-enticing top tier. "I saw that happen a few times and it always got a big cheer!" laughs Batty. Now we're talking. Now fans had a positive amongst all the doom, gloom and despondency. Something to cheer. What that something is always proves to be a good marker for the team's fortunes; and when you're cheering your own team's clearances into the upper deck, no matter how ironically, you know you are in fairly desperate straits.

First Division football returned, much to the relief of the club's under-fire owners, but the same old fractious problems occured and it would be a new manager who took over the reins as McCreadie walked out after contractual disputes and Ken Shellito took over. His tenure lasted a mere season and a half. Chelsea's 16th place finish in 1977/78 hardly had the big boys quaking in their Golas, but Droy was at his immense best and won the fans' vote as that season's Player of the Year.

AS HE gave his all on the field of play, Droy, made captain at Stamford Bridge by Shellito in Wilkins' stead, was adamant that he would do the same off of it. He of course gladly went along to the Supporters' Club to pick up his award and was no stranger to such events. To him it was a duty and a pleasure. "I would go to all the functions and meet the fans," he says proudly. "We would go along to a lot of stuff. I would make sure of that. I was in charge of the players and I would try and do it in blocks. If something came up four or five would go and then another four or five to the next thing. The fans are the important people, they are the ones who come in and pay all the money, but too many players think 'Oh, fuck that, I can't be bothered to attend or I can't be bothered to sign autographs'. I never allowed that, not when I was club captain." You had to love him.

The 1978/79 season lurched from crisis to full-blown maelstrom. Droy picked up an injury which kept him out of the side for long spells. Without him the side literally caved in. There was no spine as Chelsea wilted at Middlesbrough 7-2, nor any spunk as the Blues stumbled to a 6-0 thrashing at Nottingham Forest. When Shellito left half-way through the campaign there was confusion as to who would be there next. Peter Osgood recalls the dressing-room when Frank Upton, a coach at the club and ex-player, was appointed manager, albeit for a whole day. "Frank walked in to us and without a hint of irony said, my name is no longer Frank, it's Boss. He was deadly serious and we're all thinking "Bloody hell".

"Overnight they then installed Danny Blanchflower and Frank is no longer the manager. We're all in for training the next day and Upton's walked in looking furious. As he came in I went, 'Morning, Frank.' We were all pissing ourselves."

Relegation duly ensued, followed by a couple of years of mid-table stagnation in Division Two. The board turned to a World Cup winner, giving Geoff Hurst the hot-seat, but that didn't work, although Droy, now fully fit again did his utmost to claw the club and its fans from the gloom. His tireless efforts to at least put some fight back into the side lifted his legend from that of a good, solid hard-working pro to that of the actual backbone of the side. Without him Chelsea would bend in the wind as teams ran at (and generally past and through) them. On top of that Droy was instrumental in the two occasions at Stamford Bridge in that period that brought a skip back into the step of the Fulham Road faithful.

In 1978 Liverpool, newly crowned European Champions, came to the Bridge in the FA Cup. In 1982, they did exactly the same thing and both times were sent packing; 4-2 and 2-0 respectively.

They were incredible afternoons, unexpected and unforgettable. John Moynihan, the *Sunday Telegraph* correspondent attending the 1982 match declared Droy, "A commanding, Trojan figure in defence" who alongside 17-year-old keeper Steve Francis "inspired their colleagues in the face of the red menace."

"We had a funny hoodoo over them. I don't know why." recalls Droy, although he then went on to reveal to me precisely why. "I think maybe it was because on both occasions we had very quick youngsters and the Liverpool boys didn't like it. Mind you, they had some class. Kenny Dalglish was something else and I remember having to whack him a good few times. You had to do something to slow him down. He was bloody slippery, Kenny."

No wonder the fans sang his name. Droy had become the figure that Chelsea fans turned to, looked for to get their team going and intimidate that pesky opposition into submission. His herculean feats of tackling, oak-hewn torso and no little ability in keeping the likes of Dalglish quiet, soon led to the propogation of urban myths that he could bend metal bars and ate small children for breakfast. But they were only rumours.

Close your eyes and think of Droy and you can see his beard towering over a forward like a great grizzly bear standing its on two hind legs ready to grapple its victim to death. Then his head wins the ball at the top of a surely impossible leap for such a big man, clearing the danger, whilst simultaneously clearing the air from the poor ball with a thud and a whoosh. Think of him throwing his torso bodily in front of an onrushing forward. Forget the ball. It was vital he stopped the man. Proper "None shall pass" stuff. In 2000 a questionnaire on *The Sun's* website jokingly mocked Droy and how the everyday fan perceives his ilk:

MICKY DROY

BORN: In a cross-fire hurricane

HONOURS: Division Two title winner. Three A-levels from the School of Hard Knocks and BA (Hons) from the University of Life

FAVOURITE MEAL: Razor blades and iron filings

WAGES: Hard-earned few bob a week

HOBBIES: Looking dead hard

HAIR: Loads

BUILD: Brick shithouse

So Micky Droy didn't eat small children for breakfast. Just razor blades. Now we know.

The point being that in the land of the Cult Hero that's how we fans remember him and talk about him. As if hewn rather than born. Not of mortal being. With his ragged beard making him even more menacing than his mighty reputation.

But there was a little more to Droy than just putting his head, body and feet in where it hurts. He at times would surprise and thrill with a turn of pace or a lazy dribble. Clive Batty is no doubt that he was a far better footballer than he is given credit for. "He could be surprisingly deft on the ground," recalls Batty. "Either sending long passes forwards with his favourite left foot or occasionally embarking on earth-trembling runs along the left wing, opposition players bouncing off him as he trundled up the pitch.

"When we were losing (i.e. often) he would go up front for the last ten minutes or so playing as an auxiliary centre forward. It was a tactic that was guaranteed to cause confusion in the opposition defence as he would normally attract the attention of at least two defenders, leaving other Chelsea players unmarked."

IN 1982, a certain Ken Bates arrived at the club, purchasing it for £1 and attempting to turn around the fortunes of a place that had become so downtrodden. By then John Neal was the manager, a step away from the in-house and seemingly spontaneous appointments and a step, at last, in the right direction. Colin Lee, then the club's star centre-forward recalls the time and crowd. "Of course it was a different type of crowd, a terrace crowd," he says. "The atmosphere was good, but open, not like the surround sound that greets the players when they walk out of the tunnel today. The Shed End was famous and, at the other end of the ground, was what amounted to a little stand on stilts."

Financially, things began to improve, but on the pitch years of cash depravation had taken their toll and the 1982/83 season saw the club skid toward further relegation peril and possible extinction. It was out of control and veering toward disaster. The penultimate game of that sorry season was at Bolton, a club also struggling, but defeat for Chelsea would mean certain relegation to the depths of Division Three and so the match took on a momentous feel and, arguably, with hindsight, was a more important occasion than even Old Trafford 1970 or Athens 1971.

"It was so important," says Droy, as pragmatic as ever. "I had a chat with John Neal about it beforehand. I liked John very much – didn't like his assistant Ian McNeil much – but I liked John. He was a very clever manager. We sat down and he said to me 'What do you think about this game?' I said we should try and nick it, score a goal and then defend it out. He wasn't going to play Clive Walker at the time, but I said that if anyone would nick that goal it would be Clive.

"It was obvious we would be under pressure, but Clive could hurt them on the break. We were away from home, it was going to be hard and the bottom line was if it went wrong then this place was virtually finished." 4,000 Chelsea fans travelled to England's North-West outnumbering and out-singing the home side. Their very presence on Burnden Park's terraces underlined to everyone what was at stake. This was a giant club, with giant support. Surely it couldn't go down?

It was going to take giant men, but in Droy they didn't come much bigger. He was right. Walker was the key and it was the tricky winger's goal that won a game in which Droy defended like Hercules, Atlas and Giant Haystacks all rolled into one, driving his withered team on to survival. At the whistle, there was pandemonium. The supporters met the result with the hysteria of success and the players applauded that and a selection of them threw their shirts to the crazed support. "They were fantastic," recalled Gary Chivers, Chelsea's young striker. "They'd been cheering throughout the game and so I ran over with Mike Fillery and Clive, took our shirts off and threw them into the crowd as a show of thanks.

"When we got back to the dressing-room the manager, John Neal, asked us where our shirts were. We said we'd chucked them to the fans and thought no more about it, until we found the cost of a shirt had been deducted from our wages. Can you believe it? What a difference between then and now."

With that result came huge relief and a reprieve that the club would, at last, build upon. For the rest of the footballing community, however, there was a sense of disappointment for, if they had lost at

Bolton it would have been a case of good riddance; after all Chelsea had got itself a reputation. Its fans had been branded as hooligans.

IT IS easy to make simple associations between players on the pitch like Droy, whose masculine and thunderously committed approach bordered on the violent, with the events which dogged the club off it. There was much violence in and around stadiums wherever Chelsea played in the 1970s and 80s. Their fans weren't the only culprits, though, and it takes two to tango, but often players or referees are blamed for something which happens on the pitch sparking terrace warfare. Not so Micky Droy. He may have kicked the odd player, earned a few bookings and drawn the occasional spot of blood from an opponent, but that was all in the name of Sport, in the name of winning, or at least of not losing. Those supporters who actually believed that he was one of them had lost sight of the line which is drawn between the theatre of combat which is sport, and in particular football, and the reality of a pitch battle in the dark streets surrounding a dingy away ground in the depths of winter. Micky had nothing and wanted nothing to do with the seething hate which bubbled around the Bridge during those dark years.

To the tune of Bob Dylan's *The Mighty Quinn*, the Shed would blurt out:

You come in on your feet
You go out on your head
You ain't seen nothin' like the Mighty Shed.

However unfair Chelsea fans' reputation for actual violence may or may not have been, there was a sense that hooliganism and right wing association was prevalent on the club's terraces and it was getting out of control. Droy, contrary to what you might think for such a hard-nosed player, despaired at this ugly minority.

"There was two or three hundred who were nutters and they would be ignored by the thousands of real fans," says Droy. "The weird thing was that these guys causing trouble weren't young kids, they were grown men, a lot of them whose idea of a good Saturday was to go to football, not give a toss about the team, just as long as they had a good fight. They masqueraded as Chelsea fans, but they weren't. There was this fella, Mick Greenaway, who was the head guy and made out he was a big Chelsea fan, but I thought he was a twat. He was in his forties, he went on about how he travelled all over the country for Chelsea, but really I found him to be an idiot just looking for trouble. He might have been a fan, but he was some sort of little leader. It's easy to say I travel to watch my team, but why was it he was always getting the team into trouble? To me that is not being a supporter. They talk crap and you just get fed up with it."

FROM THE gloom, John Neal literally bought a new team, although not in the same way as the Mears brothers or Roman Abramovich, and created excitement where there had only been despair. Droy was a huge fan of Neal as a man and a manager. "I knew nothing about any of the players he brought, but John was a clever man who had been all over the place. He had spies working everywhere and looking at new talent and that summer it didn't half work."

Neal's new team excelled with Nevin, Dixon, Speedie et al writing a new chapter in the club's history. For 32-year-old Droy, who remained as club captain, while Colin Pates took over as team captain, it meant his days were numbered. This new team required different attributes. More emphasis on skill and passing, although with Graham Roberts as Droy's worthy strongarm successor, there was still penty of the rough stuff to feast your eyes upon at the Bridge. Perhaps time had moved on and rendered this most physical of defenders redundant. Irrespective of that, the manner of Droy's departure still saddens him. "It was hard, but it was all down to Ken Bates," says Droy doggedly. "He liked people that would do what they were told. I was in charge of the players and so he thought he could come to me and tell me what to do, dictate to me what he felt had to happen. I said 'You can't do that'. He would come to me and say 'This year these are the bonuses, this is this, this is that, now you go and tell your players that this is how it is'."

"I remember I'd go to him and say, 'I ain't doing that, that's wrong.'

'I'm telling you to do it, so do it,' he said.

'I don't give a fuck what you're telling me.' He thought he could tell you what to do and like a little schoolboy you would go and do it. I had to tell him that players were contracted and however much he thought he could do to players, he couldn't. We fell out, I found myself out of the side, in the reserves and all due to this schoolboy stuff with the Chairman.

"A few clubs came in for me. I could have gone to West Ham, Norwich, loads of clubs. He wouldn't let me go, though. It was ridiculous. I said 'You might as well let me go. I'm costing you money, let me fucking go. You're not going to play me.' Luckily Palace came in and he said I could go. It suited me and it was a good move. I had a good time at Palace.

"I was so sad to leave, but there is not much you can do when the boss doesn't want you to play. He ran that club, there was only one voice. It was an iron fist and if you got in his way you weren't going to win."

THAT was that. Droy, the Trojan, the Warrior was on his way. David Baddiel, comedian, writer and Chelsea fan once commented that, "Chelsea lured me in with all sorts of promises about style and excitement and Peter Osgood, but by the time I was old enough to go there actually gave me only ennui, monotony and Micky Droy."

That's a little unfair. OK, so the sideburns and crisp suits had been replaced by a full, unkempt beard and empty seats, but Droy symbolised a time when sleeves had to be rolled up and sweat had to stain those pristine blue jerseys. It wasn't pretty, it wasn't successful, but it was necessary and those who continued to love a day out at the Bridge loved him for it.

"You can't spend fifteen years at a place and not allow it to mean much," says Droy. "I have great feelings for Chelsea Football Club. They are my club. I never wanted to play for anybody else. In those bad times in the late 1970s I could have upped sticks and fucked off like so many others, but I stayed. This club had given me my chance in football, the fans were always really good to me and I felt I owed them, so I stayed. To be fair, I could have earned a lot more money leaving. I didn't earn a fortune playing at Chelsea by any means, but I'm the type of bloke that likes to stay where he is happy and that club made me happy."

JOEY JONES

'THE FIST'

1982-1985

CHELSEA CAREER

Games	91
Goals	2
Caps	72

MAGIC MOMENT

The jury was out on Joey until, while clearing a dangerous cross, he took a layer of skin off his face and simply got on with the game. From there on the fans were hooked

Never be lucid, never state, if you would be regarded great.

Dylan Thomas

FOR so long Chelsea fans had fallen for the dashing player who offered them glittering silverware with every drop of the shoulder or swivel of the hips. For so long those fans had been bowled over by their charms and gifts. For so long these players with their magnetism and their conceit had played themselves into the hearts of a set of fans unable to prevent their feelings as they fell head over heels for the men who ultimately could so disappoint them.

For so long Chelsea had been a glamorous club for glamorous people, but now those times had gone. The bubbly had gone flat and the celebrities had made their excuses and taken solace in their white-washed Marbella villas, whilst the club that had suffered from years of mis-management struggled to keep its head above water in both the financial and the football sense.

Times had changed; irrevocably altered by the twin evils of relegation and hooliganism. Now those still bothering to make the trip to Stamford Bridge found themselves faced with players less fleet of foot, less apt to be brilliant or to inspire, who instead offered endeavour and hard graft laced with true grit. But perhaps it didn't matter all that much for in the early 1980s Chelsea's fans sought idols more hewn in their own prosaic image.

JOEY JONES was not a fantastic footballer. If you put that suggestion to him he would give you a comic grimace, shake you the fist and then laugh in your face. Jones was, in fact, the very antithesis of those glamorous men in blue a decade or so earlier. To those who inhabited the seething Shed, he was the kind of player they had now learned to love, the kind of player who might just help get them out of the gargantuan hole in which they found themselves.

Jones was a Chelsea player for three seasons, his tattooed arms and lanky legs a world away from the handsome heyday of Messrs Osgood and Hudson. Raquel Welch may not have ever heard of him, but as he sprinted towards the Chelsea fans with a clenched fist acknowledging their support, he became as much a part of them as any prolific goal-getter or gifted playmaker had ever been.

In the autumn of 1982, after just three wins in their opening ten matches, Chelsea were in dire need of new players as John Neal tried to figure out how to avert the unthinkable possible relegation to Division Three and then seek to haul his team back into the First Division. Two successive bottom half finishes in Division Two indicated clearly that the Chelsea glamourpusses were now nothing more than also-rans.

The rest of the country had seen Jones immortalised in a famous Liverpool banner at the 1977 European Cup Final which neatly summed up his hardman reputation "JOEY ATE THE FROG'S LEGS, MADE THE SWISS ROLL, NOW HE'S MUNCHING GLADBACH". Wrexham's then manager Arfon Griffiths had paid a club record £210,000 (a record which still exists in late 2005) to sign him back in 1978. Neal knew all about Joey Jones from his days managing Wrexham, he'd sold him to Liverpool in the summer of 1975 for a club record sale fee of £110,000, and now approached his old club with an offer of £30,000 for the full-back.

The Welsh side were, like today, struggling financially and were interested in the deal, but Jones himself had his reservations. "The thought of travelling to London and working in London didn't appeal to me," says Jones. "I went down south to talk to Ken Bates and to have a look. I still didn't like the idea. I loved John Neal, always had done, but it was the move. I was a Northerner.

"I came back to Wales and didn't really want to leave, but that financial difficulty wouldn't go away and so the club said you HAVE to go this week. We have to sell you. Chelsea then came back with an offer of £34,500 and with lower wages for me. Money has never been my God and so that was that, I signed. "Fucking hell", I thought. "What have I done here?" I couldn't sell my house and ended up commuting from North Wales to London. Madness. What I was pleased about was the kit. I'd always loved the Chelsea kits, so that was something."

Neal had signed a man he knew well, but the fans were hardly turning cartwheels along the Fulham Road at the prospect of the Welshman's imminent arrival. Yeah, he was a Welsh International (he had been a member of the Welsh team that had beaten England 4-1 at Wrexham in 1980); yeah, he had won the European Cup with Liverpool in 1977, but to Chelsea fans he was an awkward player who had never impressed on his visits to the Bridge. "Every time I'd played at Chelsea I'd been crap," he laughs. "I remember losing there in the Cup in 1978. That was my last game for Liverpool. I was asked to mark their winger Clive Walker and he tore the arse out of me. He destroyed me and they won 4-2."

That was to prove an interesting afternoon for Jones in relation to his time at Liverpool, a club that he had grown up adoring. "I was taken off having played shit. I wasn't the only one that day by the way, but anyway, I was off. As I sat next to him on the bench, Bob Paisley threw me a tracksuit top. I was struggling to get this thing on. There I am with this top over my head, but I'm trying to get my arms through the holes when smack I've pushed my fist through and hit Bob right in the face. I didn't mean to, but it must have looked bad. I don't know if it was because of that punch or Clive Walker, but I never played for Liverpool again."

Jones seemed to have a penchant for upsetting people. He had returned to Stamford Bridge with Wrexham the following season and set about aggravating the home fans. Clive Walker was again his nemesis, but this time there was extra spice. In the build up to the game Walker had said in the press that he was glad that Jones had marked him that day and not Phil Neal as he didn't much rate the Welshman. Jones had read his words and arrived for the match seeking an apology.

"I thought he was taking the piss," says Jones. "We were waiting to kick off and I went over to him and smacked him. The ref never saw it, Clive never saw it coming, but maybe some of the fans did!" They did and that put Jones firmly in their black books. So when he signed, his arrival was severely questioned. To many this new arrrival was athletically inept, prone to punching their heroes and hardly the type of footballer to get Chelsea back on track.

PERHAPS not surprisingly then Jones' debut at Carlisle proved memorable for all the wrong reasons. "Their fans hated me too," he says. "I ran onto the pitch and I couldn't believe how many Blues fans were there, all the way up to Carlisle, bloody brilliant. But as the guy read out the teams and came to my name, both sets of fans booed. I got sent off in the second half and both sets of fans cheered!"

It was hardly an auspicious start and the club's own stuttering form didn't help his cause. Defeats at home to Shrewsbury and away at Rotherham left fans bemoaning both their fortune and a group of players seemingly doing their best to make Saturday afternoons as excruciating as possible.

"We were doing badly and my own opinion was that some of the players were not that bothered. There wasn't a lot of concern within the team about how bad we were, but I had noted how great these fans had been and thought they deserved players who were at least going to go down with a fight. That was how I had always played."

This book has underlined how so many players had to win over Chelsea's demanding supporters. Greats like Bentley, Tambling, Osgood and Harris in their time suffered the taunts of some fractious sections of the crowd, but recovered to win over their tormentors. Peter Houseman, a vital member of Sexton's team of the early 1970s had to put up with all sorts of abuse when he arrived on the scene in 1963. Soon he would be respected, but the fans claimed the credit for converting the midfielder into a player worthy of the blue shirt. One song summed up their thinking:

Peter Houseman, played terrible football
And the Shed all called him names
So they gave him
A kick in the bollocks
And now he plays in all our games

What Joey Jones lacked in god-given ability he more than made up for with a genuine tendency to battle for any cause. Everywhere he had played, he had been adored by the fans. He had stood on Liverpool's Kop as a young man and in time they had grown to love his raw effort, realising that here was a man maximising what talent he had, playing out their dreams on the famous Anfield turf. Alright, Jones hadn't been a Keegan or a Dalglish, but his efforts; culminating in his plucky display in the European Cup campaign of 1977, had the Kop lording him as one of their greats.

Now, though, in London those days and that adulation was a distant memory as the Shed groaned with each performance and each defeat. The club were perilously close to slumping into Division Three. "I thought I was a fucking jinx. It was bad. We played Bolton in a vital relegation battle and I had been getting quite a bit of stick from the fans." But Jones simply got on with his job and in that game against Bolton he gave those fans a taste of what he could give to their team. "I was in a crowded box and I dived to clear a ball and split my head open and just got up and carried on. It's only blood isn't it? From that moment the fans' attitude turned toward me. They knew and I knew I wasn't a Kerry Dixon, but they saw that I would have a go for them and they grew to love me. If I took a throw in they chanted my name, if I tied up my boots they chanted my fucking name."

The antipathy and suspicion had evaporated. Joey Jones was a bone fide Chelsea hero.

WHILST Jones' fortunes had been improved by hard graft, the club continued to struggle and were perilously close to relegation into the Third Division until that win at Bolton stopped the nightmare becoming reality, condemning the Trotters instead. Chelsea survived, but only just. With finances still shaky, and crowds still falling due to the violence which beset the club amongst sections of their supporters, it needed a special piece of managerial wizardry to pull things around.

With that in mind, John Neal set about raking the lower reaches of the Football League and Scottish leagues for untapped talent. He came up with a number of signings that would prove to be inspirational and that wind of ill-fortune that for so long had gushed through South-West London was about to die down and be replaced by a pleasantly successful breeze.

Pat Nevin, Kerry Dixon, David Speedie, Joe McLaughlin, Nigel Spackman, Eddie Niedzwiecki; each one was a gem and each one was going to help bring that air of optimism back to a ground that for so long had been stagnant and decaying. Despite their arrivals, Joey Jones remained in Neal's first choice team – testimony to his part in the club's survival the season before – building his popularity as the crowd responded to Chelsea's improvement by swelling rapidly.

Jones in turn was in awe of Chelsea's hardcore fans; a group of supporters that he felt were as good as any he had played for. "I loved the Chelsea fans," Jones says. "I loved their passion. They were always behind us. I was at Liverpool and they were superb, but what struck me was that these Chelsea boys were so passionate about us despite just how crap we had been. We were struggling, but these guys travelled everywhere and always sang."

Jones himself, the ex-fanatic who'd grown up on the Kop cheering on his Liverpool heroes empathised with the supporters as much as they empathised with him. His tattoos, his raw aggression, his passion, he was one of them and that status will always bring a high level of rapport between fan and player. But Joey's cult status was about to shoot into the stratosphere. "I had something special going with the fans, but then I started giving the fist and their love for me went through the roof."

AH, THE FIST. Jones' clinched fist was as much part of his passion and his game as his swinging lef boot. He had cultivated it at Anfield and waved it proudly to a hungry Kop as if to say, "Here I am guys, I've made it!" Now he was at the Bridge and, whilst it wasn't the Kop, Jones saw that same passion oozing from the Shed; blue had replaced red, but in terms of fervour he saw them as equals. They in turn allowed Jones to join a very elite club with just two previous members, Messrs Harris and Droy, by declaring loudly "Joey's gonna get ya" to cow opposing players.

Chelsea fans were unavoidably drawn to the fist. You couldn't help it. Jones would wave it, the fans would respond in kind. It was a ritual, but one that could land all involved in a spot of bother. In January 1984, with Neal's new team driving toward promotion, they visited Derby. Chelsea's Kevin Hales had been injured near the touchline and was receiving treatment from physio Norman Medhurst. Jones went over to check on his team-mate only to find himself the centre of a hail of coins raining down from the Derby fans.

"One hit me just above the eye and another on the head," recalls Jones. "They were little nicks and those bleed like hell, but Norman, who was known to be a bit tight, had started to pick the coins up and was putting them in his pocket!

"The referee meantime has seen me and suggested I go down. 'I'm not going down for that shower of shit,' I said. The Chelsea fans could see something was up and started chanting my name. We were in our lovely yellow away kit and as I turned to give them the fist, they saw my top was covered in blood. That was it. They went berserk and started ripping out seats and throwing them at the Derby lot and it all kicked off."

The incident led many observers to point the finger of blame toward Jones and that fist of his, so much so that a few days later whilst training, the Welshman received a couple of visitors. "I had taken stick before and thought little of it, but then the police turned up to training and arrested me for inciting a riot. I just said, 'Do what you've got to do'. Ken Bates was behind me and they eventually dropped the charges. I would happily have gone to court though. I hadn't done anything and I would have said so."

A little under two months later, Chelsea travelled to Newcastle. The Geordies, with Kevin Keegan, Terry McDermott, Chris Waddle and Peter Beardsley, were pushing hard for promotion themselves, but Jones was far more taken by the amount of Chelsea fans who had made the long journey up the A1 and who were matching the Toon Army for exuberant noise.

"The Chelsea fans had made it up to Newcastle in their thousands. They were cheering my name and as ever I went over and gave them the fist and some Geordie reported me for trying to incite a riot. Again a policeman cautioned me after the game, but again the charges were dropped. I got hauled in front of the FA though. They told me that I had to stop the fist. 'But I've always done it,' I said. I did it to the Kop, I did at Wrexham and I told them that they were coming down on me because the Chelsea fans had got themselves an unfair reputation. That was all. They were using me as a scapegoat. I said I would try, but I couldn't get used to the waving thing. I did it for a while, but soon the fist was back."

THE NEW players sparked a fantastic run of results which contrasted wildy with the previous season's desperate straits and Chelsea took the Second Division title from strong contenders Newcastle and Manchester City. Jones had been an integral part of that success and his life at the Bridge, despite that gruelling commute was now made even more manageable by the arrival of his old compadre Mickey Thomas. Jones and Thomas had grown up playing football together for club and country and even today they are inseparable.

Jones refers to Thomas as "Oh Great One," and the Chelsea fans learnt to adore their new Dragons. "Oh Great One" signed from Stoke in December 1983 having turned down Bates a couple of times before. "I told him he was a bit different to other Chairman, but the fans, they were brilliant. Mickey came and got a great reception from the supporters. He was a wonderful talent, but on the pitch I used to insist that he 'flick 'em up and I'd volley them.'"

Thomas was put up in a London hotel to ease his move and that meant some respite for Jones who at last had somewhere to crash every now and then. That roof over their heads, though, wouldn't last and in time the long drives were back on and the search for somewhere to rest was again part of their strange lives. "If we had a home game we would come down on the Friday and doss down where we could. Mickey slept in the Ref's room at the Bridge, whilst I crashed now and then in a flat in Deptford, which was full of Vietnamese boat people. They never shut up all night."

Jones and his pal weren't the kind to bemoan such drastic measures. Gold-plated hotel suites decked in satin sheets and eager glamour models were for a future generation, but the Welshmen weren't complaining and got on with their own capital adventure. "We once played pre-season at Brentford and we were sitting on the curb outside Stamford Bridge at midnight," laughs Jones. "'What the fuck are we doing? We've got nowhere to stay. The gates are locked and we've got no money.' We had nothing to do so we said, shall we go home? We'll be home by 4am. So we did, trained back in Wrexham the next day and then came back the next to train with the lads."

On other occasions they found ample ways to fill the hours. London was there to be discovered and Soho seemed the most interesting of locations for our intrepid explorers. A visit to a peep show caused much hilarity. "Me and Mickey would be in and the flap would come up and I could see Mickey's eyes across the way and we would just burst out laughing. We were leaving one place once and this guy says to me, 'Is that Mickey Thomas, the footballer?'

'I don't know mate, what does he look like?' I said hoping desperately that he didn't recognise me too. Luckily they never did."

Jones' living arrangements weren't ideal, but he wasn't going to complain. Why should he? To the fans his hardship and tortuous journey only added to his legend and for his part, the drive was worth it; although it helped to have company to help wile away the hours.

If it wasn't Mickey Thomas, Jones would often chauffeur a number of Chelsea fans that also hailed from North Wales. "There was a lad called Ajax who still has a season ticket at the Bridge and I started giving him lifts. I used to take a carload of Chelsea fans and then give them a lift home afterwards. I think a few of them got interested because they loved John Neal. They also had me, Eddie Niedzwiecki and then Mickey Thomas so there was a strong link."

WHATEVER their nationality, Chelsea fans awaited their promising side's return to the First Division with understandable relish. For about a dozen years the team and the club had suffered. The giant East Stand had loomed large over proceedings, but rather than symbolising a brave new world, it's empty blue seats had told their own depressing story. Stamford Bridge attendances were far from heaving (1984/85, their first season back in the top flight saw the club average only 23,000), but the football displayed by an attacking formation of Dixon, Speedie and Nevin was by far the best thing seen at Chelsea since Osgood, Hudson and Cooke had thrilled the locals in the 1960s and 70s.

Joey Jones wasn't part of that exciting, skilful and glamorous axis, but his time in the Chelsea kit marked the cross-over between the era of also-ran Chelsea, and a team packed with nonentities, to the beginnings of the modern Chelsea; for Nevin, Dixon and Speedie read Zola, Vialli and Gullit. Joey Jones was there at the start of it all and without his grit and fervour the club could have found itself in the wilderness of Division Three, rather than building towards its modern incarnation of glitz, glamour, spending sprees and trophies.

For now, though, the 1984/85 season back in the First Division started reasonably well for Chelsea. But Jones was suspended due to some usual over-exuberance at the end of the previous campaign. That fact, coupled with a slight dispute regarding a new contract saw him looking in on for much of that early season as Chelsea went about their business with little fuss and certainly no alarm.

Ken Bates had come to Jones in the summer of 1984 and offered him an extension to a contract that had one more year to run. "I wasn't sure about it and stalled," recalls Jones. "Ken said, 'If you don't sign I'll see to it that you never play for the first team again.' I didn't until Christmas. I liked Ken, though, he was alright. He was the top dog and I got on with him. He called me Jonesie so I called him Batesie. 'You should call me Mr Chairman,' he remarked.

'You should call me Mr Jones!' He liked that, I gave it back. I asked for an extra £50 a week. Ken wasn't sure. £50, that's all. I said I would give it back to him if we got relegated!"

That was Jones for you. Interestingly his replacement in the side which cemented Chelsea's place back in the top flight was the equally exuberant and ferocious Doug Rougvie, who arrived in the summer from Scottish Champions Aberdeen. Rougvie too became a terrace icon, like "Chopper" Harris before them; his grit and sheer bloody-mindedness carving a notch on Chelsea fans' hearts.

As for the team, they finished the season in a more than healthy sixth position. It would have been high enough to earn them a spot in the UEFA Cup, but 1985 was a tarnished year for football and its ever blackening reputation. The season culminated in the Heysel disaster when 39 Juventus fans were crushed to death prior to the European Cup Final. It was the last in a long line of shameful incidents involving English clubs and their so-called fans and resulted in a ban on English clubs competing in Europe. Chelsea, having had to deal with so many incidents and troublemakers throughout the first half of the decade, had hosted their own night of shame when Sunderland visited the Bridge in the semi-final of the Milk Cup in March.

The team's good league form had continued in the competition and Chelsea had reached the semi-final after an epic tie against Sheffield Wednesday. In the first game they drew 1-1 at the Bridge, but found themselves 3-0 down at half-time in the replay at Hillsborough. Jones had got back into the side by now and his battling attributes were brilliantly mirrored by his team-mates as they fought back to take a 4-3 lead only to squander their good work when Doug Rougvie gave away a late penalty.

Jones recalls that evening with a smile not necessarily for the remarkable comeback, but for the exploits of his pal, Mickey Thomas. "Andy Blair was playing for Wednesday. I suddenly heard this crack and Andy's on the floor. There's a big commotion, but the Ref doesn't know who is responsible. What made me laugh was the fans start singing Mickey's name and he's discreetly trying to tell them all to shut up. He gets away with it, but as we're walking off I asked him why he did that?

'He called my missus a slag.'

"We were in the bar afterwards at Hillsborough and Blair comes in and looked at Mickey and calls him a skunk. I burst out laughing. I'd never heard anyone called a skunk before.

"It calmed down, but it was all set for the Thursday and another replay, this time at the Bridge. I was left-back and Mickey was left-half. We ran out expecting some aggro, but Andy waved at us both as if to say sorry. 'We won't be having any trouble here' I laughed."

FISTICUFFS may have been avoided on the pitch, but there was little respite off it. Sheffield Wednesday were finally beaten 2-1 and so it was Sunderland who stood between Chelsea's supporters and their first trip to Wembley for thirteen years. In the first leg John Neal's side struggled at Roker Park, losing 2-0, but after their efforts against Sheffield Wednesday were hopeful of turning it around against a team who would be eventually relegated from Division One that season.

In his programme notes for the second leg, Neal wrote with eerie anticipation, "Good luck to each and every one of you, players, and supporters alike; with your help on the terraces and in the stands we can make this a night to remember." What happened next was not what the manager had envisaged, but the night went down as one of the blackest in Chelsea's infamous thug history.

The Blues took the lead through David Speedie, but the optimism that goal brought soon turned to rage as Sunderland's Clive Walker, returning to the club he had graced to devastating effect, broke away and scored a decisive away goal. He didn't help matters with a salute to the Members' benches in the West Stand and when he scored again in the second half, those very benches began to rain onto the pitch. They were joined by coins, bricks and any other debris as police horses intervened.

A third Sunderland goal compounded the misery and heightened the thugish atmosphere, so much so that one fan, known later only as "the fat man", came running onto the pitch seeking retribution against turncoat Walker. Jones, just as he had when playing for Liverpool against Chelsea's Walker in 1978, had suffered a woeful time against the winger's pace, but he managed to intercept the intruding fan with a typically ferocious tackle, this time of the rugby kind, before he reached his intended target.

Speedie and Walker continued the aggro in the players' bar afterwards (they had history and were only kept apart by the formidable Micky Droy), but Jones' efforts that night were to be his last real contribution to the club. His travel arrangements had been far from ideal and the new first team coach, John Hollins was known not to be in favour of what he saw as an unnecessary distraction.

JONES moved onto Huddersfield in the summer of 1985 before finishing his playing career with a third spell at Wrexham, where he still coaches to this day. Now he recalls Chelsea and its fans with a knowing smile. "Those supporters were the most fanatical I played in front of. There was a lot of stuff about them in the media, but I thought it was unfair. The majority just wanted to see us doing well and they would travel to the end of the earth to see it happen. You ask Mickey Thomas. He had loads of clubs, but he'll tell you Chelsea was his favourite. We had some great times down there."

It wasn't the longest or most successful spell at the club, not the most glittering, the most goal-laden or even the most triumphant, but Joey Jones brought passion back to Chelsea. The passion that had been lost for so long.

As the players run out in Blue, there he is, making that beeline for the fans, his fist clenched showing his appreciation.

PAT NEVIN

'WEE PAT'

1983-1988

CHELSEA CAREER

Games	242
Goals	45
Caps	28

MAGIC MOMENT

Newcastle were good, very good, but in 1983 Pat dribbled past them once and then went back and did it again; a star was born

Always be a first-rate version of yourself, instead of a second-rate version of somebody else.

Judy Garland

BY the mid-1980s football found itself, like a naughty schoolboy, standing firmly in the corner. Margaret Thatcher, its unimpressed headmistress, looked down her nose at what she saw as an unruly and uncontrollable part of her classroom. So there football stood, its knees grazed by continuing crowd trouble, its nose bloodied by extreme right-wing association. Thatcher saw only a game out of control. There would be no mention of some football "fans" reacting to her own hardline, right wing policies or her own war in the Falklands and using them as justification for their violence. Football was on its own, facing the wall and wearing a large dunce's pointy hat.

Riots, disasters and general ill-feeling pot-marked the decade. Whilst Thatcher's children wallowed in their high-rolling, filo-faxed lives, football's sub-culture continued to ghettoize its fans. The very real threat of electric fences, terraces that on which cattle would bemoan their comfort and the ready made tag of "hooligan" meant that being a football fan in the mid-1980s had lost a lot of its glamorous appeal.

In 1985 – the game's *anus horibilis* – the tone was set. Riots at Luton, when Millwall fans went on the rampage, Birmingham and, of course, at Heysel were all high profile thug-related incidents, whilst the Bradford disaster was another horrifying image for the game to endure. Frank Keating, respected commentator of the *Guardian* looked glumly on after the Heysel disaster at a sport he had loved for so long. "One more corpse was carried out from the Brussels stadium last night. Soccer itself – draped in the Union Jack. It deserved to be spat on."

Strong and emotive words, as were *The Sunday Times'* assumptions that here was "a slum sport, played in slum stadiums, watched by slum people." Chelsea had endured much of the needle in these dark days. They had been plagued by the reputation which had followed their fans around the country. That had been fuelled further by the riot against Sunderland and the continued presence of a small, but noticeable, extreme right-wing faction who, frustrated at failure and the loss of status, coupled with the rise of the hooligan culture, ensured Chelsea joined Millwall at the head of the list of trouble clubs.

The Chairman, Ken Bates, in his exasperation had looked closely at placing electric fences around Stamford Bridge's terraces. The very idea was like some sort of final solution as fans were finally being de-humanised as "things" to control, rather than to entertain.

IRONICALLY, events on the pitch at Chelsea over this period had brought fans flocking back to Stamford Bridge. The team was winning and one player, the complete antithesis of the game's ugly image, caught the imagination in such a fashion that his image today still provokes misty-eyed recollection from even the most tattooed hooli-fan of the time.

Pat Nevin, his shirtsleeves rolled up to his elbows like an artist at his canvas, his waif-like, frail frame jinking its way down the club's wings, before a neat trick would carve a defence open and leave his adoring crowd baying for more.

Chelsea fans had long been warmed by Scottish wingers. Men small in stature, but sky-high with wondrous skill. The Glaswegian Bobby McNeil had played for Chelsea before and after the First World

War and, whilst the fans had taken time to get used to his preference for dribbling, he soon became a crowd favourite. And in the glamour years of the 1960s and early 1970s of course there was the highland fling Chelsea enjoyed with Charlie Cook; and here now was another.

Not since Cooke had the fans been able to delight in the prospect of trickery when one of their own received the ball, and not since the early 1970s had those fans been able to delight in a team that offered very real success. Today Dave Sexton's FA Cup winning team is a nostalgic icon. A visit to the Bridge sees fans of a certain age sporting shirts with the names Osgood or Cooke proudly on their back. It is a retro look amid the club's newfound modern success, but in the mid-1980s things were extremely different.

That team, which had entertained so fluidly, was still fresh in the hearts and minds of a set of fans reeling from the nightmare that was the late 1970s and early 1980s. If that decade was touted as one that "fashion forgot", then for Blues fans it was a period that had forgotten them. Now though, under John Neal, a team to be proud of had developed and those supporters who travelled all over the country – most of whom were fanatics rather than lunatics – followed a team capable of taking them back to the First Division and ridding the gloom that had taken residence over this once effervescent part of London Town.

Entertainment? That hadn't been the motivation for coming to Stamford Bridge for many a season. Now as a fan took his or her place in the Shed, on the Members' benches or in the East Stand, they longed for the ball to be swept wide where the instant control of Pat Nevin was waiting and where he would weave his merry dance around defenders with what at times looked like effortless ease.

NEVIN played five seasons with Chelsea. It seemed like more. His time at the club spanned improvement, success, stability and then renewed failure. That's Chelsea for you, but it was five wonderful years where not only smiles returned to the Bridge, people did. Nevin's 242 appearances were all greeted with expectation for a magician who not only grabbed the imagination with those feet full of trickery, but also blew away the image of the footballer as a brainless commodity without thought or substance. In short, and this seems incredible to say of a player and his devotees from 1980s Chelsea, the fans loved him for his brains and his brawn.

Ok, so brawn is perhaps the wrong word when describing the slight, slender, mercurial Pat Nevin, but don't be fooled. Nevin's father was an Irish boxer who moved to Glasgow and ensured that his son was brought up with the necessary winning attitude to make it in professional sport. A life in the ring didn't appeal to Nevin, especially when he discovered early on that it involved being punched in the face, but nevertheless, the boxing ring is the ideal environment for realising that second is nowhere.

Nevin adored football, but the notion of pursuing it as a career was far from his driving ambition. He was playing for the Celtic Boys Club (a set-up that had given the senior team the likes of Paul McStay and Charlie Nicholas) and loved the Parkhead club, idolising the archetypal winger in Jimmy Johnstone. Interestingly though, his first kit had actually been that of Chelsea (he thinks his Dad must have found it going cheap), but it was the local men in green and white hoops who captured his attentions. Jimmy Johnstone's high jinks and later Kenny Dalglish's mercurial talents had Nevin in raptures, but he hardly dreamt of one day following in those footsteps.

That was a good thing, as Celtic would tell the young centre-forward that he was not up to scratch. That was that. Life offered many more avenues to this bright, intelligent young man willing to explore his options whilst playing football for fun on the side. That fun took him to a local amateur team called Gartcosh, who, as luck would have it, one day in 1981, played a friendly against Second Division Clyde.

To Nevin it was another chance to have a laugh with his mates, but it would prove to be a day that changed his life.

PAT NEVIN relaxes comfortably on the sofa in the living room of the flat he owned whilst at Chelsea. He is in London from his native Scotland for work in the media and recalls a time when football was a just a hobby. "I was doing a degree at Glasgow and playing some stuff on and off and one day had a game against Clyde. I had a wee bet with my mates about how many players I could dribble around and I get the ball and off I go. I beat about five of them and scored. I thought it was their reserves, but Craig Brown, who was the manager at the time, said, 'They are my first team and I want you to sign.' I wasn't keen, but then he said I could come part-time and earn £30 a week. As a student, that'll do for me."

At Clyde, Nevin perfected that nonchalant-looking style of his. The relaxed gait, the slightly limp wrist, the drooped shoulders and then the fizz of activity in his feet that had defenders reeling, punch drunk. At times he could slope about the pitch as if not quite bothered. In some ways he wasn't. Football remained a hobby even then, as he was busy studying and with that safety net he could play without stress. With that easy-going attitude to the game, he excelled.

Football fans love to play games. Over a pint, teams from differing eras are compared and current superstars are pitted against former heroes. Put Nevin in blue, fifteen years or so before he actually arrived at the Bridge, say circa 1969, and he would fit right in. Here was a player with something to say, something to give. Here was a player with that unquantifiable Chelsea something; a direct descendant of the lineage of Foulke, Gallacher and Greaves. You can picture Nevin with sideburns and a quiff, the famous old blue jersey clinging to him as the fans delight at another insouciant slalom run through defences or a pin-point cross to Ossie. That relaxed style would have lit up Tommy Docherty's or Dave Sexton's great teams and was born from the same attitude to the game that Messrs Osgood, Hudson and Cooke shared. Life existed outside of the match and, because of that knowledge, brought even more excitement to the game.

BUT ON the banks of the Clyde, Nevin's quaint abilities with the ball were just what those fans brought up around Glasgow's shipyards had been born into and as a teenager, Nevin won many plaudits. Divisional Player of the Season, promotion for the team to Scottish Division One as runaway Champions and a call up to the Scotland Under-18s were just rewards.

The international recognition saw Nevin earn the title of Player of the Tournament in the European Championships in Finland that the young Scots won (Nevin scored two in a 3-1 victory over Czechoslovakia in the final) in 1982. It was then that the studies and the game began to collide. His teachers had been told that he was ill, but excited headlines in the press suggested otherwise and when Chelsea initially came looking for his services the answer was, due to academic commitments, a firm "No".

A year later, Nevin missed some exams playing in Mexico for the Scotland Under-19s in the World Championships. Chelsea remained interested and it was now that Nevin made his unavoidable decision. He could play down in London for a couple of years and treat it as a sabbatical, come back and resume studying. He clearly didn't count on becoming one of the most intriguing and entertaining wingers in the history of a club.

It was the summer of 1983. There had been plenty of press on one Glaswegian's move to England's capital, but it wasn't anything to do with wee Nevin from Clyde. Charlie Nicholas, the scourge of the Scottish Premier League's defences was joining Arsenal amid much razzmatazz, whereas Nevin (who re-sat some exams that summer) joined Chelsea without the fans even noticing and with his team-mates wondering what this little urchin was all about.

"I arrived, but I'm sure the rest of the lads thought I was a youth team player," laughs Nevin. "John Neal hadn't said much about me. He knew that I was fit. They had done tests with the Scotland squad and I had come out on top each time. I could run. John knew that, as did his assistant Ian McNeil, who knew me quite well as he had watched a lot of me at Clyde.

"They had us playing a training match and I was up front against Micky Droy. I got the ball and stepped over it and left Micky standing there. As I'm running away I heard Micky mutter, 'I'm too fucking old for this.' I thought 'Yes! I've done a big player here.'"

That pre-season, Nevin drew more and more attention to himself. His sense of style was a world away from the "smart casual" look preferred by your average footballer. The Joy Division on his Walkman was nothing like the Phil Collins or George Benson enjoyed by his fellow players. This was however a time when the Kings Road was enjoying a renaissance, so why not its local club? But the modern area was a grittier version of its 1960s heyday. "It was 1983," wrote Kathryn Fleet recently in *Vogue*. "Swinging London the second time around. The street was filled with all sorts of people, many of them with ridiculous haircuts, wearing wild clothes." Maybe Nevin, the former punk, Nevin the stylistic would fit in after all, but there was no doubting that Nevin was conspicuous by his differences to almost all the other Chelsea players; and that didn't stop on the training ground.

"The players might have had their doubts about me and the manager must have seen this. He got all the players together, he lined up the cones and told us all to dribble through six of them, go around the end marker and repeat it four times. I had finished before they had done three and you could see the players were impressed. 'Fucking hell, this kid is OK.' It was a lovely moment as I knew that the manager was on my side and desperate to help. I was a confident thing anyway, but it gave me a lift."

IN KEEPING with almost everything about this elfin miraculist, the young Nevin had honed his silky skills not in the back yard of a Scottish tenement building with an ageing tennis ball, but whilst travelling across Europe on his way to Corfu. In Italy he and his companion had run out of money. They had a ball with them and hungry, there was only one thing for it. "I started juggling the ball and doing tricks and the locals loved it. I made enough money for a couple of lasagnes for me and my pal."

Playing for his dinner was one thing, now Nevin was hoping to play for a team desperate to improve on the hard times that had afflicted the place. Chelsea had come perilously close to relegation to the unheard of depths of Division Three in 1983, but now Neal hoped he had brought the right blend of players together from all around Britain who might just curb that slide in fortune and morale. Expectations were low, but a 5-0 opening day thumping of the bookies' favourites for promotion, Derby, immediately stamped Chelsea's authority on the Division.

Nevin had become aware in his short time at the club that some on the periphery and even in the first team were less than whole-hearted in their devotion to the team's fortunes. "I had been brought up at Celtic where there is no concept of how to lose or even accept defeat, but some of these guys seemed OK with it," says Nevin, the lessons from his boxing father clearly at the forefront of his mind. He began the season in the reserves and trotted into the dressing room at Watford that day having given his all. "I played well for the reserves and then the result came through from the first team, 5-0 and I went YES!! I was happy that the team had started the season well. The rest of the lads have their heads in their hands, disappointed that those in competition with them had won. It was a real learning curve. I thought 'You twats.'"

Neal had soon seen enough of Nevin to convince him that the lad had talent and steel enough to warrant a chance and promoted him to the first team in September 1983 for a League Cup match at Gillingham. His first goal came just weeks later at Fulham, who were supposedly the stronger team in south-west London. And it was typically impish. He latched onto a rebound, but rather than lashing it into the goal he dummied a desperate defender before tapping the ball into a bewildered net.

Suddenly Chelsea tongues were wagging about the cheeky tyke and Nevin slotted into Neal's new team, who were making a mockery of the thought that once more the club would be fighting to avoid the drop. Results continued to catch the eye as did this Scottish winger.

At Newcastle in November 1983, during a 4-0 thrashing of a fine home team boasting Kevin Keegan, Terry McDermott, Chris Waddle and Peter Beardsley amongst its ranks, Nevin recalled some fatherly advice he had once received. "Try one of your mad, mazy runs in every game you play in." So he did. He beat one, two, three men, then went back and beat them again. It was blatant showboating; the kind that would enrage opposing fans, but brings joy to one's own. It catapulted him into hero status in an instant.

Fan Katie Collins was at that game over twenty years ago, but still recalls fondly the occasion when suddenly, things were OK again. "It was absolutely fantastic," she says. "Pat is underselling himself when he cites that match as the game in which he won the fans over. He'd already done that. That match against Newcastle was the day we realised that here was a team that was coming together, but we had seen enough of Pat individually to know we had a new star. We were a cautious bunch of fans, we had good reason to be, but now things were coming together. We proved we were better than the Geordies that's for sure and as for Pat, he was brilliant. It's as simple as that."

And that day was a significant one for the young footballer for another reason. Yes, he had the skill, that was clear to everyone, but he learnt a thing or two about dedication as Kevin Keegan, a man with nothing to prove and playing in a team 4-0 down, never stopped running and never stopped trying to inspire. Nevin took that example on board and it furthered the adulation that Chelsea's fans would have for him.

NEVIN was the stand-out player in Chelsea's stand-out team. Everything had gelled so quickly and so fruitfully. Good teams were beaten, the attacking football was often wonderful to watch and in David Speedie, Kerry Dixon and of course Pat Nevin the club once more had a forward line worth trudging down the Fulham Road for.

In April 1984, Leeds United visited Chelsea, but more importantly so did 33,000 fans. A 5-0 romp confirmed how far the Blues had come in terms of capturing the imagination of the club's fans. For too long Stamford Bridge had resembled an empty and squeaky Nevada desert gas station, but now once more it was becoming Vegas. That victory secured promotion and the 1-0 final day win at Grimsby assured the fans they would be going up as Champions. Kerry Dixon latched onto great work by Nevin and the ball was in the net. The Scot created 30 of Dixon's goals that season, whilst Speedie could thank Nevin for 20 of his efforts.

It was a phenomenal season (Nevin himself managed 14 goals from the wing) and one that earned Nevin the club's Player of the Year; testament in itself to his status given that Dixon and Speedie grabbed nearly all the headlines with their goalscoring exploits. He had taken great pleasure not only in his form, but in his team's. The fans loved him, that was obvious, but what of his Chairman?

Having been plucked from the relative obscurity of Clyde, despite now playing for glamorous Chelsea, Nevin was surviving on low-ish wages and struggling to make ends meet in the expensive capital. He had played a big part in promotion and, yes, the fans loved him; he deserved a pay-rise, didn't he? Not one for the emerging new animal that was the football agent, Nevin knocked on Bates' door and begged the question himself.

"I was on £180 a week and the rental on my flat was £110. I was left with very little. I got Player of the Year, but knew others were on more than me. I went to Ken and said I wanted more, but he said he couldn't afford to and left the office with me in it. 'Sod it,' I thought and went to check the file for evidence and found that what I had asked for was less than what a number of the guys were on. He came back in and I said, 'I know you're paying that sort of money, Ken. What I want is less than the average.'

'How do you know that?'

'I know', I said and smiled. He knew what I'd done, but because I had used a little intelligence and had a glint in my eye, he didn't mind too much."

NEVIN'S intelligence and wit on and off the pitch had drawn him to many of the club's fans and his Chairman, but the sometimes blinkered world of a football dressing room can be a harder barrier to break down. Here was a footballer aeons away from the stereotype and there were bound to be eyebrows raised. "There were a few negatives and I'm sure some of them were muttering to themselves 'Fahcking weirdo,'" says Nevin with a mock cockney accent.

"I hit it off with Colin Pates and John Bumstead. They had a great off the wall Python-esque humour and we immediately got on, whilst Joey Jones and Mickey Thomas always made me laugh." Nevin admits that he had nothing in common with many of his team-mates and their world was one that didn't interest him. Consequently he could be regarded as aloof, but Jones, for one, immediately took to him.

"Like Mickey and myself he was very brainy!" chuckles Jones. "I got on great with him. I think he liked me and Mickey, he liked our silliness. He used to wear these clothes and I thought they were just weird, but then a few months later you'd realise he was the height of fashion and we weren't. What a player though. It was like the ball was stuck to his feet. He was very intellectual. He would warm up with his earphones on, listening to music. To me he was like a breath of fresh air."

Nevin was too confident in himself to be bothered by what a few less agreeable team-mates than Joey Jones thought of him, but admits that settling into London was, at times hard. "It took a while. I was lucky because a lot of my student friends had moved down to London to work. I made a lot of friends in the music scene. My first flatmate was a journalist with the NME.

"I had been a punk and loved my music, so in that respect I was different. The music scene I liked was big, but it was underground and that culture of mine just simply didn't exist in football clubs. It was marginalized, especially, strangely, in London, but it was big in the likes of Glasgow, Manchester and Liverpool."

He wasn't in any of those places though, he was in the Chelsea Football Club dressing room and he was hardly going to be able to discuss these interests with Doug Rougvie or Paul Canoville. That, however, wasn't going to perturb the resolute Nevin. The single-mindedness and confidence that electrified Chelsea's performances also got him through what could have been a very hard time.

In years to come he could offer the right advice to another Chelsea footballer who dared read the *Guardian* rather than *The Sun*. "I tried to explain it to Graeme Le Saux. He was very much an outsider with such a contrasting personality from his team-mates. I said to him, 'always be yourself, but more importantly be confident in being yourself. The worst thing you can do is try and ingratiate yourself with your team mates because they'll find you out and then there is no respect.'"

NEVIN, though, is no doubt that he could also break barriers between himself and the other players in the most simple of ways. "I suppose I was helped that I had a string of birds. I would bring these girls to the players lounge and the boys would look aghast. 'She's tasty!' I brought singers in and other girls and suddenly I wasn't the weirdo they feared I was. Strange isn't it?"

Nevin's most important weapon that year in settling into the club was a sense of humour. Thick skin and the willingness to not be thrown by those who didn't quite "get" him was vital. "I didn't take myself the slightest bit seriously. I could laugh at any stick I got and give it back. On the whole, though, I was working with a great bunch of guys and we got on. There was one fella who hated me and I hated him, but that will happen. There were 30 of us and in general it was fine.

"David Speedie and I had problems, in fact we hated each other. I initially took him as a selfish bastard, but soon mellowed in my thoughts, but he was difficult to get on with back then."

The two men were very different in so many ways, but they shared the love of the fans they played in front of week after week. In a way they highlighted the difference between two factions of fans at the club. Speedie was the fiery, argumentative and angry individual who would head-butt a wall to get what he wanted and appealed to fans of a similar ilk. Nevin was the thoughtful, culture vulture whose intelligent dribbles and intricate passing had Chelsea's more cerebral fans lapping him up. Their relationship may have been strained on a personal level, but the pair complemented each other and Kerry Dixon perfectly; forming a goal-laden triumvirate.

Looking back, though, Nevin could see that his misunderstanding with Speedie stemmed from more than their polarised styles and characters. "If I'm honest I wanted David's position. I wanted to play off Kerry and felt I could do a better job than David. I had always been a central striker and that was my preference. All my life I had been a centre-forward and suddenly I was stuck out on the wing. I went to John Neal and said, 'that position behind the centre-forward; I think I can do a good job of it.' It's a well-known tactic now, the big man knocking the ball off to a floating forward. Back then it wasn't so familiar, but I had studied Italian football where they used it a lot and really felt I could make that place my own.

"I had grown up watching Kenny [Dalglish] doing it at Celtic and was desperate to do the same. To be fair to John though, he said that he knew I could do a job in there, but he had me doing a job on the wing, I was scoring and creating goals from out there and why would he change that?"

JOHN NEAL had been around the game for years, achieving unheard of success at Wrexham and keeping Middlesbrough comfortably in the top flight in his three seasons in charge. Neal knew when a player's input was worth listening to. With that in mind he did let Nevin play a flexible winger's game, one that could utilise his ability to drift, make space and ultimately cause havoc.

"We compromised. Mickey Thomas came in from Stoke and whilst our formation looked like a 4-4-2, it wasn't. It was far more subtle than that. John said I could drift in and play across the line behind the front two. He knew I was intelligent and fit enough to do that and that when we lost the ball we would all fill in and become a midfield of four. If it was to fail though, I knew I'd be to blame!"

But the fluid, modern formation did work; it worked like a dream and in one devastating season of goalscoring the club returned to the First Division with a side that truly looked like they could stay there for a while. It seemed that Neal had set the alarm and that the club that for too long been labelled with that tag of "Sleeping Giant" was wide awake.

Neal had shown great faith in players who he plucked from relative obscurity, but who had become a strong and cohesive unit. Of them all it seemed that Nevin was his most gratifying "project". There was nothing that he felt was beyond Nevin and his willingness to get him involved in his team's play was paramount to the player's improvement.

"He really had faith in me and my ability. 'Give the ball to Pat,' he'd say. That was great, but my confidence also stemmed from the fact that if I failed, it wasn't the be all and end all. I wanted to do well, but football wasn't my whole life. I was dedicated and I loved doing it, but I knew if it went wrong I could do something else, if they failed they were stuck. Some of them anyway. I had that safety net and that helped me."

To the fan hanging on every drop of the shoulder or teasing run, they hoped with all their hearts that he would never, ever have to do something else. To them he was born to play in blue and terrorise those sent to defeat their team. It was a relationship that blossomed, but Nevin quite rightly knew that his skill alone was not enough and that was where the example set by Keegan when clearly beaten at Newcastle came into its own. "Chelsea fans appreciated me because I had a wee bit of skill, but I also worked my bollocks off. It was no more complicated than that. They always said to me that they loved the fact I kept working, I kept running and that I never give up."

That was proven on the ill-fated evening against Sunderland at Stamford Bridge when fans ran amok in anger, but the one bright spot of that dark night was Nevin running onto the ball and lifting it over the keeper into the goal, even though the tie was way beyond Chelsea at 5-1 on aggregate at the time. The game was lost, the night was one of gloom, but Nevin was still going about his business whilst a mounted policeman galloped across the penalty area.

"It was a job of work, so of course you must keep working. It doesn't matter if you're 6-0 down, you must keep going, people have paid to see you, you're getting paid to play, so play. I also had my dad coming down from Scotland for every game, so there was no way I wasn't going to put in my all."

What had been a sabbatical was now a career and one in which Nevin was doing brilliantly. That night against Sunderland was a black mark, but otherwise (especially on the pitch) the first season back in the top flight was one to be proud of. Sixth place was more than credible for a newly promoted side, especially as only one of the squad (Mickey Thomas) at the beginning of the season had ever played in such lofty surroundings.

Both Merseyside teams, Liverpool and Everton were beaten. The two clubs were dominating English football at the time, but both succumbed to John Neal's charms. Liverpool, for the third time had come to Stamford Bridge as European Champions and once more went home empty handed. In 1978, 1982 and now in December 1984 they were undone, but this occasion seemed far less of a shock. Neal's team had every right to be on this stage and beating the best.

That fact was reiterated three weeks later when the club went to the Champions-elect Everton and won a thrilling game 4-3. Nevin was having no problem doing to First Division defenders what he had done to those poor cones in training. He was always lively, always willing and constantly creating chances. Kerry Dixon won the Golden Boot that season and would be the first to say that it was Nevin's service that brought that prize to his mantle-piece.

NEVIN, as we know, was not one to get carried away. Yes, he was loving his time in the First Division. Yes, he was proud of what the club was doing, but was he awe struck, was he carried away? The simple answer to that was "No". "I would come into the dressing-room and listen to my music as ever," recalls Nevin. "With only moments to go before kick-off I would lean over to the skipper and my mate, Colin Pates and say, 'Who have we got today?' He'd look at me with this horrified look on his face. 'Man United, Pat! Manchester United!'"

Not that he didn't care, Nevin was the most terrible loser and no other took defeat as hard as him. It was just that playing came so natural, so why worry about who you're up against? He had done well for Clyde, he had excelled for Scotland's youth teams and now he had starred at Chelsea. All these teams had gained from his input, so why get overexcited about who was in the opposing dressing-room?

John Neal had been suffering with a heart condition and took a job "upstairs" on the board in the summer of 1985. John Hollins, for so long the engine to Chelsea's glamorous Rolls-Royce of the 60s and 70s had been a coach under Neal, but was now charged with taking the reins of a team that had more than got to grips with life in the First Division.

Sixth place in the table once more didn't represent progress as such, but fans just had to close their eyes and remember the way in which, only three years before their team was attracting only a handful of supporters and struggling against Rotherham and Grimsby. Nevin was part of this newfound stability and his own strengths were rewarded in March 1986 with his first cap for his country. Romania were the opposition at Hampden Park on a night when his boyhood hero, Kenny Dalglish, won his 100th cap. It wasn't enough to break into that summer's World Cup squad in Mexico, but he did make 27 more appearances for his country.

1986 did see some silverware make its way to Chelsea, albeit the Full Members Cup (a strange little competition arranged by the Football league to soften the blow of the European club ban). Nevin had his day at Wembley and created a couple of goals in David Speedie's hat-trick as Manchester City were beaten 5-4. It was silverware at least and 68,000 were there to see it.

The following season, though, was a fine example of Nevin at his best. His form was such that Chelsea hit the heady heights at the top of the First Division by Christmas, but the dizziness of old returned and down they dropped. They finished 14th that year, but Nevin had been brilliant, driving the team forward even as their form deserted them. Bug in the close season it became clear that the squad that had promised so much was going to be dismantled. David Speedie was sent to Coventry, whilst Nigel Spackman joined Liverpool.

NEVIN'S popularity never waned. The increasing numbers who turned up early enough rejoiced in his warm up that saw him demonstrating the sort of tricks that had once earned him a couple of lasagnes whilst travelling in Italy. The fans loved it and named him their Player of the Year for second time.

Nevin had forged a great relationship with those who paid to watch him entertain. He would often share banter with them when collecting the ball for a throw on, but was always aware that he was a face, a footballer, an icon, not a human being, to them. "When a young person gets fame it can be odd and you can take it for granted," he says. "You can either act like an arsehole or else you can carry on regardless and continue to be yourself. As I say, I had that bit of skill and I worked hard, but I knew it was not me they liked, they didn't know me, it was the guy kicking the football, so I knew not to get carried away with it."

It was a healthy attitude, as was his take on the nastier elements of those who called themselves fans of Chelsea. The hooligan element was there alright as it was at many grounds around the country. It wasn't just a Chelsea problem, but it was there. Sociologists and journalists have written much over the years about the phenomenon that was known as "football's disease" so we don't have to go into it here in too much detail, but Nevin was very aware of what was happening on the terraces.

Be they on the Shed or the notorious Gate 13 in the lower tier of the East Stand, those fighting in the name of the club drew only derision from Nevin. The racism levied at opposing players as loudly as it was at their own struck a horrific chord, but unlike many playing the game, Nevin was vehement in his condemnation.

"I've met them, I've spoken to them. 'How do you think we played there?' I'd ask.

'Don't know, Pat. We were having a ruck outside." I despised them for that attitude, I really did. I said how much I hated them and I suppose footballers weren't known for their opinions back then. Twenty years ago it was accepted in the game to a degree. It was seen as the norm, but not from me, I hated it."

"Before it was really trendy I was involved in anti-apartheid. I didn't vocalise my politics much and certainly wouldn't have at the club. It was something I believed in, though, and certainly at the time the two problems at the club then were the racism and the fighting.

"I felt strongly about it and sensed that the BNP, or the NF or whatever they called themselves were using our club as a vehicle and I hated them for that. These fans had no interest in football, they didn't love Chelsea. They were there for ulterior motives and that was annoying because true Chelsea fans were phenomenal. I loved them, I still do to this day. They're fantastic, but there was a sizeable minority of hooligans and racists who have latched on and they set the tone, they gained the reputation.

The club's reputation centred around its renowned hooli-crew. Chelsea's "Head-hunters" had become the face of the club, the vewpoint, the voice. That was wrong and Nevin knew it. "The club suffered. There was this thuggish picture of the skinhead and the bulldogs and the Union Jacks, but that was wrong. I knew a lot of the fans and became pals with a lot of them and they were extremely well educated, right on and committed enough to follow the team despite these arseholes who had latched on to it. They would travel in huge numbers and because of a few they would all be treated badly by the police. The majority were excellent, sophisticated and the numbers they used to travel in. My God!"

PETER COLLINS, a founder of the fanzine *Chelsea Independent* recalls just how new and exciting Nevin was. Collins, a student at the time, had interviewed Nevin for a student magazine and they remain friends to this day. "What a great footballer. I always say that the best all-round player was Gullit, the most exciting player was Zola, but I would put Nevin up with them. He wasn't necessarily there as a player, but in the context with what had gone on back then and how miserable the place had been, he was just as important and refreshing. We hadn't seen his ilk for a while. He was different."

Collins goes onto state just how refreshing it was to have someone like Nevin at the club as an antidote to the reputation and ill-feeling that had seeped its way in. "We got a reputation for having a core of racist fans. Others had then too, but we got branded as the problem club. Pat wouldn't want to be seen as a saving grace, but the best thing that can happen is firstly for there to be black players, of which there was only one at Chelsea and then Asian and black fans and then lastly perhaps a player who lets it be known where he stands and how much he detests that sort of support. Pat won't want to be symbol of hope or anything, but he certainly helped. He definitely gave the club an image boost."

That mutual appreciation was heightened by Nevin's constant involvement in the Supporters' Club's functions. Nevin, knowing that the relationship between fan and player can be a forced one was not one to let his time with them be wasted and set about trying to engage on a level playing field.

"My attitude was to go and talk to everyone. They were the club. I would be leaving Stamford Bridge after a game and would get asked for my autograph by a grown man. That was weird. 'You don't want my autograph,' I'd say. 'Lets have a chat. What did you think of the match?' I enjoyed that. You get the first 10 minutes when they are star struck, but then you could have a good conversation and that's what I did."

In fact, one of Nevin's fondest memories whilst at Chelsea was after a game as he made his way back to his Earl's Court home through Chelsea's streets. He was tapped on the shoulder and greeted by an older fan, who told him he hadn't been coming to the Bridge for about twenty years, but thanks to Nevin's style of football, he was again a regular.

That felt good, but contact with football's fans wasn't always such a pleasure. Having arrived in London as a youngster, Nevin, on evenings off, would go to Tottenham to watch a team he found more than entertaining. Mickey Hazard and Glenn Hoddle were great to watch and Nevin, then a fringe Second Division player, stood on the Shelf unnoticed and untroubled.

A year later, now in the First Division, Nevin played at White Hart Lane and informed his team-mates to leave without him, he would be taking the tube home. The players raised their eye-brows as their intrepid explorer made his way down the Seven Sisters Road. The fractious relationship between the two clubs was far from his mind as he stood on the tube train, his boots in his bag. Soon a Tottenham fan stopped staring and approached the man he was sure he recognised.

"You're Nevin," said the fan.

"I don't know what you're talking about," replied Nevin in that mockney accent of his.

"You're Nevin. You play for Chelsea."

"Not me, pal."

Who do you support?"

"Spurs of course."

"Who's your favourite player then?" he asked. Nevin laughed at the thought that if he was a professional player he wouldn't know a Spurs player. "What a twat!" he remarks today.

"Micky Hazard," said Nevin vowing to himself that he was going to start driving lessons the very next day. The tube stopped at the next station and Nevin went to get off, but was blocked by his assailant. Looking up at the man, he took a step back, pointed at the ceiling and smacked him in the face (his father would have been proud) before running off the tube and sprinting down the platform where a police presence ensured he wasn't followed.

Nevin's last season, 1987/88, ended in disappointment for both he and the club. Under John Hollins and his assistant Bobby Campbell, things hadn't gone smoothly. Nevin particularly struggled to be coached by the more conservative Campbell who lacked Neal's faith in the Scotsman's natural gifts. Despite that, and as the season descended toward relegation, Nevin continued to give his all. His form wasn't what it had been, sure, but he would have despised the fans thinking he was trying to get away from the sinking ship.

He was loved by so many, drawn to his character as well as his football. Nevin thought that sometimes the love they held for him was silly, but who was he to complain? He pushed for a new contract, despite it becoming clear that the club could soon well find themselves in the Second Division. "We'll discuss it later," came the reply time and time again from the club and Nevin was soon aware that the management might cash in on their star.

His style of play had been curbed on the training pitch and it was clear when Hollins left and Campbell took the job that his time was up. Nevin, though, wasn't one for complaining in the press or chastising a club he would have gladly played out his career at. It was time to go and after a transfer dispute that resulted in a tribunal, a £925,000 move to Everton was finally sealed.

CHELSEA once more had to say goodbye to one of its favourite sons at the height of his powers. Nevin was as sad as anyone. This was a club who had touched him as much he had touched them. Once, when injured, he'd turned down his posh seat and opted to stand alone on the Shed. "I stood there and not one person said a word. There were whispers I could hear, but nothing else. There I was, on my own, singing songs and nothing was said. I was singing 'There's only one Kerry Dixon.' I didn't sing the Speedie stuff mind! 'He's shite, get him off'"

Nevin played for Everton until the arrival for a second spell as manager of Howard Kendall, who he says, "he didn't rate me and I didn't rate him, so that's OK, but I was playing the best football of my career and he wouldn't give me a game after he arrived". After his departure from Goodison for Tranmere, Nevin was soon back at the Bridge and back on the Shed. This time the fans weren't so bashful. "I had signed for Tranmere and had a weekend off. I went along to the Shed to watch them play Everton. That was a mistake. They started singing my name and that looked bad as I'd only left Everton a few weeks before."

Who could blame them? Those chanting his name knew his worth and easily remembered what he had brought them in terms of skill and charisma. Nevin hugging the touchline, waiting for the pass, ready to razzle and dazzle an expectant and ravenous crowd. "You could hear a little raise in the noise when I got the ball, but you still don't know how you're really perceived. I never took any adulation seriously, never. I think that is a positive attitude."

Serious or not, that adulation was real. These were dark times for football, as they had been for Chelsea before Nevin's arrival. The young Scot brought some class and some dignity back to both the club and the game. Thatcher was wrong, the game needn't be banished to the corner and it ultimately wouldn't be. Joey Jones was right; Pat Nevin was "a breath of fresh air."

KERRY DIXON

1983-1992

CHELSEA CAREER

Games	420
Goals	193
Caps	8

MAGIC MOMENT

Kerry's hat-trick against Leeds in 1984 in a 5-0 win meant that promotion was theirs. "Chelsea are back!"

'GOLDEN BOY'

> **It was a blonde. A blonde to make a bishop kick a hole in a stained-glass window.**
>
> **"Farewell, My Lovely", Raymond Chandler**

JOHN Neal used to have his Chelsea men working hard up and down the Welsh sand dunes of Aberystwyth. There he would compel them to drag their weary bodies in a pre-season effort to rid them of the excess that footballers have long enjoyed over the holiday months. In the summer of 1983 that effort was going to have to be considerable. The club had survived the very real threat of relegation to the Third Division by the proverbial skin of their teeth and with it the equally real threat of complete extinction.

Now Neal was building a new team with new aspirations. It was going to take hard work. These weren't the usual Chelsea household names bought in to bring instant success. Long gone were the days when a Mears family member could open his copious wallet or write a blank cheque. Those days would not return to Chelsea until a certain Russian oil tycoon took over the reigns twenty odd years down the line. These players were going to have to sweat to succeed through good old hard work and endeavour and that was going to start up and down those sand dunes.

As the players worked hard to rid their bodies of the summer's sangrias and barbeques, a new face arrived. The chairman, Ken Bates had brought him to Wales personally in an effort to convince him of the benefits of signing for Chelsea and now he was kitted out and ready for work.

His square jaw and mop of blonde hair were immediately noticeable as he set about climbing the dunes like Peter O'Toole in Lawrence of Arabia. It was tough, but he was here to impress, he had never done any training like this, but he was here to impress. As he pounded those dunes, Neal took a breath and muttered, "Bloody hell, if he can play like he runs, I've got myself a world beater."

TYPICALLY Kerry Dixon laughs at the idea that he could have possibly made an impression that day on a Welsh beach. "If you consider last on the beach run and second last on another run world-beating, then maybe," he laughs. "John must have looked at the fact that despite my obvious struggles, I kept going and therefore he liked me."

Over the next nine seasons, Chelsea's fans would join their manager in appreciation for the centre-forward. The effort he showed during that first day's training was a hallmark of the following decade and his presence in the team and in the club's forward line always meant that goals were never far away. Dixon filled that famous blue Number 9 shirt with ample authority. His blonde hair, rounded shoulders and barrel chest gave him a swashbuckling swagger whilst his pace, delicate touch, clinical finishing and ability in the air meant that the sturdiest of centre-backs would, after an encounter with Chelsea, retreat to the communal bath assured that they had just earned every penny of their wages.

Add together Dixon's Roy of the Rovers looks and the 193 goals he scored for the Blues, each greeted by two clenched fists aimed at the sky, it is no surprise to learn that this is one of Chelsea's most enduring heroes

Dixon didn't possess the best first touch ("but my last isn't bad," he once declared), but he had purpose. He was the ideal target man, but with more to his game than simply heading on long balls or holding up play for more nubile performers á la Peter Crouch. He would get at defences, outpace them and had an eye for a finish that was as good as any in a decade brimming over with fine goalscorers.

He wasn't the most outlandish dresser, his politics were his own business and he wasn't one to be seen out with glamorous women dripping from each arm. But perhaps because of that Dixon became the pin-up; the golden boy and Chelsea fans loved him for old-fashioned reasons – namely goals and glory. For a generation of supporters who'd grown up with mediocrity and had been forced to sit and listen to endless tales of brilliant centre-forwards, winning trophies, cups and celebrity, Dixon was the perfect antidote.

For those on the Shed, there was "Only one Kerry Dixon,", but that didn't prevent the inevitable, but flattering comparisons. "There was bound to be," says Dixon. "Ossie was *the* big Chelsea number 9, and there was Roy Bentley, so it was great to be talked about in the same breath as those guys." It was the latter who first encountered Dixon when he was club secretary at Reading and Dixon was their young striker only just beginning to suggest his huge potential by banging in 25 goals in his first two seasons as a teenager. "When I was a young man, Roy used to tell all about Stamford Bridge, what he had achieved there and how the fans used to cheer his every goal. It was nice to eventually be compared to him."

TOMMY LAWTON, Roy Bentley, Peter Osgood; all legends in blue and all centre-forwards, but it was the less abrasive inside-forward Bobby Tambling who Dixon most wanted to emulate. That goalscoring record of his, 202 in 370 games, loomed large on an ever-decreasing horizon and it was Dixon who, more than any other player, threatened to make it his own. It didn't happen and today, thirteen years after leaving the Bridge, the very topic of what he regarded as his destiny evokes emotion. "That is the greatest regret of my life," he says and a fixed stare tells you that he isn't joking. "I spoke to Bobby and he agrees that I should have beaten it.

"I think it will stand now forever. It will be very hard for a young forward to come here and play over a period of years and score so consistently. That isn't the modern game. This is one of the best clubs in the world so maybe a great forward might come here and do it, but I doubt it.

"I was so sad to not beat it, though. Maybe I was going out to play with it on my mind. I hope I went out there and got on with the game, but I guess it might have been lingering in the back of my mind. I had been kicked out of two clubs as a kid. Luton and then Tottenham said I wasn't good enough, so you learn to take the knocks, but that still hurts."

Dixon finished his Chelsea career nine goals shy of Tambling's total, not bad at all for one who as a young man trying to make his way in the game was told "Thanks, but no thanks", by those not one, but two league clubs. David Pleat had regarded him not suitable for his Luton Town side and, having gone on aged only 16 and scored plenty of goals for Chesham United in the Isthmian League, it was Spurs who took a closer look, offering him an apprenticeship. Again, though, Dixon was deemed surplus to requirements.

Non-League football, as well as an engineering course took up Dixon's time, but 52 goals in one season for Dunstable in the Southern League ensured League clubs would at last take notice and in July 1980 it was Maurice Evans, the manager of Third Division Reading, who parted with £20,000 (the then second highest fee for a league club to pay a non-league outfit for a player).

THE WORLD of engineering would have to do without Dixon's input as league football began to benefit from his arrival and in his first full season he finished as Reading's top scorer with 13 goals. It wasn't as easy as it sounds. Dixon was getting used to life as a pro, but, being a determined individual, once he found his feet, there was no looking back.

He scored 28 goals in the 1982/83 season, finishing top scorer in the very Division that John Neal's men were fighting so hard to avoid dropping into. Despite housing the most prolific scorer in their league, Reading were relegated (they let in as many as they scored – a fact highlighted by one match against Doncaster in which Dixon scored four, Reading scored five, but Doncaster managed seven) and it was obvious that their striker was going to have to move on and better himself.

His goalscoring feats had attracted a lot of attention. Bobby Gould at Coventry, Howard Wilkinson, the new man at Sheffield Wednesday, and Bobby Ferguson at Ipswich had all shown an interest, but it was Chelsea who moved with the most purpose. "Ken Bates arrived at the club and drove me up to the training camp in Aberystwyth. I had agreed to train with them and have a look at the set up, but Ken pretty much convinced me on the drive in his red carpeted Roller to sign for them.

"Having me running up and down those dunes wasn't the most endearing method of convincing me to come, but the rest of it went well. Ken was a great salesman for the club, John Neal was clearly a great football man, Ian McNeil his assistant, John Hollins too, and they all convinced me to sign."

£175,000 convinced Reading and Kerry Dixon was a Chelsea player. He wasn't the only new boy. Neal brought in a glut of new players that summer to attempt to break the cycle of mediocrity which had so afflicted the club, but that spree in the transfer market wasn't necessarily geared toward the immediate success that followed. "They mentioned what their hopes were," recalls Dixon. "They didn't mention winning anything or going up, they just wanted to improve on the season before which hadn't been acceptable. They hoped that us new players would give the place a much-needed boost. They said this club was a sleeping giant and I knew that."

THE CURTAINS had been drawn and the light switched off after the memorable days under Dave Sexton, halcyon days that had touched Dixon as a young football fan. As a boy he had watched the FA Cup Final replay against Leeds in 1970 and marvelled at Osgood's flying header and the glamour of the eye-catching club. With that in mind, the hard sell hadn't been too necessary.

But Dixon was not alone in believing that he had the talent to return at least a modicum of good times to the deeply depressed Bridge. The arrivals of the likes of Speedie, Nevin, Niedzwiecki and Rougvie packed the side with blossoming talent and fiery determination. It was to prove a potent mix.

Sometimes in life groups of people come together to form a sum greater than the parts. That summer's arrivals gelled exquisitely on Chelsea's training pitch playing like lifelong team-mates from the off. Simply from the way they clicked in training those low expectations began to grow. It was a strong league. At the outset Chelsea's expectations may have been no higher than to avoid the struggles of the season before, but the likes of Derby, Sheffield Wednesday, Newcastle and Manchester City set about fighting for promotion.

"They were all decent. Future world stars were involved. Chris Waddle, Peter Beardsley. Man City had great players, but funnily enough it was Sheffield Wednesday who would become our great rivals over the next few years. Expectations were low, but for me personally they were high. I put pressure on myself, I wanted to know if I could make this step up a division and score goals again. Could I get in the side, could I play well, could I score?"

The answer to that last question was an emphatic and immediate "YES". Peter Taylor brought his Derby team to London on a warm August opening day, ready to prove that he was more than Brian Clough's shadow. The Rams were strong promotion contenders according to those in the know, but what they didn't know was that John Neal's modestly assembled squad *were* about to bring smiles back to the Bridge, a place that had become as hearty and optimistic as the vast Brompton cemetery that flanks its East Stand.

Chelsea immediately got about their visitors. Clive Walker began to tantalise, Speedie began to terrorise and Dixon was on hand to capitalise. The new centre-forward scored twice in the 5-0 win, each time showing off both his power and pace. Chelsea had a new goal-getter and about time too! As far back as 1974, Chelsea's *Official Yearbook*, edited by Albert Sewell (for so long the club's programme editor) bemoaned the lack of a regular goalscorer. Osgood had been sold and Greaves, Bridges and Tambling were nothing but black and white photographs in the Down Memory Lane section.

"As far as individual requirements are concerned, one Chelsea need stands out above all others at the start of 1974-75," declared Sewell. "They must find a goalscorer. No, not a striker or a front-runner, to use the modern idiom, but a real, old-fashioned goalscorer...Chelsea's problem is greater than most and must be solved quickly if their two million pound stand is to be brought to life – noisy, cheering, throbbing, exciting life – on Saturday afternoons.

Now, almost ten years later, it seemed that request had been met in the form of Kerry Dixon. That stand had reflected the clubs gloom off the pitch for the latter part of the 1970s, but now fans returned to fill it and enjoy a "throbbing" and "exciting" new dawn.

GOALS aplenty arrived as games were won 3-2, 4-0 and 5-3. The latter was the result at Fulham's Craven Cottage in October 1983 when, despite a Gordon Davies hat-trick for the hosts, Chelsea revealed their credentials as serious promotion contenders. That day, Dixon proved there was much more to him than just a burly target man. He bagged two, his first a fine run and shot and his second a similar run, but this time topped off with a deft, curling effort into the corner. Classic Kerry.

As Chelsea continued winning and Dixon continued scoring, promotion beckoned and in April, with over 33,000 fans at the Bridge, Leeds United were dismantled 5-0 (Dixon got a hat-trick) and the Blues were going up. It was a joyous day, the Shed was at its raucous best as the spring sun beamed down. Despite Bates' pleas on the loudspeaker fans streamed onto the pitch – peacefully – after each goal on an occasion that John Neal declared "You could write a book about."

The epilogue to such a work would be scribed two weeks later when, in the last game of the season Grimsby were beaten 1-0 and Chelsea, by virtue of goal difference, were going up as Champions. Again it was Dixon who got the decisive goal having latched onto more fine work from Pat Nevin. The good times were rolling in, after five long and depressing years when further relegation and very possible extermination had loomed high over the Bridge.

Of course a team of such characters wasn't without its internal problems. The fire and brimstone that the team could offer on the pitch was reflected by the personalities off of it. Dixon was a docile and approachable man off the pitch. He played to win, but generally he wasn't in the market for bust-ups and tribulation. Having said that, he could defend himself surprisingly vigorously for a man more at home during his off-field activities on a catwalk than in a boxing ring.

Having lost a vital game at the Bridge that season to their rivals Manchester City the team trudged off disappointed and at odds at the reasons for their defeat. David Speedie, the antithesis of the more laid-back Dixon, was in no doubt. "Why didn't you pass to me, big man?" he decried to his partner. "You really are a greedy bastard." With that tempers blew and fists flew. Joey Jones recalls being in the dressing-room contemplating breaking up the ensuing melée, but then thinking better of it. "I grabbed a cup of tea and enjoyed the show as Speedo and Kerry went for it, hammer and tongs.

"Speedie was a great player, but boy, could he moan. Moan, moan, moan, moan. That man could moan for Scotland. Anyway Kerry twatted him and it kicked off and all I'll say is, if it was going to go off, Kerry was someone you would like behind you. Never mind those baby-faced good looks, he was a tough boy, you know. I'd back him to beat most."

To both men it had been nothing but a brawl between colleagues. The kind of thing that happens more commonly than we might think and is only brought into national focus when some incident or other is witnessed, such as John Hartson's infamous training ground kick in the face of West Ham team-mate Eyal Berkovic. Dixon and Speedie's spat was forgotten, especially amidst the furore of promotion. The fans were ecstatic, lauding their favourites to the hilt in song, but their blonde goalscoring hero was all too aware – again because of his unsure route into the game – that things can change in an instant.

"I know that fans can be a fickle bunch," he laughs. "You are only as good as your last game. It is a cliché, but it's right. Things change and things happen. It was lovely though. I noticed early on that they were singing my name and cheering me as I ran out. It's a wonderful thing, it really is and if you have it, it doesn't half help. I had a great relationship with them throughout my time at Chelsea. Of course there were some bad times, but not many. We got relegated in 1988 and there were the obvious grumbles, but on the whole they didn't single me out for that. By and large over nine years I had a great rapport with them and that has continued to this day."

DIXON meets me to chat outside what is now the Shed Bar at Stamford Bridge on the evening of a Champions League fixture. It is a galaxy away from the fabric of the club he once plundered goals for. The restaurants, the bars, the money, top-flight European football, and a thronging gift shop epitomise the modern game, but as he prepares to entertain the evening's corporate visitors he can't escape his past. We stroll along the original Shed wall that stands as a reminder of a more straightforward era, not so very long ago. Some fans more interested by what they have just bought from the shop wouldn't recognise him, but to those with memories of the big-man's exploits there is a knowing look, a cry of "Kerry" and a friendly handshake in way of thanks.

And here is Dixon's true claim to cult status. Unlike Speedie, the more obvious choice for Chelsea fans of the day, who adored his pugilistic approach and equal ability to find the net, Dixon's stature has endured. They may have been a fearsome partnership on the pitch; Dixon and Speedie became a by-word for dangerous strike partnerships during the mid-1980s, but when all is said and done, Speedie was not loved, not even liked. In fact he was admired purely because he was an annoying git; Chelsea's annoying git. OK, at the time Chelsea's fans adored Speedie arguably even more than Dixon, as evidenced by Speedie's Player of the Season award in 1984/85 (Dixon would never win that honour), but as soon as he departed for Coventry in 1987, Speedie was no longer part of Chelsea FC. He was a deserter; that annoying Scots git.

Dixon's memory is founded on much more solid foundations. He didn't have the fire and brimstone of Speedie, but he was admired for longer-lasting qualities; skill, dedication, longevity and, most importantly, all those goals. The contrast could not be plainer; just as the adoration which still comes Dixon's way is as golden in hue as the striker's flowing locks and that characteristic chain around his neck.

Back in the summer of 1984, Chelsea laughed in the face of press expectation of a season of struggle and prepared for First Division Football. Not much had changed since they had gone down, Liverpool were still European Champions and had won the League title yet again, but now Neal's new Chelsea were coming up with belief. Dixon's 34 goals in the promotion season had earned him the Second Division's Golden Boot, but could he take yet another step up?

"People look for you to fail," he says. "That's the way of the world. You are built up to be knocked down. Even when I played for England people were saying I wasn't good enough, but I'm thick-skinned enough to not worry about other people. Not everyone in the world is going to like everyone, but I just got on with trying to prove that I was up for the challenge."

That challenge began at Highbury, never the happiest of stomping grounds for Chelsea's faithful, but as good a place as any to test one's credentials and aptitude for life back with the big boys. For Dixon it was to be a day that answered any doubters, including himself. "That was one of the great games for me. We drew 1-1, which wasn't bad start and I scored past Pat Jennings and immediately felt I was going to be OK. It wasn't the most spectacular goal, but it wasn't bad and I reckon it may have been the most important of my career."

From Highbury the goals, Dixon's stock in trade, didn't stop flowing. Chelsea competed with purpose, their players each proving they were more than able top-flight competitors. Their eventual sixth place finish was highly commendable and Dixon – alongside Gary Lineker – finished up as the league's top scorer with 24.

There could be no doubt. Even with quality centre-forwards such as Lineker, Graeme Sharp, Peter Withe, Mark Hughes and Mick Harford around, Chelsea supporters could cite their own as among the best. England manager Bobby Robson agreed and was intent on having a look at a player who must have reminded him of the men he himself would have played against. John Charles, big and skilful; Nat Lofthouse awesomely athletic, Dixon had something of their ways about him and Robson rewarded him with a cap in a close-season pre-World Cup tour to Mexico in 1985.

Dixon made his debut as a substitute against the home nation in a 1-0 defeat, becoming in the process the first Chelsea player since Ray Wilkins in 1979 to represent England. But better was to come. Picked to start the next game against West Germany in smoggy 100-degree temperatures, Dixon proved himself once more and scored twice in a 3-0 win. Robson could take note, here was a man able to live on a world stage, let alone at Luton or Tottenham, and Chelsea fans were brimming with pride.

THE BEGINNING of the following season continued to bring goals and more goals. By Christmas, Dixon had scored an incredible 21 times, but then in January he tore a stomach muscle in a Cup defeat to Liverpool and was out for two months. Like Alan Hudson before him, he feared a World Cup trip to Mexico may be lost, but on his return he managed to get back in the groove – including two goals at Old Trafford – and bagged a spot in Robson's final squad of 22.

Dixon only managed a handful of minutes that summer and only won eight caps in total. The four goals he scored in those few games underline a man with an eye for goal, but in the end he was a victim of the times he lived in, unable to get ahead of Gary Lineker, who had forged a lethal partnership with Peter Beardsley, in the pecking order.

"I was pleased to get a cap or two, but of course I would have loved 100," Dixon says. "I was playing at a time when there were an awful lot of good, good forwards about vying for only two places in the team. That is not the case right now, I don't think, but back then it was extra tough. Clive Allen, Lineker, Tony Cottee, John Fashanu and Steve Bull later, Alan Smith. They were all very good."

Whilst these men were trying to manoeuvre themselves into the International set-up, the nation's clubs were all in a quest to have them playing in their colours. Ian Rush was leaving Liverpool for an Italian job and would have to be replaced. George Graham was building a new team at Arsenal and wanted a target man to base his style of play around, whilst the likes of Tottenham and Manchester

United were always on the look-out for the kind of quality players they hoped would make their fans' dreams reality and also live up to their footballing traditions.

Dixon's name was never far away from the back pages. He was an obvious choice for many of these clubs (Bates scared some off, including United, with an incredible £5 million price-tag, which dwarfed the £800,000 paid by Everton for Lineker that summer), but it was clear that he may have a price. Not that he was eager to leave. "I was close enough to going without ever being extremely close. I never wanted to leave, not ever, but whilst I was always being linked with clubs I guess there was always a possibility. During the John Hollins era it seemed a distinct possibility, but, as I say, I never wanted to go."

CHELSEA fans detected that and Dixon's stock rose as someone at last who would stay and try and finish the job that had been started. Speedie didn't. Speedie left – and for Coventry. They may have won the FA Cup the season before, but it was hardly the kind of move to launch his career into the stratosphere and it ensured that his memory was instantly blackened in Chelsea fans' eyes. Rumours of Dixon's sale, however, were never far away as the club's management flirted with the idea of cashing in. "I spoke to West Ham and I talked to Arsenal because I had been informed that the club were prepared to sell me. I had to talk to clubs whether I liked it or not.

"Real Madrid were keen too. Raddy Antic was the manager and fancied me, but soon it was all irrelevant as Ken Bates stepped in. He was prepared to give me a new deal and was adamant that we got on with the job at hand."

That task was becoming harder. Chelsea had again come sixth in 1986, but the following season saw the team begin to break up. Dixon may have been staying, but Speedie and the unsung Nigel Spackman weren't. To Dixon it was a vital error to let such players go. "I thought it was the big tragedy that players were allowed to leave. I think it was a massive mistake selling those guys. Then John Neal got ill and was moved upstairs. Hollins came in and, in my mind, wrong decisions were taken, but that happens. You have to get on with it, but I felt that what had been built under John Neal was a very solid foundation and now integral parts of that were being sold on and the team broke down."

Despte Dixon's goals, 36 in the league over the next three seasons, results began to stagnate; so much so that once more the roller-coaster ride that is being a Chelsea fan was descending rapidly toward another relegation. They finished fourth from bottom, but that meant a play-off against Middlesbrough due to the league cutting the size of the top flight by one club to bring it down to the current size of 20. That was lost amid further crowd trouble and Dixon (who scored 14 goals that season) would again have to ply his trade in a lower league. It was another chapter in the club's history darkened by trouble, but, as depressing a time as it was, Dixon remained faithful to his faithful fans.

"I was aware of what was going on and whilst you don't like some of the things you hear you can only react to how the fans are with you and they were brilliant to me. I don't like violence, but it was a sign of the times and every club had it to some extent. They were unfairly blamed at times because of previous misdemeanours."

This defence of Chelsea's moronic minority may be slightly misplaced, but reveals a steely determination in this model (and that's the catwalk kind) footballer that belies the first impression that may lead one to believe that pretty boys such as Dixon don't like the rough stuff. That exists within the likes of David Beckham today. Those blessed with boyish good looks and skill never carry much of a reputation for the steely side of their game and yet Dixon, like Beckham, possessed plenty of grit to go with the glamour and the looks. Mind you, Dixon had the temperament to keep his tantrums to himself, unlike both Beckham and his fire-breathing contemporary, Speedie. And that quality only endears him more to his fans.

JOHN HOLLINS departed Chelsea's managerial chair after relegation and it was Bobby Campbell who set about working to build a team that would once more get the team back to the First Division. He forged a new strikeforce as Gordon Durie and Kevin Wilson arrived and between the three of them goals flowed. "Kevin and Gordon did very well. I adapted to their styles. Neither of them were Nevin or Speedie, but they were their own men and we all got a good amount of goals. In fact there was quite a keen tussle for goals that promotion year, but I came out on top with 25."

Dixon continued with 20 goals in the 1989/90 including a wonderful hat-trick at Millwall toward the end of the season when he once more proved his array of centre-forward attributes with his drive, his purpose and his aerial ability. Chelsea ended the season on a high, finishing 5th, their best performance since 1970. Both of his teams that had won and consolidated promotion were exciting, but which does Dixon consider the best?

"League positions would suggest that the 1989 team were better, but the flair of the 1984 side makes them the better team for me. Both topped the table at one time, but the potential, the exciting nature, the unpredictability of John Neal's lot makes them stand out."

The first few years of the 1990s were also the last few seasons of football as the country knew it. Premiership glamour was just around the corner and TV saturation, along with foreign imports, was about to take the nation by storm. Dixon represented the old school. He continued to find the back of the net regularly, but by 1992 the club were looking to spend available funds on new faces and that meant his days were numbered; and with that decision went his chances of breaking Tambling's record.

"Mick Hartford had come, Tony Cascarino and Robert Fleck had arrived and they're my mates, but I was willing to stay and fight for my place and break Bobby's record. I was told, though, that I was going to be playing in the reserves and felt I would just waste away waiting for a chance that wouldn't come. I wasn't prepared to do that and when the chance came along to play in the new Premiership with Southampton I took it. It was a bloody tough decision though."

Did he leave a bitter man? "I'm not a bitter person, I do accept life and football for what they are. It was the saddest thing, though, not breaking that record." He was so close, but his last goal, in March 1992 at Norwich, was a reminder of what the club was letting go. With his back to goal Dixon killed a long ball with his right-foot, turned the centre-back and curled a delightful left-foot shot into the top corner. Thank you and good night.

HE'D be back of course. His spell at Southampton didn't last long, but in 1994 he took a decent Luton side to the semi-finals of the FA Cup. "It was dreadful. We had done well in the Cup; we had a good little side. We were in the draw as were Chelsea, Man United and Oldham. You can imagine who we wanted. That was the dream, to beat Oldham and get Chelsea in the final, but it never happened, we got Chelsea and there I was playing my old team."

Glenn Hoddle's side won comfortably 2-0 at Wembley, but after the final whistle, amid his obvious disappointment, Luton's centre-forward heard his name echoing from the end packed with Blues fans. "It was the greatest moment of my football career, not the game, but afterwards when the Chelsea fans gave me that most amazing reception. That was up there with scoring for England on my full debut.

"The place means everything to me and my family. My family are from Luton and we like Luton Town, but we are all Chelsea fans and Chelsea have become my life. The club has done so much for me and I would like to think I have more than paid them back. The fans still sing my name. Even today. I like to think I treat them with respect and long may that continue."

And Dixon's memory lives on to this day, along with Osgood, Hudson and Harris, in song. A cry that reverberates occasionally around the Bridge to this day; a fitting epitaph for Chelsea's Golden Boy. There is, after all, "Only one Kerry Dixon."

DENNIS WISE

1990-2001

CHELSEA CAREER

Games	445
Goals	76
Caps	21

MAGIC MOMENT

Humbling the supposedly mighty AC Milan at the San Siro by scoring the late equaliser in 1999 which helped the Blues qualify for their first ever Champions League Quarter-final

'DENNIS THE MENACE'

> **Mr Dawkins's appearance did not say a vast deal in favour of the comforts which his patron's interest obtained for those which he took under his protection; but, he had a rather flighty and dissolute mode of conversing and furthermore avowed that among intimate friends he was better known by the sobriquet of "The Artful Dodger..."**
>
> **"Oliver Twist", Charles Dickens**

IN early October 2005, Geremi, Chelsea's Cameroonian midfielder lifts the ball over Liverpool's Spanish goalkeeper "Pepe" Reina and Chelsea, the reigning Champions and runaway leaders despite being only eight games into the season, are 4-1 up at Anfield. It's a rout as the Blues knife-like counter-attacks cut through the Merseysiders' buttery defence. The war of words that has erupted between the two clubs is settled by the men on the pitch as Chelsea fans rejoice in time honoured fashion. "One man went to mow!"

It didn't used to be like this, because there was a time when a trip to Anfield offered almost certain defeat, at best a hard fought draw, at worst, utter humiliation. A 5-1 hammering in September 1996 put paid to Chelsea's unbeaten start to the season and any thoughts that Glenn Hoddle's men were the next big thing.

Chelsea's record at Anfield had been appalling. They hadn't won at the old ground in a league game for a whopping 56 years, 1935, in fact, when they beat the Reds 3-2 thanks to two goals by Eric Oakton and one from Harry Burgess. Then, in 1992, the Blues arrived at Liverpool, who under Graeme Souness, were about to suffer a downturn in fortunes, but who still housed some of the most famous names and feet in the game. Ian Rush, Jan Molby, Mark Wright, Dean Saunders, they would guide the club to that year's FA Cup and so a trip there for Ian Porterfield's side seemed fraught with peril.

But this Chelsea team was not one to be cowed by illustrious reputation or precedent. Vinnie Jones, renowned debunker of supposed superiors, was relishing the argy-bargy of the occasion and Paul Elliott and Erland Johnsen steadily marshalled the back four, whilst Dennis Wise drove the side forward and snapped into the tackle. Jones scored a wonderful opening goal, but Liverpool levelled matters. No problem; Chelsea were well in this match and Blues fans sensed they were here for more than a day trip and a ritual defeat.

Then Wise latches onto a loose ball and fires Chelsea into a decisive lead to send those in the away section into raptures. The Kop is silenced, as Wise runs to the fans in blue. This was more than a simple badge-kissing occasion; this was the moment that the little midfielder had been waiting for. At last he had given the supporters reason to cherish him and his cheeky game. Kissing the badge would be purile. His joy was unconfined, so instead he launched himself into their throng and lapped up their adulation. He was one of them now; literally and he was never going to look back.

Wise was Man of the Match that day (an away team member claiming that honour at Anfield was virtually unheard of), he had been everywhere, he had even found time to miss a penalty, but it was a sign of Chelsea's form that day that such erroneous shortcomings mattered little to the joy of such a memorable occasion.

That moment made Dennis Wise a hero. The fact that it happened at Anfield only made it bigger news as those who'd witnessed the celebration at first hand boasted of how they had hugged the pocket-sized midfielder in equal glee. It's become one of those "I was there" moments. Apparently about 50,000 pairs of hands claim to have been there at last count. That's how much it means to fans to have witnessed the moment that Dennis Wise, the scamp, the dodger, won his Chelsea spurs.

THE FUTURE captain of the club had hardly inspired those very fans in the early part of his Stamford Bridge career, but that was nothing new was it? Love affairs between those on Chelsea's terraces and in the blue kit were often drawn out affairs. Like a Hollywood Rom-Com, love never blossomed easily and many hurdles were crossed before real affection was mutually offered and received.

Wise had found it hard to sell himself and his game to the fans, who were still more inclined to adore class, skill and swagger above industry and brawn, despite the hero-worship of the likes of Droy, Jones and Rougvie. It would take perseverance, but fortunately for everyone involved, Wise had that commodity in abundance and the supporters, who couldn't help but admire a player's raw effort, were soon sold on his obvious desire to do well for their team.

To Wise fans are "Punters". They are men and women who come to a football ground, pay good money and deserve to be entertained. Chelsea's "punters" clocked on to that attitude and loved him for it. To some players fans are a faceless and nameless bunch of people, there to create noise; a mob rather then individuals. Not to Wise though. Over the eleven years that he graced the blue shirt, he took time to see the crowd as individuals who deserved more. He was hardly a saint, but he appealed to the fans' sense of urgency, fun and commitment. He gave them the attention they deserved and in turn they adored him with all their hearts.

In Rick Glanvill's *Rhapsody in Blue*, Wise reiterates the point. "It's nice to be liked by the crowd," he said. "It's a great feeling. Wherever I've played I don't think I've been hated – I hope I never will be. People come to be entertained, basically, and to enjoy it. You play football, but you want to be part of it as well. You want all the punters not just to come, say, 'Oh, we've watched the game' and go home."

Wise offered the punters just that. Like Ian Wright at Arsenal or Bruce Grobbelaar at Liverpool, Wise was of that ilk. With that cheeky grin and with an air of menace about him as well as fine shot or pass, he was the link between fan and team. Players such as these make the experience of watching football more than just a soulless day gazing at untouchable and untenable superstars. Fans thrive on the interaction they get from these men and through them feel far more involved in what is, remember, *their* football club. And in the era of the Premiership, when footballers have become further and further distanced from their fans, a player like Wise was a rarity rather than the norm.

WHAT'S more, Wise was one of them. He hailed from West London. Brought up near Queen's Park Rangers in Shepherd's Bush, he excelled at football, despite his size and was snapped up by Southampton. It wouldn't work out on the South Coast and Chelsea were close to signing him as an 18-year-old in the spring of 1984, but stalled and so he joined Wimbledon, who, under Dave Bassett's command, were making their torrid way up the Football League. It was the perfect set-up for a player who played on his role as a street urchin; stealing the ball as if a nicking an apple from his Mum and Dad's fruit store in Shepherd's Bush market (knowing QPR fans used to sing "Fruit 'n' Veg, Fruit 'n' Veg" to the man who used to support their team).

Wise, along with the likes of John Fashanu, Vinnie Jones and Dave Beasant, thrived in the anarchic atmosphere of Plough Lane. They won promotion to the top flight and against all odds stayed there. Then the Dons had the temerity to win the FA Cup in 1988. Their story gave hope to millions that a small club could break the incessant domination of the few. Mind you, that was in the pre-Premiership era. Most of the Crazy Gang would, of course, move on to pastures new, and in Wise's case that would mean the short journey along the District Line to Fulham Broadway. It was the summer of 1990. Times at Stamford Bridge weren't exactly care-free. The club had won promotion in 1989 and whilst they looked unlikely to be in trouble at the wrong end of the table there was a distinct lack of flair within Bobby Campbell's set-up; no Nevin, no Speedie and with Dixon nearing the end of his career.

Heroes were at a premium, panâche even more so and so when the club forked out a club record £1.6 million for Wise – a member of those spoilers from deepest South-West London – it was hardly a move that had them skipping down the Fulham Road in expectation of a momentous season.

Wimbledon players came with a reputation. Like disruptive schoolboys, they were to be avoided. From a distance they could be fun, but when they arrived at your club, a place where a certain quality was expected, then that became embarrassing. Wise was treated with suspicion.

That day at Anfield though in February 1992, was a seminal one. Yes, Wise scored, threw himself at the fans and was forthwith idolised, but it was also an afternoon when the cheek of the players was accepted and even lorded. Vinnie Jones had stuck a piece of paper under Liverpool's famous "This is Anfield" sign. The scribbled note read, "We're Bothered" and aroused venom from the home club whilst the visiting fans, on hearing of the mischief couldn't help but be buoyed by their impish heroes. Wise was a good player, he had just proved that, but he was also something else as well, naughty, devilish and mischievous; and from then on the fans would love him for it.

BUT WHY did it take 18 months for Wise to find a place in Chelsea fans' hearts? The little midfielder's start to his first season at the bridge, 1990/91, was mixed. His debut was promising as he won the Man of the Match in a 2-1 win over a decent Derby County team. The second game, though, saw him sent off in a 2-1 defeat at Crystal Palace. What sort of player had the club taken on? Wise was playing in a central role, not the wide position that he had excelled in whilst at Wimbledon. He was finding his feet and the jury (i.e. the fans) remained well and truly out.

He was the most expensive player in the club's history, putting him on a par with record signings Hughie Gallacher, Steve Wicks and David Hay and therefore eyes were on his every move. The pressure had told on previous bearers of that particular load and did so once more with Wise. Mistakes were highlighted, whilst positive play was merely expected. That is the pressure top players find themselves under. The best take that pressure and use it as their match day petrol. Could Wise?

That first season, though, was typical Chelsea. A tremendous 3-2 win at Old Trafford in December 1990 triggered a five game winning streak which included a remarkable 6-4 victory at Derby, but there were too many blips; most notoriously the 7-0 defeat at Nottingham Forest in April. "Always look on the Bright Side of Life" sang the travelling fans (an occasion that has been cited as the first time Monty Python's tune made an appearance at a football ground).

During the barnstorming run Wise had shown enough for England to give him a chance and in May 1991, Graham Taylor handed him his first cap in a European Championship qualifier in Istanbul. England won 1-0 and Wise scored the goal, albeit with the aid of his arse.

Whereas Wise had done enough, Chelsea hadn't and Bobby Campbell departed under a cloud of mediocre football to be replaced by Ian Porterfield, the nice guy who had won the Cup for Sunderland in

1973, but who would struggle to impose his personality on the club. These were frustrating times. The football was tepid. Robert Fleck arrived and whilst popular in the stands, was hardly living up to his £2 million fee. At least his misery took the pressure of Wise as he passed on the poisoned chalice of record signing. Mick Hartford, Tony Cascarino, they were strong, but they weren't playing the silky stuff that Nevin, Dixon, Speedie and even Gordon Durie had offered not long before.

In 1991, the team reached the semi-final of the League Cup, but slipped up against eventual winners Sheffield Wednesday. The first leg at Stamford Bridge had finished 2-0 to the Yorkshiremen. In Glanvill's book, Wise bemoans the small crowd for such a big game, but in fact there were 34,000 there, not bad at all for the time, but their lack of enthusiasm in terms of noise spoke wonders for the apathy on the terraces at the time. By February 1993, a year after that win at Anfield, things hadn't improved. In 1992, the club had reached the quarter-final of the FA Cup for the first time in ten years, but had slipped up against Second Division Sunderland and so, halfway into the Premiership's inaugural season, 1992/93, Porterfield made way for old-favourite David Webb.

Wise himself had improved as a player under Porterfield (he finished as top-scorer with 15 goals in 1991-92). He found Porterfield a nice bloke, but maybe too nice and at least under Webb results improved. But still the style remained stagnant. Club Chairman Ken Bates was always one for style (his famous fur coat, so reminiscent of Fatty Foulke's, is testimony to that) and there was one young manager who was available and who could change the profile and the fortunes of the club around almost over night.

GLENN HODDLE was always Tottenham. Think Glenn Hoddle and you think of him with that famous lily-white shirt loosely hanging over his shorts and against his permanently tanned legs. Could a Tottenham man make his way at Chelsea once more? Well, perhaps surprisingly, yes he could. Suddenly the media were interested in what was going on at Stamford Bridge. Hoddle was a keen, young player-manager with strong ideas about how he wanted to run a club and how he wanted his teams to play. Hoddle brought an educated passing style, with himself as the fulcrum at sweeper, pinging long, raking passes out to the wings. Although embryonic, it brought comparisons to by-gone eras of swaggering style.

29,000 turned up for Hoddle's first game at Stamford Bridge, and despite a defeat at the hands of Blackburn Rovers, Ken Bates would have noted the spring back in the step of the club's supporters. Wise had been the one success story between fan and team in those oddly grey seasons in the early 1990s. Playing in the hole behind the front two, like Wilkins before him, he was vital to how the team progressed. He became the fans' voice on the pitch, covering every blade. His petulance and cheek remained and often he faced the wrath of an impatient referee, but the fans saw that stemmed from a real passion for his team's fortunes. They would scream at a linesman's flag or a misplaced whistle, so why shouldn't Wise?

He was headstrong, he was prone to rash, woeful decision-making that belied his own surname, but he was, by now, Chelsea through and through and Hoddle saw in him a man who could lead the new club. Like Fagin in a tracksuit, Hoddle charged Wise, his Artful Dodger, with the task of leading the young gang on the pitch in their quest to pick-pocket a glut of Premiership points.

Like Dickens' gang, this SW6 version was a fractious assortment. Things were far from eye-to-eye as Hoddle set about trying to stamp his very personal way of doing things onto a squad that often struggled to put his thoughts into practice. Liverpool and Manchester United had both been beaten at the Bridge, but the big teams were always given a game there by Chelsea; it was against the easier fodder that the club habitually struggled and, as the season took shape, this was still clearly the case.

Oldham won at the Bridge, whilst Chelsea lost at Sheffield United, Blackburn and, on the 27th December at Southampton 3-1 and stared up from their yuletide failings as the penultimate team in the Premiership. It was a meandering display at the Dell. As if playing in porridge, Hoddle's men couldn't get going and received all they deserved. Nothing, except a panning in the papers.

THIS, though, was a turning point, as Wise, along with Steve Clarke confronted Hoddle and convinced him, amid some angry exchanges that the manager's methods lacked the steel required to win points at this level. Wise had taken the tenacity that he showed week in and week out on the pitch and brought it into a dressing-room desperate for some fire and brimstone. The club's fortunes were at the forefront of his mind. There was no self-serving reason for challenging his manager; this was a fan voicing his concern and the punters that he played for loved him even more for it.

The following day, Newcastle were beaten 1-0 and Chelsea went onto win their next two matches. Such form saw them slowly climb the Premiership table and embark upon a cup run that brought them within reach of glory. A 4-0 tonking at the hands of a Cantona-inspired Manchester United in the 1994 FA Cup Final meant it wasn't to be, but it was a run that proved that Hoddle could work with this club and with these players. The vacuum between them and he had suggested a bleak future, but in their run to Wembley, the players had shown their fans that they could all pull together and once more bring good times to the Bridge, and at the very throbbing heart of that was the skipper, Dennis Wise.

That visit to Wembley was Chelsea's first for 22 years, not counting the slightly spurious Full Members Cup final against Manchester City in 1986. Before the game many fans commented that the club were on their way to becoming the masters of the country's new glitzy football world and Hoddle's men had nothing to fear, for they had achieved a league double over Alex Ferguson's men and many fancied that they would once more turn over their Mancunian rivals.

The clouds that opened over Wembley that day were dreary omens for the Blues and their supporters. Wise led the team out, but that proved to be the highlight as this, unlike his occasion in 1988 with Wimbledon, brought no glory.

THE POSITIVES were there, though. Hoddle had created a team worthy of Chelsea's name, and in Wise he had a player whose perpetual motion was the driving force to the team's ambitions. Hoddle realised – as the fans had been forced to do – that you couldn't change Wise's often futile behaviour. That was his game; that was what made him tick. Embrace him and embrace it.

In 1993, just weeks after accepting the role as captain, Wise had been sent off against West Ham for a reckless tackle on David Burrows and was publicly derided by the new manager. Come his second season, when Wise was once more given his marching orders, this time at Newcastle for foul language, Hoddle stood by his man, questioning the officials' ability to hear any obscenities over the drone of 40-odd-thousand Geordies. Chelsea were now a unit, now together; and now moving onwards and upwards into Europe.

Not for a generation had Chelsea's supporters had to pack a passport and travel over land and sea to watch their heroes. Now, due to Manchester United's double they were off on a European adventure in the Cup Winners' Cup, the trophy that they had so famously won in Athens 23 years earlier. Now, fans swarmed to obscure venues such as Jablonec on the Czech–Polish border, then onto Vienna, Bruges and finally Zaragoza in Spain for a hard-fought semi-final.

There was no shame in losing to a very good Real Zaragoza side (Wise missed the tie due to a long-term injury) especially as most of the players – Wise included – had never experienced European football before. The form on the home-front, however, wasn't as fruitful as on their continental travels.

But there was always Dennis Wise to bring a smile to a Chelsea fans' lips and warmth to his heart.

Toward the end of a tense League Cup game at Newcastle, Wise won his team a goal-kick amid some last gasp pressure from the home side. In front of the black and white striped hoards of Geordie fans he picked up the ball, kissed it and lifted it toward the heavens. It's what we'd all like to do given the chance, Wise got booked for it, but by then, who cared?

It was typical Wise. Young kids were lifted from the crowd before the game by the captain and invited to join in the warm up. On one occasion, whilst a team-mate was being treated for an injury, Wise retrieved the ball from the crowd, but having had a fan throw it back he headed it back in and began to play head-tennis with those in the stand. By such actions, legends are born.

IT DIDN'T stop there. In 1995, Wise scored the winner at Villa Park and ran away past the home fans slapping his forehead. Why had he done it? Well, a Villa fan who had been dishing out a load of abuse to Wise and his team-mates was lacking in the hair department and if anyone was going to remind him of his misfortune upstairs, then it was Wise. The fans revelled in such mischief.

"Why not?" asked Wise in Rick Granvill's book. "It's just making it a bit more enjoyable for the punters...You think 'That's great that.' I sometimes think that's what it's about: you've got to let them enjoy it and show a bit of passion and a bit of appreciation to them for their loyalty to you and the club."

He continues, "It's just that some players are like that and some players ain't like it. You don't see it much now: there's Ian Wright at Arsenal and that's about it you know? I think certain clubs have one of them, and most clubs have none of those players who the supporters can respond to. You give your all and you want to win. I think that's what they mostly appreciate, and that's all I want to do."

If all he wanted to be was appreciated, then Wise would have left Chelsea a very satisfied footballer. His efforts on and off the pitch were never in question. He was the joker in the dressing-room, always the first to get a game of cards going on the team-bus, always the closest to torrid footballing antics. He had always been like that.

Tony Adams, in his autobiography *Addicted* recalls an Under-15 trial for England when eight London boys made their way to Lilleshall on the train:

> They included Steve Potts, Dennis Wise, Michael Thomas, John Moncur and myself, all of whom went on to a professional career. That night I remember praying to be in the England team. I had this strange feeling about the trial match that took place. At previous trials, all the people in charge had been friendly towards me. Now there was a strange, frosty atmosphere. Nobody spoke to me. I was handed a No.13 shirt and was told to stand behind the goal, out of the way. It was the same for five other London boys. We were discarded. They had found an easy way to whittle the squad down.
>
> We were told that we had been seen misbehaving on the train journey the previous day by an education officer travelling independently and who had reported us. There had been some minor, high-spirited scuffling among the lads, which involved some coffee being thrown and some bad language by one or two. Dennis Wise also had his ear bitten. I had certainly not been any part of it, though.

Whatever happened on that occasion it reiterates the point that whatever Wise did, trouble was often his shadow and one that would too often get our man into misfortunate situations. In 1990 he had been fined £200 and banned from driving for a year and there had been those frequent trips to answer charges at the Football Association headquarters, But Wise's most notorious flirtation with the law of this land took place in 1995, outside Scribes, a London club owned by Terry Venables. Like that unnamed team-mate of George Hilsdon all those years before, Wise was reported by a taxi driver for an incident that had allegedly left said driver and his car in a less than healthy state.

He was sentenced to three-months in prison, but released on bail pending an appeal in which he was exonerated and set-free. The cabbie, labelled "a liar" by Wise's council, was devastated as Wise amid football-like cheers in Southwark Crown Court left with that wry smile across a previously anxious face. "I am so relieved," he said. "I have been shattered by this and I just want to put it all behind me. I am an innocent man."

Days later, a Sunday newspaper reported that Wise was about to make a £4 million move to Liverpool, but that fell through and instead a new, and exciting chapter was about to start at Chelsea with the arrival of Ruud Gullit. Before that momentous signing by Hoddle, he was forced – due to the adverse publicity from that court case – to rescind Wise's captaincy and give it to the far more serene Gavin Peacock.

THESE were changing times. The ground, thanks largely to the money of super-fan and club director Matthew Harding, was being developed; players such as Gullit now sported the club's blue and more were set to follow. The swagger was back, but now it was gaining a cosmopolitan flavour. Wise, though, remained the old-school component. He got on with the new foreign influx, was never overawed by the greatest of players and enjoyed taking them under his wing and showing them how to behave in the wild world of the English dressing-room.

On the face of it he was the antithesis of the continental approach of classy passing and slick movement, and whilst the fans genuinely loved the flowing, sweeping moves that the team were adopting, they were glad to have the tenacious Wise back after a season when the glint in his eye was dimmed by injury and off-field complications.

1995/96 was a little off from vintage Wise. The previous year's tribulations had taken their toll, but he still managed flashes, scoring two goals at Southampton to seal a 3-1 win, plus a vital one at Old Trafford to nick a 1-1 draw. He also helped the team reach the semi-final of the FA Cup, in which they lost 2-1 to Manchester United.

Gullit for one was very impressed. "He plays differently now," the Dutchman said at the time in Glanvill's book. "He used to run with the ball more; now he plays one-twos and short touches and he played very well last season." In the summer of 1996, Gullit, who had become close bedfellows with the likes of Wise and John Spencer, revelled in the task of analysing Wise's game even further when he became manager after Glenn Hoddle took the vacant job of England boss.

"He is so important in the locker room," was one of Gullit's first assessments of Wise as manager and he immediately re-issued the captain's armband to the little midfielder. The Artful Dodger was back in charge and this was to prove to be a season when the fans once more – after 26 years of only dreaming of success – were able to wallow in their team's efforts.

AND WHAT of Wise? Under his Dutch-master, Wise's game – his off field plights now behind safely him – blossomed even further and that season he looked even more the complete midfield player. Football snobs may scoff at the idea of Wise as complete, but week in and week out he carried his team's fight. He would be the holding player one week, nullifying the opposition, and then the playmaker, the next at the sharp end of a midfield diamond.

The new England manager, a certain Glenn Hoddle, resisted the temptation to pick his ex-skipper (it would be Kevin Keegan who would award Dennis the majority of his 16 caps), but Wise continued to wear the one Lion with pride even if his chances with three looked slim.

In early January 1997, Wise slipped the ball into West Brom's net (Alan Hudson would have cheered) to set Chelsea on their way on an ultimately glorious Cup run. Chelsea won that game 3-0 (Gianfranco Zola scored the third having joined the club the previous November) and their chalenge for silverware was off and running.

Of course the League was another matter. As good as Gullit's team could be on their day, inconsistency, as ever, was a season ticket holder at the Bridge and the side would finish sixth in the Premiership. That wouldn't offer European football, but Cup success would.

The fourth round of the FA Cup saw Liverpool beaten 4-2 at the Bridge after a fantastic comeback from 2-0 down and from there it seemed that Wise was destined to get those hands on the famous old trophy. "When Dennis goes up, to win the FA Cup, we'll be there, we'll be there," sang the fans. Leicester were beaten 1-0, before Portsmouth were discarded 4-1 at Fratton Park with Wise getting two of the goals in a wonderful personal and team performance.

Next came the semi-final and it was Wise's old comrades at Wimbledon who would provide the opposition. The venue was Highbury, home of an old enemy and scene of mixed fortunes for Chelsea over the years. Arsenal and their North Bank had long had reason to cheer cruel victories over their London cousins, but, for that day in April 1997, it was Chelsea's playground. Blues fans packed the famous old stands and sang their hearts out (something that its usual habitants had seemingly found it harder and harder to do over the years) to cheer on a fine 3-0 win.

CHELSEA were going back to Wembley. This time they were clear favourites (Middlesbrough, their opponents had endured a torrid season which would end in relegation) with a team brimming with talent, both bought and nurtured and a team spirit that belittled the notion that foreign players couldn't bed into the strange world English football.

As the final neared and Cup fever gripped the blue corner of London (flags and balloons were as prevalent as chic women along the Kings Road that May) the players relaxed, with Wise dishing out the stick as only he knows. "Our Frank is not the brightest player in our squad," he said of Frank Sinclair to the BBC's cameras. "But he would walk through a door for you – only because he hasn't worked out how to open it!"

Sinclair was having none of it. "We all know what Wisey is like, but to be fair he has to take a lot of stick himself," said the unfortunate defender. "Let's face it, he is not the brightest man himself! And all the flak he dishes out is just a cover-up. They all try to make out I'm the thickest player in the team, but I come back with, 'The most intelligent people are the ones who make others think they are silly.' Anyway, all I would say to Wisey and the other players is that I've got two GCSEs in English and Design & Tech, how many have you got? Some of the lads think I'm making it up about my English certificate, but I have proved it to them a few times and that normally shuts them up. I wouldn't know how many GCSEs Wisey has got because he is not that clever, but he is very streetwise so you've got to watch him all the time. Anyway, I might not be able to work out how to open a door, but I certainly know how to get in a taxi!"

Streetwise? (Sinclair, as proud holder of a GCSE certificate, qualifies in football terms as a wordsmith after all). What Wise was that season was a driving force, a real captain and a player capable of bringing the best out of those around him. The final was effectively over before the Royal guests had dented their royal cushions with a goal by Chelsea's Italian midfielder Roberto Di Matteo after 43 seconds (still the fastest ever Cup Final effort although Bob Chatt was credited with Aston Villa's winner against West Brom after 40 seconds in 1895, but as David Lacey wrote in the *Guardian* in 1997, "Who was counting and on what?"). Wise had begun the game at his terrier-like best, as if chasing a bone he chewed the ball from Borough's Robbie Mustoe and sent the Italian away, hurtling toward the goal and a date with statto history.

CHELSEA and their captain controlled the game, the Teesside Brazilian, Juninho, was a threat, but ultimately not a lethal one. Eddie Newton, an underrated and arguably unlucky professional gave himself a lifetime of opportunity to dine out cheaply with a late sealing goal from close-range to make it 2-0 and it was party time.

Wise made his way up the steps. He had made that glorious journey once before for Wimbledon, but this time he was skipper. He had that same cheeky smile that had adorned his face in 1988, but now there was more to him, a touch of responsibility about him as a man and a player. He took the Cup in his hands (how Ron Harris would have loved to have done the same at Wembley rather than Old Trafford) and lifted it towards the Blues fans who, with the help of Suggs' Cup Final song, were well and truly making this a *Blue Day*.

Cup final celebrations are always high-tempo and joyous affairs, of course they are, but in 1997, there was extra spice. Chelsea Football Club had lain dormant for too long, trying to be considered as a big boy in English and even European football, but failing in a choppy sea of underachievement and inconsistency. Now as Wise paraded the cup there was an incredible feeling of glory and, more than an inkling that this was the start of something special. Des Lynam, in the BBC studio declared it as the most enthusiastic Cup success he had ever seen. Enough said.

THERE was more to come. Like Ron Harris before him, Wise went on to lift the Cup Winners' Cup the following season, but this team also added the League Cup, whereas the kings of the Kings Road had lost the 1972 final to Stoke. Suddenly, in a matter of months, once the European Super Cup was clinched by a 1-0 victory over Real Madrid, Wise had become the club's most successful ever captain (although a certain Mr Terry may soon have something to say about that). The European run had gained momentum from its early stages with wins over Slovan Bratislava and Tromso of Norway. The latter side had won 3-2 on home soil, although soil was hardly the operative word as the game was played on a mixture of snow and mush which manager Gullit referred to as "cowshit."

The Norwegians had taken offence and words were exchanged in the press, but as ever Wise had the last laugh. His team won 7-1 back at the Bridge and he declared, "They said a few things after the first-leg we weren't too happy about, but just as they know how to play on snow more than we do, we showed we are better on grass then them."

With that the team marched on and won against Spanish, Italian and in the final German opposition (to complete the set against the continent's strongest leagues) as Stuttgart were beaten 1-0 in Stockholm. Wise lifted his third trophy toward the Swedish sky as fans roared his name. This winning lark was becoming a doddle and each time it was their hero, Wisey offering them the silverware.

By now Gullit had gone amid the kind of media storm that was beginning to accompany every development at the Bridge. He was replaced from within the club by Italian international striker Gianluca Vialli. The Italian was very fond of Wise (at Chelsea, who wasn't?). Once, when sitting depressed on the substitute bench, Vialli's mood had been lifted by a celebrating Wise, who, having scored a goal, ran across to his forlorn team-mate and hoisted his jersey up to show a T-shirt bearing a message that read, "CHEER UP LUCA, WE LOVE YOU xx". It was typical Wise. That was why you couldn't help but love this infectious little scamp.

GULLIT'S demise had begun the day he left Wise on the bench for a visit to Everton. His side were second in the league that day, but lost 3-1 and it was then that insiders and fans began to wonder if maybe he was "losing the plot." The Dutchman made the same mistake a couple of years later when he put Geordie God Alan Shearer on the bench for Newcastle. Take the fans' heroes away and you lose part of their support.

Wise was simply too popular to be left out. He enjoyed a testimonial in 1999 (the 27,000 that turned up for the 0-0 draw against Bologna was a record for such games at the Bridge) and bought each of the Chelsea staff watches and pens from Cartier, costing him £50,000. He was, to many in the press, a brash scally and maybe sometimes he was exactly that, but what wasn't written so frequently about was how much time he spent after games signing autographs and having pictures taken with adoring young fans. He *was* Chelsea to so many fans.

Success followed under Vialli with an FA Cup win over Aston Villa in the last final to be played under Wembley's twin towers in 2000. It was a momentous season. Still not strong enough collectively to take the Premiership, Chelsea, having finished third in 1998/99, enjoyed a fine run in the Champions League before losing in an incredible tie against Barcelona in the quarter-finals. It was against another European giant, AC Milan, that Wise gave the fans perhaps his greatest moment. There was no silverware to lift, but his equaliser in the San Siro handed the travelling contingent a night to remember, which they duly celebrated with unbounded glee. That result helped the team qualify for the quarter-finals at their hosts' expense. Chelsea – thanks to their little captain from Shepherd's Bush – were truly on the map.

Wise departed the Bridge in the summer of 2001 for Leicester, having played 445 games and scored 74 goals. He left a hero. The cheeky scamp bridged Chelsea history from Vinnie Jones and David Lee to Ruud Gullit and Gianfranco Zola. He was the link between the side which established itself in the Premiership after winning promotion in 1989 and that which progressed to the latter stages of the Champions League. As skipper, he had driven the team on with a smile, a clenched fist and a snarl, lifting more silverware than Chelsea's fans had ever seen. Prior to the unprecedented success of today, he did what all great entertainers aspire to do; he left the punters wanting more.

Wise was known amongst the players at Stamford Bridge as the Rat, due to those sharp features. He's been called worse by irate opposition and fans alike, but to those at the Bridge who cheered on every minute of his eleven years at the club he was far from a Rat, he was the pied-piper and wherever he went they followed, dancing to his tune.

RUUD GULLIT

'THE STAR'

1995-1998

CHELSEA CAREER

Games	64
Goals	7
Caps	66

MAGIC MOMENT

Player-manager Ruud led his team out at Wembley in 1997 and ended that damn 26 year trophy drought with the FA Cup victory over Middlesbrough

Happiness... it lies in the joy of achievement, in the thrill of creative effort.

Vincent Van Gogh

THE party has moved inside. Champagne splashes against Wembley's old dressing-room walls as a drinking spree gets under way that would have made even the club's Class of 1970 hiccup. The captain, Dennis Wise, sits surveying the mayhem that he will soon take great delight in joining. His socks are rolled around his ankles and his hands have at last loosened their grip on the FA Cup and it now makes its way around his team.

The press have been satiated and now the player-manager and club guru, Ruud Gullit, strolls through the door (he always strolls doesn't he?) and takes in what he has achieved in his first season as a manager. There are cheers, of course there are, Gullit has just led his men to their first major trophy in 26 years, but from Wise there is only playful banter. "It's the Yeti," he cries amid raucous laughter – even now Gullit must contend with jokes regarding his appearance.

Wise, ever the comedian, may have been onto something here. Gullit arrived at Stamford Bridge at a time when the place was as desolate of swaggering celebrity as a Himalayan mountain-range and desperately in need of a creature that would bring some hype and street credibility to its four creaking corners. Somehow it happened. Gullit arrived in May 1995 amid impressed and envious glances from outsiders, but far from being the abominable Dutchman, he was the saviour. As he glided into the club, with one flick of those famous dreadlocks, the place was instantly revamped into a member of that elite desirable group of clubs; a place for winners and for the best to be.

SURE, footballing celebrities had inhabited the Bridge for many years. Of course, the likes of Terry Venables and Peter Osgood had created a certain joie de vivre, but they were young stars developed by the club, for the club, whilst other young men, from Cooke to Nevin, arrived as one-time footballing nobodies ready and eager to learn and developed into heroes. No, not since Hughie Gallacher had a genuine world star and household name arrived at the club at the height of their pomp. Not since the wee Scot had a man so at ease on football's red-carpet been persuaded to pull on the blue shirt and entertain the troops.

Glenn Hoddle was a major football name, but not on Gullit's global scale and he had reached the very twilight of his illustrious career. Tommy Lawton had arrived from Everton in 1945, the country's most notorious goal machine and every English schoolboy's hero, but times had changed, this was now a global game and, like it or not, we in this country were no longer the doyens of the sport we had gladly invented. In 1978, after a friendly with the New York Cosmos at Stamford Bridge there was some talk about Johan Cruyff joining the Blues, but it was a fitful fantasy concocted by those who had spent millions on a new giant stand and needed to see it full. Not since Nils Middelboe, a Danish star playing at the club in the 1920s, had there been such fervour surrounding a foreign import.

Now, astonishingly, the club and its fans were dealing in the reality of boasting a true world superstar and oh, how sweet it was. The game had changed and Chelsea had to keep up if they were going to compete. By the summer of 1995, Sky TV had become part of the footballing furniture. Love them or loathe them, Rupert Murdoch's cameras were here to stay and that meant clubs were afforded the chance to add to their squads the sort of players that would attract the cameras and sponsors as well as your average punter.

THE PREMIERSHIP had begun to glimpse the fervour a giant of the world game can create. Jürgen Klinsman had enjoyed a wonderfully exciting season at Tottenham that year. He had won the Football Writers Player of the Year and, whilst Eric Cantona's jury was out due to his need to interact with the country's more Neanderthal football fans, there was room in the game for more, real stars. Cynics cited their opinion that these players had enjoyed wonderful careers with top Italian clubs where they could win Europe's top honours and now, as they approached the OAP years of their careers, they would swan over to these shores for that last bumper pay-cheque.

There may have been something in that, but what wasn't in doubt was that whatever stage of their careers these guys were at, they had talent that could only tingle the fingers of Britain's too-long, bored supporters. The glitz of the new game was too much for some. Sky TV had kicked off with awful half-time bands playing – make that miming – baton-twirling, pom-pom swirling cheerleaders and general US-style razzmatazz. Thankfully that was quickly rescinded, but there remained cynics. How could some be convinced that football was still a game to fall in love with, how could the most irate of old-school fans be persuaded that there were players, brought over from foreign shores that were worth the effort?

Stadiums were improving – Chelsea themselves were beginning to put into the shape the ground that today so proudly houses the major force in the game – and so the players began to arrive who could add a new sheen to the glitz that for so long had draped itself around Stamford Bridge.

Without doubt Ruud Gullit was the catalyst for Chelsea's successful 1990s and beyond. Fans loved this colossus of the game for simply taking the time to play for their club with their badge caressing his left breast. In a way, his cult worship began with almost embarrassed gratitude, which slowly turned into love-struck awe.

SO WHAT was all the fuss about? Who was this footballer strutting into town like a peacock, whilst all and sundry tried to get a glimpse of his exquisite feathers? Ironically, Chelsea's sea of fans could have answered that question years before he dread-locked his name to the global game. In 1984 John Neal's busy assistant Ian McNeil was scouting at a youth game between Denmark and The Netherlands. He was there to run the rule over a couple of Danes, but returned drooling over an athletic, powerful teenager, individual in looks and in talent.

McNeil and Neal had been busy picking out obscure names from nowhere and creating a fervent team that was pulling the club from its slumber. They'd already plucked the likes of Dixon, Nevin and Speedie from the depths of the lower leagues, so their track record was second to none. This time, though, a more suspicious board had its doubts (Gullit was valued at £300,000 even back then – a lot for a kid – and more than the then club record fee of £225,000 paid to Celtic for David Hay), however good his potential may be. "John Neal told me that young Ruud was one of the players he wanted to bring to London," wrote the then chairman Brian Mears in his recent chronicle of the club. "The other board members dumbly stared at him. It was just unheard of to try to sign foreign teenagers. Before anything could develop, Johan Cruyff snapped him up for Feyenoord." Fortunately, Nigel Spackman and John Bumstead's progress softened that blow. But who knows what riches the rather less prosaic Gullit would have brought to SW6 had the board backed their managerial team.

Gullit's game blossomed in Holland where he moved on to PSV Eindhoven before a massive 17 million guilders (£5.7 million) move to the might of AC Milan. It was with the Rossoneri that the distinctively dread-locked Ruud Gullit became a household name as he linked up with his fellow compatriots Marco van Basten and Frank Rijkaard and set new standards in skill and awesome power.

European Cups, Scudettos, World and European Footballer of the Year awards, as well as scoring the opening goal as he captained his country to the European Championships in 1988, were all beautifully penned onto his impressive CV. He left Milan in 1993 to join calmer seas in Genoa with Sampdoria, but, come 1995, he was after a new challenge. He had undergone serious knee surgery and lacked that explosive power that had steamrolled through defences for so long. But the surgeon's knife had not removed his most telling asset, pure class. With a ball at his feet he still oozed that commodity from every pore. His signature would be well sought after.

French and Japanese clubs (the latter had become a kind of football star's graveyard in the early 1990s) were keen, but England? Now that was a challenge. Stylish Gullit was always most likely to choose London's more cosmopolitan streets and it was Chelsea, whose stylish environs stood out and appealed to this discerning cool cat about town.

Not that it was only the Kings Road's boutiques and cafes that did the trick. Glenn Hoddle had gained quite a reputation as a young coach wanting to do things the right way, and, of course, his name alone appealed to players of a certain generation who, when breaking into the game as youngsters would have marvelled at his methods on the field of play.

HODDLE had been on the look out. Chelsea had made positive strides, but it lacked the fizz that he and so many fans desired; a star, a real star, now that would go some way to putting the bubbles back in a somewhat flat club. Ken Bates had, for a long time, wanted the club to reflect his sense of brash high-achievement.

"This is a glamour club," he said. "Half of the showbiz world were here on freebies courtesy of the Mears. What I like is style. Glamour is The Spice Girls. I prefer style. I'm not interested in fashion. Fashion comes and goes. Style is timeless. We're one-and-a-half miles from Harrod's. Everyone in the world knows Harrod's. I want everyone in the world to know about Chelsea. And it's got a better ring to it than one-and-a-half miles from Tesco's, hasn't it?"

With that Bates took out his charge card and went on a shopping spree for someone more Harrod's than Tesco's. A global star. Paul Gascoigne was touted as a possible target and would have no doubt been a very popular choice, but Hoddle wanted Gullit, a man who could play in his midfield or as a sweeper, a system favoured by Hoddle and easily adopted by the Dutchman who had started out in that very same role.

Bates and Hoddle got their man. Tthe latter found out whilst on holiday in Florida with a message from the club's Managing Director Colin Hutchinson that said, "The man from Italy, he say yes!" Gullit was on his way to London. Fans couldn't quite believe it. Ruud Gullit? Are you sure? Coming to Chelsea?

The ground itself was hardly up to his scratch with renovation and workmen adding to the dishevelled feel of the place. The Shed had been demolished to allow the Bates motel to be constructed, forming the first part of Ken's much vaunted Chelsea village. Bringing Ruud Gullit here was like meeting the most beautiful of women, inviting her back to your place, opening the door and discovering your dog isn't as house trained as you'd hoped. Gullit must have arrived at the Bridge wondering about his decision, but by meeting the staff and the eager fans he was sold on progress. Here was a place moving forward. This was going to be fun.

Hi arrival sparked incredbile scenes. Gullit's face adorned everything from t-shirts to flags, whilst more fun-loving supporters donned Stevie Wonder-like wigs in an attempt to mimic their new icon. "We all wanted to see him in the UK," wrote Rick Granvill. "Meet him. Touch him. Thank him." The only men and women with smiles as wide as those of the fans and Ken Bates were the merchandisers working the surrounding streets. "Judge Dread: Chelsea's Ruud Boy: Judge, Jury and Executioner", "The Ruud Boys," and a huge flag that gave the old Chelsea lion a full head of dreadlocks were just a few examples to the fever pitch that had surrounded his move.

Never before had a player's hairstyle caused such a furore around Stamford Bridge. It was like William Foulke's weight; Gullit's hair stood him out and fans had their "special one" (as we all now know he wouldn't be the last). And when he finally made it onto the pitch Gullit shone like a beacon, his passing crisp, his reading of the game giving him vital extra seconds in the melée of a rumbustious Premiership game. Rob Hughes of *The Times* noted that he was "like liquid on a parched tongue", whilst the fans left with their thirst for class part satiated, but longing for their next trip to the well.

CHELSEA made a half-decent start to the season, but it was in mid-September that they finally got to cheer a goal from the new man as he volleyed home the second in a 3-0 win over Southampton. He comprehensively upstaged Matt Le Tissier (a player repeatedly linked with a move to Chelsea) on a day that the club celebrated their 90th anniversary and paraded squad members from both the 1955 title winning team and their 1970 FA Cup lifting counterparts. Alan Hudson, for one, liked what he saw.

"I saw Gullit in a friendly at Birmingham before the season began and I got goose pimples. I can't remember the last player who really excited me; Paul Gascoigne to a point, but he's not in this man's class. I was getting pretty disillusioned with football, hearing average players described on television as great players, but Ruud is one truly great player. At Birmingham, he hit one ball out of defence that never went above six feet in the air. No-one could head it because it was going too quick and it landed in the other box, right at the feet of Mark Stein. I've never seen a player like Gullit; Hoddle was probably the nearest at hitting passes like that, but this fellow goes even further."

The supporters had not seen anything like it. This man could play, really play and if some players are worth the day's admittance fee, then this Dutch master was worth a season ticket.

Gullit had taken to his new home, both in the dressing-room, on the pitch (despite playing in front of a building-site) and within England's capital where he felt at ease and less set-upon than in Italy where god-like affection from your public can suffocate rather than inspire. "I have no doubt that I've made the right choice in coming to Chelsea," he said. "I have adapted very quickly and having come from Amsterdam and also having lived in Milan, it is quite easy for me to live in a big city like London."

Here, Gullit could disappear far easier than he had in Milan or even Genoa. He had suffered from a marriage break-up, but here he could enjoy a personal life, take in the restaurants, see live music (Gullit is a keen guitarist) and play a bit of golf in relatively serene surroundings.

IT WASN'T, however, just Chelsea's male fans who took an interest in the new man. Women in the all-seater, post-Nick Hornby, Sky TV era were becoming far more prevalent both at football matches and as armchair fans. It would be churlish and wrong to suggest that they were at games to admire a new breed of pin-up, but Gullit did turn heads and his mastery of the ball, combined with his Olympian body and flamboyant style made him a hit with those female supporters. Apparently one female fan, who just happened to live above Gullit in his new London home, went so far as to pour a bucket of water through her floorboards, trog downstairs and introduce herself armed with a bucket and helpful mop.

The fervour surrounding Gullit's arrival and the fine form that he had given the team showed little sign of abating, but as ever things wouldn't run smoothly. This was Chelsea and even the arrival of the Dutch Master couldn't paint over the cracks that appeared in the team. Newcastle, hurtling toward a Premiership challenge that would eventually run out of steam, beat Chelsea 2-0 at St James' Park, whilst that season's double winners, Manchester United hammered Hoddle's men 4-1 at the Bridge.

The following week, Chelsea were again humiliated, this time with a 3-0 defeat at Blackburn. It was tough. Once more the Blues looked about to lose their way on the arduous journey from potential to actual challengers. Along with a League Cup defeat at home to First Division Stoke, October had been a month to forget for the club. One tabloid hack couldn't hide his disdain.

"Sometimes body language can say more than a thousand diplomatic words – just take Ruud Gullit. For 90 minutes the big man had been trying to keep his finger in the leaking dyke of a defence before moving to midfield. By the end this was one very cheesed off man from Holland. Shoulders slumped, head shaking, Gullit could not get off Ewood Park quick enough.

"And for an hour the dread-locked superstar sat in the away dressing room as he tried to face the harsh realities of his new surroundings. Because now all the bright hopes of his summer move from Sampdoria have disappeared. Stuffed by Stoke, mauled by Man United and battered by Blackburn! Gullit cannot possibly need this, playing with team-mates who are simply not at his level.

"When he moved into the midfield for the last half hour it was pure poetry, but also rather sad. Such a talent is squandered at the back and is totally wasted at Chelsea."

IT WAS bound to happen. Outsiders were bound to look down their nose at what they saw as a world star marrying outside of his station. Gullit's Mr Darcy and Glenn Hoddle's Elizabeth Bennett were always going to suffer from both pride and prejudice, but what the real fans could sense was that deep down Gullit was enjoying learning a quicker style of football, whilst also thriving on passing on his knowledge to obviously and unashamedly inferior players such as...well, such as everybody.

Gullit had become good pals with Dennis Wise and John Spencer who disregarded his fame and affectionately nicknamed him "Big Nose." And it was these off pitch friendships which would begin to bind this Chelsea team of disparate talent together.

League form remained patchy (the club finished 11th), but they got going in the FA Cup after drawing 2-2 at Wimbledon in the quarter-final at the Bridge. It was going to be a tricky replay at Selhurst Park, the sort of wet night on which the unconvinced xenophobes – wary of an invasion of "our" game – were convinced that Johnny Foreigner, namely Gullit, would go missing.

But Gullit was magnificent, controlling the pace of the play – never easy against any Wimbledon team – and dictating Chelsea's 3-1 win. Was this the year they would finally win some silverware? The semi-final saw them drawn against an in-form Manchester United who now had their own Johnny Foreigner, Eric Cantona, pulling their strings, having earlier in the season returned from his ban for the infamous Selhurst Park kung-fu kick. It was off to Villa Park to find out.

Chelsea fans created a wonderful atmosphere that day. Flags and banners adorned the stadium, whilst blue balloons, ticker-tape and streamers had the United contingent hoping (amid deafening noise) their players would win the battle on the pitch that they were patently losing off of it.

Chelsea came out for the match as the brilliant incarnation of their inconsistent selves. They harried, they passed crisply, and they tore into United's defence before Gullit deservedly put them one up with a ferocious header past Peter Schmeichel that had the pundits harking back to his effort in the 1988 European Championship final.

They were playing well, but fate once more decreed that Chelsea would be the bridesmaids and not the brides. After key injuries to Steve Clarke and Terry Phelan, United scored twice and were on their way to Wembley for the third successive season. Gullit was pragmatic. "The team did everything to win," he said. "The supporters were tremendous for us. Unfortunately it didn't go well, but Wembley can wait – there are bigger goals to achieve." God he was cool.

THAT SEASON the chance would arise for Gullit to become more to the club than merely an example of how the game should be played. Glenn Hoddle had done enough for the Football Association to offer him the England job. Terry Venables was leaving, Hoddle couldn't say no and so all eyes were on the Bridge and Ken Bates. Who would take over? George Graham was available, but despite the style he had brought to the club in the 1960s, his managerial name was hardly synonymous with the approach that the fans hoped to continue to grace their new-look stadium and team.

"You can stick George Graham up your arse," they pointedly sang to the Chairman before the end of the season and cries of "We want Ruudi" and massive banners suggesting the same sentiment underlined that they had only one man on their minds. Since Gullit had arrived, he couldn't put a foot wrong, so why not give him the job and let the team blossom in his image? He had been virtually running the show as it was. Their love hadn't been lost on Gullit. He was almost embarrassed by their cheers and later admitted that the fans' appreciation was a key factor in him accepting the position.

"Without doubt the reception the fans gave me was very important," he gushed. "Before, when the rumours started, of course as a football player already you start thinking about it – that's obvious. So when they wanted me that bad I was, oh!…It was a big surprise to me. You know it was a very strange experience and of course when I was thinking about the job the reaction of the fans made it a lot easier for me to make the decision. And also I knew I had a lot to do back for them."

A JOKE was doing the rounds at Stamford Bridge. Glenn Hoddle, Ruud Gullit and Dennis Wise are on their way to training together when the car breaks down. There is a river between them and the training ground and no bridge in sight. Glenn decides they should run across and agrees to go first.

Glenn runs and skips across, remaining just above the surface. Next is Ruud. He too glides across the river and joins Glenn. So to Dennis, who leaps onto the river, but sinks without trace. "Do you think we should have told him about the stepping stones just under the surface?" asks Glenn.

Ruud looks confused. "What stones."

It summed up just how in awe the fans were when it came to Gullit. He was something special. It was just they had never seen a player with such a command of how the game should be played and now he was both playing in and managing their team.

Gullit took over a healthy-looking club. Average attendances went up in each of the three years of Hoddle's tenure after a steady decline in the years prior to his arrival. With Gullit at the helm, good ship Chelsea could now set about attracting more and more world stars. After all Gullit, more than anyone, had a contact book brimming with panâche and fame.

The man who would later coin the phrase "Sexy Football" was bringing a style to a club that had metamorphosised itself – with the help of some cash and a makeover to the ground – into a sexy place to play the game. It wasn't only Chelsea fans enamoured by Gullit. In large part his glamour convinced the nation – still high from a fantastic Euro 96 – that here was a Premiership worth crowing about, whilst convincing those with allegiances to Chelsea that here was a team who might (a byword for weary Chelsea fans) just win things.

GULLIT immediately set about bringing in new faces. Even his forays into the transfer market oozed style. Franck Leboeuf, a French libero from Strasbourg, Roberto Di Matteo, an Italian midfielder from Lazio, Gianluca Vialli, a recent Champions League winner from Juventus and then in November 1996, the best of the lot, Gianfranco Zola from Parma. Suddenly Chelsea was a hip, cosmopolitan and simply successful place to be. It hadn't been that since 1970 and the fans couldn't get enough.

It was in the FA Cup that this team – brilliant one week, but of course only ordinary another – would finally achieve. Unlike the year before, this was going to be Chelsea's season after 26 years (sorry to keep mentioning that). And it was in the fourth round tie against Liverpool that Gullit earned his managerial spurs. The visitors had ghosted into a 2-0 lead at half-time and were dictating the pace of what was proving an easy game. Gullit noted that Liverpool's back-four had not been troubled by lone striker Vialli. Veteran warhorse Mark Hughes was on the bench and there was nothing he liked more than terrorising defenders (usually Liverpool's) and so the Dutchman sent him on for the second half in place of left-back Scott Minto. Chelsea went two up front. Bish, bash, wallop. Hughes pulled one back immediately and drove the team forward whilst goals from Zola and two from Vialli sealed a famous Sunday afternoon.

That day left everyone believing that this was it, this was their year. Chelsea drove on to Wembley remorselessly with fate seemingly playing off their front two. Gullit walked out of that tunnel looking even more imperious than usual. That stroll was there, and a smile etched on his face; here was a man who knew that this was a moment to savour. Poor Bryan Robson in comparison, the weight of Middlesbrough's relegation on his shoulders, with sunken eyes looking like a man at a party where he knew no-one.

Gullit was the first black man to make that walk as manager of a Cup Final team and in 90 minutes' time he was to become the first foreign manager to win the trophy. It was a great day. It was Gullit's day. It was his team's day, but most of all it was the fans' day and the party went well on into the night.

The team celebrated their 2-0 win at the Waldorf Hotel amid what seemed like a thousand toasts, but it was Gullit's speech that struck the biggest chord. "It was wonderful," recalled Ken Bates, the gleaming chairman. "He picked out every single person individually, down to the groundsman, the kitman and 'our girls at the training ground who cook for us'. We had Pele as our guest and Jimmy Tarbuck as our host." Pele and Tarby? Now there's a double act, but both for once were upstaged by the proud manager who, in his first season, had achieved where so many since Dave Sexton had failed.

There had been some criticism that Gullit had opted for overseas flair over the young crop of talent at the club, but if you had stopped a dizzy-looking Chelsea fan along the Fulham Road at 2am that night he would have slurred on and on about the wonderful marriage between that day's goalscorers, the Italian Roberto Di Matteo and the homegrown Eddie Newton.

The following morning, hangovers not yet allowed to take hold, 100,000 fans greeted the team in an open-top bus as they made their way through Chelsea's streets. Gullit stood beaming whilst Bates was on hand to tell anyone and everyone about his team's moment in the sun. "This has been the greatest party in the history of English football," he boasted. "I thought I'd seen the greatest party on the pitch at Wembley. We've seen so much knocking over the years and this is the best answer to it all."

Gullit was, as is his want, a little cooler when he grabbed a microphone and spoke to the fans. "We're happy to make your dreams come true. We love you all." It was mutual. Gullit's stock peaked that summer. The Cup had made its merry way back to the Bridge, Gullit had brought incredible players like Vialli and Zola to the club and in the interim had managed 14 appearances on the pitch and a goal that helped beat Tottenham. He had written himself into legend. But the question realists were asking was: Could it get even better?

PERHAPS. The 1997/98 season should have been Gullit's next brilliant chapter in Blue, but instead, just when it seemed that this man really could walk on the Thames, the club drew its pistol firmly out of its holster, took aim and shot itself accurately in the foot once again. Gullit was sacked.

It was a shock even in a game that had become more and more fickle in this new era where success was sought hysterically amid a feeding frenzy from the fans, papers and money-men alike.

That, though, was surely what Gullit was providing. Success. The season started well with only one defeat in their first eleven games. Then came a trip to Liverpool. The home side won 4-2 (a defeat that Gullit put down to a terrible sending off decision from David Elleray – not the most popular official at the Bridge due to the penalties he had awarded Manchester United in the 1994 FA Cup Final). What stood out in that game was Gullit's decision to replace Zola with himself once they were down to ten men within the first half an hour. The travelling fans booed the decision; suddenly the man who could walk on water was seen only as a mere mortal.

What followed was an odd few months. Cup runs, league wins, it didn't matter, Gullit was alienating himself from his players, the fans and more importantly his bosses, But that is what makes his status at the club all the more iconic. That is the whole point. Gullit's star came into view and shone so bright that for 18 months the fans practically needed sunglasses. For that year and a hal, Gullit brought glamour, honour and pride to the club, but such shooting stars always burn out and eventually his did.

As 1997 drew to an close, Chelsea were going strong. They were right up there with perennial challengers Manchester United and Arsenal. The old enemy, Tottenham had gleefully been dispatched 6-1 on their own patch. Happy days? You would have thought. The results over Christmas were patchy and then, in January, Gullit's men were knocked off their FA Cup high-horses by Manchester United who won 5-3 at the Bridge. There were murmurs of discontent, but not necessarily from the stands.

Later that month, Gullit dropped Zola and Wise for a trip to Everton. High-treason to some at the club and the fact that the team lost 3-1 was another factor in a rising trend amongst those who wondered if the Dutchman was becoming drunk on power. Ten days after that defeat Chelsea visited Arsenal in the semi-final first-leg of the League Cup (crisis, what crisis? They had reached a semi-final) and were beaten 2-1. Mark Hughes grabbed a late goal to keep the Blues in it, but really the team had been outplayed. The players called a meeting.

The senior pros weren't sure about the direction the team were taking (League Cup semi-final, European Cup Winners' Cup quarter-finalists and second in the Premiership wasn't clear enough, lads?) and their unrest wasn't unnoticed at board level; the very level where a new contract for Gullit was being thrashed out.

WHAT happened next is a blur. Gullit wanted £2 million a year, a figure that Chelsea could ill-afford, especially as they had doubts about his commitment to them whilst he was also indulging in a sea of commercial activity (Gullit launched his own brand of underwear, which merely cemented his place as the coolest of debonair foreign footballers as far as most were concerned, but was seen as a distraction by others) and working alongside that other irresistible smoothy Des Lynam on the BBC. In truth, Gullit was very committed, turning down big offers of work abroad for the chance to finish what he had so emphatically started at Chelsea Football Club.

To Gullit, any problems he was now facing were all part of his new journey. "This for me is the most interesting and important stage of my managerial career," he said at the time. "I've always said that the first year is the easiest because nobody knows what you can achieve and the second is the hardest because you are under more pressure as people expect a lot more."

In early February 1998, Chelsea once more lost at Arsenal, this time in the League by two goals to nil. It was to be Gullit's last game at the club. Four days later Chelsea announced to the world that they were letting their superstar go. His contract negotiations and the problems they had thrown up had become irreversible. He was sacked with immediate effect and one of his most high-brow signings, Gianluca Vialli would be replacing him as the team manager. Thank you and good night.

Colin Hutchinson, the club's Managing Director, made the following statement:

> Once it was clear Ruud would not be with us next season, we had to act swiftly. We have decided to make a clean break immediately and Gianluca Vialli is the new player-manager of Chelsea with immediate effect. While we were prepared to give Ruud a contract which we believe would have made him the best paid manager in the Premiership, we were not able to meet what he wanted and expected. We simply could not afford what he was asking. Ruud was told that unfortunately the gap was too wide to allow for further meaningful negotiations and that we would actively pursue lining up a replacement. Gianluca was offered the position of player-manager last night and took all of five minutes to accept.

English football was shocked. Bates, like his Hitchcockian namesake, had swung the knife and, to the outsider, ruthlessly dispatched a man who could theoretically have been one of their great, great managers. What was not yet widely known was that unrest surrounding commitment, team-selection and money had been swelling for months. It had now been dealt with.

Hours after the announcement fans quickly started congregating around the Stamford Bridge gates. Images of their hero smiled at them from the club shop, but now he was only that, an image. There was initially shock rather than anger, but later, James Edwards, the editor of the *Chelsea Independent* fanzine summed up many feelings when he said, "As far as I'm concerned we should pay Ruud as much as he wants. He is the best manager we have had around here for a good decade or so. I'm quite amazed by it."

AND SO Gullit was gone. He sat in his rented flat a dejected and rejected man. These weren't feelings that he'd had to endure with in his professional life, but now they were rampant. He talked to the press of lies and conspiracies and of how the club had used claims about his wage demands as "a big stick to beat me with." It was an undignified end to a Chelsea career that had offered fans only charm, skill and success. They would miss him. He too would miss them.

And yet Gullit's replacement in the Stamford Bridge hotseat, Vialli, would take the club on to new levels of success in terms of winning trophies. With five in all he is still the club's most successful manager. But you cannot possibly argue that his success could have happened without Gullit's groundwork, the force of his personality and the shaping of his team.

But therein lies the rub of Ruud Gullit's Chelsea legacy. Someone else benefited from what was rightfully his.

Here was a man who'd arrived as a world hero, played brilliantly in blue and brought an abundance of talent to the party, but now, it was over; he had been thrown out of the soirée that he had helped make such fun.

Gone, but what an impact.

GIANFRANCO ZOLA

'FRANCO'

1996-2003

CHELSEA CAREER

Games	312
Goals	80
Caps	35

MAGIC MOMENT

Take your pick, but was there a better goal at the Bridge than Franco's cheeky flick against Norwich? Genius.

Well I'm not the world's most physical guy
But when she squeezed me tight she nearly broke my spine
Oh my Lola, lo-lo-lo-lo Lola

"Lola", The Kinks

THERE seems to be a little problem. On opening the dictionary and looking up the word "Cult", I came across the following definitions. "Intense interest in and devotion to a person, idea or activity." That is fine. When it comes to Stamford Bridge and Gianfranco Zola was there ever more intense an interest or devotion? No, it's this next definition that concerns me. "Something regarded as fashionable or significant by a particular group." Again, Zola was the most fashionable and significant commodity in SW6 for the eight wonderful years that he was there. It's the words "particular group" that are a little concerning. There seems little doubt that Zola is Chelsea's number one Cult Hero (a BBC poll confirmed that) it's just that he was cherished by all. Not just a section of the fans, not worshiped by a devoted minority, but universally and in that you can even bracket a slightly envious but admiring away support. So, Cult Hero? Should the little maestro have made the final cut at all?

THE 1990s will be remembered for a new wave of footballer plying his trade in this country. There were some atrocious players from overseas (Harry Redknapp will tell you that), but there were some great ones too. The thing was a lot of them, however good they were, were so easy to dislike or ridicule. Jürgen Klinsman, a fantastic striker, was lambasted for his tendency to go down in the penalty area like the proverbial sack of potatoes. It didn't help that he was German either. Monsieur Eric Cantona, a mercurial talent, no doubt; but hated for his arrogance by those not supporting Manchester United.

Then there is David Ginola. Again, a dazzling performer, but a little too vain perhaps. Patrick Vieira, his perpetual motion dazzled Highbury, but to those in the away seats he was a bit of a thug. Then there was Zola. He played the game with impish skill, delighted those he played for, but did what these others couldn't and that was to endear himself to the footballing community as a whole. Unfortunately, the fact that he is Italian rather than French or German might have something to do with it on these shores, but he also played his sport with dignity and a smile.

For those who pay good (at Chelsea it's very good) money to watch their football team perform, a connection to those who play is longingly sought. It doesn't always come off, you can't always really feel at one with even those you call your players, but in Gianfranco Zola, Chelsea fans discovered an icon whose like had never before been seen before at the Bridge. They loved him for what he did with a football, they loved him for what he did for the team and the club and they loved him for the humble way he did it all.

He was brilliant, but he was approachable. Watching Zola, you felt you could sit and gaze at his wonderful ability for 90 minutes and then meet him after, shake his hand and have a conversation, albeit in pidgin English or Italian. You sensed that the windows of his car wouldn't be tinted to keep out prying eyes. It was clear, Zola was a man of the people, for the people. "There's not one person who hates Franco Zola is there?" asks Tim Lovejoy of *Soccer AM* fame.

"Players, old pros, managers, away fans, the opposition, everybody loves Zola. The great thing about Zola was he came over at a time when these guys were all labelled mercenaries, coming over to England for the money. Zola, though, stayed for eight seasons and clearly fell in love with us as much as we did with him. There was no nasty side to Franco. Fans from all sides could enjoy watching him play the game. He had flair, pure skill, pure football, nothing else. He was genuinely loved by all."

And what a footballer. The image of Zola, the ball tantalisingly at his feet, as excited as the crowd at what it might be made to do next, is an enduring one. The little Italian could pass, he could dribble, he could bend a ball, he could strike the ball, he even managed the odd header, not bad for someone who made Dennis Wise look like Peter Crouch!

Ask Chelsea fans who the best player is they have ever seen in Blue and the majority will say Franco Zola; and they'll say it with a smile as broad as the little man's as they fondly retrace in their minds countless occasions when the Italian drew gasps from the crowd with another example of his genius. He married the club's swaggering past with its exciting present effortlessly, managing to make thousands of new friends along the way.

At Wembley in 1997, a Zola inspired Chelsea were just minutes away from FA Cup glory. 2-0 up against a deflated Middlesbrough side and on cruise control, Zola began to make his way toward the bench. His friend and compatriot, Gianluca Vialli was substitute. Despite endearing himself to the fans with goals and passion, Vialli had made way for Zola to start in the team that day and could only watch forlornly from the bench as his team-mates strolled to victory. His name had begun to be chanted around the blue sections of Wembley and now he would get his chance. It was Zola who offered his place on the famous pitch and embraced Vialli as he passed him. Ruud Gullit, the manager, didn't make that substitution, Zola decided that Vialli deserved his moment and humbly made way for him. Amid the hullabaloo of glory, it was a simple and genuine moment. Everybody loves Franco.

THAT SUNNY afternoon was a wondrous finale to Zola's fantastic first season. As far as the Italian's form was concerned it was matched only, funnily enough, by his last as immediately the fans at Stamford Bridge and those around the country fell under his spell.

The 1996/97 season had started off well for Chelsea and their new manager. He had brought in Vialli, partnered him in attack with the old warhorse Mark Hughes and goals ensued with effective regularity. But Gullit had plans. He wasn't going to sit on what he had, especially when it became clear that a player he had long admired whilst playing in Italy and been interested in signing for months had become available. That player was Zola. The diminutive Sardinian had become disillusioned with life at Parma. Life in a city known for its ham and cheese, and increasingly for its Parmalat yoghurt, had become less of the picnic than it once was. He was being played in an alien role out on the wing by the coach Carlo Ancelotti and the two had fallen out (I know, the idea of Zola falling out with anyone is difficult to believe).

But even then Zola demonstrated his dignity by stating calmly that things had not been handled altogether to his liking. "If, at the beginning of the season," he said, "they had told me that I would have to change roles, I would have discussed it and probably we would have come to an agreement, but these are things that should be worked out at the start. Before the game against Inter, Carlo Ancelotti asked me to play on the right. He said to me, 'Try it up to half-time,' and I did try. I certainly gave it all I'd got, even if I thought that I could have given more in another position." It was time to go, and like many of his fellow Italian players, eyes were drawn toward these shores.

Roberto Di Matteo and Vialli had settled into London life with typical Italian aplomb. They looked as at home amongst the grandeur of Chelsea's bistros and boutiques as they did on the pitches of the

Premiership, their willingness to graft in the pell-mell of the English gane dispelling the myth that these foreigners "Don't like it up em".

In October 1996, tragedy struck when Matthew Harding, a fan and businessman who had pumped money into the club, was killed in a helicopter accident having watched his beloved Blues in a League Cup tie at Bolton. The tender response from fans highlighted his effect on the club, as did the financial clout that Gullit was now able to work with in a transfer market he perused like a hungry shopaholic. Some wondered if he should bother. Vialli and Hughes were doing brilliantly. Manchester United, the champions, had once more been beaten 2-1 at Old Trafford. So why make changes?

When Zola became available, he was reportedly touted by his agent to Tottenham, but Alan Sugar and his manager Gerry Francis dithered, wondering about wage structures. Gullit had no such concerns and swooped to bring yet another Italian to the Bridge, paying Parma £4.5 million for the services of a 30-year-old. As the new signing stepped off the plane with his wife Gianfranca on 11th November 1996 he immediately received a call from Vialli who invited him to his favourite Italian restaurant in Chelsea. This was going to be fun.

"I decided to come to England because I wanted another experience in football," he tells me now. "I knew very little about the club, but to be honest I didn't know much about Engish football in general. I had seen some on television, but I had never even played much against English opposition. I was very excited to come though."

The fans would have been excited about the prospect of another big-money signing, but few would have envisaged the impact that this small man (Zola stands at 5 feet 6 inches) was going to have on their hearts. Having been introduced to his team-mates, Zola quickly was given a taste of dressing-room life. They had him line up, back to back with Jody Morris, a talented prospect from the youth ranks and also vertically challenged. Measurements were taken and it was official, Zola was now the smallest player at the club. Club captain Dennis Wise loved it, immediately brandishing the new boy (and someone with whom he struck up an instant rapport) "a fairground freak". What's Italian for Pot Calling the Kettle Black?

WHAT Zola lacked in inches he more than compensated for in god-given talent. That same first day at the training ground saw the squad congregate for a spell of keepy-uppy. There were plenty at the club handy with the ball, notably Di Matteo and Dan Petrescu, but both were among a throng of well-paid superstars drooling like visiting schoolboys at their new team-mate's talent. It wasn't just the fans who were in awe of Zola, his colleagues were too.

Zola made a more than promising debut in a 1-1 draw at Blackburn before taking to his new London stage for the first time in another draw, this time with Newcastle and Chelsea's goal came when his free-kick was glanced in by Vialli. In Chelsea's next home game against Everton, Zola turned the deft touches and bamboozling dribbles into gold-dust. He struck a wicked 30-yard free-kick that defeated big Neville Southall in the Everton goal before nestling, like a punch drunk boxer, dizzily in the net. The buzz about the Bridge was all about their new star.

And yet Chelsea have always had stars. To be simply a star is commonplace in SW6. What Gianfranco Zola is, though, is a God. And with good reason too. Combine his phenomenal talent and his appealing personality and you have a superstar. And what's more, one that appreciated every minute of his adulation.

"There is something very special about English fans," he says "and my relationship with the Chelsea supporters was absolutely briliant. I wasn't expecting anything like that. Italian supporters can be very focussed, but I really wasn't prepared for the kind of devotion I received in London. I had great respect from all fans and that was just spectacular."

Despite his impact, Zola had yet to play in a winning Chelsea team after five games. But then came that moment, the moment that hoisted Zola into the stratosphere. Chelsea hosted West Ham, Zola's first experience of a London derby, and it was to be the day that the fans, who had already aimed admiring glances his way, fell head-over-heels in love.

If Zola is the type of player Chelsea fans can't help but applaud then Julian Dicks was a competitor they found hard not to disparage. At the Bridge, Dicks' agricultural take on the game had the home fans barracking his every contribution. Like a pantomime villain, Dicks seemed to thrive on the fans' distaste of his abilities, never shirking from his task and giving as good as he got. Today, though, he was going to find it tough.

Mark Hughes had given Chelsea a sixth minute lead, but after only ten minutes Zola stepped into the fray with a brilliant piece of skill that was made even better by the fact that his sorry victim was none other than Julian Dicks. He picked the ball up and made a beeline for Dicks, something others dared not do, and turned him one way and then beautifully another before unleashing an arcing shot that whizzed past Ludek Miklosko into the net. It was a fantastic moment, one that today is still talked about today by fans unable to forget their little hero.

It didn't end there. Zola continued to torment the full-back nicknamed "Terminator" with baffling skill. Even when Dicks tried the rough-stuff he was kicking only air where once there was soft flesh. Chelsea ran out 3-1 winners, a win that was greeted by rapturous applause, the majority of it especially for the brilliant Sardinian. Had he been warned about Dicks, for his display suggested otherwise? "I think they could have told me about him before the game!" he joked at the time, "Had they done that I would have played for the other side."

ZOLA was the talk of the town. His fabulous form on the pitch being mirrored by how his family was adjusting to their new life in London.

"I loved the place. I was enjoying my work so much that everything else fell into place. My wife, my kids, they were all pleased with Chelsea and London and so things were perfect." His performances coincided with a wonderful spell of results as Zola goals and Chelsea wins went hand in hand into the New Year. The club had stumbled upon a gem, and coach Graham Rix was in no doubt that his very presence at the club was a benefit to all. "His attitude is very professional, on and off the field," he said. "I'm not sure if I can teach him anything new. I try to keep him confident and the last thing I say to Franco when he goes onto the pitch is 'Play with a smile on your face.' He does, all the time. He's a great footballer, wonderful lad and signs all the autographs. Franco hasn't come here just for the money. He wants to show people what he can do."

Zola had found a home near the ground, his two children settled into local schools and his wife, unlike some higher profile other-halves, notably those who'd moved to Middlesbrough, was more happy with her new home. "We are here to stay," Franca Zola declared. "I come from Sardinia and compared to that, London is a great and wonderful city, one of the best in the world to live in. It is very exciting for the whole family to be here and there is a big Italian community for us, and that will help us settle in."

Zola's happy home life was reflected in his game and he reiterated how pleased he was to play for these fans. "In London you can walk about calmly in the streets; no one bothers you or follows you for hours. When supporters recognise you, they greet you, they politely encourage you, and that's all. The English are very reserved, like we Sardinians, and very respectful."

That respect and polite manner was to be transformed into mob-like adulation over a season that saw Zola just get better and better. The fans had a player that brought world class action to their doorstep. Like Gullit, the man who had brought him to the Bridge, Zola demonstrated the game week in and week out at a level that had only been afforded in the past on videos of distant and past masters.

DEFENDERS struggled in vain to get to grips with his game. Like men attempting to catch Whitebait with their bare hands, they huffed and puffed, but he seemed to slip through their grasp each time. Over the Christmas period, Sheffield Wednesday visited the Bridge, their yuletide gift to Zola was to have Peter Atherton man-mark him. Zola opened the scoring, but had the big defender as a constant companion for the entire game. How did he find it? a journalist asked. "I prefer my wife," quipped Zola.

Chelsea continued to challenge. If the West Ham game had informed fans just how special Zola was, then it was his effort against Manchester United in a Premiership match at the Bridge that confirmed the fact to the entire nation. He picked the ball up in the box, skipped past Gary Pallister, turned like a shot and beat the gargantuan Peter Schmeichel at his near post.

Now the nation too were hooked, but rued that very same ability weeks later when Zola scored the only goal of a World Cup qualifier between Italy and England at Wembley. He took his chance brilliantly, latching onto a pass and swivelling to shoot clinically past Ian Walker in England's goal. It had been a tight game between the qualifying group's two major players, but Zola's spark of deft brilliance had won it for the Italians. "The night Italy beat England was a great one;" he says. "For me, playing and living in England to score the winner at a great stadium like Wembley was spectacular. It is something very special. Not for England, though, obviously." Don't tell me that those Chelsea fans who lapped up his every move didn't feel just a twinge of pride that it was their little Franco who had scored the goal to defeat their own country.

Chelsea's special moments that year came in the FA Cup. The comeback against Liverpool from 2-0 down at half-time to win 4-2 was a highlight and to many, the jewel in that particular crown was Zola's wonderful equaliser that bent unerringly past the outstretched David James. The excitement built as fans realised that now they had a team that could compete for trophies. The major trophies; and it was another wonderful Zola effort in the semi-final against Wimbledon at Highbury that once more had fans drooling over the best Italian they had tasted in a very long time.

With a Cup Final appearance booked, Zola's name began to be touted as a candidate for Footballer of the Year and it was in May, just days before that final, that he received that very award from the nation's football writers. He was the first Chelsea man to win such an honour. "I was very honored to win the Footballer of the Year and it was such a bonus to receive the award from Sir Stanley Matthews. He was a legend." His father was utterly amazed that Zola was presented with that special award by Stan Matthews, a man he had grown up hearing about and who now, on his first visit to the country, he was witnessing honour his talented son.

ZOLA had grown up in Sardinia before taking his talents over the water to Naples, where he was the apprentice to Diego Maradona's demonic sorcery. With Maradona, Napoli won the Scudetto in 1986/87 and the young Zola was on hand to watch the Argentinean who one day he would be mentioned with in the same dazzled breath.

Zola played for Naples until 1993, helping lift the UEFA Cup in 1989 and the Scudetto once more in 1989/90. Then he moved to Parma and impressed further alongside Faustino Asprilla and Thomas Brolin (the svelte pre-Leeds and Crystal Palace version). He had broken into the Italian national side and was regarded one of the real talents in the World game. Now, in the blue of Chelsea, he was proving that wonderful theory correct.

The Cup was, of course, won against Middlesbrough and the smile etched onto Zola's face was as bright as the spring sunshine. "I had seen the FA Cup Finals on television as a boy, but the TV doesn't do justice to the occasion. You have to be there to take in the noise, the tension and the colour. I have always said that I think winning that first Cup for Chelsea was the best achivement. I knew it was an important event, of course, but I was't expecting anything like that. [I have] absolutely fantastic memories of that game," he continues. "I remember everything – the tunnel, the noise, the crowd, the colour. Gianfranca was sitting to the right of the Royal Box, but I did not see her until after the game. I was so tuned in. It is not easy to explain, but I think each time I remember how lucky I am to know this day, to have played in such a game. That is why I must thank Chelsea, all those supporters. When you live as a footballer, you do everything you can in the hope that one day you can experience a day like that. What a party we had, esepcially the day after."

How can you fail to love a man who thanks you for what delight he has given you? Blues fans simply upped their adulation to the highest possible level.

Chelsea were on their way to a period of success, but for Zola the second season was to prove tougher then the first and he had to get used to rampant attention from the nation's defenders, whilst struggling to emerge from a dip in form as he attempted to reach the plateau of the previous campaign. "I'm getting more attention now from defenders," he noted. "They know me, and it's harder for me to find space, to find the freedom that I found last year, but if I'm a great player, I have to sort it out."

AND SORT it out he did; with aplomb, flair and that huge smile. For now Zola found himself on the bench as Vialli earned a spot in the starting line-up and repaid his manager's faith, like all quality forwards do, by scoring plenty of goals in return. It was tough for Zola, but even as a substitute, he found ways of pleasing his adoring crowd. He and Tore Andre Flo, the new Norwegian centre-forward, were both warming the bench, but, instead of retreating to the dressing room at half-time at the Bridge, they would delight the crowd by playing what was known as the "Crossbar Game".

They would attempt to hit the bar, firstly from the penalty spot, then the eighteen-yard line, moving slowly back until they were at the halfway line striking the ball with pin-point accuracy at the bar, now 50 yards away. Zola was incredible, regularly hitting the bar and bringing hearty cheers from enthralled fans. This was better than a tepid pie and overpriced beer, the usual half-time fair. Tim Lovejoy loved it so much he stole the idea and today's "Crossbar Challenge" on *Soccer AM* is the result.

Clearly Zola hadn't lost his class, as we all know class is permanent, but his spells in and out of the team showed that even the greats can suffer bad days at the office. Again this feeling of ordinary mortal, turned god, added to fans' warm feelings about the Italian.

Or perhaps his temporary lack of form was down to a new haircut. Dennis Wise was so taken with it he opened his programme notes with references to his team-mates' newly-coiffed look. "We thought the reason Gianfranco had such a bad haircut was that he had big ears and was hiding them," he wrote. "So we said to him after the new one, 'Gianfranco, you've got lovely ears. Why have you always covered them up?' He couldn't quite understand what we were on about. So we said, 'We thought you had really, really big ears, and that's why you had such a bad haircut and why it had to cover the majority of your face.' He looks like a little boy. It suits him. Have a close look today."

What didn't suit Zola was that tracksuit. He had shown flashes of brilliance, scoring a wonderful hat-trick against Derby at the Bridge. Zola waited afterwards like a schoolboy to collect the match ball then took it into the shower with him just so it wouldn't go missing before getting his team to sign it. "My son wanted to play with me and the ball, but I had to tell him I couldn't." There was no way he would allow those memories to be erased from the ball's surface by a kickabout. It was moments like that so drew fans to Zola. He was as passionate about the place as they were and when a fan knows that about a player the bond cannot be broken. On top of that, despite his enforced spell on the sidelines, Zola never once mooted a move away from Chelsea or expressed dissatisfaction with the situation; a rarity in this day and age.

Results were going well at home and abroad. Zola signed a two-year extension to his contract in February 1998, again underlining his affection for his new employers and on the field the team looked well placed to add further honours to the once lonely trophy-cabinet. Then, almost immediately, Gullit, the man who had lured Zola to the club, was asked to leave. It was a shock, especially to Gianfranco, but the players got on with – under their pal, Vialli – what proved to be the most exciting climax to a season for years.

THE LEAGUE Cup was won in March and the pursuit of another European trophy grew stronger and stronger as the likes of Real Betis and Vicenza bit the dust. Zola had put his blip behind him and Vialli used him for the big games in the run into the season. A hamstring injury in Chelsea's 4-1 April drubbing of Liverpool caused him to miss the last couple of league games, but Zola had almost three weeks in which to receive intensive therapy from an Italian specialist before the Cup Winners' Cup Final in Stockholm against Stuttgart. Ultimately he only recovered enough to start the game watching from the substitute's bench.

Vialli would cite tactical reasons and it was a night when cracks in the relationship between the two began to show. They would deepen, but for now, as a tense, goalless game looked like to be heading for stalemate, decisions had to be made. It was Chelsea coach Graham Rix who suggested bringing on everyone's favourite little maestro after 70 minutes and what a decision it turned out to be. Within 30 seconds of joining the action Zola ran on to a through ball from Wise, drew Stuttgart's Austrian keeper, Franz Wohlfahrt, and let rip a humdinger of a shot that scorched into the roof of the net. It proved to be the only goal of the game.

"The 1997/98 season hadn't been great for me," Zola recalls. "Scoring the winner in the Cup Winners' Cup FInal made amends a little, but really I hadn't been playing as well as I knew I could and there had been injuries. I started the game on the bench and got my chance. God, it was something when I scored right away. It really was".

The thousands of Blues supporters who had made the trip over the North Sea agreed as Zola's sweet strike sent them into apoplexy. It was another defining moment in the little genius' wonderful Chelsea adventure. The celebration of that goal, both on the pitch and in the stands, was a release of all that pent up tension. It was one in the eye to his old pal and now unsteady boss Vialli, and it confirmed Zola's place right in the centre of fans' hearts. Athens in 1971 had been great, now they had done it once more and Zola, Dennis Wise, Steve Clarke, Ed de Goey, Danny Granville; these names could be placed alongside Peter Osgood, Charlie Cooke, Eddie McCreadie, Peter Bonetti and Ron Harris.

LIKE an Italian hoodlum, Zola's status was untouchable at Chelsea. There was nothing he could do that wouldn't please the fans. Charlie Cooke once noted that the supporters at the Bridge would have applauded him for standing in a strong wind; Zola no longer needed to stand. He had 50,000 shoulders willing to hoist him wherever he needed to go.

The Kinks' *Lola* reverberated around Stamford Bridge:

He's only five foot six and that's not tall
But we all love him 'cause he's good on the ball
We call him Zola la-la-la-la-la Zola...Gianfranco Zola

Zola had that way about him. Wherever he had played he had been adored. In Naples he had lost his dog and appealed for knowledge of its whereabouts. After another spine-tingling display for the Azzurri, the pet was returned safely. Now, in England, that worship continued and grew to new levels. Tesco even named a Pizza, The Gianfranco Zola. "I don't think there has been a player as loved as him at Chelsea," says Lovejoy.

It was a two-way love affair and one that may last forever. "From the first day, I've been touched by the atmosphere surrounding these matches," said Zola. "Here, the supporters go to the stadium as if they were going to church. They come to commune with the players. The match is a festival, the chance to live a day in good humour."

The three trophies the team had won in two seasons were a fantastic return and were added to in May 2000, with another FA Cup victory, this time a 1-0 win over Aston Villa in the very last such occasion at the old Wembley. That old devil called inconsistency meant that the Premiership was a bridge too far for the Zola era, but his ability on the pitch lit up the seasons saddling a new Millennium.

His relationship with his old pal Vialli had become strained. So much so that in 2000 Zola very nearly left the club, with Napoli the most like to gain from the fall out. Vialli publicly announced that Zola should run more, work harder on the pitch, in short, play more like Vialli himself had. "If you have Zola in your team," rebuked the Sardinian brilliantly talking of himself in the third person, "you don't ask Zola to play like somebody else." Fair point, and one that you would have expected someone like Vialli to grasp, but pressures of management had begun to chip away at the manager's good humour and the increasing tension behind the scenes over the increased expectation levels which Chelsea's success brought saw the axe falling just three months after that FA Cup had been lifted at Wembley.

WHEN Claudio Ranieri took over, there had been noises and optimistic punts that it would be Zola who would replace Vialli in the hotseat.

"There were reports of me taking over the job, but I had never even considered it. I was enjoying playing too much," he says. So instead it was Ranieri, the coach who had symbolically handed Zola the number 10 jersey at Napoli when Maradona had departed.

Moments of magic continued to flow within the new-look ground. The first match of the 1999/2000 season brought a 4-0 win over Sunderland, the last goal from Gus Poyet winning that year's Goal of the Season. Poyet majestically volleyed the ball into the net, but the sublime chipped pass from Zola meant he needn't have checked his stride. There is putting the ball on a plate, but this was silver service at its best. It even had Sunderland fans standing to a man in appreciation of Zola.

That was the great thing about the Italian. He brought the best out of the often maligned football fan. Supporters up and down the country would applaud him; he received a standing ovation from an entire Anfield crowd after a League Cup tie that he had excelled in, even the notorious Galatasary fans couldn't help but cheer the man as he orchestrated a wonderful 5-0 win in Istanbul. He'd been walking on water at the Bridge for years, but now Zola could even cool the flames of Istanbul's supposed "Hell".

IN 2001 Zola had to ponder a new contract. He felt he had a few top flight years left in him and was happy to stay in London, but he would have to talk it over with his wife Franca. Nails were bitten to the quick as Chelsea fans awaited the result of the pow-wow. Two days before the last game of the season Zola announced that he and his family would love to stay, the contract was signed and as the team took an end of season lap of honour the fans showed their delight.

There's only one Mrs Zola, one Mrs Zola! There's only one Mrs Zola.

"My last two seasons were very special to me. I wanted to go out playing very well and I did. The pleasure I got from that last season in particular. It was unbelievable".

To those fans who were at the Bridge in January 2002 for a seemingly humdrum midweek FA Cup replay against Norwich "very well" fell way short of a suitable description for what most of us would call genius. Yes, there is no other word for it. Genius.

From a Graeme Le Saux corner, Zola ran to the near-post seemingly letting the ball run by him before, with the speed of a frog catching a fly, flicking the ball with his right foot past a dazzled keeper. It was a wonderful moment. Even the Norwich manager, Nigel Worthington, declared himself thankful for being in the stadium to witness such audacious skill.

And he bade farwell to his adoring fans by adding to his long term legacy of genius as Chelsea beat Liverpool 2-1 to ensure qualification for the following season's Champions League. Zola had the crowd in raptures, especially when he left Jamie Carragher, no mug as a defender, dazed and confused by the corner flag. A matter of weeks later, Roman Abramovich arrived and immediately tried to convince Zola to stay, but the Sardinian had already agreed terms with his hometown club of Cagliari and wasn't one to go back on his word. It was a fitting way to part company from a good and decent man.

ZOLA arrived at the Bridge that July to say a proper goodbye to the staff and the fans who crammed through the gates to get a last glimpse of their favourite. Amid all the photographs and autographs, one fan just dropped to his knees hailing his hero as if greeting a god. There is a famous picture of Bill Shankly at Liverpool faced with the same adulation after winning the 1974 FA Cup; a Liverpool fan kneeling in front of him in worship. Zola had achieved that level of affection and adulation, but now it was time to say "Ciao".

Fans' messages swarmed the club's website in support and gratitude. "I have witnessed, first hand, opposition fans standing to applaud you," wrote one. "You have been, and will always be, loved by the Chelsea faithful and true football fans around the world." Whilst another simply said, "You are the only Chelsea player I have ever watched as an adult who made football seem as magical as it did when I was a child."

That was Zola. That was his true genius and that was his legacy. That is why you cannot refuse him his place amongst this pantheon of Chelsea's Cult Heroes. He not only had that certain something, he engendered in fans the raised pulse, the quickening breath and half-rise out of the seat every time he took possession of the ball. When he played you left the ground having fallen in love with this great game all over again. Today Zola is a welcome guest at Stamford Bridge. He, like Vialli, Poyet and others can often be seen at a ground they loved playing in as much as those that filled its seats enjoyed them being there. But what of the future, surely Zola's work at Chelsea is not yet done? A coach; even manager one day? "There is definitely a place at the club for Zola as coach or maybe more," says Lovejoy hopefully.

Gianfranco Zola, manager of Chelsea Football Club. Now that would be special.

JOHN TERRY

'THE COLOSSUS'

1998-PRES

CHELSEA CAREER

Games	259
Goals	23
Caps	20

*up to and including 15 October 2005

MAGIC MOMENT

John's true moment may still be to come, but his face when he lifted that Premiership trophy and the party that ensued lingers long in the memory

> **The iron man stood at the top of the cliff. Where had he come from? Nobody knows....**
>
> **"The Iron Man", Ted Hughes**

MULTI-million pound superstars dressed in blue trudge off the pitch, their heads bowed in disbelief. They are out of the Champions League at the cruellest stage of all, the semi-final. To make matters worse, the victors are Liverpool, a team who will finish a full 37 points behind them in the Premiership, but who now celebrate wildly with ecstatic fans.

Those Chelsea players – many of whom lost at the same stage the previous year – slope away towards their dressing-room. These men are professionals, they will get over this, they will come again and eventually European glory will surely, inevitably belong to the club and their billionaire owner Roman Abramovich.

That's the problem.

To outsiders, these men are robots in a robotic club. One oiled by hard cash, one that has been bereft of a soul or emotions ever since it sold itself to the very highest of bidders. Those players will get over it. It won't bother these über-men at this new über-club.

As the Liverpool players rush to the Kop, amid ground-shaking noise, one man in blue remains fixed to the centre-circle, unable to move, unable to take solace, even from the cashmere-covered arms of his manager, Jose Mourinho. That man is John Terry, Chelsea's giant of a man, giant of a defender and inspirational leader. Once more, his Champions League dreams have been dashed and, whatever those outsiders may think about his supposed soulless club, his tears tell a different story.

As each one splashes onto the Anfield turf we are reminded that, to some, there is more to this game than the billions of roubles pumped into the fortunate coffers of Stamford Bridge. Each tear streaming down Terry's face reminds us that there is more to this team than the Galactico-like stream of players through the gates, or the tinted-lensed exotic businessmen that watch from the stands these days with their Bond-girl ladyfriends.

Terry's tears prove that the club is in touch with its roots, the fans who care so passionately about its fortunes. That may sound crazy to some, but in Terry, the leader of the pack, Chelsea have a player who desires, no, craves success for a club that taught him how to excel in the game he loves.

WHILE 'stars' and 'celebrities' are everywhere in modern society, true heroes are at a premium; and that's not only at Stamford Bridge. The old place will obviously take the majority of the stick dished out by an increasingly cynical football public. After all, in the time it takes Jose Mourinho to click his fingers and Comrade Abramovich to flip open that cheque-book, another world class footballer has drawn up at the gates on Fulham Road in his gold-plated Chelsea-tractor.

In John Terry, though, Chelsea possess a man and a footballer who harks back to another era. An era of your Harris or Hilsdon; Greaves or Gallacher. When passion was what won you games and made you an icon. For obvious reasons, John Terry is the modern God of the Stamford Bridge altar. He is the captain. The armband swells around his bulging biceps as he leads his team to yet another victory; his defence to another clean sheet. His pumping performances create a contagious will to win among his team-mates and supporters alike. Young fans eager for success and desperate for someone to idolise (and probably sick of being told just how great the game used to be) adore Terry's athleticism.

You wouldn't blame a youngster for adorning his or her bedroom wall with his image, but what of the older generation of fans? What of the men and women who have been coming to this eager, funny, underachieving club for so long? Supporters who have witnessed greatness and mediocrity in equal measures, who today must get used to the idea that their club may just stand on the edge of total European domination. What of them?

These fans also look to the skipper. He is their link between a fun past and a glorious future. Chelsea Things have changed. Fans have changed. Where once the Headhunters ran amok, now suits proliferate. Where once the Shed End bubbled like a cauldron of hate, now stands the Chelsea Village Hotel, corporate dining facilities and the Away End. Yes, the sacrilege of it; the Away End. But in Terry, supporters of any flavour, any creed, any culture, any background have a constant; one who will make their dreams come true without completely altering their love affair with Chelsea Football Club, that strange old place where anything can happen.

When looking at Terry these fans squint their eyes and see this home-grown, local (in today's game Essex is local) boy and fantasise about him being spotted, in the early 1960s on a Barking playing field by legendary scout Jimmy Thompson and nurtured by Dick Foss like so many before him. John Terry could have played with any of the men in this book. He is of that ilk. Hewn from the same rock which gave us Foulke and Osgood, Hudson and Droy, Nevin and Wise. He is a reminder of why so many love this club and why so many did long before a certain Russian came along. Peter Collins, a founder of the original Chelsea fanzine, *Chelsea Independent,* simplifies the reasons why, amongst the current squad, a special cheer is reserved for the skipper. "First of all, he's quality," he says. "Secondly he's kind of local and lastly he obviously cares."

It's that last reason that stands out. We live in a badge-kissing era. Players have to pucker up and kiss that badge in an attempt to let cynical fans know they care. It doesn't always work, of course. One minute a player is kissing one badge, the next he is – like an 18-30 holidaymaker – slobbering over a new one. Terry doesn't really go for all that nonsense. It is obvious that he cares, so no amount of demeaning shirt-snogging is going to reiterate the point. Instead more natural acts proclaim his love for the club and its fans. Terry is more often than not the last player to leave the pitch. He remains out on the arena clapping the fans who have grown to adore him unconditionally (not that he often makes the kind of mistakes that can test a supporter's patience).

He, like Roy Bentley, has that presence about him. The two men who have lifted the crown of Champions for the club are similar entities. One scored goals, of course, whilst another – just as emphatically – stops them, but both are the sort of men that supporters can't help but adore. Like a protective big brother, these players make you feel safe. With them around, a fan knows that things will be ok, and if they aren't, then it won't be for the want of trying. You can almost close your eyes and see Terry in that team of 1955, his hair brylcreamed, his shorts baggy around his knees, but the leather-laced ball is still given the Terry treatment and sent unerringly on its merry way out of the penalty area.

Tim Lovejoy, hardened Chelsea fan and presenter of Sky TV's *Soccer AM*, knew immediately that this was a special player; the type fans will always cherish. "I remember I used to watch John warming up at Stamford Bridge when he was much younger," he recalls. "It would be the middle of winter and everyone else, all the foreign players, they were head to toe in polar-neck jumpers, jackets, tracksuit bottoms and there would be John warming up in a t-shirt. I asked him once, 'Why do you do that?' he told me that it just made him feel more comfortable. They've stopped him now, though. They don't like him being so bold these days. It was that sort of attitude; he was such a British kind of player if you like. I love the foreign players, you can't help but love them, but what John offers is passion. He will throw any part of himself in front of the ball, he'll tackle with his face if need be and that is why us fans adore him."

John Terry *is* the modern Chelsea. He was here long before the much-maligned new regime got involved and fans can hope that if it all went tits up tomorrow and Abramovich chose to squander his fortune on some other plaything, Terry would still be here; leading from the back, driving the team and the club on. As Sam Pilger wrote in *FourFourTwo* in spring 2005, "[Terry] has become symbol of the whole club. Chelsea may be funded by Russian money and guided by Portuguese wisdom, but it still speaks with a cockney accent."

IT IS true; Terry represents everything that the new club stands for. He is young, strong, rich and very ambitious, but unlike Chelsea, circa 2005, he is almost universally popular. Players, managers, pundits, press-men, rival fans; they are all forming an orderly queue to have a dig at the club and what it now stands for, but you won't hear a bad word for Terry. Indeed his fellow professionals voted him as PFA Player of the Season in 2004/05. You can't say fairer than that.

As for the club, even the mild mannered on the BBC sports sofas, such as ex-Arsenal defender Lee Dixon, have chipped in. When asked whether he thought that their success was devalued by Abramovich's millions, Dixon replied, "As a purist, yeah, I do. You can't deny they've bought the Championship because without the money they wouldn't have won it, it's as simple as that. And in doing so they've completely changed every aspect of English football, for the worse. It was good to have another team to break up the Manchester United – Arsenal dominance, definitely, but the transfer market has been completely distorted. Everybody else is signing players Chelsea don't want."

Whatever the thoughts of these "purists" no-one can deny the impact of the man who captains the club. Theoretically he should be the evil pirate who skippers this tyrannical ship, raping the national game of its identity and prosperity. Graeme Souness didn't court popularity as Liverpool captain, nor did Roy Keane when Manchester United were dominating. Terry is the same tough breed of player, but you won't hear outsiders complaining about his style of play or leadership. On the contrary, he is touted as the team's saving grace and even a future captain of the national team.

AS I write this chapter, England have just qualified – rather tepidly it must be said – for the 2006 World Cup in Germany. The build up to the game against Austria was dominated by the question of which two players would make up the centre of England's defence. There was a very recent time when it was a given that Sol Campbell and Rio Ferdinand were joined at the hip. No-one else, unless due to injury, was going to get a look in, but how things have changed. Now it is which one of that two-some will partner John Terry, the commanding figure who has played himself onto the spine of the nation's football team.

Most fans wouldn't disagree. They may detest the new Chelsea and vociferously bemoan the club's success, but many are drawn to Terry's style of play, a style that appeals to the St George in all of us, however un-PC that may be. Some have had their doubts. Some cite a possible lack of pace that may find him wanting at the highest of international levels, but isn't that what they said of another young defender from Barking in Essex, one Bobby Moore?

Whatever the doubts, England coach Sven-Göran Eriksson seems to think Terry is the real deal, as does his assistant, Tord Grip. "John Terry is a leader. He's captain at Chelsea and is still very young," says the latter. "He has been a regular in Chelsea's team and has played a lot of international games.

That will improve you. To play and train with great players, good strikers, that improves you. You have to be on your toes to compete in training and to take a place in the team."

When Frank Lampard volleyed home the goal which defeated Poland to clinch the qualifying group for England, Terry's central defensive partner for the evening, Rio Ferdinand, raced to the goalscorer, ensuring he was the first to arrive on the scene to celebrate and be caught by the cameras, fist clenched, posing. His stock was at its lowest in his career, even lower than during his suspension for failing a drugs test, as now his place in the England side was being called in to question by John Terry's irrepressible form. Ferdinand had been dropped for the previous game against Austria and only returned because of injury to Sol Campbell. This is what John Terry has achieved through his sturdy and resolute performances at the heart of England's defence. He has usurped the perennial incumbents, voted as the best pairing of centre-backs in the 2002 World Cup. His form has been so consistent for so long that he could not be denied and has reduced the likes of Rio Ferdinand to trying anything to get in the public eye again and boost his Celebdaq ratings. You can't imagine John Terry stooping to such methods to garner attention. He prefers old fashioned ways, like playing well.

Terry has been likened to Tony Adams, a player he admired as a child and whose example of never-say-die defending has clearly rubbed off on our new hero. Grip, though, sees even more positives in the young protégé. "He's probably better on the ball than Tony Adams," he enthuses. "But, as a leader he's the same type of player. He can one day be captain of England."

No wonder Chelsea fans swell their chests when their player, a boy who grew up wearing their blue, is talked about as a leader of the country. He is their two fingers up at a mistrusting public and for that he is adored.

CHELSEA fans, like all fans, want to see exciting, fast, skilful flowing football. This book has proven that generations of supporters who have made a habit of standing and sitting regularly at Stamford Bridge have been spoilt by men bringing a swagger and a touch of class to a Saturday afternoon. Results and success haven't always been regular bedfellows at Chelsea, but no-one can deny the style that has long taken residence at the Bridge right since the Mears brothers bought its very first icon, "Fatty" Foulke, a century ago. Now the club has success and more will surely follow, although ironically it has come at a time when some have questioned the very essence of the place. Now sustained trophy winning is a reality, where is the fun, where is the style?

Perhaps that's the next stage. Chelsea have proved that they can win. In the past there's been bags of style with little to show for it. With Abramovich's squillions perhaps Chelsea can learn to win in style. What is a certainty is the rock-solid foundation that Mourinho's team is built on and the main paving stone in that structure is John Terry. Dribbling, show-boating, body-swerving and goalscoring; all have been admired, loved even, over the years, but now you can add to that defending; and in Terry it is real, old-fashioned defending and the fans love it.

Chelsea conceded a mere 15 goals on their way to the Premiership title in 2005 and look well placed to fare even better that this 2005/06 season. It is the sort of form that leaves fans going to the game knowing there is little chance of conceding a goal. Boring to some, but not to those who actually support the club. To them it is a source of great celebration and because of that they hero-worship the dogmatic, the diligent, the dogged John Terry.

Born in Barking in early December 1980, John Terry can't help but be compared to Bobby Moore. Both hail from that part of Essex that Jeff Powell – in his biography of the ex-England captain – calls "the rough and tumble border town on the cusp of Essex and East London." As soon as Terry showed an aptitude for the game and for leadership such comparisons were inevitable and have yet to cease. Terry grew up, like all the boys in his area knowing all about the England legend, the local guy who had lifted the World Cup. "It was a big deal," said Terry. "All the kids knew where his mum's house was. I was always pedalling up there. It was an experience just to stand outside and look at it. His mum was still there and I'm sure she got fed up with it, but he was the local hero."

Inspiration can be found in the most ordinary looking of places and Terry went on to shine in local football and it soon became obvious that here was a kid who could go all the way. He was playing on the fields of Wanstead and beyond for an incredible boys' team called Senrab. The side blossomed, but then again they did house a selection of future Premiership and England players. Paul Konchesky, Ledley King, JLloyd Samuel, and Bobby Zamora all joined Terry in a side that couldn't help but prosper.

The manager, Paul Rolls, was in no doubt about the talents of his young defender. "John was a phenomenal talent," he said. "He was the pick of all the kids I have ever come across and it really hasn't surprised me to see him captain Chelsea." With that, professional clubs came sniffing and Terry actually began his career at the more local West Ham, but it didn't work out at Upton Park due to someone thinking that the young defender had a strange running action. It's what you might charitably call a misjudgement. A bit like that bloke who turned down the Beatles because he thought guitar groups were on their way out. The point being that no-one can actually remember either fool's name.

Oh how Chelsea have benefited from West Ham's academy. From George Hilsdon to John Terry, players have come from claret and blue and prospered in just plain blue. It must rankle the east end club whilst delighting the Chelsea fans always willing to prosper from the misgivings of a London rival, whatever the persuasion.

And so John Terry arrived at Chelsea where, under Ruud Gullit, Gianluca Vialli and then Claudio Ranieri, he would begin to grow as Chelsea began to flower before blossoming into the bounteous rose-bush of the English game. That journey from youth-team hopeful to first-team brilliance is one that will always endear a player to his army of fans. Terry like Jimmy Greaves and Ray Wilkins, Ron Harris and Alan Hudson can truly count himself as one of the club's own.

THERE was never any doubt that here was a young man willing and able to lead men. Even at the tender age of sixteen, out on the football pitch there was nothing sweet about this driven and confident boy. Just minutes into Terry's first ever training session with the club's first-team the youngster was screaming orders at renowned and established world stars. He was tackling like a veteran. The likes of Mark Hughes and Luca Vialli were almost left dumbfounded.

"If they needed to be told they were doing something wrong or not putting the effort in I'd do it," recalled Terry recently. "From the very beginning it didn't matter that I was a young lad and they were superstars, because in my eyes we were all the same on the pitch and I thought I should tell them what was what. What's the point of wandering around star-struck? You're no use to anyone then."

It became apparent to anyone with half a brain that here was a player who would, given time, be very useful to everyone. Having captained the club at youth level, Terry got his first-team chance under Vialli in October 1998 in a League Cup tie against Aston Villa. The Italian had just completed a hat-trick in a 4-1 win when he called for the youngster. It was only four minutes, but it was a taste of the big time and, still aged seventeen, that was priceless for Terry.

There was another substitute appearance, this time at Southampton, before, in January 1999, he made his first start in an FA Cup third round match at Oldham. Chelsea won 2-1 and would remain unbeaten in all of the seven matches that the youngster was involved in that season. Fans were taking notice. They voted him as the club's Young Player of the Year that campaign and there was no looking back. The new millennium ushered in his big chance and how he took it. Terry was voted the club's Player of the Year in 2000/01 as, under new manager Claudio Ranieri, he proved that the burden of securing Chelsea's defence was far from daunting. He even managed a goal at Highbury, one of the most welcome of venues for Chelsea players to do well.

Marcel Desailly was in no doubt that here was a youngster he could pass on some of his gallic know-how to. "He is young, but he has grown up. I hope I've taught him that off the pitch he has to be a leader." With John Terry's emergence, World Cup winner (and oh how he enjoyed informing people) Franck Lebeouf became surplus to requirements. The position belonged to Terry and who knows when he will relinquish it.

The 2001/02 campaign saw Terry break into his country's under-21 set-up and become skipper, make just shy of 50 appearances for Chelsea, sometimes even being handed the captain's armband on the odd occasion when Marcel Desailly was out injured and score winning goals in both the FA Cup quarter and semi-finals. His goal to clinch a 3-2 victory at West Ham in the quarter-final arrived in injury time and completed a thrilling fightback from 2-1 down. Terry was finding a place in his supporters' hearts and for weeks afterwards they celebrated his winner by singing:

Oh John Terry
Scored a fucking great goal
In that fucking shithole
With one minute to go

Chelsea lost the final 2-0 to Arsenal and it is Terry's personal worst moment in football that he missed out on playing at the Millennium Stadium due to an illness on the morning of the match, which confined him to the bench.

SOON the players looked up to him, despite his callow 21 years. It may be that their opinion was all the higher due to his ability to turn around and tame the wilder side of his personality. Because, of course, as a young man in the goldfish bowl of modern football, it hadn't been an easy ride.

Terry was among the band of Chelsea players who reportedly hurled abuse at Americans in a hotel bar just hours after the attacks on New York in September 2001. That wasn't all. In 2002, the defender was forced to appear in court to answer charges about his role in a nightclub brawl with bouncers that also involved fellow youth team protégé Jody Morris. These were tough days and whilst the case was heard, his international chances were frozen.

Tim Lovejoy empathises with players whose every moves are so tightly scrutinised. "I have a lot sympathy for footballers," he tells me. "I'm not the most saintly man on this earth. I did things as a young man that I'm not proud of, but that is being young for you. Footballers have a lot of pressure to be these perfect role models. I'm a pretty good person, I don't do drugs, but I learnt those morals from my parents not Kerry Dixon.

"Of course they should act responsibly, but on the whole they do as they grow up and as a kid you just go through wild stages. They are just normal guys with an incredible capacity to play football."

Terry did mature, taking his morals and behaviour with him. Perhaps having witnessed the very public downfall of Tony Adams, he did not wish to follow the same route. Perhaps someone had a word in his shell-like "not to cock it up". Whatever, his domestic form remained well in tact despite his run in with the law and the tabloids, and as Chelsea edged closer toward being the country's finest, his form was a driving force. In 2003, with his problems well behind him, Terry won his first full England cap in a friendly against Serbia and Montenegro at Leicester.

AND THEN came a Russian named Abramovich. In a flash, Chelsea had lost their debts, discovered vodka was even nicer than champagne, and could look ahead to a future full of rich promise. Fans played fantasy football, wondering which of the game's greatest players would be next to come and play for them. With that though, the spine of the club and its importance was even further highlighted and home-grown men such as Terry were as rich a commodity as the oil that was funding the whole caboodle. "When a player comes through the ranks and does well, it makes such a difference to the fans," says Lovejoy. "If you ask the fans who their favourite players are then the answers are usually the same. John is right up there, whilst some might go for Lampard or even Joe Cole because these are London boys and you can see how much they want to do well for us. They're such good players and they so badly want to win."

Ron Harris, that most daunting and successful of Chelsea captains also sees just why the fans have a soft spot for Terry. "I used to have a great relationship with the lads on the terraces and in the stands at Chelsea. Week in, week out, whether you're winning 4-0 or being done seven-nought you have to still have a go. I did and so does John. I imagine he's the same in training. Us types of players don't want to lose, even five-a-sides. Supporters aren't stupid. They know when fellas are pulling out of tackles and being a bit milky and that's why John is so appreciated."

In Abramovich's inaugural season at the club, Chelsea had to put up with only second in the league (their highest position since they won it in 1955) and a place in the semi-final of the Champions League. It wasn't enough and Ranieri, a popular figure at the club was off. The new man was a special one. He had won the Champions League with Porto that year and so was the obvious choice for the Russian owner with an eye for the delectable.

Jose Mourinho arrived as manager in the summer of 2004. Terry had enjoyed a run in the heart of England's defence for the European Championships held in his new manager's home country of Portugal and had clearly impressed his boss. Mourinho's first act was to make him team captain. He had carte blanche to sign any skipper in the world and Mourinho made Terry captain. There had never been any doubt, it had always been a case of when would Terry skipper Chelsea? Mourinho had answered that question. By finding he had John Terry at the heart of the team and its dressing-room Mourinho was able to save Roman a small fortune (at the very least a small cruise liner).

Ron Harris is in no doubt that the young man wearing his old armband is a chip off the old captain's block. "I'm always telling people that I think John is very similar to myself," says Harris like a father describing a son. "He came through the youth ranks, he captains Chelsea, he lacks a yard in pace which is very similar to my own game. The only difference is, when I tackled someone, the bastard never got up.

"John is a tremendous inspiration and I see him one day captaining England. He definitely deserves it. If you look at the other defenders such as Rio Ferdinand and Sol Campbell, John is the one throwing himself into the tackles, blocking the ball any way he can whilst the others are probably a little worried about their looks. John would run through a brick wall for the cause."

So, would Chopper have liked to have played under John? "No, mate, I would have been captain, he could have been my understudy. I would have chipped up the inside-forwards and he could have volleyed them back."

JOSE MOURINHO had work to do. When he arrived he declared that here was a club without the smell of victory. "I'm at a club which is not a winner, which has won nothing in the past five years," he declared. "I feel that they need someone to give them self-belief and self-esteem and I will do that." Too right he will.

Terry himself seemed to grow even broader shoulders, his already square jaw becoming more chiselled by the arrival of Mourinho. "After I was made captain, my confidence flew up during pre-season, and with him telling you that you are the best, you feel a million dollars and are on top of the world."

Fans delighted in the marriage between player and manager and built upon the feel-good factor emanating from the dressing-room and made it their own. Manchester United were beaten 1-0 at the Bridge on the opening day of the 2004/05 season and there seemed an inevitability (even with Arsenal – the unbeaten invincibles – looking so good) that here was a resolute team who would lift silverware. At the heart of that, of course, was John Terry.

Nil became the most widely used word when summarising the opposition's performances against the Blues and John Terry, along with a beautifully marshalled defence, was the proud owner of more clean-sheets than Habitat.

Whilst Arsenal stumbled under the strain of living up to their own impressive achievements, Chelsea strode nonchalantly on. In October they lost at Manchester City, but that was that. Terry was supreme; especially in the first half of the season when the club was finding its rhythm. He led, he directed, he cajoled, he dragged when they needed to be dragged. His were performances that would win him that Player of Year award. That is why he is England's first choice centre-back; the choice of many to lead his country.

In November 2004, Chelsea were playing a London derby at Charlton. The Valley is never the easiest of venues to visit and even having scored an early goal through Damien Duff, the Blues were up against it as the home team came at them, their fans demanding goals. Step up John Terry. In three minutes, Terry had planted two purposeful headers into the Addicks' net and the three points belonged to Chelsea.

The goals against column continued to drip goals with frightening irregularity as it became obvious that the club were going to win only their second title. By February it became a more a case of which trophies would they not win in this most memorable of seasons. The end of the month gave Terry the opportunity to lift his first pot as Liverpool were beaten 3-2 in the League Cup Final. Silverware again at last.

Just twelve days later Barcelona were beaten 4-2 at the Bridge and knocked out – against many observers' predictions – of the Champions League. It had been Terry himself who had risen with dynamic power to head home the winning goal on that amazing night. If confirmation were needed, now it was official; John Terry was a Chelsea legend, even at the tender age of 24. It seemed that Chelsea and Terry were going to sweep the board.

That never quite happened; Newcastle beat them in the FA Cup and ultimately Liverpool would shock everyone by winning that Champions League semi-final, invoking those tears which tell us so much about why Terry stands apart in Chelsea fans' affections.

Just days before that game, Bolton were beaten 2-0 at the Reebok to confirm the Premiership win. On their 100th birthday, just as had happened on their 50th, Chelsea were crowned Champions of England. The fans could rejoice as Terry beat his chest in appreciation of their efforts over what had been a quite exhilarating nine months.

ON THE final day of the 2004/05 season, Stamford Bridge witnessed a pre-match party. Chelsea's all-conquering heroes were called one by one onto the pitch, where those white-haired men who had achieved the same iconic status in 1955 waited for them. It was, for an army of fans, a delight to behold.

Roy Bentley received a booming cheer, only matched by Terry's, when he strolled on last to pick up the trophy amid a cacophony of blue and white ticker tape. His place in the club's record books and in the hearts of those present and watching at home was complete.

Times change, supporters change, their class, their background, their wealth, their attitude to life, but fans' motives for idolising a player don't. Like Joey Jones scraping his face, Micky Droy heading away concrete if it would help the team or Ron Harris causing havoc in the name of Chelsea Football Club, Terry is loved for being out there with as much will and desire for success as those with a rattle, a scarf, yet another replica shirt, or just a lump of celery. "John Terry is so passionate," says Tim Lovejoy with obvious affection. "He plays with such a will to win that you just know that here is a player that cares. That means everything to us."

Picture the scene. In 50 years time, fans will be packed into the Ken Bates Memorial Stand in the new 150,000 seater Abramovich Stadium somewhere near Heathrow. They're there to celebrate the club's 35th Premiership crown, and 11th consecutive (breaking their own record). Before the eager young captain receives the trophy, members of the 2005 team that first won this very honour all those years ago are welcomed onto the pitch by Abramovich (who, thanks to the wonders of modern surgery looks exactly as he does today). Cheers rattle around the huge stadium, but the last is saved and most raucously given to the old skipper. The man who led the team by the scruff of its collective neck toward endless glory.

That man is John Terry. A Colossus. A legend.

Bibliography

Addicted
(Collins Willow 1998) by Tony Adams with Ian Ridley

Billy Wright: A Man for all Seasons
(Robson Books 2002) by Norman Giller

The Chelsea Story
(Arthur Baker 1982) by John Moynihan

Chelsea: The 100 Year History
(Mainstream 2005) by Brian Mears with Ian Macleay

Concerning Soccer
(Longmans Green and Co 1952) by John Arlott

Football and the English
(Carnegie Publishing 1997) by Dave Russell

Footballers Don't Cry
(Virgin 1999) by Brian Glanville

The Goalscorers
(Cassell 1978) by Tony Pawson

Greavsie: The Autobiography
(Time Warner 2003) by Jimmy Greaves

Kings of the Kings Road: The Great Chelsea Team of the 60s and 70s
(VSP 2004) by Clive Batty

London: The Biography
(Vintage 2001) by Peter Ackroyd

Masters of Soccer
(Naldrett and Heinmann 1960) by Maurice Edelston and Terence Delaney

The Mavericks
(Mainstream 1994) by Rob Steen

Rhapsody in Blue: The Chelsea Dream Team
(Mainstream 1998) by Rick Granvill

The Soccer Syndrome
(McGibbon and Kee 1966) by John Moynihan

Stamford Bridge Legends: Chelsea Champions
(Legends Publishing 2003) by David Lane

Stanley Matthews: The Authorized Biography
(Pavilion 1989) by David Miller

Tommy Docherty Speaks
(Pelham Books 1967) by Tommy Docherty

Upfront with Chelsea: The Inside Story of the Forward Line, From Cooke to Osgood, Nevin to Zola
(Mainstream 2001) by Chris Westcott)

Zola: The Inside Story of the Italian Maestro
(Robson Books 2003) by Harry Harris

Subscribers

Aherne, June & John	Peter Bonetti
Anderson, Paul	Gianfranco Zola
Brenner, Jeff	Kerry Dixon
Cox, Matt	David Speedie
Drury, Dominic	John Terry
Edwards, Sean	Jimmy Greaves
Farmer, Tommy	Frank Lampard
Finnigan, Stephen	Micky Droy
Green, Patrick	Charlie Cooke
Griffiths, Martin	Gianfranco Zola
Hare, Jez	Peter Osgood
Heanor, Brett	Gianfranco Zola
Hearn, TW	Peter Osgood
Heeley, Ed	Frank Lampard
Hollybush, John	Frank Lampard
Hull, David	David Webb
Jones, Peter	Frank Lampard
Kimble, Jim	Jimmy Greaves
Knight, Leigh	Gianluca Vialli
Light, Suzanne	Peter Osgood
Lomas, Terry	John Terry
Lyons, David	Peter Osgood
MacCorkhill, Trevor	John Terry
McNamee, Holly	Gianfranco Zola
McTavish, Stephen	John Terry
Neill, Andy	Gianfranco Zola
O'Riordan, Paddy	Alan Hudson
Paul, Ed	Charlie Cooke
Peerman, Christine	Dennis Wise
Pendridge, Bill	Peter Osgood
Phillips, Colin	Frank Lampard
Pringle, Jane	Gianfranco Zola
Ransome, Terry	Jimmy Greaves
Roper, Don	Gianfranco Zola
Ryan, Billy	John Terry
Thomas, Trevor	Gianfranco Zola
Thompson, Stephen	Kerry Dixon
Treweke, Gordon	
Unwin, Peter	Gianfranco Zola
Voss, Michael	Gianfranco Zola

Top Five Players Voted For

Gianfranco Zola	10 votes
John Terry	5 votes
Peter Osgood	5 votes
Frank Lampard	5 votes
Jimmy Greaves	3 votes